POWER-GLIDE
FOREIGN LANGUAGE COURSES

Welcome to the exciting adventure of Power-Glide Foreign Language Courses. We're thrilled to have you aboard and we are determined to help you succeed. As you go through the course, keep these two things in mind:

1. Keep it simple
2. Have fun

Most of us have studied language in traditional ways, where methods emphasized listening and lots of memorizing. Power-Glide's approach is very different. We offer a variety of activities all aimed at making natural learning possible.

So, rather than trying to master everything in a given lesson, find accomplishment in small successes and realize that learning a language is most effective when it's enjoyable.

One more note: Our mission is to revolutionize language learning. Everything in the course is aimed at helping students communicate in a new language. Here are some tips for you:

- Don't think you have to master everything in an exercise before you can move on. Or as we say, "Don't die on a page."
- Don't be afraid to make mistakes—learn as a child does!
- Feel free to jump around in the course.

This project would not have been possible without the assistance of many people. The help of those mentioned below was invaluable.

Editorial, Design, and Production Staff

Project Coordinator: James Blair

Cover Design: Darren Albertson

Editors: Ingrid Kellmer, Troy Cox, Nathalie Arrieus, Richard Tice

Editorial Assistants: Annick Bellemain, Dell Blair, Julia Blair, Renaud Coulliens, Craig Harman, Bruce Young, Margaret Young

Head Compositor: Troy Cox

Translators: Nathalie Arrieus, Annick Bellemain, Robert Blair, Renaud Coulliens

Voices, Audiocassettes: Dell Blair, Julia Blair, Robert Blair, Renaud Coulliens, Kent Hurcules, Isabelle Tarazone, Bruce Young, Margaret Young

Illustrator: Apryl Robertson

Musicians: Marty Hughes, Scott Mills

Recording Engineers: Bruce Kirby, John Brady, Benjamin Blair

Workbook and Cassettes © 1992-99 Power-Glide Language Courses. This Workbook revised and updated, March 1999.

All rights reserved. No part of this book may be reproduced in any form or by any means without permission in writing from the publisher, Power-glide Language Courses, 1682 W 820 N, Provo, UT 84601.

Printed in the United States of America

10　9　8　7　6　5　4　3　2　1

Table of Contents

Table of Contents		ii
Introduction		1

Tape 1, Side A

1	Mission to *l'île de Providence*	5
2	The Puzzle	10
3	Listening to a Reading of the Puzzle Sentences	16
4	Self-Test	17
5	Points, Lines, and Figures	18
6	More on Numbers	22
7	Toward Fluency	25
8	From Word to Discourse	29
9	Chatter at a Royal Ball	34
10	A Diglot-Weave Story	37

Tape 1, Side B

11	*La fenêtre cassée*	39
12	More on Numbers	41
13	*Points, lignes et figures*	44
14	Thinking *en français*	46
15	Toward Fluency	49
16	Chatter at a Royal Ball	52
17	Focus on the Language 1–8	55
18	*Au sujet de la prononciation*	59
19	Story Time: The Key of the King's Kingdom	61
20	*Points, lignes et figures*	63
21	From Word to Discourse	66
22	Chatter at a Royal Ball	69
23	Focus on the Language 9–14	72
24	Self-Test	77
25	Questions and Answers	79
26	Telling Stories	82
27	Creating Your Own Ministory Plots	85

Tape 2, Side A

28	*Points, lignes et figures*	87
29	*Une mère parle à son bébé*	90
30	From Word to Discourse	93
31	In the Classroom: A French Lesson	95
32	Lecture on Geography	96
33	More on Numbers	98
34	Thinking *en français*	101
35	A Lecture on the Alphabet	105
36	Chatter at a Royal Ball	106

37	Focus on the Language 15–23		107
38	*Ma première visite au Québec: première partie*		111
39	The Key of the King's Kingdom		113
40	Much Communication with Limited Means		114
41	Focus on the Language 24–28		116
42	Stringing Together Your Own Narratives		121

Tape 2, Side B

43	*Points, lignes et figures*		123
44	Story Time: The Keys of Rome		126
45	A Geography Lesson		128
46	A Mother Talks to Her Baby		129
47	A French Lesson in a Classroom		131
48	*Points, lignes et figures*		132
49	Thinking *en français*		134
50	*Ma première visite au Québec: deuxième partie*		137
51	A Lecture on the Alphabet		139
52	From Word to Discourse		140
53	More on Numbers		142
54	Focus on the Language 29–33		143
55	Stringing Together Your Own Narratives		145
56	Easy Words to Learn and Important Words to Know		147

Tape 3, Side A

57	Focus on Action		151
58	Thinking *en français*		154
59	*Une leçon de géographie*		157
60	*Proverbes*		158
61	*Une leçon de français*		159
62	*Une mère parle à son enfant*		160
63	Child Talk 1		162
64	Chatter at a Royal Ball		163
65	Focus on the Language 34–39		163
66	Review		167
67	Test Your Performance		168
68	Wrap-up Activities		170
69	Generating Sentences for Oral Practice		172
70	*L'alphabet romain* (continued)		177
71	Child's Talk		178
72	A Surprising Discovery		179
73	*Une leçon de géographie*		180
74	Storytime: The Three Little Pigs		182
75	*Ma première visite au Québec: troisième partie*		184

Tape 3, Side B

76	Focus on Action	187
77	*Une leçon de géographie*	192
78	A Dream about a Little Girl	193
79	*Dans la salle de classe: une leçon de français*	194
80	Chatter at a Royal Ball	195
81	Focus on the Language 40–44	197
82	Talking to a Small Child at the Zoo	201
83	*Des questions posées par un enfant*	203
84	A Note of Humor: A Critical Mother	204
85	A Note of Humor: A Polite Rebuke	205
86	*Ma première visite au Québec: quatrième partie*	205
87	From Word to Discourse	209

Tape 4, Side A

88	Focus on Scene	211
89	Chatter at a Royal Ball	215
90	Focus on the Language 45–49	216
91	Focus on Action	222
92	Chatter at a Royal Ball	228
93	*Une leçon de géographie*	229
94	Storytime: Little Red Riding Hood	230
95	A Child's Questions	232
96	What a Beautiful Sight!	233
97	Storytime: The Three Bears	234

Tape 4, Side B

98	A Geometry Lesson	238
99	*Un petit garçon et une fleur*	241
100	*Une leçon de géographie*	242
101	In the Aquarium	245
102	Focus on Scene	247
103	Storytime: The Story of the Three Thieves	249
104	*Dans la salle de classe de chimie*	251
105	Voice in the Darkness	254
106	A Note of Humor: *Un fils paresseux*	254
107	Chatter at a Royal Ball	255

Tape 5, Side A

108	A Note of Humor: The Crocodile	257
109	Storytime: The Farmer and the Turnip	259
110	The Story of Chicken Little	261
111	No One Pays Any Attention to Me!	263
112	Conversations and Snatches of Conversations	264
113	Beautiful Girl at the University	266
114	Openers and Rejoinders	268

Tape 5, Side B
- 115 Second Meeting at the University — 271
- 116 Isabelle and Vincent — 275
- 117 Chatter at a Royal Ball — 276
- 118 Afanti and the Pauper — 278
- 119 The Story of the Hare and the Tortoise — 280
- 120 Five Blind Men Describe an Elephant — 282

Tape 6, Side A
- 121 Three Little Pigs (Version One) — 283
- 122 Three Little Pigs (Version Two) — 284
- 123 The Hunter and the Thief — 287
- 124 The Silent Fishermen — 290
- 125 *Les pêcheurs silencieux* — 293
- 126 The Three Billygoats Gruff — 293
- 127 Mercury and the Woodcutters — 296
- 128 *Proverbes* — 298
- 129 The Little Red Hen — 299
- 130 Treatment for Melancholy — 300
- 131 Learning Words in Clusters — 301

Tape 6, Side B
- 132 Little Red Riding Hood — 304
- 133 A Milkmaid's Fantasy — 308
- 134 Two Stubborn Goats — 309
- 135 The Little Red Hen — 310
- 136 A Hungry Giant — 313
- 137 Poor King Midas — 316
- 138 A Greedy Dog — 320
- 139 The Most Beautiful Thing in the World — 321

Appendix—Answer Keys — 327

Appendix II Verbs — 337

Introduction

WHAT MAKES A POWER-GLIDE LANGUAGE COURSE UNIQUE?

Our course is developed by linguists, not marketing strategists. Many commercial language companies promise a super shortcut. They put together a selection of useful words, phrases, and dialogues that simulate situations a tourist might face. They have you listen to natives deliver the lines and repeat what they say. And that's it. However, such little scraps aren't enough to get to the core of a language, to develop a strong sense of how it works and feels, and to build the habits, skills, and strategies that make efficient learning possible. This Power-glide language course gives you real language learning—the kind where you actually internalize the language, and begin to use it as your own. And with the capability you will have after completing the course, you can readily acquire the special language you need for business or other purposes.

Dr. Robert Blair, PhD in Contrastive Linguistics, is the developer of Power-glide language courses. His methods are informed by current language acquisition theory and rooted in the work of world-renowned language teaching innovators. These pioneers created holistic, nonlinear models focused on the learner, the learning process, and on natural acquisition strategies. Dr. Blair has adapted their contributions to his own creative work to make superb language courses.

This course is fun and engaging because it gives rich experience in communication; it does not rely on mazes of grammar rules, rote memorization, and mind-numbing drills. Instead, you'll find:

- Music
- Stories
- Memory aids
- Diglot weaves
- You-are-there adventures
- Kinesthetic, visual, and audio activities
- Pictographs

What's more, Power-glide language courses can be used:

- with or without a teacher.
- in groups or individually and self-paced.
- for many different learning styles and aptitudes.

PHILOSOPHY

Power-glide courses cover grammar without emphasizing it. Our approach lets students gradually soak up the language. The course has exercises designed to help students discover the grammar for themselves. They learn grammar by listening to and seeing the language, much like small children do. Power-glide students have two main objectives: understanding, and speaking & writing. It's critical that they follow the learning methods.

How to Use This Course
- Recognize the tape on and tape off symbols.
- **Understand** the text.
- **Say it** and **write it**.

The tape on and tape off symbols:

The symbol 📼 is used to indicate that the text is on the tape, whereas ⊗ indicates that the text is off the tape.

To **understand**, students should:

1. Look over the material and compare the French to the English.
2. Listen to the tape while following the written text.
3. Listen to the tape a couple of times *without* looking at the written text.

Don't be shy: Use the pause button to stop the tape for a moment if you want a bit more time.

To **say** it, do this:

1. Read the story or material out loud in chorus with the tape, and keep the meaning in mind.
2. Turn the tape off, read each French sentence out loud, and then look away and say it. Think of the meaning.
3. Now cover up the French, look at the first English sentence, and try to say it in French. Check to see if you did it right. Do that for all of the sentences.
4. Play the recording of the text, but pause the tape after each English sentence and say the French.
5. Using notes of key words only, try to say the French sentences the best you can.

To **write** it, do the same as above, but write your sentences instead of speaking them.

LEARNING SUGGESTIONS

Here are some ideas that will help you learn the language better.

General tips

1. Use the course daily. Ten minutes per day is far better than an hour once a week. Sporadic use leads to lower retention and motivation. You may forget previous material, have difficulty developing crucial habits, and eventually become frustrated if you use the course sporadically.
2. Follow the instructions carefully. Use the advice given in the How to Use This Course. It will result in greater understanding, faster learning, and better

retention of the material. If you do not follow the prescribed order, you will not only not learn well—you will not learn *how* to learn.

3. Take weekly quizzes. This will encourage you to study and take responsibility for your learning. It will also give the teacher an indication of your needs and help keep you on the schedule they've created for you.

4. Pause and review as needed. Although it's not necessary to know everything perfectly before moving on, it's also not necessary to hurry through the course. Take some time to review, and play and replay the audio tapes as often as needed. The more exposure to the target language, the better.

Tips for Teaching Groups

1. Encourage creativity. Let students dramatize or act out their exercises as much as possible. Use games, role-plays, songs, poetry, or any other ideas that get students to immediately apply what they've learned.

2. Encourage a high level of interaction among students. Give students some time to help each other, to talk to each other in the language, and to otherwise support each other in their learning.

3. Allow students some personal learning time. This will let them absorb the material in their own particular way. Students' strengths vary greatly, so some will take longer or do better than others for certain kinds of activities.

4. Help students learn the steps given in the How to Use This Course section. Write them on the board, or on a poster. Review them often and make sure students follow them whenever they work on an exercise.

5. Give frequent positive feedback. Don't worry that the kids are having too much fun for learning to happen. The more fun they have, and the more positive encouragement they receive from their teacher, the better they will do.

Tips for Teaching Young Students

1. Emphasize listening and positive exposure to the language. Younger children need extra reinforcement.

2. Skip the more complex grammar ideas. Focus instead on stories, games, role-plays, ditties, and songs. Give them as much exposure to the language as possible. Children learn grammar by listening and speaking, not by consulting grammar books.

3. Try some of these activities:

    a. Diglot Weaves

    b. Well-known stories such as *The Three Bears* and *Little Red Riding Hood*

    c. Points, Lines, and Figures

NEW SUPPLEMENTARY MATERIAL AVAILABLE!

You can now buy a Teacher's Supplement/Learner's Guide that contains:

1. Clear objectives for every exercise. Now you'll know what you're supposed to learn and when you have accomplished the objective—so you can confidently move on to the next section.

2. A package of twelve tests: pre- and post-tests, listening comprehension tests, and suggestions for quizzes to keep you on your toes.

3. Tests at the end of each side of your cassette tape.

If you have questions, please contact us at (801) 373-3973.

Answers to your questions may be on our web page: www.power-glide.com, or you may email us.

Tape 1, Side A

1

🎧 Mission to *l'île de Providence*
Day One—05:15 Hours

It is just before dawn. You and your companion are intelligence officers assigned to parachute onto *l'île de Providence,* an island in the western Caribbean Sea. It has been seized by invaders from an unknown place of origin. Your mission is to discover why this tiny speck of land was singled out for capture. What is there there that is of such value? A submarine is to pick you up in ten days at midnight at the north point of the island.

You are to be met by three agents, code-named "Zsa-Zsa," "Bonbon," and "Joujou." You were given the code name "Rumpelstiltskin" and your fellow officer the name "Stumpelriltskin." The people of the island speak French. You and your fellow officer, "Stump," have never studied the language, but you know that English has borrowed words from French: *château, souvenir, saboteur, éclair,* and thousands of others. From films, books, and just living in America you have picked up some phrases like It's me...*C'est moi,* right?...*n'est-ce pas?,* Have a nice trip!...*Bon voyage!,* Do you speak French?...*Parlez-vous français?,* pardon me...*pardonnez-moi,* yes sir...*oui, monsieur,* no ma'am...*non, madame,* after you, miss...*après vous, mademoiselle,* please, "if it please you"...*s'il vous plaît,* thanks a lot...*merci beaucoup,* hello...*bonjour,* goodbye...*adieu.*

You review these, concentrating on pronunciation:

C'est moi.	*N'est-ce pas?*	*Bon voyage!*	*Parlez-vous français?*
Pardonnez-moi.	*Oui, monsieur.*	*Non, madame.*	*Après vous, mademoiselle.*
S'il vous plaît.	*Merci beaucoup.*	*Bonjour.*	*Adieu.*

Just before departure, you are given six new phrases to learn:

Do you speak English?	*Parlez-vous anglais?* (Resembles PAR LAY VOO ON GLAY)
What is this?	*Qu'est-ce que c'est?* (Resembles CASK A SAY)
I don't know.	*Je ne sais pas.* (Resembles ZHUN SAY PA)
What does ___ mean?	*Qu'est-ce que veut dire ___?* (Resembles CASK OF A DEER)
How does one say ___?	*Comment dit-on ___?* (Resembles COMB ON DEE TONE)
In French.	*En français.* (Resembles ON FRON SAY)

You review these, focusing on pronunciation:

Parlez-vous anglais?   *Qu'est-ce que c'est?*   *Je ne sais pas.*

Qu'est-ce que veut dire ___?   *Comment dit-on* "window" *en français?*

🎧 Review all the above expressions until you can say the French.

🎧 You jump into the dark ahead of "Stump" and land just fifty yards offshore. You hide behind some rocks. "Stump" is nowhere to be seen. You wait for dawn, worried about him, hoping he landed nearby. As it begins to get light, you see a woman walking up the beach toward you. With her are two Russian wolfhounds. As she comes near, you take a chance. You step out of hiding and ask, "*Pardonnez-moi, madame, parlez-vous anglais?*" Startled, she hesitates but then answers, "*Anglais? Non…français…Je parle français.*" Then she extends her hand and says, "*Bonjour, monsieur, je suis madame Pétard.*" Pointing to the dogs, she adds with a smile, "*Voici Bonbon, et voilà Joujou.*"

Recognizing the dogs' names as the code names *Bonbon* and *Joujou*, you figure this lady is your contact. "*Zsa-Zsa?*" you ask. "*Je suis Zsa-Zsa Pétard. Et vous êtes monsieur…?*" You give her your code name. She nods, then, looking up and down the beach, asks, "*Et l'autre…Stumpelriltskin?*" You shake your head. She motions you to follow: "*Venez avec moi, monsieur, s'il vous plaît.*" You take it to mean, "Come with me, sir, please."

As you follow her up to her beach house, you reflect on her words *avec moi* "with me," *venez avec moi* "come with me," then on her words *je parle français* "I speak French," contrasting it with *parlez-vous anglais?* and *parlez-vous français?* You deduce that "I speak English" would be *je parle anglais*, and that "I am French" would be *je suis français*, but you're unsure how to pronounce "*Je suis* American." You comment, "*Je suis*…American." She nods: "*Mmm, vous êtes américain. Je sais.*" Of course she knows. You practice saying, "*Je suis américain*," and she corrects you, "*Je sui<u>s(z)</u> américain.*" You practice these expressions, concentrating mainly on pronunciation: *Je sais. Je ne sais pas. Vous êtes américain. Venez avec moi, monsieur. Je parle français. Je suis français. Je suis américain. Je suis anglais. Parlez-vous anglais? Oui, je parle anglais.*

Notice the tape-off sign. Read and follow instructions.

▣ Practice saying these expressions several times, always with meaning. Picture an appropriate context.

▣ Arriving at the door, Mme Pétard bids you enter, "*S'il vous plaît, monsieur, entrez.*" You bid her go ahead of you, saying: "*Après vous, madame, s'il vous plaît.*" She smiles and goes in, expressing thanks with "*Merci.*"

Notice the tape-off sign. Read and follow instructions.

▣ Review the above until you can read the French expressions and know what they mean. After that, see if you can call to mind the French equivalents of the following:

Good day!	Please, sir, go in.	After you, ma'am.
After you, ma'am.	Thanks.	Do you speak English?
No sir.	Do you speak French?	Yes, I speak French.
I am French.	I am Zsa-Zsa.	And you?
It's me, Rumpelstiltskin.	I am American.	Yes, I know.
You are American.	And the other?	I don't know.
Come with me.	This is Bonbon.	That is Joujou.
Hello, Bonbon and Joujou.	If you please, sir.	Thanks a lot.
You are Zsa-Zsa, right?	Yes sir, I am Zsa-Zsa Pétard.	Good-bye, sir.
I don't know.	What is this?	In English.
How does one say…?	In French.	

How does one say "king" in French?
How does one say "*je suis anglais*" in English?
What does "*je suis anglais*" mean?

🔊 As you enter, you meet a gentleman who welcomes you with the word "*Bienvenue,*" and then introduces himself: "*Je suis Monsieur Pétard, Henri Pétard.*" You ask, "*Parlez-vous anglais?*" He replies, "*Non, monsieur, mais vous parlez français. Vous parlez bien. Vous êtes américain, n'est-ce pas?*" Before you can respond, a girl comes in and speaks with the man and lady of the house. In a moment they excuse themselves and leave. The girl introduces herself as Jacqueline and offers to help you. Together you work on pronunciation and spelling. You prepare the following list of expressions.

No.	*Non.*	You are American.	*Vous êtes américain.*
Yes, please.	*Oui, s'il vous plaît.*	I am American.	*Je suis américain.*
Here's Joujou.	*Voici Joujou.*	I speak English.	*Je parle anglais.*
There's Bonbon.	*Voilà Bonbon.*	I am French.	*Je suis français.*
Enter!	*Entrez!*	Come with me.	*Venez avec moi.*
Thanks, sir.	*Merci, monsieur.*	Mr. Henry Pétard.	*Monsieur Henri Pétard.*
Welcome!	*Bienvenue!*	And the other?	*Et l'autre?*
Do you speak French?	*Parlez-vous français?*	I know.	*Je sais.*
I am English.	*Je suis anglais.*	I don't know.	*Je ne sais pas.*

You also prepare a list of your previously learned expressions.

It's me.	*C'est moi.*
Right?	*N'est-ce pas?*
After you, ma'am.	*Après vous, madame.*
Thanks much.	*Merci beaucoup.*
Have a good trip!	*Bon voyage!*
Pardon me.	*Pardonnez-moi.*
You speak well.	*Vous parlez bien.*
How does one say…?	*Comment dit-on…?* (COMB ON DEE TONE)
In English.	*En anglais.*
In French.	*En français.*
What is this?	*Qu'est-ce que c'est?* (CASK A SAY)
What does ___ mean?	*Qu'est-ce que veut dire ___?* (CASK OF A DEER)
Hello (good day!).	*Bonjour.*
Goodbye.	**Adieu.* (lit. "Unto God")

Tape off.

🔊 *Note: Another more common way to say goodbye in French is *au revoir*, which sounds like "oh vwa."

After reviewing the words, cover the English column. How many of the French words do you recognize? Don't get caught up trying to memorize the words. You will see them often throughout the course. As you see them used in different contexts, you will gradually acquire their meaning.

🔊 As you and Jacqueline sit, lacking words with which to communicate, you initiate some language exploration. Pointing to the door you ask, "*Qu'est-ce que c'est?*" She says what sounds like "*la porte,*" and you relate it to the word <u>port</u> or sea port, a door to a country. She writes it: the door = *la porte*, and then asks: "*Comment dit on «la porte» en anglais?*" and you tell her. In minutes, you've acquired eight new words:

	Spelling	🔊 **Helpful Hints**
the feet	*les pieds*	(sounds a bit like P.A.)

the hands	*les mains*	(manual, handbook)
the head	*la tête*	(*tête à tête* = head to head)
the face	*le visage*	(massage your visage)
the nose	*le nez*	(nasal)
an eye	*un œil*	("an eye" in a strange dialect)
the mouth	*la bouche*	(swoosh into the boosh)

Tape off.

Jacqueline puts these in a playful question form and teaches you to answer appropriately.

Avez-vous (les pieds)?   Do you have (the feet)?
Oui, j'ai (les pieds).   Yes, I have (the feet).

Take time to learn these words.

While you're arranging these words into your memory storage, Mme Pétard comes in with a concerned look on her face. She looks at you and says something you don't understand about Stumpelriltskin. You guess she's made contact with him.

End of Episode 1

Review the previous section until you feel comfortable with the French phrases.

SELF-TEST

How many of the French phrases can you recognize? See if you can match the English and the French phrases. The answers are in the appendix.

1. c   *Adieu.*   a. After you, ma'am.
2. a   *Après vous, madame.*   b. Enter!
3. j   *Bienvenue!*   c. Goodbye.
4. d   *Bon voyage!*   d. Have a good trip!
5. e   *Bonjour.*   e. Hello (good day!).
6. i   *C'est moi.*   f. How does one say…?
7. f   *Comment dit-on…?*   g. In English.
8. g   *En anglais.*   h. In French.
9. h   *En français.*   i. It's me.
10. b *Entrez!*   j. Welcome!

11. a *Et l'autre?*   a. And the other?
12. e *Je ne sais pas.*   b. I am American.
13. g *Je parle anglais.*   c. I am English.
14. f *Je sais.*   d. I am French.
15. b *Je suis américain.*   e. I don't know.
16. c *Je suis anglais.*   f. I know.
17. d *Je suis français.*   g. I speak English.
18. i *Merci beaucoup.*   h. Mr. Henry Pétard.
19. j *Merci, monsieur.*   i. Thanks much.
20. h *Monsieur Henri Pétard.*   j. Thanks, sir.

21. d *N'est-ce pas?*   a. Do you speak French?
22. b *Oui, s'il vous plaît.*   b. Here's Joujou, there's Bonbon.
23. c *Pardonnez-moi.*   c. Pardon me.
24. a *Parlez-vous français?*   d. Right?

25.	_f_	*Qu'est-ce que c'est?*	e.	What does ____ mean?
26.	_e_	*Qu'est-ce que veut dire ___?*	f.	What is this?
27.	_j_	*Venez avec moi.*	g.	Yes, please.
28.	_b_	*Voici Joujou, voilà Bonbon.*	h.	You are American.
29.	_h_	*Vous êtes américain.*	i.	You speak well.
30.	_i_	*Vous parlez bien.*	j.	Come with me.

THE ADVENTURE CONTINUES

Day One—0900 hours

Nine Days to Rendezvous

Your reception has taken a strange twist. The invaders are searching the area, so Jacqueline leads you to a hiding area in the basement. She gives you a notebook, a tape player, and several cassette tapes. Jacqueline shuts the heavy door softly behind her, and you are left alone. You open the notebook and find a brief note scrawled across the first page.

> Hidden on this island is a treasure—one that offers its finder wealth and fame. It is a great prize and a local trademark. The invaders seek this treasure to steal it, but they do not know this treasure's location. Since an understanding of the French language and French-speaking culture is essential in learning the treasure's location, chances are that they will not find it. Hidden in this room is a map that will help you in your search for the treasure. To learn the location of this map, complete the puzzle that begins on the next page.

You wish Stump were here to help you, but you decide to do all that you can without him. You begin the first puzzle in the book.

2
The Puzzle
Le puzzle

The purpose of this puzzle is to make you prove your ability to tackle the language on your own, figuring out by yourself some fundamental things about the language. If you are sufficiently robust you will persevere until you succeed in breaking the code of French. And if you are sufficiently smart, you will keep alive the information you gain from this challenging exercise and use that information in learning more French.

Instructions: In Part 1A below, you will find sentences in normal French, except that the spaces between words have been deleted. Your first task is to figure out where the word breaks are. Do this by comparing the French phrases with their English translations and hypothesizing the scope of the individual words. Mark with pencil or pen the word breaks that you hypothesize.

When you are convinced that you have identified all the words, compile a dictionary by writing the French words and phrases in the blanks in Part 1B on the next page. If you cannot come up with a hypothesis, check the HELP section (Part 1C).

PART 1A

1. *PauletMarie.* — Paul and Marie.
2. *VoiciPaul.* — Here's Paul.
3. *VoilàMarie.* — There's Marie.
4. *Unhommeetunefille.* — A man and a girl.
5. *Paulestunhomme.* — Paul is a man.
6. *Ilestjeune.* — He is young.
7. *Ilestunjeunehomme.* — He is a young man.
8. *Ilaunesœur.* — He has a sister.
9. *Marieestunefille.* — Marie is a girl.
10. *Elleestpetite.* — She is little.
11. *Elleestunepetitefille.* — She is a little girl.
12. *Elleaunfrère.* — She has a brother.
13. *PaulestlefrèredeMarie.* — Paul is Marie's brother.
14. *MariestlasœurdePaul.* — Marie is Paul's sister.
15. *LamèreetlepèredePauletMarie.* — The mother and the father of Paul and Marie.

PART 1B—TRANSLATION

Instructions: Fill in the translation equivalents. Leave space between words you have identified.

here's _Voici_   he is _Il est_   young _jeune_

there's _Voilà_   she is _Elle est_   of _de_

a brother _un frère_ he has _Il a_   Paul's _de Paul_

a sister <u>une sœur</u>   she has <u>Elle a</u>   Marie's <u>de Marie</u>

a man <u>un homme</u>   the father <u>Le père</u>   and <u>et</u>

the mother <u>La mère</u>

PART 1C—HELP SECTION

The English word *the* is invariable, no matter what it refers to: <u>the</u> brother, <u>the</u> sister, <u>the</u> parents. Its French counterpart, however, is variable, depending on the gender and number of the noun referred to: <u>le frère</u> but <u>la sœur</u> and <u>les parents</u>.

Similarly: *a* brother, *a* sister (with the same word *a*), but its counterpart in French has two forms: <u>un frère</u>, <u>une sœur</u>. The selection of <u>un</u> or <u>une</u> depends on the gender of the noun referred to.

PART 2

Instructions: The sentences in the second column are marked with an asterisk, which indicates that they are grammatically incorrect. Compare each of these with its correct counterpart on its left (from Part 1A), hypothesizing what the error is. Then take the self-test to see how well you can distinguish well-formed sentences from ungrammatical ones.

	Normal Sentences		Ungrammatical Counterparts
8.	*Il a une sœur.*	8.	**Il a un sœur.*
9.	*Marie est une fille.*	9.	**Marie est un fille.*
11.	*Elle est une petite fille.*	11.	**Elle est une fille petite.*
12.	*Elle a un frère.*	12.	**Elle a une frère.*
13.	*Paul est le frère de Marie.*	13.	**Paul est la frère de Marie.*
14.	*Marie est la sœur de Paul.*	14.	**Marie est le sœur de Paul.*

Self-Test

Instructions: Identify which sentences below are incorrect. The answer key is in the appendix.

1. *Paul est une homme.*
2. *Elle est un homme.*
3. *La mère est petite.*
4. *Il est une fille.*
5. *Il a une sœur.*
6. *Paul a une frère.*
7. *Elle est une petite fille.*
8. *Paul est la frère de Marie.*
9. *Marie est la sœur de Paul.*

PART 3

Instructions: Figure out, as you did before, where the word breaks are and mark them. When you are convinced your hypotheses are correct, compile a word list by writing the French words and phrases in the blanks below.

1. *Paul aide sa sœur.* Paul helps his sister.
2. *Il l'aide.* He helps her.
3. *Il aime l'aider.* He likes to help her.
4. *Il aime aider sa sœur.* He likes to help his sister.
5. *Marie aide son frère.* Marie helps her brother.
6. *Elle l'aide.* She helps him.
7. *Elle aime l'aider.* She likes to help him.
8. *Elle aime aider son frère.* She likes to help her brother.

9. Ils peignent ensemble.   They paint together.
10. Ils cuisinent ensemble.   They cook together.
11. Elle aime son frère.   She likes her brother.
12. Il aime sa sœur.   He likes his sister.
13. Il aime ses sœurs.   He likes his sisters.
14. Elle aime ses frères.   She likes her brothers.

Translation

Instructions: Fill in the translation equivalents. Leave space between words you have identified.

he helps __Il aide__   he likes to help __Il aime aider__

his sister __sa sœur__   she likes __Elle aime__

they cook __Il cuisinent__   her brother __son frère__

they paint __Il peignent__   her brothers __ses frères__

she helps him __Elle l'aide__   he helps her __Il l'aide__

together __ensemble__   they paint together __Il peignent ensemble__

Help Section

	1	2	3
The normal order of sentence parts is the same in English and French:	<u>Paul</u>	<u>likes</u>	<u>Marie</u>.
	Paul	*aime*	*Marie*.
However, in French if the object is a pronoun, the order changes:	<u>Paul</u>	<u>her</u>	<u>likes</u>.
	Paul	*l'*	*aime*.

Observe the contrast between the English possessive pronouns *his* and *her* and the corresponding French possessive pronouns *son, sa,* and *ses*.

English	**French**	**English**	**French**
<u>his</u> brother	<u>son</u> *frère*	<u>her</u> brother	<u>son</u> *frère*
<u>his</u> sister	<u>sa</u> *sœur*	<u>her</u> sister	<u>sa</u> *sœur*
<u>his</u> parents	<u>ses</u> *parents*	<u>her</u> parents	<u>ses</u> *parents*

Note that "his" and "her" are invariable, no matter if they are tied to a singular masculine or feminine referent or to plural referents: "his" brother, "his" sister, "his" parents; "her" brother, "her" sister, "her" parents. In contrast, *son* is the equivalent of "his" or "her" before masculine referents, *sa* is the equivalent of "his" or "her" before feminine referents, and *ses* is the equivalent of "his" or "her" before plural referents.

Part 4

Instructions: Compare each of the starred sentences with its correct counterpart on the left, forming a hypothesis as to what the error is. Then take the test to see how well you can distinguish normal sentences from ungrammatical ones.

Normal Sentences	Ungrammatical Counterparts
1. *Paul aide sa sœur.*	* *Paul aide son sœur.*
2. *Il l'aide.*	* *Il aide elle.*
3. *Il aime l'aider.*	* *Il aime aider elle.*
4. *Il aime aider sa sœur.*	* *Il aime aide sa sœur.*
5. *Marie aide son frère.*	* *Marie aide sa frère.*
6. *Elle l'aide.*	* *Elle aide il.*
7. *Elle aime l'aider.*	* *Elle aime il aider.*
8. *Elle aime aider son frère.*	* *Elle aime aide son frère.*
9. *Ils peignent ensemble.*	* *Il peignent ensemble.*
10. *Ils cuisinent ensemble.*	* *Ils cuisine ensemble.*
11. *Elle aime son frère.*	* *Elle aime sa frère.*
12. *Il aime sa sœur.*	* *Il aime son sœur.*
13. *Il aime ses sœurs.*	* *Il aime son sœurs.*
14. *Elle aime ses frères.*	* *Elle aime sa frères.*

Self-Test

Instructions: Identify which translation is correct. Time yourself. The answer key is in the appendix.

1. They help.
   (a) *Ils aident.*
   (b) *Ils aide.*

2. She has a brother. Yes, Paul is her brother.
   (a) *Elle a un frère. Oui, Paul est sa frère.*
   (b) *Elle a un frère. Oui, Paul est son frère.*

3. He has a sister. Yes, Marie is his sister.
   (a) *Il a une sœur. Oui, Marie est son sœur.*
   (b) *Il a une sœur. Oui, Marie est sa sœur.*

4. Paul likes his sister. Yes, he likes her.
   (a) *Paul aime son sœur. Oui, il l'aime.*
   (b) *Paul aime sa sœur. Oui, il l'aime.*

5. She likes her brother. Yes, she likes him.
   (a) *Elle aime son frère. Oui, elle l'aime.*
   (b) *Elle aime sa frère. Oui, elle l'aime.*

6. Marie helps her brother. And he helps her.
   (a) *Marie aide son frère. Et il l'aide.*
   (b) *Marie aide son frère. Et il aide.*

7. They paint together. And they cook together.
   (a) *Ils peignent ensemble. Et ils cuisinent ensemble.*
   (b) *Ils peint ensemble. Et ils cuisine ensemble.*

8. He likes his sisters. She likes her brothers.
   (a) *Il aime son sœurs. Elle aime sa frères.*
   (b) *Il aime ses sœurs. Elle aime ses frères.*

⌚ Completion time: 48 sec.

THE CHALLENGE: PART 1

French Pronunciation

Instructions: Study these tables describing the sounds and spelling of French. Listen closely to the French words and examine closely how the spelling of sounds correspond.

Note: Don't be discouraged if you feel this is too much to learn at once. Come back to this reference often as you go through the course. The more exposure you have to the sounds of French, the better your pronunciation will become.

Table of Vowels and Vowel Sounds

Spelling of Sound	Examples
a, à, â, as	*travail* (work), *là* (there), *pâte* (pastry), *pas* (not)
e, eu, oeu	*le* (the), *peu* (little), *soeur* (sister)
é, ei[1]	*societé* (society), *pleine* (full)
è, ai[2]	*mère* (mother), *j'ai* (I have)
i	*ici* (here), *qui* (who)
o, ô, eau	*dos* (back), *vôtre* (yours), *beau* (handsome)
au[3]	Paul
u	*rue* (street), *but* (goal)
ou	*vous* (you), *beaucoup* (much)
y	*y* (there)

[1]This sound is also created when an "e" is followed by a consonant at the end of the word, as in the word "*pied*".

[2]This sound is also created:
- when there are double consonants following an "e", as in the word "*elle*".
- when the form of the verb "*être*" is conjugated, as in "*es*" and in "*est*".
- when other verbs have an "e" followed by an "s" and another consonant, as in "*espérer*".

[3]This sound is also created when there are double consonants following an "o", as in "*donne*".

Table of Semi-Vowels

Spelling of Sound	Examples
ie	*pied* (foot)
y[1]	*yeux* (eyes)
oi	*voilà* (there it is), *moi* (me)
oui	*oui* (yes)
ui	*lui* (him), *cuisine* (kitchen)

[1]This sound is also formed when a vowel (or a vowel sound) is followed by "il" as in "*soleil*", "*travail*", "*oeil*", or a word finishing in "*ille*" as in "*famille*" and "*fille*". One exception to this general rule is "*ville*".

Table of Nasal Sounds

Spelling of Sound	Examples
on, om	*bon* (good), *ombre* (shadow)
en, em, an, am	*enfant* (child), *temps* (weather), *flan* (pudding), *ambassade* (embassy)
in, im, yn, ym, ain, aim, ein	*prince* (prince), *impossible* (impossible), *synthèse* (synthesis), *sympathique* (friendly), *pain* (bread), *faim* (hungry), *plein* (full)
un, um	*un* (one)

Table of Consonants

Spelling of Sound	Examples
b	*bon* (good), *robe* (dress)
c[1], k, q, qu	*cable* (cable), *coeur* (heart), *kilo* (kilo), *coq* (cockerel), *quatre* (four)
cc	*accident* (accident), *occident* (occident)
d	*dans* (in), *mode* (fashion)
f, ph	*fille* (daughter), *photo* (photograph)
g[1]	*garçon* (boy), *guide* (guide)
j, g[2]	*jouer* (to play), *géométrie* (geometry), *girafe* (giraffe)
l	*lettre* (letter), *belle* (beautiful)
m	*mère* (mother), *somme* (sum)
n	*notre* (our), *tonne* (ton)
p	*papa* (dad), *soupe* (soup)
r	*rue* (street), *roi* (king)
s[3], c[2], ç	*sans* (without), *cible* (target), *ce* (this), *ça* (that)
t	*tableau* (picture), *note* (note)
v	*vous* (you), *voir* (to see)
x	*exister* (to exist)
z, s[4]	*zéro* (zero), *cousin* (cousin)
gn	*vignette* (vignette), *signe* (sign)
ch	*cher* (dear), *bouche* (mouth)

[1] This sound is pronounced this way when followed by any letter other than "*i*" or "*e*".
[2] This sound is pronounced this way when followed by an "*i*" or "*e*".
[3] This has an "s" sound when at the beginning of the word and between a vowel and a consonant.
[4] This has a "z" sound when between two vowels.

THE ADVENTURE CONTINUES

You complete the first segment of the puzzle to receive the map. You wish that Stump were here. Just then, Jacqueline softly opens the door and leads Stump into the room. She motions for both of you to be quiet, then she silently leaves the room and closes the door behind her.

You inform Stump of what has happened in his absence. Then the two of you tackle the rest of the challenge.

3

📼 Listening to a Reading of the Puzzle Sentences
Écouter la lecture des phrases du puzzle

Tape off. Read instructions.

THE CHALLENGE: PART 2

Instructions: Listen carefully to the reading of the puzzle sentences. The first group of sentences are from Part 1, the second group from Part 2.

📼 *Paul et Marie.*
Voici Paul.
Voilà Marie.
Un homme et une fille.
Paul est un homme.

Il est jeune.
Il est un jeune homme.
Il a une sœur.
Marie est une fille.
Elle est petite.

Elle est une petite fille.
Elle a un frère.
Paul est le frère de Marie.
Marie est la sœur de Paul.
La mère et le père de Paul et Marie.

Paul aide sa sœur.
Il l'aide.
Il aime l'aider.
Il aime aider sa sœur.
Marie aide son frère.

Elle l'aide.
Elle aime l'aider.
Elle aime aider son frère.
Ils peignent ensemble.

Ils cuisinent ensemble.
Elle aime son frère.
Il aime ses sœurs.
Elle aime ses frères.

4

Self-Test
Auto-évaluation

THE CHALLENGE: PART 3

Part A: Translation from French

Instructions: Translate the following sentences from French to English. Check your answers in the appendix.

1. *Elle cuisine.* <u>She cooks</u>

2. *Paul aime sa sœur.* <u>Paul likes his sister</u>

3. *Il aime l'aider.* <u>He likes helping her</u>

Part B: Translation from English

Instructions: Translate the following sentences from English to French. Check your answers in the appendix.

1. He is a young man. <u>Il est un ^Jeune homme</u>

2. She has a brother. <u>Elle a un frère</u>

3. Paul is Marie's brother. <u>Paul est le frère de Marie</u>

4. She likes to help him. <u>Elle aime l'aider</u>

5. They cook together. <u>Ils ~~cuisent~~ ensemble cuisinent</u>

5
📼 Points, Lines, and Figures
Points, lignes et figures

Tape off to read explanation.

📼 The following tasks invite you to develop critical skills in inferring meaning. The aim is (1) to lead you to exercise your learning-by-ear faculties to learn inductively, as you did naturally as a child, (2) to help you push the envelope of listening comprehension, and (3) to lead you to perceive and use basic patterns of sentence formation.

📼 A. SCATTER CHART

		2		
	6	*deux*	4	
	six		*quatre*	
1		3		5
un		*trois*		*cinq*
4 5 2 3 6 1		•		&
chiffres		*point*	_____ *ligne*	*et*

B. LOOK, READ, AND LISTEN

📼 Instructions: Follow along with the tape. In part F you will check your understanding of the English equivalents to these phrases.

📼 1. • Un point.

2. ___ Une ligne.

3. 1 Un chiffre, le chiffre un.

4. • • ___ Deux points et une ligne.

5. ___ ___ ___ • • 3 Trois lignes, deux points et un chiffre, le chiffre trois.

6. 3 2 1 ___ ___ Trois chiffres, les chiffres trois, deux, et un et deux lignes.

7. • • • • ___ ___ 2 Quatre points, deux lignes, et un chiffre, le chiffre deux.

8. ___ ___ ___ 3 4 Trois lignes et deux chiffres, les chiffres trois et quatre.

9. 1 2 3 4 5 • • • • • Cinq chiffres, les chiffres un, deux, trois, quatre, cinq et cinq points.

10. • • • • • ___ ___   *Cinq points et deux lignes.*

11. ___ • • • • • •   *Une ligne et six points.*

12. 1 2 3 4 5 6   *Six chiffres, les chiffres un, deux, trois, quatre, cinq et six.*

C. LOOK AND LISTEN

Instructions: Check the appendix for the script of this activity.

1. •	5. ___ ___ ___ • • 3	9. 1 2 3 4 5 • • • • •
2. ___	6. 3 2 1 ___ ___	10. • • • • • ___ ___
3. 1	7. • • • • ___ ___ 2	11. ___ • • • • • •
4. • • ___	8. ___ ___ ___ 3 4	12. 1 2 3 4 5 6

D. CONCENTRATION AND MULTIPLE-CHOICE FRAMES

Tape off. Read instructions.

Instructions: Below, you see a series of frames, each with four sections. You'll hear the frame letter (A through J) and then a sentence referring to what is in one of the four sections (section a, b, c, or d). In the following pause, point to the correct section, and then listen for the answer. Control the pace by stopping and starting the tape. When you are finished, check your answers in the appendix.

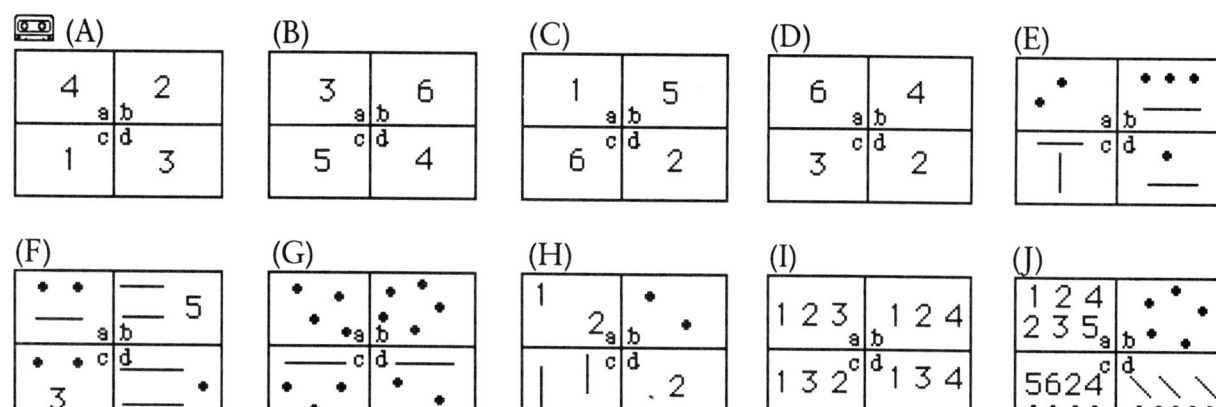

E. LISTEN AND DRAW

Instructions: Listen to the descriptions on tape and draw what is described. Stop the tape if the pace is too fast. When you are finished, check your answers in the appendix.

(A)   (B)   (C)   (D)   (E)

19

⚙ F. Comprehension Check

Instructions: Check your comprehension of the twelve sentences in part B.

1. A dot.
2. A line.
3. A number, the number one.
4. Two dots and one line.
5. Three lines, two dots, and a number, the number three.
6. Three numbers, the numbers three, two, and one, and two lines.
7. Four dots, two lines, and a number, the number two.
8. Three lines and two numbers, the numbers three and four.
9. Five numbers, the numbers one, two, three, four, five, and five dots.
10. Five dots and two lines.
11. A line and six dots.
12. Six numbers, the numbers one, two, three, four, five, and six.

If you can understand the French spoken on the tape, you have achieved most of the aims for this section. If you feel ready to enhance your production, you may wish to do the following: (1) See how well you can render the sentences of Part F back into French. (2) Go back to Part B, cover the French, look only at the items pictured, and make statements about them similar to those made on the tape.

The Adventure Continues

As you finish the last part of the puzzle, one of the shelves in the room slides back to reveal a hidden compartment. You and Stump examine the compartment. Inside, you see the map that you are supposed to find. To your surprise, it is a regular road map of the island. Several locations are numbered in red on the map. You wonder what these locations could be. You and Stump remove the map from its shelf and push the shelf back in place.

No sooner have you done this than Mme. Pétard enters the room. "The invaders have left this area," she tells you in softly accented English. "We hope they have gone for good."

You and Stump stare. "I thought you didn't speak English," you gasp.

Mme. Pétard smiles. "I do not speak it well, and I would not risk that our enemies might hear me speak in your language. Now, come. I have prepared a lunch, and we French believe in savoring every morsel."

You and Stump glance at each other. You can smell delicious odors wafting through the open door of the basement room. You grin and follow Mme. Pétard upstairs, where she served you a light, delicious quiche. After the meal, you ask Mme. Pétard if she will share her recipe with you. She smiles and agrees.

Recipe: *Quiche Lorraine*

1 9-inch unbaked pie crust

1 c shredded Swiss cheese

6 slices bacon

1 small onion, chopped

1/2 green pepper, chopped

3 eggs, slightly beaten

1 c evaporated milk or light cream

1/2 t lemon peel

1/2 t salt

dash pepper

1/4 t dry mustard

Cook bacon. Reserve 2 T bacon fat. Crumble bacon and set aside. Cook onion in reserved bacon fat until tender and browned. Set aside.

Line unbaked pie crust with foil. Put dry beans or other lightweight items in bottom of pan to prevent large air pockets from forming in crust. Bake unpricked pie crust in 475 degree oven for 5 minutes. Remove from oven. Arrange cheese, bacon, onion, and pepper in bottom of crust.

Combine eggs, cream, lemon peel, salt, pepper, and mustard. Pour over cheese mixture in crust. Bake at 325 degrees for 45 minutes or until set. Remove from oven. Let stand about 10 minutes before serving. Cut quiche into 6 servings to serve. Makes 6 servings.

THE ADVENTURE CONTINUES

You thank Mme. Pétard for teaching you her recipe. Then you tell her what you have accomplished so far and show her the map. She reads the note thoughtfully.

"Since the note tells you to learn my language as well as French-speaking cultures, perhaps I should help you to begin your learning now," she begins. "Would you like that?" You and Stump gladly accept her offer. She begins by introducing you to the French numeral system. Then she assigns you two exercises from your notebooks to help build your vocabulary and your understanding of French sentence structure.

6
More on Numbers
Plus au sujet des chiffres

Tape off. Read very carefully.

TEN / DIX - HUNDRED / CENT

In French, the word for 6 is written *six* and pronounced (by itself) like *cease*. The word for 10 is written *dix* and pronounced (by itself) like *deese*. Say: "Mr. DEESE has 10 GEESE." Incidentally, *dix* comes from Latin *decem*, which we recognize in "decimal," "deci-liter," and other words.

The French word for 100, *cent*, comes from Latin *centum*, which we see in "century" and other words having to do with the concept hundred. No t- or n- consonant is pronounced.

Listen and repeat:

1	2	3	4	5	6	10	100	101	102	103	104	105
106	110	200	300	400	500	600	100+10=110		100+1=101		100+100=200	

Point to the number called:

```
                              105
                   300                400
             10           100              104
                   500          200
                        110
```

Tape off. Say those numbers, then read the numbers below:

cinq cents	quatre cents	six cents	deux cents	trois cents	cent trois
cent un	cent quatre	cent deux	cent cinq	cent dix	

THOUSAND / MILLE

Like *dix* and *cent*, the word for 1000 (*mille*) is from Latin. We see it in words like "millimeter" and "millennium," having to do with the concept thousand. Sounds like "meal" except for the lighter "l" sound.

Listen and repeat:

1000	100	10	2000	3000	4000	5000	6000	10000	100000	1100	1101
1102	1103	1104	1105	1106	1110	2200	3300	4400	5500	6600	

🔊 Note that *dix* is pronounced [dee] and *six* is pronounced [see] before a word beginning in a consonant.

📼 Point to the number called:

			1200		
		3000		4000	
	100		1000		10000
	5000		2000		
		1100			

Say those numbers, then read the numbers below:

🔊 *cinq mille*   *quatre mille*   *six mille*   *trois mille*   *mille trois*
mille un   *mille quatre*   *mille deux*   *mille cinq*

SEVEN / *SEPT*

The French word for 7 *(sept)* is related to "<u>Sept</u>ember," the seventh month in the Roman calendar.

NINE / *NEUF*

The French word for 9 *(neuf)* is pronounced a bit like "nerf" but without the *r*. It is related to "<u>No</u>vember," the ninth month in the Roman calendar.

📼 Listen and repeat:

| 7 | 9 | 700 | 900 | 7000 | 9000 | 10000 | 1 |
| 2 | 3 | 4 | 5 | 6 | 7 | 9 | 10 |

Say those numbers, then read the numbers below:

🔊 *neuf*   *sept mille*   *trois mille*   *mille trois*   *mille un*   *mille quatre*   *mille deux*   *mille cinq*
mille

EIGHT / *HUIT*

📼 The word for 8 *(huit)* rhymes with "wheat" but begins in a different sound. Listen: *huit*. Not "wheat" but *ooeat*.

Listen and repeat:

| 7 | 8 | 9 | 700 | 800 | 900 | 7000 | 8000 | 9000 | 10000 |
| 1 | 2 | 3 | 4 | 5 | 6 | 7 | 8 | 9 | 10 |

Point to the number called:

```
                                    1900
                          1700            1200
                  7000          10000           8000
                          8100            1800
                                    9100
```

Say those numbers, then review.

● PRACTICE AND APPLICATION

1. Count down from 9 to 1, then by hundreds from 900 to 100, and then by thousands from 9000 to 1000.

2. Choose random numbers in the cluster below to make up number sequences in the hundreds and thousands. For example: 600, 407, 2000, 7310, 8409. Say each number sequence as you make it up.

```
              8       7       5
          4       1       2       6
              3               9
```

3. Practice counting, gradually increasing your speed.

4. Time yourself saying the string of numbers below from left to right. Then from right to left. Par time is 26 seconds after five trials. Can you attain it?

2 4 6 8 7 9 3 10 400 600 800 700 900 300 4000 2000 10000 1800 1300 1700

⌚ Time on first trial: 1:15 seconds   ⌚ Time after five trials: 50 seconds

24

7
📼 Toward Fluency
Vers la facilité de parole

1. WORDS AND PATTERNS

📼 Instructions: Learn these vocabulary words and see them in use in the sample sentences below.

📼 Who?	*Qui?* (KEY)
Who is Pierre?	*Qui est Pierre?*
Who is he/she/it/this?	*Qui est-ce?* (KEY-S)
And	*et* (silent "t")
But	*mais*
The other (one)	*l'autre*

Sample Sentences

Who is this? It's a friend.	*Qui est-ce? C'est une amie.*
And the other, who is she? It's Nanette.	*Et l'autre, qui est-ce? C'est Nanette.*
Nanette who? Nanette d'Avignon.	*Nanette qui? Nanette d'Avignon.*
Oh yes, it's Nanette d'Avignon.	*Oh, oui, c'est Nanette d'Avignon.*
The other one is Josette.	*L'autre est Josette.*

Tape off. Oral translation.

📼 Oral Translation Exercise 1

Instructions: Cover the English column with your hand. Translate the following sentences from French to English as fast as you can. Once you feel confident in your ability to do that, cover the French side and try to produce the French equivalent as fast as you can.

1.	*Qui est-ce? C'est Jacques.*	Who is it? It's Jacques.
2.	*Qui est Jacques?*	Who is Jacques?
3.	*Et qui est Joséphine?*	And who is Josephine?
4.	*Mais qui est Nanette?*	But who is Nanette?
5.	*Et Marie, qui est-ce?*	And Marie, who is she?
6.	*Qui est-ce? C'est l'autre.*	Who is she? She is the other one.
7.	*Qui est-ce? Oh oui, c'est Marie-Antoinette.*	Who is this? Oh yes, it's Marie Antoinette.

Review

1. Go through the oral translation exercises again, aiming for fluency. Speak with expression and confidence. Imagine you are telling a story to children.

2. Close your eyes, breathe deeply, and relax, letting your mind create sentences made up of material from this lesson. See how many meaningful statements you can generate from this material in two minutes. Par is 7 statements in 2 minutes. If you can equal par you will have no difficulty with what is to come.

⌚ First 2-minute trial: _7_ statements   ⌚ Second 2-minute trial: _10_ statements

2. WORDS AND PATTERNS

Instructions: Learn these French vocabulary words and see them in use in the sample sentences below.

a prince	un prince	he/she/it is...	c'est...
a princess	une princesse	No indeed!	Mais non!
a friend	un ami (m)	Yes indeed!	Mais oui!
a friend	une amie (f)	a foe, adversary	un/une adversaire
or	ou	right?	n'est-ce pas?
either...or...	ou...ou...	neither the one nor the other	ni l'un ni l'autre
neither...nor...	ni...ni...		

Sample Sentences

Pierre is a prince.	Pierre est un prince.
He is a friend, right?	C'est un ami, n'est-ce pas?
No indeed. He's an adversary.	Mais non. C'est un adversaire.
And Marie, who is she?	Et Marie, qui est-ce?
A friend or a foe?	Une amie ou une adversaire?
Either a friend or a foe.	Ou une amie ou une adversaire.
Neither a friend nor a foe.	Ni une amie ni une adversaire.
Oh yes, she is a formidable adversary.	Oh oui, c'est une adversaire formidable.
But she is also a friend.	Mais c'est aussi une amie.

Tape off. Oral translation.

Oral Translation Exercise 2

Instructions: Cover the English column with your hand. Translate the following sentences from French to English as fast as you can. Once you feel confident in your ability to do that, cover the French side and try to produce the French equivalent as fast as you can.

1. Pierre is a friend. — *Pierre est un ami.*
2. He is a prince. — *Il est un prince.*
3. Josette is a princess, right? — *Josette est une princesse, n'est-ce pas?*
4. Yes indeed, a princess and a friend. — *Mais oui, une princesse et une amie.*
5. And Josephine, who is she? — *Et Joséphine, qui est-ce?*
6. She is an adversary. — *C'est une adversaire.*
7. But she is a princess, right? — *Mais c'est une princesse, n'est-ce pas?*
8. She's a princess, yes, but she's also an adversary. — *Elle est une princesse, oui, mais elle est une adversaire aussi.*
9. Yes indeed, Josephine is an adversary. She is a formidable adversary. — *Mais oui, Joséphine est une adversaire. C'est une adversaire formidable.*
10. And Robert? He is either a friend or a foe, right? — *Et Robert? Il est ou un ami ou un adversaire, n'est-ce pas?*
11. No, neither. — *Non, ni l'un ni l'autre.*

Review

1. Go through the oral translation exercises again, aiming for fluency. Speak with expression and confidence. Imagine you are telling a story to children.

2. See how many meaningful statements you can generate from this material in two minutes. Par is 7 statements in 2 minutes. If you can equal par you will have no difficulty with what is to come.

⌚ First 2-minute trial: _10_ statements   ⌚ Second 2-minute trial: _11_ statements
⌚ Third 2-minute trial: _8_ statements   ⌚ Fourth 2-minute trial: _9_ statements

3. WORDS AND PATTERNS

Is it (true) that…?	*Est-ce que…?*
Who knows if…?	*Qui sait si…?*
I don't know if…	*Je ne sais pas si…*
I know that…	*Je sais que…*
Well	*Bien*
It's fine/that's fine.	*C'est bien.*
Well then/Well/Anyway…	*Et bien…*
A good friend (m)	*Un bon ami*
A good friend (f)	*Une bonne amie*
Me too.	*Moi aussi.*
Is not…	*n'est pas…* (compare to Right?—*N'est-ce pas?*)

Sample Sentences

Is Nanette a good friend?	*Est-ce que Nanette est une bonne amie?*
I don't know if Nanette is a good friend.	*Je ne sais pas si Nanette est une bonne amie.*
I know who Jacques is.	*Je sais qui est Jacques.*
Me too, I know who Jacques is.	*Moi aussi, je sais qui est Jacques.*
I know well that he is a good friend.	*Je sais bien que c'est un bon ami.*
No, Jacques is not a friend, he is a foe.	*Non, Jacques n'est pas un ami, c'est un adversaire.*
Friend or foe, who knows? I don't know.	*Ami ou adversaire, qui sait? Je ne sais pas.*
Who knows if Jacques is a friend?	*Qui sait si Jacques est un ami?*
Is that all right? Yes, it's fine.	*C'est bien? Oui, c'est bien.*

Stop the tape. Oral translation.

Oral Translation Exercise 3

Instructions: Cover the English column with your hand. Translate the following sentences from French to English as fast as you can. Once you feel confident in your ability to do that, cover the French side and try to produce the French equivalent as fast as you can.

1. Who is it? It's Jeanette, isn't it? — *Qui est-ce? C'est Jeanette, n'est-ce pas?*
2. Is Jeanette a princess? — *Est-ce que Jeanette est une princesse?*
3. No, Jeanette is not a princess. — *Non, Jeanette n'est pas une princesse.*
4. Is Josette a friend or a foe? — *Est-ce que Josette est une amie ou une adversaire?*
5. I know that Josette is not a good friend. — *Je sais que Josette n'est pas une bonne amie.*
6. Jacques is not a prince, but he is a friend, a good friend. — *Jacques n'est pas un prince, mais il est un ami, un bon ami.*
7. But Robert is not a friend, he is an adversary, a formidable adversary. — *Mais Robert n'est pas un ami, il est un adversaire, un adversaire formidable.*
8. Well then, who's a good friend? — *Eh bien, qui est un bon ami?*
9. Well, I know Marie is a friend, but I don't know if she is a good friend. — *Eh bien, je sais que Marie est une amie, mais je ne sais pas si c'est une bonne amie.*
10. Is that all right? That's fine. — *C'est bien? C'est bien.*

Review

1. Go through the oral translation exercises again, aiming for fluency. Speak with expression and confidence. Imagine you are telling a story to children.

2. See how many meaningful statements you can generate from this material in two minutes. Par is 8 statements in 2 minutes. If you can equal par you will have no difficulty with what is to come.

- First 2-minute trial: __8__ statements
- Second 2-minute trial: __10__ statements
- Third 2-minute trial: __9__ statements
- Fourth 2-minute trial: __6__ statements

OVERALL REVIEW

1. Go through the three oral translation exercises again, aiming for smoothness. Speak with expression and confidence. Imagine you are telling a story to children.

2. Close your eyes, breathe deeply, and relax, letting your mind create sentences made up of material from this lesson. See how many meaningful statements you can generate in two minutes from this material. Keep a tally. The goal is twelve statements in two minutes. Can you reach this goal?

8
From Word to Discourse
Du mot au discours

This is an activity that focuses on sentence formation. Its purpose is to push you toward independence in figuring things out and in discerning what is correct or incorrect. Your investment of time and effort here will pay off richly.

Below is a scatter chart of words that you can string together properly into sentences. For each word, you are given the spelling. On the next page, some sample well-formed strings using words from this scatter chart are contrasted with ungrammatical strings.

Instructions: (1) Look over the words in the scatter chart. (2) Study the sample strings of words from the scatter chart. (3) Complete the three tasks listed after the sentences.

SCATTER CHART

petite(s)	*et*	*grande(s)*
voici		*est/sont*
est-ce que (qu')...?	*c'est*	*cette/ces*
les autres		*une*
des	*chose(s)*	*l'autre*
blanche(s)		*noire(s)*
la/les	*oui*	*non*

English Equivalent

small	and	big
here is		is/are
yes-no question marker (Is this...)	this is	this/these
the others		a/one
some	thing(s)	the other
white		black
the	yes	no

29

Sample Strings

Instructions: Carefully study these sentences, <u>including the ungrammatical ones</u>. Work out in your mind the rules for the correct formation of these kinds of sentences. (The ungrammatical sentences are starred.)

English	French	Ungrammatical Form
A thing. The thing.	*Une chose. La chose.*	
The things. Some things.	*Les choses. Des choses.*	**La choses. *De choses.*
Here is a thing.	*Voici une chose.*	**Voici est une chose.*
Here is a white thing.	*Voici une chose blanche.*	**Voici une blanche chose.*
And here is a black thing.	*Et voici une chose noire.*	**Voici une noire chose.*
Here are the things.	*Voici les choses.*	**Voici la choses.*
Here are the other things.	*Voici les autres choses.*	**Voici l'autre choses.*
Some white things and some black things.	*Des choses blanches et des choses noires.*	**Des choses blanche et des choses noire.*
One thing is black.	*Une chose est noire.*	**Une chose est noires.*
One thing is white, the other is black.	*Une chose est blanche, l'autre est noire.*	**Une chose sont blanche, l'autre sont noire.*
The black thing is large.	*La chose noire est grande.*	**La noire chose est grande.*
The white thing is small.	*La chose blanche est petite.*	**La blanche chose est petite.*
This thing is small and this thing is large.	*Cette chose est petite et cette chose est grande.*	**Ces chose est petite et ces chose est grande.*
These things are small.	*Ces choses sont petites.*	**Ces choses est petites.*
These small things are white.	*Ces petites choses sont blanches.*	**Ces petites choses est blanches.*
These large things are black.	*Ces grandes choses sont noires.*	**Ces grandes choses est noires.*
Is the black thing large? Yes.	*Est-ce que la chose noire est grande? Oui.*	**Est la chose noire grande? Oui.*
Is the white thing large? No.	*Est-ce que la chose blanche est grande? Non.*	**Est la chose blanche grande? Non.*
Are these things large and white? No.	*Est-ce que ces choses sont grandes et blanches? Non.*	**Sont ces choses grandes et blanches? Non.*
Are these things small? Yes.	*Est-ce que ces choses sont petites? Oui.*	**Sont ces choses petites? Oui.*

TASK 1

Preparing to deal with real objects: For each sentence, give the French equivalent <u>and</u> a different sentence of parallel structure.

A white thing. Here is a white thing. (Parallel structure: A large thing. Here is a large thing.)

And here is a black thing. One white thing and one black thing.

Here are the white things. Some white things and some black things.

This thing is small. These things are large.

These large things are black. The other things are white and small.

TASK 2

Looking at the scatter chart, compose a number of grammatically correct sentence strings. Work toward building speed and fluency in the sentences you compose.

30

Task 3

Set out on a table before you a number of small white things and large black things. They can be pieces of paper or whatever, as long as the smaller things are white and the larger ones are black. (You can even write "black" on larger pieces of white paper to represent black things.) Referring to these objects in front of you, see how many meaningful statements you can generate about them in two minutes. Start with very short statements, then advance to more ambitious ones. Par is twelve statements in two minutes.

The Adventure Continues

After you complete the exercises, Mme. Pétard speaks again. "Let's see . . . you are to learn culture as well. The French-speaking world is so beautiful, so varied and complex. A brief summary cannot do it justice, but I will try."

You thank her for her efforts and listen attentively as she gives you an overview of French-speaking cultures.

Facts and Figures on French Speakers of the World

- French is the official language of France, its overseas territories, and its associated states.

- French is also an official language in Belgium, Canada, Haiti, Luxembourg, Senegal, Switzerland, and Tahiti.

- French is so widely spoken that it ranks with English as an international language.

- More than 90 million people speak French as their native language, and many more speak French as a second language.

- French is called a Romance language—not because it is nicknamed "the language of love" but because it developed from Latin. (Italian, Portuguese, Romanian, and Spanish are some other Romance languages.)

When Mme. Pétard finishes, she refers you to a homepage where you can learn more about French-speaking cultures around the world: http://www.power-glide.com. Then your conversation lapses into small talk. You ask her where she grew up. When she tells you she grew up in Algeria, you ask her if she will tell you about her homeland as well. She smiles and agrees.

Algerian Culture Overview

The Algerians are generally formal and traditional, but they also value individuality and expressiveness. People are expected to speak their minds, but they are expected to do so in a polite manner. Many Algerian people struggle with questions about their country's future. This ongoing debate has created deep divisions between different social classes and political groups. In urban areas, both men and women usually wear Western clothing. However, many Algerians continue to wear traditional North African Muslim clothing. Though French is not an official language in Algeria, it is widely spoken and understood. In 1830, France invaded Algeria. France's control lasted until 1954, when an independence movement erupted into warfare. After eight years of fighting, Algeria received its independence on 3 July 1962.

FACTS AND FIGURES ON ALGERIA

• Arabic is Algeria's official language, but French and various Berber dialects are widely spoken and understood.

• Islam is Algeria's state religion. Nearly 99% of the population are Sunni Muslim.

• The meeting of Arabic and French cultures in Algeria makes hospitality an important part of Algerian culture.

• Almost 90% of Algeria's population lives in the northern coastal area that is called "The Tell." "The Tell" has a mild Mediterranean climate.

• The Atlas Mountains and the Haut Plateau separate "The Tell" from the vast Sahara Desert that covers the southern part of the country.

• Algeria's main exports are oil, petroleum products, natural gas, and wine.

Mme. Pétard smiles as she thinks of the land where she grew up. "I hope that information will help you," she says. "If you want, you can talk to my husband about Belgium. That's where he's from. He and I met in Algeria while he was serving in the Foreign Legion."

You thank Mme. Pétard for her help and for her suggestion. Then you go in search of her husband, Henri. You find him in the kitchen working on a popular food that originated in Belgium—french fries. He nods and greets you as you approach. You and Stump ask him if he would be willing to tell you about Belgium. He hesitates and explains that he doesn't want to leave his cooking. You offer to help him. He nods and agrees to tell you the recipe as well as facts about Belgium if you help him.

BELGIUM CULTURE OVERVIEW

Belgians value hard work, cultural appreciation, and family ties. In general, they believe in living life to its fullest, devoting themselves to work and play with equal zeal. Belgian culture is divided into two main groups—Walloons and Flemish. The Flemish speak a form of Dutch called Flemish, and the Walloons speak French. Belgium is famous for its chocolates, mussels, waffles, and french fries. In Belgium, french fries are served with mayonnaise rather than ketchup. The extended family remains an important part of Belgian life. Almost 75% of Belgium's population belongs to the Roman Catholic church.

FACTS AND FIGURES ON BELGIUM

• French and Dutch (Flemish) are Belgium's official languages. Most Belgians also understand English.

- Brussels, Belgium's capital city, serves as headquarters for the North Atlantic Treaty Organization (NATO) and the European Community (EC).

- Belgium has a system of dikes and seawalls along its coast to prevent tidal flooding.

- Belgium is a constitutional monarchy. The king shares executive power with the prime minister, and a bicameral parliament holds legislative power.

- Belgium's main exports are steel, wool, meats, automobiles, chemicals, diamonds, crystal, and glass.

RECIPE: *LES FRITES*—FRENCH FRIES

4 potatoes

oil for deep frying

seasoned salt

Cut pared potatoes lengthwise in strips. Fry small amounts at a time in hot oil (360°F) for 6-7 minutes or until crisp and golden. Drain on paper towels. Sprinkle with seasoned salt and serve at once. Makes 8-12 servings. Note: Do not French-fry new potatoes.

THE ADVENTURE CONTINUES

You munch several of Henri's delicious fries as Stump finishes copying Henri's recipe. Then Zsa-Zsa enters the room.

"I have prepared something to help you in your search," she tells you. "Come with me, please."

You follow Zsa-Zsa Pétard to the basement's other room. This room, though small, is modern and well-lit. On a desk sits a powerful computer. Stump, who loves computers, sits at the chair in front of the computer.

"This is great!" he exclaims. "This machine has secure email. We'll be able to update the submarine captain and check out the webpage Zsa-Zsa mentioned."

You agree that this is wonderful, and both of you thank Zsa-Zsa for her thoughtfulness. She nods and smiles.

"Il n'y a pas de quoi," she tells you. "I must go now, but Jacqueline will come and work with you on your French. Pay close attention to her. Remember that you must learn language and culture to find the treasure you seek."

Zsa-Zsa leaves. You find another chair and sit by Stump at the computer. Soon, Jacqueline enters the room and asks you to open your notebooks. She helps you work through several French exercises.

9
📼 Chatter at a Royal Ball
Bavardages au bal royal

Tape off. Read the instructions very carefully.

📼 Instructions: The aim of this activity is to lead you to discover for yourself how to map your thoughts into French. This is an altogether different approach to grammar, one so simple and nontechnical that a child can do it. So if you don't know a verb from a noun, don't let that concern you. The goal here is not to make a grammarian out of you, but to help you discover how to make meaning with French. Your enthusiastic performance with the material of this key module is of utmost importance. Push yourself to use your pen and your voice to create new sentences. You're preparing to engage in the telling of tales and the weaving of narrative.

TASK 1

Familiarize yourself with the words and pictographs. Very quickly draw each pictograph on a separate card or piece of paper. You'll need these for constructing sentences and stories.

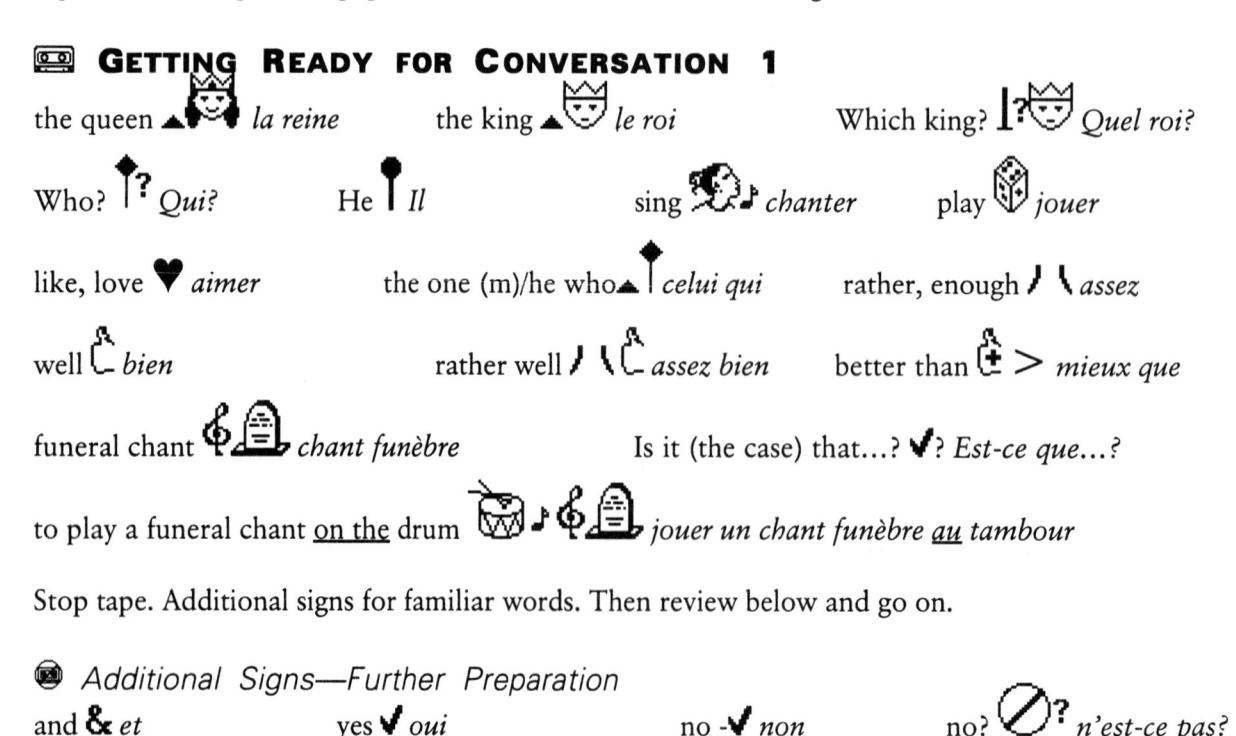

📼 GETTING READY FOR CONVERSATION 1

the queen *la reine*   the king *le roi*   Which king? *Quel roi?*

Who? *Qui?*   He *Il*   sing *chanter*   play *jouer*

like, love *aimer*   the one (m)/he who *celui qui*   rather, enough *assez*

well *bien*   rather well *assez bien*   better than *mieux que*

funeral chant *chant funèbre*   Is it (the case) that…? *Est-ce que…?*

to play a funeral chant on the drum *jouer un chant funèbre au tambour*

Stop tape. Additional signs for familiar words. Then review below and go on.

📼 *Additional Signs—Further Preparation*

and *et*   yes *oui*   no *non*   no? *n'est-ce pas?*

to sing   *chanter*   he sings   *il chante*

to play   *jouer*   he plays   *il joue*

34

to love	*aimer*	she loves	*elle aime*
better than she sings	*mieux qu'elle ne chante.*		

REVIEW OF PICTOGRAPHS

Instructions: Match the pictographs with the word list below.

Word List

aimer	*assez*	*assez bien*	*Qui?*	*bien*	*celui qui*
chant funèbre	*chante*	*est-ce que?*	*et*	*il*	*quel roi?*
joue	*qui*	*la reine*	*le roi*	*mieux que*	*n'est-ce pas?*
non	*oui*	*quel*			
jouer un chant funèbre au tambour					

TASK 2

Listen several times to the reading of this dialogue until you can understand the conversation fully with your eyes closed.

The setting: A royal ball is under way in a palace. Two servants (• and ••) are observing and commenting about the goings on.

CONVERSATION 1

••: Who is singing?   *Qui chante?*
 •: The king. The king is singing.   *Le roi. Le roi chante.*
••: Which king?   *Quel roi?*
 •: The one who likes to play funeral chants on the drum.   *Celui qui aime jouer des chants funèbres au tambour.*
••: The king who likes to play funeral chants on the drum is singing?   *Le roi qui aime jouer des chants funèbres au tambour chante?*
 •: Yes, and he sings well, doesn't he?   *Oui, et il chante bien, n'est-ce pas?*
••: Well enough. He sings better than he plays.   *Assez bien. Il chante mieux qu'il ne joue.*

Tape off. On to the task below.

TASK 3

Use your hands as puppets and dramatize the dialogue, looking only at the English. Throw yourself into this performance. Aim for "Frenchiness" and fluency.

Task 4

Do the same as in Task 3, but this time look only at the following pictographic representation of the dialogue. Ham it up. Try to say the dialogue without thinking in English.

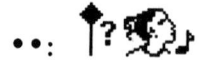

Pictographic Representation

10

A Diglot-Weave Story
Une histoire bilingue

The story of the diglot-weave reader is interesting (*diglot* is a word meaning two languages, like *polyglot*, which means many languages). Professor Rudy Lentulay of Bryn Mawr University was invited to teach a class in Russian for twenty minutes a day, two days a week, to six-year-old children. Lacking previous experience teaching small children, he hesitated to accept the invitation. For one thing, he doubted children could learn any significant amount of language under such a limited schedule.

By chance, he had just finished reading Anthony Burgess's novel *A Clockwork Orange,* in which teenagers use almost two hundred slang words—all of them Russian words in English spelling. The reader, as well as the teenagers in the story, must learn the meaning of these words from context. From this came the inspiration to make a game out of learning Russian, a word game that even small children could play. So he accepted the job.

From the first day he made telling stories the focus of the course. Each week he told a story with Russian words sprinkled here and there—at first sparsely, then gradually more and more abundantly, each story using as much as possible of the vocabulary employed in previous stories. Since the learners were children just beginning first grade, nothing was written for them in English or Russian. They had to understand the words and their meanings not through translation, but through visual and verbal context.

Through the use of pictures as well as verbal and nonverbal context, Professor Lentulay engaged these young learners in playful but meaningful use of new expressions. The game was this: once a new expression was started in circulation, the children were expected to use it in place of its English equivalent thereafter. The "game" was to catch someone using an English word or phrase where the Russian equivalent was called for. The rules of the game of Musical Chairs were sometimes used to eliminate from play those who slipped. Central to the activity was the story.

Before the end of the term, he was telling complete stories—even stories from Russian literature—entirely in Russian, and the six-year-old American children were understanding them.

STORY TIME: *LA FENÊTRE CASSÉE* (THE BROKEN WINDOW)

Would *vous* like me to tell *vous une histoire? Eh bien,* let me tell *vous une histoire* about some naughty *enfants* who were playing with *une balle* in *la rue* in front of *une maison.* In this *illustration, vous* cannot *voir les enfants,* but *vous pouvez voir la maison, la rue devant la maison, et la balle dans la rue. Cette histoire* tells about what happens when *un des enfants* throws *la balle, et elle* shatters *une des* glass *fenêtres de la maison.*

Besides telling about *des enfants* playing *balle dans la rue* and breaking a glass *fenêtre*, this *histoire* tells about *un homme, le propriétaire de la maison,* who *est dans la maison. Vous* can't see him. *Non, vous ne pouvez pas le voir dans l'illustration. L'histoire* also tells about *une* kind old *femme* who is walking down *la rue* toward *la maison et* looks up *et voit* what happens.

Et bien, now I'll *raconter la première partie de l'histoire.* Prick up your ears *et écoutez! Des enfants* are playing *balle dans la rue devant la maison.* Probably *les enfants* are not aware of what can *se passer. Et bien,* as I *vous* have already told, one *des enfants* throws *la balle très* hard, *et elle* sails up high.

> To be continued
>
> End Tape 1, Side A

Tape 1, Side B

11

📼 *La fenêtre cassée*
(The Broken Window, continued)

Let us look at some of the *détails de l'illustration. La maison a une porte.* Every *maison a* at least *une porte, n'est-ce pas? La maison a un toit. Le toit, naturellement,* is on top of *la maison.* What usually sticks up out *d'un toit? Une cheminée, n'est-ce pas?* Sure enough, sticking up *du toit de cette maison,* there is *une cheminée. Et,* billowing out *de la cheminée, il y a de la* black *fumée.* What other things has *la maison* besides *des portes, un toit, et une cheminée?* Of course, *la maison a des fenêtres.* From what *vous* can *voir sur cette illustration, la maison a deux fenêtres.*

If *vous* could look through *cette fenêtre-ci, vous* could *voir que* there is *un homme dans la maison,* sitting *à la fenêtre. L'homme est le propriétaire de la maison. L'homme* is sitting *à la fenêtre,* reading. Growing near *la maison, il y a un* apple *arbre—un pommier.* Hanging on *l'arbre, il y a une pomme. Et* on the other side *de la rue, il y a une forêt.*

Et bien, now let's *continuer l'histoire.* What do *vous* think will *se passer? Pensez-vous que la balle* breaks *la porte? Non, la balle ne* breaks *pas la porte. Pensez-vous que la balle* lands on *le toit? Non, la balle n'atterrit pas sur le toit. Pensez-vous que la balle descend* through *la cheminée? Non, la balle ne descend pas* through *la cheminée. Pensez-vous que la balle* crashes through *la fenêtre? Pouche! Oui, c'est exactement ce qui se passe. La balle* crashes through *la fenêtre et* hits *l'homme* right on *le nez. Oh là là!*

Now what *pensez-vous* will *se passer? Pensez-vous que les enfants* will run away? *Pensez-vous que l'homme* will punish them? *Pensez-vous que les enfants* will have to *payer* for *la fenêtre?*

After *la balle* breaks *la fenêtre et* smacks *l'homme* on *le nez, il* jumps up *et* looks out *de la* broken *fenêtre.* What does *il voit? Il voit les enfants.* Now what *sorte* of *homme pensez-vous qu'il soit? Pensez-vous qu'il* doesn't mind if *une balle* smacks him *dans le nez?*

Le visage de l'homme est red, *très rouge* because *l'homme est très fâché.* When *vous* get *très fâché,* your *visage* gets *rouge* too. Why is *l'homme fâché?* Well, wouldn't *vous* get *fâché* if *des enfants* threw *une balle et* broke *la fenêtre de* your *maison, et la balle* smacked *vous* right on *le nez?*

What *se passe* after that? *Pensez-vous que l'homme* jumps out *de la fenêtre et chasse les enfants? Pensez-vous que l'homme* climbs up *la cheminée* onto *le toit et* then jumps off? *Pensez-vous que l'homme téléphone à la police, et un policier* comes *et arrête les enfants et* throws them *en prison?*

Et bien, what does *l'homme* really do? *Il* throws *la balle* back out *de la fenêtre et* calls out gruffly, «*Les enfants!*» *Et* what *supposez-vous que les enfants* do? *Pensez-vous que* they pick up *la balle et* go knock *à la porte et* apologize *à l'homme*? *Ou, pensez-vous que les enfants* leave *leur balle et* run away? *C'est exactement* what *ils* do. *Ils* run away. *Ils* run up *la rue*.

Est-ce qu'ils sont fâchés? Non, ils ne sont pas fâchés. Ils have nothing to be *fâchés* about. *Ils* are afraid. *Oui, ils ont peur que l'homme* will catch them. *Ils ont peur qu'ils* will be punished, *sévèrement punis. Ils ont peur qu'ils* will have to *payer la fenêtre cassée*.

Pensez-vous que l'homme a le right *de punir les enfants? Pensez-vous qu'il a le droit de* make *les enfants payer la fenêtre cassée?* What about *la fenêtre? Qui* should *payer, le propriétaire de la maison, le garçon* who threw *la balle qui a cassé la fenêtre, ou* should *tous les enfants payer?* Have *vous* ever thrown *une balle qui a cassé une fenêtre ou qui a cassé* somebody's *nez*?

Et bien, to *continuer l'histoire*. Down *la rue une* old *femme* is walking. *La femme voit les enfants* running up *la rue*. She calls out to them, «*Les enfants! Attendez!*» *Que pensez-vous que la femme* wants to do? *Que pensez-vous que les enfants* will do?

A close look at *la forêt* will reveal something sticking out from under *un arbre*. There's a *petite* arrow…*une petite flèche* pointing to it. *Vous voyez? Voilà la petite flèche.* What could *la petite flèche* be pointing to? A tail? *Oui, une queue.* Could it be *la queue d'un loup? Pensez-vous que la petite flèche* is pointing to *la queue d'un loup?* Perhaps…*peut-être…un* big bad wolf, *un grand loup méchant*, is hiding *dans la forêt! Vous avez peur que le grand loup méchant* is going to eat *les enfants, n'est-ce pas?*

Et bien, écoutez as my *histoire* unfolds, *et vous* will find out *ce qui va se passer. Voici ce qui s'est passé:* After *l'homme* calls out: «*Les enfants!*» *les enfants* don't stop. *Ils* run away up *la rue, et* when *ils voient la femme* walking down *la rue* toward them, *ils* run off to *la forêt. Ils ont peur de l'homme* more than *ils ont peur du loup!*

Just as *ils* enter *dans la forêt, ils voient* something hiding behind *un arbre*. Could it be *le grand loup méchant?* Or *est-ce* only *Bobi, un* big dog, *un gros chien* that loves to play *dans la forêt* with *les enfants. Non, ce n'est pas Bobi. C'est le loup. Et il est très* hungered, *très affamé. Il* intends to eat *ces enfants*.

Just as *le loup* charges, *les enfants voient le gros chien qui* loves to play *dans la forêt avec les enfants.* «*Bobi! Bobi!*» *ils* cry. *Bobi* comes running, *chasse le loup, et sauve les enfants. Bobi est un héros! Les enfants* run out *de la forêt. Ils* go right back to *la maison*, knock *à la porte, et offrent de payer la fenêtre cassée.* Now *l'homme n'est plus fâché. Il dit* to *les enfants*, "That's all right. *La fenêtre cassée n'est pas importante.* I'm just happy *que le loup* did not eat *vous. Allez* home *et dites à* your *parents tout ce qui s'est passé.*»

12
More on Numbers
Plus au sujet des chiffres

Stop the tape and read the explanation.

Seventeen / *Dix-sept*, Eighteen / *Dix-huit*, Nineteen / *Dix-neuf*

In French, the numbers 17, 18, and 19 are structured like Roman numerals:

ten-seven	ten-eight	ten-nine
XVII *dix-sept*	XVIII *dix-huit*	XIX *dix-neuf*

Remember that the sound of the final consonant in *dix* is lost before the *s* in *sept* and becomes [z] in 18 and 19.

Listen and repeat:

17   18   19   17000   18000   19000   17700   18800   19900   1717   2818   3919

Point to the number called:

```
                          19000
                   1700          1200
            7000          10000         17000
                   18000         1800
                          8000
```

Say those numbers and read below.

dix-sept mille	17000	*six mille six*	6006	*dix-neuf mille neuf cent neuf*	19909
dix-huit mille	18000	*trois mille neuf*	3009	*dix-sept mille quatre cent quatre*	17404
neuf mille dix	9010	*neuf mille neuf cent*	9900	*dix-huit mille huit cent huit*	18808
dix mille dix	10010				

Eleven through Sixteen

The numbers 11–16 are built in a different way. There one common feature, the part that corresponds to *teen* in English, is a final [z]- sound.

Listen: 11   12   13   14   15   16

It may be helpful to compare these with English sound-alikes:

(11) owns   (12) dues   (13) trays   (14) cat oars   (15) cans   (16) says

Listen and repeat:

11	11000	11101	16	16000	16606
14	14000	14404	13	13000	13303
15	15000	15505	12	12000	12202

Point to the number called:

```
                        12000           16000
              15000           10000           14000
                        11000           13000
```

Stop tape. Say those numbers! Read below.

treize mille trois cents	13300	*douze mille deux cent deux*	12202
cinq mille cinq cent cinq	5505	*quatorze mille quatre cent quatre*	14404
seize mille six cent six	16606	*onze mille cent onze*	11111

PRACTICE AND APPLICATION

1. Count down from 19 to 10. Then by thousands from 19000 to 10000.

2. Choose randomly from the numbers in the cluster below to make up number sequences in the hundreds and thousands.

```
                       18
               17      11      15
        14          (0)(0)(0)          12
               16              13
                       19
```

3. Practice counting from 1 to 19, gradually increasing your speed. Then from 100 to 900 and from 1000 to 19000 the same way.

4. *Speed-runs.* Time yourself saying the first string of numbers below from left to right. Then time yourself saying it from right to left. Par time is 15 seconds (either direction) after five trials. See how much you can improve your time. Then do the same with the second string. Par time for that is 25 seconds after five trials.

1st string
13 11 15 14 12 17 19 18 16 10 100 110 1000 2000 13000 16000 19000
⌚ Time on first trial: ____seconds   ⌚ Time after five trials: ____seconds

2nd string
15000 12000 11000 14000 18000 13000 16600 17717 18818 14414 13313
⌚ Time on first trial: ____seconds   ⌚ Time after five trials: ____seconds

THE ADVENTURE CONTINUES

By the time you finish working with Jacqueline, you are really getting excited about learning French, and you are already starting to see some progress in your language ability. After a delicious dinner, you and Stump decide to work through a few more French exercises on your own, and you resolve to visit the first place marked on your map the next day.

13

Points, lignes et figures
Points, Lines and Figures

Instructions: As explained before, this learning activity is designed to help you push the envelope of listening comprehension and develop critical skills in inferring meaning. Look for patterns of sentence formation.

A. SCATTER CHART

gros point	longue ligne	ligne courte
ligne épaisse	ligne fine	petit point

B. LISTEN, LOOK, AND READ

1. Un gros point et un petit point.
2. Une longue ligne et une ligne courte.
3. Une ligne épaisse et un petit chiffre, le chiffre cinq.
4. Un gros point et une ligne fine.
5. Deux petits points et deux lignes courtes.
6. Cinq gros points et deux petits chiffres, les chiffres six et un.
7. Ce point est petit. C'est un petit point.
8. Ce point est gros. C'est un gros point.
9. Cette ligne est épaisse. C'est une ligne épaisse.
10. Ces points sont petits. Ce sont de petits points.
11. Ces deux lignes sont fines. Ce sont de fines lignes.
12. Ces trois points sont petits et ces trois sont gros.

C. Look and Listen

🔊 Instructions: Check the appendix for the script of this activity.

1. • •   2. _____ __   3. ▬▬▬▬ 5
4. • __   5. •• __ __ __   6. •••••• 6 1

D. Multiple-Choice Frames

🔊 Instructions: Below, you see a series of frames, each with four sections. You'll hear the frame letter (A through J) and then a sentence referring to what is in one of the four sections (section a, b, c, or d). In the following pause, point to the correct section, and then listen for the answer. Control the pace by stopping and starting the tape. When you are finished, check your answers in the appendix.

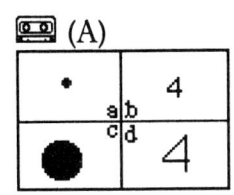

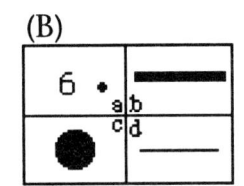

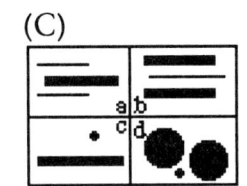

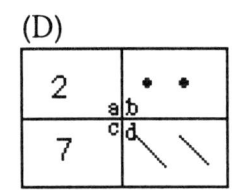

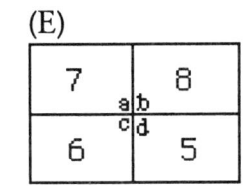

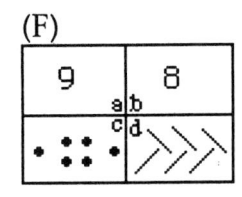

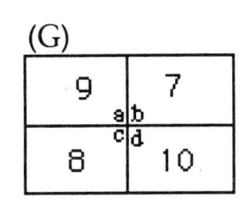

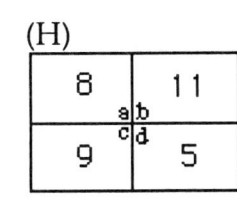

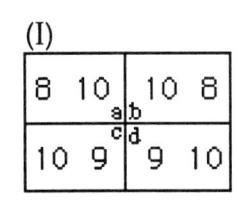

(A) (B) (C) (D) (E) (F) (G) (H) (I) (J)

E. Listen and Draw

Instructions: Stop the tape if the pace is too fast. The answer key is in the appendix.

1.   2.   3.   4.

F. Comprehension Check

Instructions: Check your comprehension of the twelve sentences in Part B.

1. A big dot and a little dot.
2. A long line and a short line.
3. A thick line and a small number, the number 5.
4. A big dot and a thin line.
5. Two little dots and two short lines.
6. Five big dots and two small numbers, the numbers 6 and 1.
7. This dot is small. It is a small dot.
8. This dot is big. It is a big dot.
9. This line is thick. It is a thick line.
10. These dots are small. They are small dots.
11. These two lines are thin. They are thin lines.
12. These three dots are little and these three are big.

14
🎞 Thinking *en français*

This module is for your special enjoyment. It is entirely tape-off. If you give it your best, it will help you begin to think in French.

🎞 Instructions: As you become bilingual, you learn to turn your thoughts, intents, and feelings directly into French without translation from English. You also learn to understand spoken and written French directly without translation into English. What follows is designed to lead you toward that goal. Using pictographs rather than words as stimuli, you will first create short, simple sentences, then longer, more elaborate sentences. You are to go through it on your own. Give it your best shot! You will make strides toward thinking *en français*.

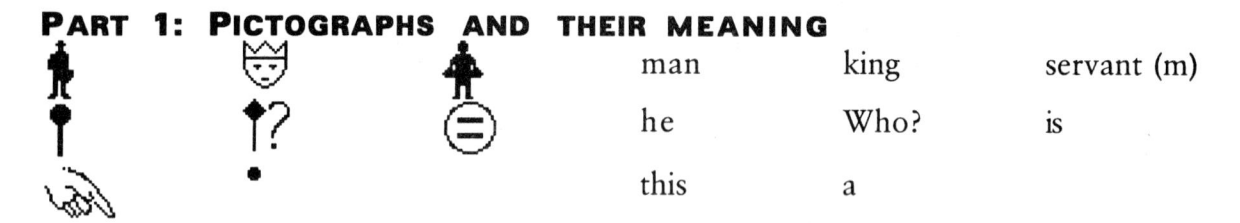

PART 1: PICTOGRAPHS AND THEIR MEANING

man	king	servant (m)
he	Who?	is
this	a	

Building Blocks—Words

UN CE(T)	ROI HOMME SERVITEUR	EST	(UN) CE(T)	ROI HOMME SERVITEUR
IL	QUI?			

Note: *Cet* before a vowel sound.

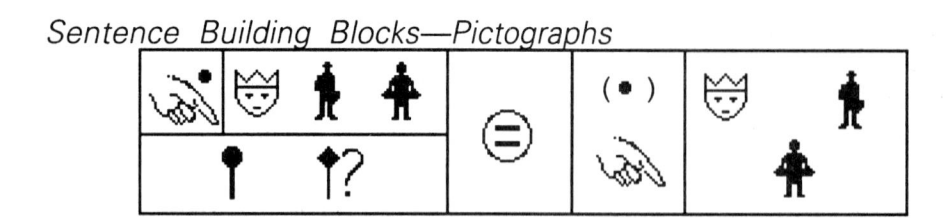

Sentence Building Blocks—Pictographs

Sample Sentences

Un roi est un homme.

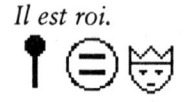

Qui est cet homme?

Il est roi.

Un roi est un serviteur.   *Qui est ce serviteur?*   *Il est roi.*

Nine Sentences to Read Out Loud 1

1. 2. 3.
4. 5. 6.
7. 8. 9.

If you need help to read the pictographs, check the appendix. Then read the same pictograph sentences a second and a third time, pushing yourself to read fluently.

PART 2: PICTOGRAPHS AND THEIR MEANING

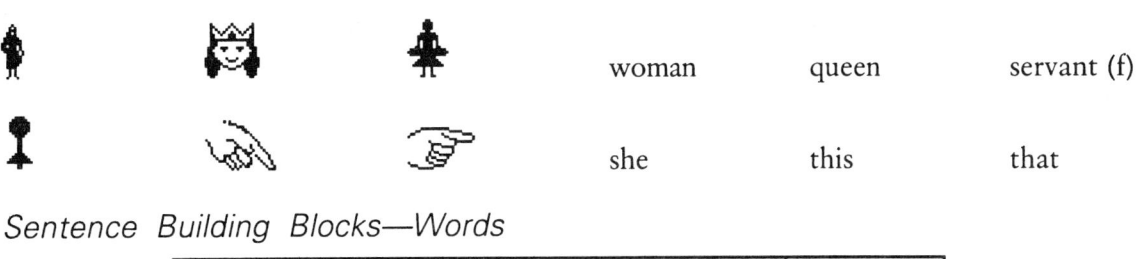

woman   queen   servant (f)

she   this   that

Sentence Building Blocks—Words

UNE CETTE...-CI CETTE...-LA	REINE FEMME SERVANTE	EST	(UNE) CETTE...-CI CETTE...-LA	REINE FEMME SERVANTE
ELLE	QUI?			

Sentence Building Blocks—Pictographs

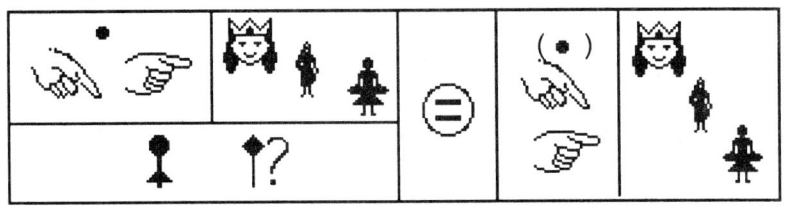

Sample Sentences

Une femme est une reine.

Qui est cette femme-là?

Elle est reine.

Une servante est une reine.

Qui est cette servante-là?

Qui est cette femme-ci?   *Elle est servante.*

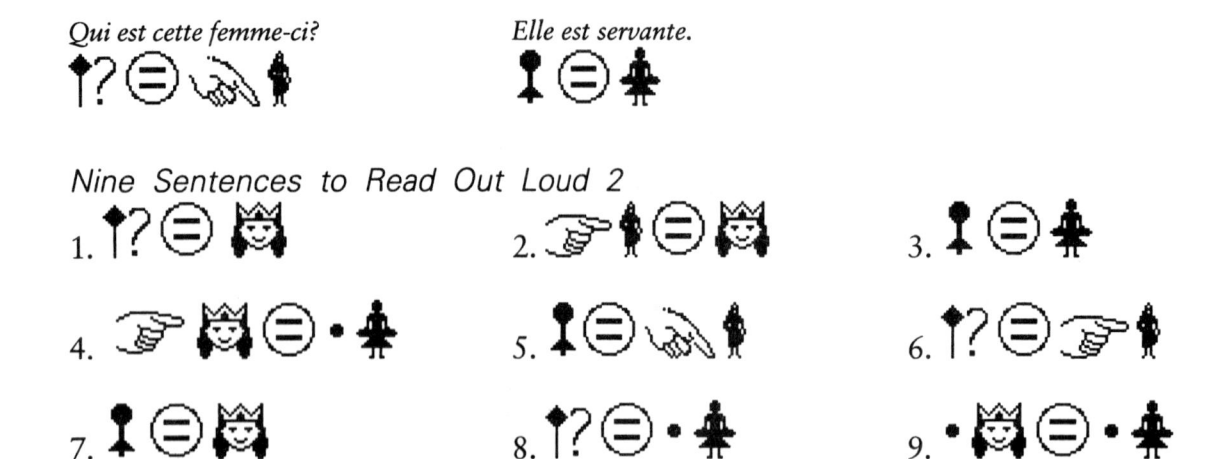

Nine Sentences to Read Out Loud 2

1. ⚑? ⊜ 👑
2. 👉 ⚑ ⊜ 👑
3. ⚑ ⊜ ♣
4. 👉 👑 ⊜ · ♣
5. ⚑ ⊜ 👌 ⚑
6. ⚑? ⊜ 👉 ⚑
7. ⚑ ⊜ 👑
8. ⚑? ⊜ · ♣
9. · 👑 ⊜ · ♣

If you need help reading the pictographs, check the appendix. Then read the same pictograph sentences a second and a third time, pushing yourself to read fluently.

Instructions: Form several sentences from these icons.

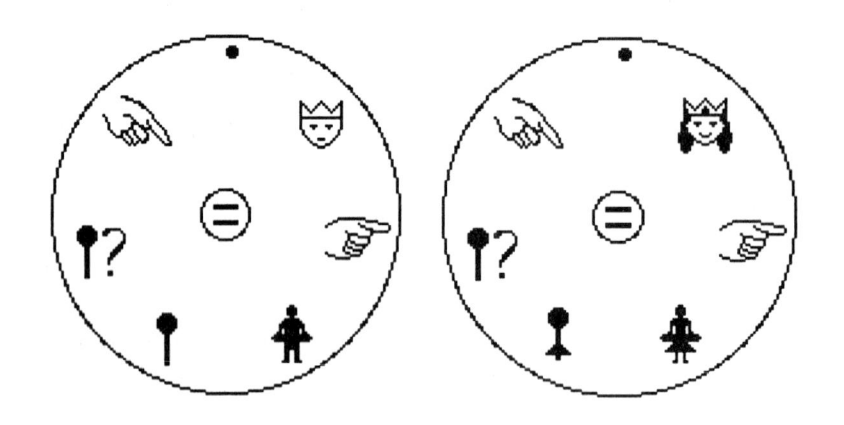

15

Toward Fluency
Vers la facilité de parole

WORDS AND PATTERNS 1

Instructions: Read through these words and see them used in the sample sentences below.

a gentleman	*un monsieur*	(he/she) was	*était*
the gentleman	*le monsieur*	(he/she) was not	*n'était pas*
a young lady	*une demoiselle*	You know...	*Vous savez...*
the young lady	*la demoiselle*	Do you know...?	*Savez-vous...?*
of Joseph/of Albert	*de Joseph/d'Albert*	with	*avec*
of the princess	*de la princesse*	here	*ici*
perhaps, maybe	*peut-être*	he/she/it/this	*ce*

Sample Sentences

You know who Albert was, don't you?	*Vous savez qui était Albert, n'est-ce pas?*
I know that Albert was a prince.	*Je sais qu'Albert était *un prince.*
And do you know who Richard was?	*Et savez-vous qui était Richard?*
He was not a prince.	*Ce n'était pas un prince.*
Richard was a friend of the princess.	*Richard était un ami de la princesse.*
Do you know if he was a friend of Albert?	*Savez-vous s'il était un ami d'Albert?*
Do you know if Pierre was here?	*Savez-vous si Pierre était ici?*
A gentleman was here with Nanette.	*Un monsieur était ici avec Nanette.*
Perhaps it was Pierre.	*Peut-être [que] c'était Pierre.*
The gentleman who was here was not Pierre.	*Le monsieur qui était ici n'était pas Pierre.*
Yes, I know. He was the prince who...	*Oui, je sais. C'était le prince qui...*

*Note: Most often French speakers do not say the definite article when they refer to occupation titles. For example, you might hear: *Albert est prince. Albert est docteur. Nanette est chanteuse.*

Stop tape. Translation exercise.

Translation Exercise 1

Instructions: Translate the following sentences from English to French. Check your answers in the appendix.

1. Joseph is a friend of Josette, who is a princess.
2. Nanette's friend isn't a princess.
3. Pierre's friend was a prince, yes.
4. He was here with Robert, who is a friend of the princess.
5. Who is Josette? She's the princess who was here with Robert.
6. Roland was a prince and is a prince.
7. Richard was not a prince and is not a prince.
8. Who was here with Nanette?
9. It was a gentleman who is perhaps a friend of the princess.

Review

1. Go through the translation exercises again, aiming for fluency.

2. Close your eyes, breathe deeply, and relax, letting your mind create sentences made up of material from this lesson. See how many meaningful statements you can generate from this material in two minutes. The goal is to create 7 statements in 2 minutes.

⌚ First 2-minute trial: ____statements   ⌚ Second 2-minute trial: ____statements

WORDS AND PATTERNS 2

Instructions: Familiarize yourself with these vocabulary words and see them in use in the sample sentences below.

of the prince	*du prince (de le - du)*	not me	*pas moi*
for sure, surely	*bien sûr*	they	*ils*
in the room	*dans la chambre*	they were	*ils étaient*
without me	*sans moi*	(they) were not	*n'étaient pas*
not without him	*pas sans lui*	there	*là*

Note: The verbs *était* "was" and *étaient* "were" sound exactly alike.

Sample Sentences

Pierre was a good friend of Albert.	*Pierre était un bon ami d'Albert.*
And Marie was also a good friend of the prince.	*Et Marie était aussi une bonne amie du prince.*
She was the friend of Robert and Albert.	*Elle était l'amie de Robert et d'Albert.*
They were in the room without me.	*Ils étaient dans la chambre sans moi.*
But the prince was not there.	*Mais le prince n'était pas là.*
For sure he was not there.	*Bien sûr qu'il n'était pas là.*
Who was it? It was me and him.	*Qui était-ce? C'était moi et lui.*
Who was there? Not me. And not him.	*Qui était là? Pas moi. Et pas lui.*
He is not there, he is here.	*Il n'est pas là, il est ici.*
He was not there, he was here.	*Il n'était pas là, il était ici.*

Stop tape. Translation exercise.

TRANSLATION EXERCISE 2

Instructions: Translate the following sentences from English to French. Check your answers in the appendix.

1. Josette is a friend.
2. Marie too, right?
3. Is Marie a friend?
4. Yes, she is also a friend.
5. But the princess who was here is not a friend.
6. Mademoiselle Renard is a princess without friend.
7. Marie and Robert were not here with the prince.
8. They were with the friend (f) of the princess.
9. Who was here and who was there?
10. I don't know, but for sure they were not there.
11. It was me.

Review

1. Go through the translation exercises again, aiming for fluency.

2. See how many meaningful statements you can generate from this material in two minutes. The goal is to create 9 statements in 2 minutes.

First 2-minute trial: ____ statements   Second 2-minute trial: ____ statements

3 WORDS AND PATTERNS

Where?	*Où?*	They are...	*Ils sont...*
Where is Marie?	*Où est Marie?*	the friends	*les amis*
Where from?	*D'où?*	now	*maintenant*
Where is Albert from?	*D'où est Albert?*		
He is from Paris.	*Il est de Paris.*	the princes and	*les princes et*
He is from here.	*Il est d'ici.*	the princesses	*les princesses*

Note: In written French, a plural noun has a plural suffix (s or x): ami<u>s</u>, tableau<u>x</u>, etc. But in spoken French, that suffix is silent. So how can one distinguish singular nouns from plural? Observe how *le* (luh) and *la* (la) indicate singular, but *les* (lay or lays) indicates plural even when the noun sounds the same.

Le prince : les princes   *la princesse : les princesses*   *l'ami : les amis*

Sample Sentences

Me, I'm from here. I'm not from Paris.	*Moi, je suis d'ici. Je ne suis pas de Paris.*
Me too, I'm from here.	*Moi aussi, je suis d'ici.*
Where is Albert from? From America? No.	*D'où est Albert? D'Amérique? Non.*
Where are the princes now?	*Où sont les princes maintenant?*
Where are the princes from?	*D'où sont les princes?*
Where is the prince who is from Paris?	*Où est le prince qui est de Paris?*
Is Josette from here?	*Est-ce que Josette est d'ici?*
Not from here, not from Paris...from Monaco.	*Pas d'ici, pas de Paris...de Monaco.*
Do you know if she is with us now?	*Savez-vous si elle est avec nous maintenant?*
I know that she and Robert are with you.	*Je sais qu'elle et Robert sont avec vous.*
For sure the princesses are with you.	*Bien sûr que les princesses sont avec vous.*
They were with you. Now they are with us.	*Ils étaient avec vous. Maintenant ils sont avec nous.*

Stop tape. Translation exercise.

Translation Exercise 3

Instructions: Translate the following sentences from English to French. Check your answers in the appendix.

1. Where is Robert from?
2. Is he from Paris?
3. Who's from here and who's from Paris?
4. Where's the prince who was here with the princess of Monaco?
5. The princess is not from Monaco, she is from Paris.
6. From where? From Paris...not from Monaco.
7. The prince and the princess are here.
8. The princes are from Paris, but the princesses are from Monaco.
9. Are they here? Not now, but they were here.

16

Chatter at a Royal Ball
Bavardages au bal royal

GETTING READY FOR CONVERSATION 2
You're on your own here. Tape off. Prepare well.

TASK 1

Instructions: Draw each pictograph on a separate card or piece of paper. These cards will help you to construct sentences and stories. Learn the words and their pictographs.

the tower *la tour*

the bath *le bain*

the bathroom *la salle de bain*

with *avec*

also, too *aussi*

to cry *pleurer* (imPLORE)

princess *la princesse*

prince *le prince*

in *dans*

the one [f] who... *celle qui...*

but *mais*

more or less *plus ou moins*

much, a lot *beaucoup*

Which queen? *Quelle reine?*

Why? *Pourquoi?*

she *elle*

to know (something) *savoir*

(🧠 = brain with a speck of knowledge)

Who knows? *Qui sait?*

REVIEW OF PICTOGRAPHS

Instructions: Match the pictographs with the word list.

52

Word List

joue/jouer	beaucoup	mieux que	Qui?	aime/aimer	la reine	chante/chanter
assez bien	celui qui	celle qui	il	Pourquoi?	Qui sait?	chant funèbre
le prince	la princesse	pleurer	la tour	aussi	le roi	la salle de bain
elle	et	avec	mais	savoir	plus ou moins	Quelle reine?
n'est-ce pas?	le bain	dans				

TASK 2

Listen several times to the reading of this dialogue until you can understand the conversation fully with eyes closed or by looking only at the pictographic representation below.

CONVERSATION 2

Instructions: Recite the English before the French voice speaks on the tape!

••: The queen is singing also.   *La reine chante aussi.*
•: Which queen?   *Quelle reine?*
••: The one who was crying in the bathroom with the princess.   *Celle qui pleurait dans la salle de bain avec la princesse.*
•: The queen who was crying in the bathroom with the princess is singing?   *La reine qui pleurait dans la salle de bain avec la princesse chante?*
••: Yes, she's singing in the tower with the king.   *Oui. Elle chante dans la tour avec le roi.*
•: The king and the queen are singing funeral chants in the tower?   *Le roi et la reine chantent des chants funèbres dans la tour?*
••: Yes. And don't they sing well?   *Oui. Et ne chantent-ils pas bien?*
•: Well yes, they sing more or less well. But why do they sing funeral chants?   *Bien oui, ils chantent plus ou moins bien. Mais pourquoi chantent-ils des chants funèbres?*
••: Who knows?   *Qui sait?*

TASK 3

Use your hands as puppets and dramatize the dialogue, looking only at the English. Drop all shyness and inhibitions and throw yourself into this performance.

TASK 4

While looking only at the pictographic representation of the dialogue, express your thoughts in French without thinking in English.

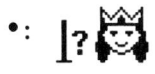

Pictographic Representation

17

Focus on the Language 1–8
Concentration sur la langue 1-8

The next three-and-a-half pages contain important activities and information. Give them your very best. They are tape-off.

◉ Focus 1

Masculine and feminine nouns with indefinite articles: *un, une* and plural *des*.

un roi et une reine	a king and a queen
un roi et une reine	one king and one queen
un étudiant et une étudiante	a student (m) and a student (f)
un chat et une chatte	a cat (m) and a cat (f)
un tambour et une tour	a drum and a tower
des rois et des reines	some kings and some queens
des rois et des reines	kings and queens

1. Every French noun is either feminine or masculine. A noun such as *roi*, referring to a male, is masculine; one such as *reine*, referring to a female, is feminine. Such person nouns are said to have "natural gender"—their gender matches their sex. Likewise with other animate nouns, there is a different form for males and females. (The feminine counterpart of *chat* is *chatte* and of *chien* is *chienne*.) Feminine nouns require feminine-marked modifiers (*une reine*) and masculine nouns require masculine-marked modifiers (*un roi*).

2. Nouns like *tour* and *tambour* do not have natural gender but have assigned gender: *une tour* (not *un tour*), *un tambour* (not *une tambour*). Every noun in French is either masculine or feminine. No one knows why tower is "she" and drum is "he"—they just are.

3. In English, the plural of "a king and a queen" is "kings and queens" or "some kings and some queens." The French plural is not *rois et reines* but *des rois et des reines*. (The *s* of *des* is silent except before a vowel sound, when it is pronounced [z]: *des étudiants*.) *Des rois et des reines* can mean either "kings and queens" or "some kings and some queens."

Translate Orally from and into French

(some) kings and (some) queens	*des rois et des reines*
a drum and a tower	*un tambour et une tour*
(some) drums and (some) towers	*des tambours et des tours*
a duke and a duchess	*un duc et une duchesse*
dukes and duchesses	*des ducs et des duchesses*
some dukes and some duchesses	*des ducs et des duchesses*
a male student and a female student	*un étudiant et une étudiante*
male students and female students	*des étudiants et des étudiantes*

Focus 2

The definite article "the": *la, le, l', les.*

the king and the queen	*le roi et la reine*
the kings and the queens	*les rois et les reines*
the American and the Arab	*l'américain et l'arabe*
the Americans and the Arabs	*les américains et les arabes*

1. Whereas the English definite article "the" never changes, its French counterpart has four forms: *le, la, l',* and *les.*

2. *Le* always goes with masculine and *la* with feminine. You'll never hear *la roi or **le reine!*

3. Both *la* and *le* drop their vowel before a word that starts with a vowel: not *le américain but *l'américain.*

4. The plural form of *la* and *le* is *les: les rois, les reines, les affaires.* (The *s* of *les* is silent except before a vowel sound: *les américains.*) There is no gender distinction in the plural.

Translate Orally from and into French

the king and queen	*le roi et la reine*
the kings and queens	*les rois et les reines*
the bar and the towers	*le bar et les tours*
the student (m) and the student (f)	*l'étudiant et l'étudiante*
The students sing in the tower.	*Les étudiants chantent dans la tour.*
Students sing in the tower.	*Des étudiants chantent dans la tour.*

Focus 3

Linking singular with singular, plural with plural (regular verbs).

The king sings.	*Le roi chante.*
The kings sing.	*Les rois chantent.*
NOT: *The king sing.	NOT: **Le roi chantent.*
NOR: *The kings sings.	NOR: **Les rois chante.*

1. Though speakers of nonstandard English say "They is here, he sing there," etc., in French (as in standard English), verbs have different forms for plural and singular subjects. This is called subject-verb agreement: singular with singular, plural with plural.

2. The plural form of *(il) chante* "he sings" is *(ils) chantent* "they sing." Both *chante* and *chantent* are pronounced the same. The singular and plural forms are pronounced identically in all regular verbs.

Focus 4

Linking singular with singular, plural with plural (irregular verbs).

The king is in the tower.	*Le roi est dans la tour.*
The kings are in the tower.	*Les rois sont dans la tour.*
NOT: *The kings is in the tower.	NOT: **Les rois est dans la tour.*

NOR: *The king <u>are</u> in the tower.	NOR: *Le roi <u>sont</u> dans la tour.
The king <u>knows</u>.	Le roi <u>sait</u>.
The kings <u>know</u>.	Les rois <u>savent</u>.

The plural of *(il) est* "he is" is *(ils) sont* "they are." The plural of *sait* (pronounced [say]) is *savent* (pronounced [sav] as in <u>SAV</u>VY): *il sait; ils savent*.

Translate Orally from and into French

The king is in the tower.	*Le roi est dans la tour.*
The dukes are also in the tower.	*Les ducs sont aussi dans la tour.*
The prince knows.	*Le prince sait.*
The princes know.	*Les princes savent.*

FOCUS 5

"Loves (desires, prefers) to sing," - *aime (désire, préfère) chanter*.

He loves (or likes) to play.	*Il aime jouer.*
She desires to play.	*Elle désire jouer.*
He prefers to play.	*Il préfère jouer.*

1. Verbs such as *(he) intends, wishes, expects, hopes, plans, proposes* combine with a second verb to form phrases. Phrases like "loves to sing," have two parts. The first part is a verb ("loves") that is tied to a subject; the second part consists of "to" plus a verb. This construction is called the infinitive form of the verb. (Take away the "to" and you have the base form of the verb.)

2. The infinitive form of most verbs ends in the sound [e], spelled <er>: *pleur<u>er</u>, chant<u>er</u>, jou<u>er</u>, aim<u>er</u>, préfér<u>er</u>, désir<u>er</u>, parl<u>er</u>*.

3. Just as in English one says "he loves <u>to sing</u>" and not "he loves <u>sings</u>," so also in French one says "*il aime <u>chanter</u>*" and not "*il aime <u>chante</u>*."

Translate Orally from and into French

He likes to play in the tower.	*Il aime jouer dans la tour.*
The dog likes to talk in French.	*Le chien aime parler en français.*
The cat prefers to talk in English.	*Le chat préfère à parler en anglais.*
The princess desires to sing.	*La princesse désire chanter.*

FOCUS 6

Which?

Which king and which queen?	*Quel roi et quelle reine?*

1. *Quelle* precedes a feminine noun: *Quelle reine?* "Which queen?" *Quel* precedes a masculine noun: *Quel roi?* "Which king?" *Quel* and *quelle* do not differ in pronunciation.

Translate Orally from and into French

Which princess and which prince?	*Quelle princesse et quel prince?*
Which king and which queen?	*Quel roi et quelle reine?*
Which duke and which duchess?	*Quel duc et quelle duchesse?*

Focus 7

Pointing words: *cette, ce, cet, ces.*

this king and this queen	*ce roi et cette reine*
this student (m) and this student (f)	*cet étudiant et cette étudiante*
these kings and these students	*ces rois et ces étudiants*

1. *Cette* goes with a feminine noun: *cette reine* "this queen"; *ce* goes with a masculine noun: *ce roi* "this king."

2. When it precedes a word that begins in a vowel sound, *ce* becomes *cet*: *cet étudiant* (NOT: *ce étudiant* or *c'étudiant*).

3. The plural form of both *cette* and *ce* is *ces*: *ces reines* "these queens," *ces rois* "these kings." The *s* of *ces* is silent except before a vowel sound: *ces affaires* is pronounced "says a fair." Note that there is no gender distinction in the plural; *ces*, like *des* and *les*, does not vary.

Translate Orally from and into French

this prince and this princess	*ce prince et cette princesse*
this duke and this duchess	*ce duc et cette duchesse*
these dukes and these duchesses	*ces ducs et ces duchesses*
These Americans (m). These Americans (f).	*Ces américains. Ces américaines.*
This American (f). This American (m).	*Cette américaine. Cet américain.*

Focus 8

The one who: *celui qui, celle qui.*

| This king is the one who sings. | *Ce roi est celui qui chante.* |
| This queen is the one who cries. | *Cette reine est celle qui pleure.* |

Note: *ce* and *cette* cannot stand alone; they are always linked to a following noun: *ce beau prince* "this handsome prince," *cette belle princesse* "this beautiful princess." But *ce* and *cette* have counterparts *celui* and *celle* that do not link to a following noun. These translate "the one" (or "he" or "she") and refer back to a previously named person or thing.

Translate Orally from and into French

The duke is the one who sings.	*Le duc est celui qui chante.*
The duchess is the one who plays.	*La duchesse est celle qui joue.*
Which princess cries? The one who is singing.	*Quelle princesse pleure? Celle qui chante.*
Which prince sings? The one who is crying.	*Quel prince chante? Celui qui pleure.*
He who sings cries. She who cries sings.	*Celui qui chante pleure. Celle qui pleure chante.*

18

🎵 *Au sujet de la prononciation*
On Pronunciation

The sequence of letters <ou> consistently represents the sound [u], as in what a Frenchman cow says, *mou*, *Pérou* (Peru), and *voudou* (voodoo).

THE [Ü]-SOUND

The vowel letter <u> that we call [ju], the French call [ü]. By itself, the letter <u>, as well as the sequence <ue>, consistently represents a vowel sound like that of *Vee* or *knee*, but with lips rounded: [vü, nü]. Listen to the contrast between these words:

bout : bu   *vous : vu*   *nous : nu*

The final vowel sound in the underlined member of these contrasts is not the [u] of b<u>oo</u>, v<u>oodoo</u>, g<u>nu</u>, nor is it the [i] of b<u>ee</u>, V<u>ee</u>, kn<u>ee</u>. It is rather [ü], that is, a "rounded [i]," lips rounded to say [i], [ü].

THE [Ø]-SOUND

Listen to these words: *feu, adieu, milieu*. To approximate this [ø] sound, say "bird" without the r-sound, or say <u>uh</u>, but with rounded lips. Listen and repeat.

fu : feu : fou   *pu : peu : pou*   *du : dieu : d'où*   *adieu, milieu, Monsieur.*

🎵 *Goals*

The purpose of these accelerated language courses is to help the learner achieve four main goals. These are (1) discover the delight and excitement of learning a language; (2) become a robust, independent learner using effective learning strategies; (3) acquire skill and confidence in understanding a great deal of normal native speech and in producing a great deal of spontaneous, creative speech; (4) acquire the kinds of skills, knowledge, and experience that can best undergird the continuing pursuit of mastery.

THE ADVENTURE CONTINUES

Day Two—0800 hours

Eight Days to Rendezvous

The next morning, you consult with Jacqueline and find out how to reach the first place on the map. She tells you that the marked place is a café. It will not open until noon.

"If you like, I can help pass the time by telling you about Canada," she offers. "I studied abroad in Québec for a little over a year."

You gladly accept her offer, and Jacqueline tells you about Québec.

Québec Culture Overview

The province of Québec is the only province in Canada that is primarily French-speaking. Québec has experienced more European influences than Canada's other provinces because of its past cultural and linguistic ties to France, Switzerland, and Normandy. Québec's population of almost 7 million makes up 25 percent of Canada's total population. Of these 7 million people, less than one million claim English as their first language, though many are bilingual. The French-speaking people of Québec even have a name for themselves: *Québécois*. A separate English-language school system exists in Québec, but most schools in this province conduct all classes in French. Food in Québec has a heavy French influence, and food connoisseurs consider Québec's food to be among the best in North America. Maple syrup is produced in Québec, and many people have parties centered on syrup making.

Facts and Figures on Québec

- English and French are both official languages in Canada, but French is used almost exclusively in many parts of Québec.

- Catholicism is the dominant religion in Québec.

- There is a sizable minority of Inuit Indians in the northern part of Québec. They have their own language called Inuktitut.

- Mining, forestry, and manufacturing are major industries in Québec.

- Montréal is known for its excellent subway system.

- Popular sports throughout Canada include hockey, baseball, curling, rugby, skiing, tennis, and lacrosse (Canada's national sport).

The Adventure Continues

After she finishes teaching you about Québec, Jacqueline teaches you a short story in French.

"It is an old Swedish folktale," she explains. "Its simplicity and repetitiveness make it easy to remember."

19

🎧 Story Time: The Key of the King's Kingdom
French Only
La clé du royaume du roi

🎧 Instructions: Listen to and read this story. Then try to retell it by only looking at the illustrations.

Here is a key, a small key.
Here is a king.
And here is the king's kingdom.
In this kingdom, there is a town.
And in this town, there is a park.
And in this park, there is a house.
And in this house, there is a room.
And in this room, there is a vase.
And in this vase, there's a flower.
   The flower in the vase,
   the vase in the room,
   the room in the house,
   the house in the park,
   the park in the town,
   the town in the kingdom,
   and here is the key of the king's kingdom.
Just imagine!
	🎧 *Voici une clé, une petite clé.*
	Voici un roi.
	Et voici le royaume du roi.
	Dans ce royaume, il y a une ville.
	Et dans cette ville, il y a un parc.
	Et dans ce parc, il y a une maison.
	Et dans cette maison, il y a une pièce.
	Et dans cette pièce, il y a un vase.
	Et dans ce vase, il y a une fleur.
	   La fleur dans le vase,
	   le vase dans la pièce,
	   la pièce dans la maison,
	   la maison dans le parc,
	   le parc dans la ville,
	   la ville dans le royaume,
	   et voici la clé du royaume du roi.
	Imaginez donc!

This little gem is a breeze to learn. Sit back and listen to it again, taking in the music of its expression.

Voici une clé, une petite clé.
Voici un roi.
Et voici le royaume du roi.
Dans ce royaume, il y a une ville.
Et dans cette ville, il y a un parc.
Et dans ce parc, il y a une maison.
Et dans cette maison, il y a une pièce.
Et dans cette pièce, il y a un vase.
Et dans ce vase, il y a une fleur.
La fleur dans le vase,
le vase dans la pièce,
la pièce dans la maison,
la maison dans le parc,
le parc dans la ville,
la ville dans le royaume,
et voici la clé du royaume du roi.
Imaginez donc!

LEARNING ACTIVITIES

1. Listen to the story while keeping one hand on the pause button. See if you can give a quick English translation for each sentence.

2. With one hand on the pause button, look at the English and see if you can anticipate the French equivalent for each sentence.

3. Use the material to make statements not found in the story itself.

4. Read sections out loud with the voice on the tape.

5. Memorize some parts of the story.

6. Do something creative with the material, such as write a modified story.

7. Invest some time in learning to tell this story to a child on your lap.

THE ADVENTURE CONTINUES

When Jacqueline has finished the story and you can repeat it fairly well, you check the time. It still isn't time to visit the café. Jacqueline takes a sheet of paper, draws some simple shapes, and uses this page to teach you more vocabulary and some new sentence patterns.

20

Points, lignes et figures
Points, Lines, and Figures

A. SCATTER CHART

| | | |

ligne verticale   *ligne diagonale*   *ligne horizontale*

un point suivi d'une ligne   *une ligne suivie d'un point*

B. LISTEN, LOOK, AND READ

1. | *Voici une ligne verticale.*
2. _____   *Voici une ligne horizontale.*
3. \   *Et voilà une ligne diagonale.*
4. \ / \   *Ces lignes sont diagonales.*
5. \\ /   *Ces lignes sont aussi diagonales.*
6. _____   *Est-ce que cette ligne est verticale? Non, elle est horizontale.*
7. _____   *Est-ce que cette ligne est aussi horizontale? Oui.*
8. / /   *Est-ce que ces lignes sont horizontales? Non, elles sont diagonales.*
9. | | | *Est-ce que ces lignes sont verticales? Oui.*
10. | *Ce n'est pas une ligne diagonale.*
11. • | *Voici un point suivi d'une ligne verticale.*
12. | | •   *Voici deux lignes verticales suivies d'un point.*

C. LISTEN AND LOOK

1. | 2. ____   3. \   4. /\
5. / \ /   6. ____   7. ____   8. / /
9. | | | 10. | 11. • | 12. | | •

D. Multiple-Choice Frames

Instructions: Below, you see a series of frames, each with four sections. You'll hear the frame letter (A through J) and then a sentence referring to what is in one of the four sections (section a, b, c, or d). In the following pause, point to the correct section, and then listen for the answer. Control the pace by stopping and starting the tape. When you are finished, check your answers in the appendix.

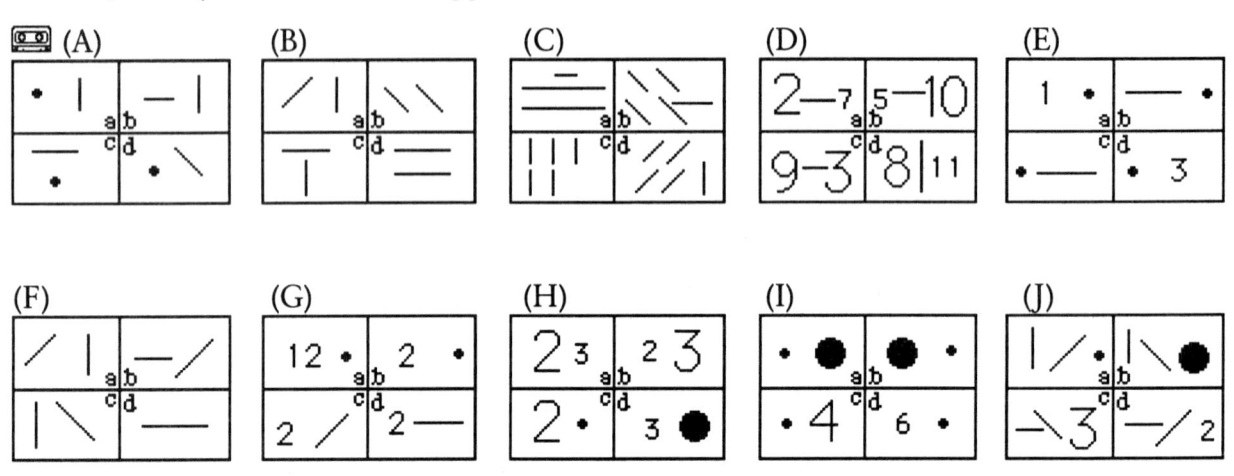

(A) (B) (C) (D) (E)

(F) (G) (H) (I) (J)

E. Read and Draw

Instructions: Draw the following descriptions and then check your answers in the appendix.

1. *Une ligne horizontale suivie d'une ligne verticale courte et fine.*

2. *Deux lignes diagonales, trois lignes verticales, et deux lignes horizontales.*

3. *Un gros chiffre neuf suivi d'un petit chiffre sept.*

4. *Un petit point suivi d'un gros point suivi de quatre lignes diagonales.*

F. Comprehension Check

Instructions: Check your comprehension of the twelve sentences in Part B.

1. Here is a vertical line.
2. Here is a horizontal line.
3. And there is a diagonal line.
4. These lines are diagonal.
5. These lines are also diagonal.
6. Is this line vertical? No, it is horizontal.
7. Is this line also horizontal? Yes.
8. Are these lines horizontal? No, they are diagonal.
9. Are these lines vertical? Yes.
10. This is not a diagonal line.
11. Here is a dot followed by a vertical line.
12. Here are two vertical lines followed by a dot.

THE ADVENTURE CONTINUES

You complete this exercise without difficulty. You notice that it is almost time to leave for the café. You and Stump thank Jacqueline for her help.

She smiles. "Look for a man named Gilles," she tells you as you walk out the door. "He is from France."

You and Stump walk to the café. A waiter seats you at a quaint outdoor table. The only other customer is a man with dark hair and a well-trimmed mustache. He is seated at the table next to yours, drinking water and gazing pensively at the street beyond.

"I wonder how we should start looking for Gilles," Stump says softly.

"Maybe we can ask the waiter when he comes back," you reply.

The gentleman seated at the next table starts out of his reverie and looks at you and Stump. *"Pardonnez-moi,"* he inquires, "but did you say you are looking for Gilles?"

"Oui," you reply.

He nods. *"Je suis Gilles Dupont,"* he introduces himself. "Please, join me at my table. Why do you seek me?"

You and Stump explain your search as well as you can. Just as you finish, the waiter returns to take your orders. You order french onion soup and plenty of fresh baguettes.

After the waiter leaves, Gilles leans toward you. "I have your first clue," he explains. "In order to receive this clue, you must complete my challenge." Gilles assigns you a series of French exercises and a few questions about the French-speaking cultures you have learned about so far. You only finish two of the exercises before your food arrives.

21

From Word to Discourse
Du mot au discours

As explained previously, this activity focuses on the mechanics of sentence formation. You're given a scatter chart from which you must learn to string words into sentences. Samples of well-formed sentences—as well as some ungrammatical ones—are given for you to study before constructing your own.

Instructions: (1) Study the scatter chart. (2) Read the sample sentences. (3) Do the practice, then the tasks.

SCATTER CHART

	il y a	
entre	*sur*	
	voici	*blanche(s)*
là	*ici*	
est / sont	*est-ce que (qu')…?*	*longue(s)*
	c'est	
n'est-ce pas?	*cette*	
ces	*des*	*une / deux*
		noire(s)
chose(s)	*couchée(s)*	
debout	*regardez!*	*l' / la / les*
non	*toute(s)*	*aussi*
autre(s)		*petite(s)*
	oui	*mais*
	et	

66

ENGLISH EQUIVALENT

	there is	
between	on	
	this is	white
there	here	
is /are	is it the case that...?	long
	it is	
isn't it so?	this	
these	some	one / two
		black
thing(s)	laying down	
(standing) upright	look!	the
no	all	also
other(s)		small
	yes	but
	and	

SAMPLE SENTENCES

Instructions: Carefully study these sentences, including the ungrammatical ones, which are starred. Work out in your mind the rules for the correct formation of these kinds of sentences.

There is a thing, a white thing.

Here is the white thing.

There is another thing, a black thing.
This thing is black.
Is this black thing small?
No, this black thing is long.
Between a white thing and a black thing.
A black thing between two white things.

Il y a une chose, une chose blanche.
  * *Il y a une chose, une blanche chose.*
Voici la chose blanche.
  **Voici la blanche chose.*
Il y a une autre chose, une chose noire.
Cette chose est noire.
Est-ce que cette chose noire est petite?
Non, cette chose noire est longue.
Entre une chose blanche et une chose noire.
Une chose noire entre deux choses blanches.
  **La chose noire est entre deux chose blanche.*

A black thing on a white thing.	*Une chose noire sur une chose blanche.* **Une noire chose sur une blanche chose.*
The black thing is on the white thing.	*La chose noire est sur la chose blanche.*
It is a small thing.	*C'est une petite chose.*
This small thing is here, (standing) upright on the black thing.	*Cette petite chose est ici, debout sur la chose noire.*
This other thing is here too, (standing) upright between the black thing and the white thing.	*Cette autre chose est ici aussi, debout entre la chose noire et la chose blanche.*
Some white things are (standing) upright on the black thing.	*Des choses blanches sont debout sur la chose noire.*
The black thing is long.	*La chose noire est longue.*
The white things are small.	*Les choses blanches sont petites.*
All the white things are (standing) upright.	*Toutes les choses blanches sont debout.*
The black thing is lying there.	*La chose noire est couchée là.*
These two white things are (standing) upright, but these two are lying.	*Ces deux choses blanches sont debout, mais ces deux sont couchées.*
These black things are long, but these white things are small, right?	*Ces choses noires sont longues, mais ces choses blanches sont petites, n'est-ce pas?*
Yes, one is small and the others are long.	*Oui, l'une est petite et les autres sont longues.* **Oui, une est petite et des autres sont longues.*
Are all the black things long? No, there are long and small things.	*Est-ce que toutes les choses noires sont longues?* *Non, il y a des choses longues et des petites.* **Est-ce que toutes les noires choses sont longues?* *Non, voici longues et petites choses.*
Are the white things black? No, the white things are white, and the black things are black.	*Est-ce que les choses blanches sont noires? Non, les choses blanches sont blanches, et les choses noires sont noires.*

PRACTICE

Instructions: Translate each of these sentences into French. The answer key is in the appendix.

1. There is another thing, a black thing.
2. Is this black thing small?
3. No, this black thing is long.
4. The black thing is on the white thing.
5. This small thing is here, (standing) upright on the black thing.
6. The black thing is lying there.
7. These black things are long, but these white things are small.
8. Yes, one is small and the others are long.
9. Are all the black things long? No, there are long and small things.
10. Are the white things black? No, the white things are white, and the black things are black.

Task 1

Looking at the scatter chart, compose a number of grammatically correct sentence strings. Work toward building speed and fluency.

Task 2

Set out on a table a number of white and black things. For each color, there should be a large object, a small one, a long one, and a short one. These may simply be pieces of paper cut to size. See how many meaningful statements you can generate about them in four minutes. Move the objects about so you can also make statements concerning position.

22
🎞 Chatter at a Royal Ball
Bavardages au bal royal

🎞 GETTING READY FOR CONVERSATION 3

the dog 🐕 *le chien*

the cat 🐈 *le chat*

It appears that... 👻 *Il semble que...*

in fact... ✛ *en fait...*

Imagine 💡! *Imaginer*

not well ✗ *pas bien*

worse than 💊 > *plus mal que* or *pire que*

better than 💊 > *mieux que*

of course ⚠ *bien sûr*

more than + > *plus que*

Review of Pictographs

Word List

joue/jouer	Il semble que	pire que	Qui?	il	le chat	la salle de bain
aime/aimer	le chien	assez bien	en fait	celle qui	dans	avec
imaginer	qui sait?	beaucoup	le prince	la princesse	pleurer	chant funèbre
aussi	le roi	oui	elle	et	quelle reine?	mieux que
bien sûr	plus que	pas bien	savoir	plus ou moins	n'est-ce pas?	chante/chanter
la tour	mais	pourquoi	le bain			

CONVERSATION 3

Instructions: Recite the English before the French voice speaks on the tape.

••:	Bobi and Misti are singing too. They are singing with the king and queen in the tower.	*Bobi et Misti chantent aussi. Ils chantent avec le roi et la reine dans la tour.*
•:	Bobi and Misti?	*Bobi et Misti?*
••:	The cat and the dog.	*Le chat et le chien.*
•:	A king and a queen with a dog and a cat? They're singing in the tower?	*Un roi et une reine avec un chien et un chat? Ils chantent dans la tour?*
••:	It appears so.	*Il semble que oui.*
•:	Do they sing well?	*Est-ce qu'ils chantent bien?*
••:	Yes, they sing well enough.	*Oui, ils chantent assez bien.*
•:	And the princess, is she singing too?	*Et la princesse, chante-t-elle aussi?*
••:	No, the princess isn't singing. She cries more than she sings. She doesn't sing well. In fact, she sings worse than the dog!	*Non, la princesse ne chante pas. Elle pleure plus qu'elle ne chante. Elle ne chante pas bien. En fait, elle chante plus mal que le chien!*
•:	But better than the cat, right?	*Mais mieux que le chat, n'est-ce pas?*
••:	Of course. Imagine!	*Bien sûr. Tu t'imagines!*
•:	Oh gee!	*Oh là là!*

TASK 1

Use your hands as puppets and dramatize the dialogue, looking only at the English. Drop all shyness and inhibitions and throw yourself into this performance. Aim for "Frenchiness" and fluency.

TASK 2

Do the same, looking only at the pictographic representation of the dialogue and bringing thought down in French without thinking in English.

Pictographic Representation

•• : ✓ 👧 ne 🐑 pas.

⚱︎☺ + > ⚱︎🐑.

⚱︎ ne 🐑 pas 🍾.

◎ ⚱︎🐑 > 🐕.

•• : ⚠️ 💡!

• : 1 > 🐈 ⊘ ?

• : *Oh là là*

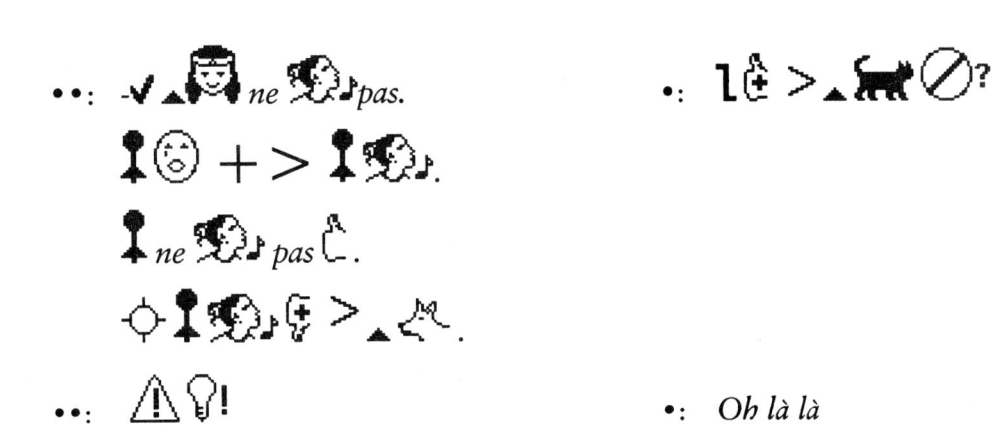

THE ADVENTURE CONTINUES

When you have completed two French exercises, your food arrives. You pause in your work to make room for the meal. To your surprise, Gilles still has no food—just the water he had earlier. The waiter refills his cup.

"How long ago did you order your food?" **Stump asks.** "Maybe you should complain— you've been waiting longer than we have."

"I haven't ordered any food yet," **Gilles tells you.** "I like to sit and sip my water and enjoy the beautiful day." He smiles at your surprised looks. "It's a very French thing to do."

"Oh," is all you can say. Stump still looks confused. The two of you take time to enjoy your lunch before returning to work on Gilles's challenge.

23

Focus on the Language 9–14
Concentration sur la langue 9-14

FOCUS 9

He VERBs, they VERB; he VERBed, they VERBed.

Supposing the English verbs "pay," "taunt," "blur," and "moo" were borrowed into French verbs (but retained English pronunciation), here's how they'd work. Consider the pronunciation column, then the spelling column.

	Pronunciation	Spelling
The king PAY-s.	*Le roi PAY.*	*Le roi PAY-e.*
The kings PAY.	*Les rois PAY.*	*Les rois PAY-ent.*
The king PAY-ed.	*Le roi PAY-ay.*	*Le roi PAY-ait.*
The kings PAY-ed.	*Les rois PAY-ay.*	*Les rois PAY-aient.*

Note how nice and simple the pronunciation is for present and past. Differences are found in the spelling (*PAY-e* and *PAY-ent*—both pronounced *pay*—and *PAY-ait* and *PAY-aient*—both pronounced the same *pay-ay*.) Read the pronunciation column, then compare the spelling.

Present	Pronunciation	Spelling
The king TAUNT-s.	*Le roi TAUNT.*	*Le roi TAUNT-e.*
The kings TAUNT.	*Les rois TAUNT.*	*Les rois TAUNT-ent.*
The king BLUR-s.	*Le roi BLUR.*	*Le roi BLUR-e.*
The kings BLUR.	*Les rois BLUR.*	*Les rois BLUR-ent.*
The king MOO-s.	*Le roi MOO.*	*Le roi MOO-e.*
The kings MOO.	*Les rois MOO.*	*Les rois MOO-ent*

Past	Pronunciation	Spelling
The king TAUNT-ed.	*Le roi TAUNT-ay.*	*Le roi TAUNT-ait.*
The kings TAUNT-ed.	*Les rois TAUNT-ay.*	*Les rois TAUNT-aient.*
The king BLURr-ed.	*Le roi BLUR-ay.*	*Le roi BLUR-ait.*
The kings BLURr-ed.	*Les rois BLUR-ay.*	*Les rois BLUR-aient.*
The king MOO-ed.	*Le roi MOO-ay.*	*Le roi MOO-ait.*
The kings MOO-ed.	*Les rois MOO-ay.*	*Les rois MOO-aient.*

The verbs *chant-*, *pleur-*, and *jou-* work just like *taunt*, *blur*, and *moo*.

CONJUGATION EXERCISE

Following the French pattern above, make up sentences in present and past tense with singular and plural subjects, using the verbs provided.

The cat moos. The cat _____ (blurs, taunts).

The cat mooed. The cat _____ (blurred, taunted).

The cats moo. The cats _____ (blur, taunt).

The cats mooed. The cats _____ (blurred, taunted).

FOCUS 10

One French verb form translates two or more English tenses.

1a.	Who sings and who cries?	*Qui chante et qui pleure?*
1b.	Who is singing and who is crying?	*Qui chante et qui pleure?*
2a.	He sang and she cried.	*Il chantait et elle pleurait.*
2b.	He was singing and she was crying.	*Il chantait et elle pleurait.*
2c.	He used to sing and she used to cry.	*Il chantait et elle pleurait.*
	Note: He is singing.	*Il chante.* NOT: **Il est chante.*
	He was singing.	*Il chantait.* NOT: **Il était chante.*

Caution: Any attempt to put in a translation the words "is," "are," "was," "were" in sentences like "He is singing," and "They were crying" will result in incomprehensible French! "He sings" and "He is singing" are both normally rendered by "*Il chante.*" Similarly, "he sang," "he was singing," and "he used to sing" are normally rendered by the one form: *Il chantait*.

Translate Orally from and into French

Who plays and who sings?	*Qui joue et qui chante?*
Who is playing and who is singing?	*Qui joue et qui chante?*
Who was singing and who was crying?	*Qui chantait et qui pleurait?*
Who sang and who cried?	*Qui chantait et qui pleurait?*
He used to play and she used to cry.	*Il jouait et elle pleurait.*
He played and she cried.	*Il jouait et elle pleurait.*

FOCUS 11

Comparison: better than, more than, etc.

He sings better than the prince plays.	*Il chante mieux que le prince joue.*
He sings better than he plays.	*Il chante mieux qu'il <u>ne</u> joue.*
	NOT: **Il chante mieux qu'il joue.*

The particle *ne* is used in comparisons like these when the subject of both clauses is the same (I sing better than I cry); *ne* is not used when the subject of the two clauses is different (I sing better than the cat sings).

Translate Orally from and into French

She plays well...more or less well.	*Elle joue bien...plus ou moins bien.*
She plays better now.	*Elle joue mieux maintenant.*
She plays better than the cat.	*Elle joue mieux que le chat.*
She plays better than she sings.	*Elle joue mieux qu'elle ne chante.*
He sings badly.	*Il chante mal.*
He sings worse now.	*Il chante moins bien maintenant.*
Worse than the dog.	*Moins bien que le chien.*
She plays worse than the cat sings.	*Elle joue moins bien que le chat chante.*
She played worse than she sang.	*Elle jouait moins bien qu'elle ne chantait.*

Focus 12

Two ways to form a yes-no question.

1.	*La reine pleure.*	The queen is crying.
1a.	*Est-ce que la reine pleure?*	Is the queen crying?
1b.	*La reine pleure-t-elle?*	Is the queen crying?
2.	*Le roi et la reine pleuraient.*	The king and queen were crying.
2a.	*Est-ce que le roi et la reine pleuraient?*	Were the king and queen crying?
2b.	*Le roi et la reine pleuraient-ils?*	Were the king and queen crying?
3.	*La reine chante.*	The queen is singing.
3a.	*Est-ce que la reine chante?*	Is the queen singing?
3b.	*La reine chante-t-elle?*	Is the queen singing?
4.	*La princesse chantait.*	The princess used to sing.
4a.	*Est-ce que la princesse chantait?*	Did the princess use to sing?
4b	*La princesse chantait-elle?*	Did the princess use to sing?

Note: In 1a, 2a, 3a, and 4a, a question is formed by simply putting the question phrase *Est-ce que* in front of a sentence. In 1b, 2b, 3b, and 4b, a pronoun follows the verb, connected to it by a *t*-sound. If the verb does not end in the letter *t*, one is attached using a hyphen; if the verb ends in the letter *t*, there is no extra *t* attached between the verb and the pronoun.

Study Task

Instructions: Cover columns B and C except for the first sentence. Translate each sentence according to the patterns given in columns B and C.

A	B	C
Does the king cry?	*Le roi pleure-t-il?*	*Est-ce que le roi pleure?*
Did the queen cry?	*La reine pleurait-elle?*	*Est-ce que la reine pleurait?*
Do they sing?	*Chantent-ils?*	*Est-ce qu'ils chantent?*
Did they sing?	*Chantaient-ils?*	*Est-ce qu'ils chantaient?*
Do the king and the queen sing?	*Le roi et la reine chantent-ils?*	*Est-ce que le roi et la reine chantent?*
Did the king and the queen sing?	*Le roi et la reine chantaient-ils?*	*Est-ce que le roi et la reine chantaient?*
Is the king singing?	*Le roi chante-t-il?*	*Est-ce que le roi chante?*
Does he cry more than the dog?	*Pleure-t-il plus que le chien?*	*Est-ce qu'il pleure plus que le chien?*

FOCUS 13

L'imparfait des verbes "être" et "savoir": speaking of what was (irregular verbs *était, savait*).

1a.	The king was in the tower.	*Le roi était dans la tour.*
1b.	The kings were in the tower.	*Les rois étaient dans la tour.*
2a.	The prince knew.	*Le prince savait.*
2b.	The princes knew.	*Les princes savaient.*

The plural of *était* is *étaient*. The plural of *savait* is *savaient* (both forms are pronounced identically).

Translate Orally from and into French

One princess was in the tower.	*Une princesse était dans la tour.*
She is no longer in the tower.	*Elle n'est plus dans la tour.*
The king and the queen knew.	*Le roi et la reine savaient.*
No, she didn't know.	*Non, elle ne savait pas.*
She knew and the dukes knew.	*Elle savait et les ducs savaient.*
She knows and the dukes know.	*Elle sait et les ducs savent.*

Translate Orally from and into French

Caution: Any attempt to translate the words "do," "does," "did," etc. in sentences like those below will result in quite incomprehensible French! Give close attention to the French way of asking questions.

Does the king sing?	*Est-ce que le roi chante?*
Did the queen cry?	*Est-ce que la reine pleurait?*
Do the king and the queen cry?	*Le roi et la reine pleurent-ils?*
Did the prince and the king sing better?	*Le prince et le roi chantaient-ils mieux?*
Is the princess singing or crying?	*Est-ce que la princesse chante ou est-ce qu'elle pleure?*
Do the king and the princess sing?	*Le roi et la princesse chantent-ils?*

FOCUS 14

How to make a negative statement: Take an affirmative sentence and transform it into a negative one by sandwiching the verb between the two-part negative frame *ne...pas*.

He cries. No, he doesn't cry.	*Il pleure. Non, il ne pleure pas.*
He doesn't cry much.	*Il <u>ne</u> pleure <u>pas</u> beaucoup.*
	NOT: **Il ne pleure beaucoup pas.*
Not much.	*Pas beaucoup.*
	NOT: **Ne beaucoup.*
She doesn't sing well.	*Elle <u>ne</u> chante <u>pas</u> bien.*
Don't they sing well?	*Ne chantent-ils pas bien?*
	NOT: **Ne chantent pas ils bien?*

Note: Both *ne* and *pas* are negative markers, each with its own rules of occurrence. "Not bad!" is "*Pas mal!*" (not *ne mal*). To negate anything other than verbs, use *pas*: *Pas Misti.*

Not Misti. *Pas le roi.* Not the king. *Pas beaucoup!* Not much! *Pas mal!* Not bad! *Pas moi!* Not me!

Translate Orally from and into French

He is not a king.	*Il n'est pas un roi.*
The princess is crying.	*La princesse pleure.*
No, the princess isn't crying.	*Non, la princesse ne pleure pas.*
Does she cry a lot?	*Pleure-t-elle beaucoup?*
Not much.	*Pas beaucoup.*
Doesn't she cry a lot?	*Ne pleure-t-elle pas beaucoup?*
Not in the tower.	*Pas dans la tour.*
The king and queen don't cry.	*Le roi et la reine ne pleurent pas.*

24

Self-Test
Auto-évaluation

REVIEW

Instructions: Look over the sentences below. Make two passes as follows:

1st pass: Read each French sentence out loud, then look away and repeat it, thinking of its meaning.

2nd pass: Cover the French and see if you can quickly render the English into French.

GROUP A

Which king with which queen?	*Quel roi avec quelle reine?*
That king and that queen.	*Ce roi et cette reine.*
Which king sings?	*Quel roi chante?*
Which king and queen are singing?	*Quel roi et quelle reine chantent?*
Which king sang?	*Quel roi chantait?*
Which king and queen were singing?	*Quel roi et quelle reine chantaient?*
Who was singing and who was crying?	*Qui chantait et qui pleurait?*
He sings better than the queen.	*Il chante mieux que la reine.*
She sings better than she plays.	*Elle chante mieux qu'elle ne joue.*

GROUP B

He is king. She is queen.	*Il est roi. Elle est reine.*
They are king and queen.	*Ils sont roi et reine.*
The one (she) who sings cries.	*Celle qui chante pleure.*
The one (he) who plays sings.	*Celui qui joue chante.*
The queen and the princess cried.	*La reine et la princesse pleuraient.*
Who sings better, the princess or the dog?	*Qui chante mieux, la princesse ou le chien?*
The prince is the one who sings well.	*Le prince est celui qui chante bien.*

SELF-TEST

Part 1

Instructions: Translate orally from and into French (covering the opposite column).

GROUP A

1.	A duke and a duchess.	*Un duc et une duchesse.*
1a.	Which duke and which duchess?	*Quel duc et quelle duchesse?*
1b.	Dukes and duchesses.	*Des ducs et des duchesses.*
1c.	The dukes and the duchesses.	*Les ducs et les duchesses.*
2a.	A tower and a drum.	*Une tour et un tambour.*
2b.	Drums and towers.	*Des tambours et des tours.*
3.	The bars and some towers.	*Les bars et des tours.*
4.	This prince and this princess.	*Ce prince et cette princesse.*
5a.	The duke is the one who cries.	*Le duc est celui qui pleure.*
5b.	The duchess is the one who plays.	*La duchesse est celle qui joue.*
6a.	Which duchess cries? The one who is playing.	*Quelle duchesse pleure? Celle qui joue.*

6b.	Which duke sings? The one who is crying.	*Quel duc chante? Celui qui pleure.*

GROUP B

1.	The king and queen are singing **well** now.	*Le roi et la reine chantent bien maintenant.*
2.	Do the king and queen sing?	*Est-ce que le roi et la reine chantent?*
2a.	Do the king and queen sing?	*Le roi et la reine, chantent-ils?*
3.	Did the queen sing with the king?	*Est-ce que la reine chantait avec le roi?*
3a.	Did the queen sing with the king?	*La reine, chantait-elle avec le roi?*
4.	Does the king cry?	*Est-ce que le roi pleure?*
4a.	Does the king cry?	*Le roi, pleure-t-il?*
5.	Does he cry a lot?	*Pleure-t-il beaucoup?*
6.	He's king. No, he's not king.	*Il est roi. Non, il n'est pas roi.*
7.	A king sang, some queens played.	*Un roi chantait, des reines jouaient.*
8.	Kings sang and a queen played.	*Des rois chantaient et une reine jouait.*
9.	Is the princess singing or is she crying?	*Est-ce que la princesse chante ou est-ce qu'elle pleure?*
10.	Do the king and queen sing?	*Le roi et la reine, chantent-ils?*

GROUP C

1.	Doesn't she cry?	*Est-ce qu'elle ne pleure pas?*
1a.	Doesn't she cry?	*Ne pleure-t-elle pas?*
2.	The cat doesn't sing well.	*Le chat ne chante pas bien.*
3.	He sings worse than the dog.	*Il chante moins bien que le chien.*
4.	He sings worse than she plays.	*Il chante moins bien qu'elle ne joue.*
5.	He sings better than the prince.	*Il chante mieux que le prince.*
6.	One princess was in the tower.	*Une princesse était dans la tour.*
7.	Some princesses were in the room.	*Des princesses étaient dans la chambre.*
8.	A duke and a duchess were singing.	*Un duc et une duchesse chantaient.*
9a.	The duke is in the room.	*Le duc est dans la chambre.*
9b.	The dukes are in the room.	*Les ducs sont dans la chambre.*

Part 2

Instructions: See how well you can **create** the following conversation. Two kings are chatting about who is where and **what they are doing.**

King 1 asks:
    who is in the bathroom
    who is in the tower

King 2 replies:
    princess, bathroom
    queen, tower

King 1 asks what each is doing there:
    duke, singing
    princess, crying
    queen, playing

King 2 replies:
    no, duke, playing drum
    yes, princess, crying
    no, queen, singing

King 1 asks:
    who's in the tower with the duke
    who is in the bathroom with the princess
    who is in the tower with the queen

King 2 replies:
    dog, tower, duke
    cat, bathroom, princess
    duchess, tower, queen

King 1 asks:
    dog, play, duke
    cat, cry, princess
    duchess, sing, queen

King 2 replies:
    yes, dog, play, duke
    yes, cat, cry, princess
    no, duchess, play drum, queen

25

Questions and Answers
Questions et réponses

QUESTION WORDS AND THEIR ICONS

These symbols or icons for these interrogative words will help you gain mastery of this crucially important area of French. Here are the symbols.

	Icon	Memory Aids
Who?—*Qui?*	↑?	
Which?—*Quel, quelle?*	↓?	
What?—*Que?*	▨?	(thing or wrapped box)
What kind of?—*Quelle sorte de?*	**S?**	(**S** for "sort")
Why?—*Pourquoi?* (for what?)	**R?**	(**R** for "reason")
How?—*Comment?*	**M?**	(**M** for "manner")
Where?—*Où?*	**@?**	(**@** for "location at")
When?—*Quand?*	**X?**	(**X** "hour glass" for time)
How much?—*Combien?*	**$?**	(**$** for quantity)

SUMMARY

Instructions. Read the *résumé* and prepare to respond to the questions that follow it.

Dans cette histoire il y a un roi et une reine. Voici le 👑 *et voici la* 👸 *.* ▨*? font-ils dans l'histoire? Ils chantent. Ils chantent ensemble dans la tour.* ▨*? chantent-ils? Ils chantent des chants funèbres avec le chien et le chat. Oui, le roi, la reine, le chat, et le chien chantent ensemble dans la tour.* **M?** *chantent-ils? Ils chantent plus ou moins bien. Le roi chante mieux que la reine, la reine chante mieux que le chien, et le chien chante mieux que le chat.*

Il y a aussi une princesse. Voici la princesse 👧*. Est-ce que la princesse chante aussi? Non, elle ne chante pas.* **R?** *ne chante-t-elle pas? Elle n'aime pas chanter. Elle ne chante pas bien. En fait, elle chante moins bien que le chien. Moins bien que le chien?! Oui, mais mieux que le chat. La princesse pleure dans la salle de bain.* **R?** *pleure-t-elle dans la salle de bain?* ↑? *sait? Il semble qu'elle aime pleurer dans la salle de bain. Et la reine, pleure-t-elle aussi dans la*

79

salle de bain avec la princesse? Oui, la reine et la princesse pleurent ensemble dans la salle de bain.

QUESTIONS

1. *Dans cette histoire il y a un roi et une reine, n'est-ce pas?*
   Sample Answer: *Oui, il y a dans cette histoire un roi et une reine.*
2. ▨*? fait le roi? Est-ce qu'il chante?*
3. *Joue-t-il du piano?*
4. *Et la reine,* ▨ *? fait-elle? Est-ce qu'elle chante aussi?*
5. **l?** *instrument joue-t-elle? Joue-t-elle du tambour?*
6. **@?** *est-ce que le roi et la reine chantent? Chantent-ils dans la tour ou dans la salle de bain?*
7. **S?** *chants le roi chantait-il? Des chants populaires ou des chants funèbres?*
8. *Le roi,* **M?** *chante-t-il, bien ou pas bien?*
9. *Est-ce qu'il chante mieux que le chien? Mieux que le chat aussi?*
10. *Et la reine, chante-t-elle mieux que le chien? Et mieux que le chat aussi?*
11. *Avec* ♦*? pleure la reine? Avec le roi ou avec la princesse?*
12. **@?** *pleurent la reine et la princesse? Dans la salle de bain ou dans la tour?*
13. *La princesse, ne pleure-t-elle pas dans la tour?*
14. **x?** *est-ce que la princesse chante avec le roi?*
15. **R?** *la princesse ne chante-t-elle pas? Est-ce qu'elle n'aime pas chanter?*
16. **M?** *chante la princesse? Est-ce qu'elle chante mieux que le chat?*
17. *Chante-t-elle mieux que le chien et le chat?*
18. **R?** *la princesse pleure-t-elle dans la salle de bain?*
19. *Le chien et le chat chantent avec le roi et la reine, n'est-ce pas?*
20. *Est-ce que le chien et le chat chantent avec le roi et la reine dans la tour ou dans la salle de bain?*
21. *Est-ce que le chien et le chat pleurent dans la salle de bain avec la princesse et la reine?*
22. ♦*? chante mieux, le chien ou le chat?*
23. ♦*? chante plus mal, le chat ou la princesse?*

READING AND TRANSLATION

Instructions: Read the following for meaning (see translation which follows).

1. *Qui chante dans la tour?*
2. *Le roi chante dans la tour.*
3. *Il joue aussi dans la tour.*

4. *Le roi chante et joue dans la tour.*
5. *La reine chante-t-elle aussi dans la tour?*
6. *Oui, elle chante aussi dans la tour.*
7. *Elle chante et joue aussi dans la salle de bain, n'est-ce pas?*
8. *Le roi et la reine chantent et jouent dans la tour.*
9. *Est-ce que Bobi et Misti chantent et jouent aussi dans la tour?*
10. *Oui, ils chantent et jouent aussi dans la tour.*
11. *Bobi pleure dans la salle de bain, mais il ne pleure pas dans la tour.*
12. *Bobi chante et joue dans la tour, mais la princesse ne chante pas dans la tour.*

Now render the sentences back into French.

1. Who sings in the tower?
2. The king sings in the tower.
3. He plays in the tower too.
4. The king sings and plays in the tower.
5. Does the queen also sing in the tower?
6. Yes, she also sings in the tower.
7. She sings and also plays in the bathroom, right?
8. The king and the queen sing and play in the tower.
9. Do Bobi and Misti sing and play in the tower too?
10. Yes, they also sing and play in the tower.
11. Bobi cries in the bathroom, but he doesn't cry in the tower.
12. Bobi sings and plays in the tower, but the princess doesn't sing in the tower.

26
Telling Stories
Raconter des histoires

GENERATING YOUR OWN SENTENCES

Suppose you knew only four nouns, "butcher," "baker," "dog," "cat," and five possible impacts between them, "hates," "loves," "catches," "bites," "hugs." Suppose also that you had this simple rule for combining these elements into meaningful statements: Place a noun before an impact word (a verb), and place a noun after the verb. Here is a combination chart of those elements. (Pick any item in column 1, then any in column 2, then any in column 3, and say them in that order.)

Sentence Generation Chart

Agent (noun)	**Impact** (verb)	**Patient** (noun)
the butcher	hates	the dog
the baker	loves	the cat
the dog	catches	the butcher
the cat	bites	the baker
	hugs	

Here are some sample outputs from this sentence-generation chart or sentence-production "machine":

The butcher hits the baker. The cat loves the butcher. The dog catches the butcher.

To string several sentence combinations from this chart into a story line, you need only to give attention to the logic or the story possibilities of the sequence. Here, for example, is a story line:

The baker loves the cat. The baker loves the dog. The dog hates the cat. The cat hates the dog. The dog bites the cat. The baker hates the dog.

If you were learning English, you would gain much by practicing telling such stories (and longer ones) fluently and expressively.

Here now is some more powerful help in organizing your own sentence production. And from the statements you form by combining these words, you can create stories. This creating and telling of stories (or ministory plots) will play a major role in your learning to speak French. Give it your best effort. Use your pictograph cards for this exercise, if you'd like.

FOURTEEN FUNCTIONS YOU KNOW HOW TO EXPRESS

AGENT/PATIENT NOUNS: *roi, reine, princesse, chat* (Misti), *chien* (Bobi)
MODIFIERS: *le, la, ce, cette*

PRONOUNS: *il, ils, elle, elles*
LOCATION NOUNS: *la salle de bain, la tour*
LOCATION OR ACCOMPANIMENT: *dans, avec*
ACTION-VERB STEMS: *chant-, pleur-, jou-*
VERB ENDINGS: {present} *-e, -ent* (silent); {past} *-ait, -aient* ("ay")
INFO-QUESTION WORDS: *Que? Qui? Quel(le)? Où? Comment? Pourquoi?*
ANSWERS OR REJOINDERS: *Oui. Non. Imagine-toi! Bien sûr!*
MANNER: *bien, mal, ensemble*
TEMPORAL: *maintenant, encore, déjà*
QUANTITY: *beaucoup, assez*
YES-NO QUESTION MARKERS: *Est-ce que…? N'est-ce pas?*
OTHER WORDS: *et, ou, mais, aussi*

You may now want to arrange all your pictograph cards in separate piles (nouns, verbs, and so on).

Instructions: Using the words listed above (represented by your pictographs on cards), do the following:

1. Take three agent nouns (*roi, homme, princesse*) and three action-verb stems, (*pleur-, chant-, jou-*). By adding the proper grammatical details, make up three quick sentences on the model of *le roi pleure*. Arrange the pictograph cards you have prepared. Strive to say your sentences smoothly.

1a. Put the question phrase *est-ce que…?* in front of those sentences, asking, for example, *Est-ce que le roi pleure?* Remember to produce your sentences smoothly, without hesitation.

1b. Put the tag question *n'est-ce pas?* at the end of your sentences, as in *Le roi pleure, n'est-ce pas?* (The king is crying, right?)

2. Make three sentences plural, as in *Les rois pleurent*. (Visualize the plural marker *-nt* in the spelling of the verbs, even though it is not pronounced.)

2a. Put the question phrase *est-ce que…?* in front or the tag question phrase…*n'est-ce pas?* at the end of those sentences as in 1a and 1b.

3. Turn your sentences into who, which, where questions as in *Qui pleure? Quel roi pleure? Où pleure la reine?*

4. Change the sentences to what-action questions as in *Que fait le roi?* (What is the king doing?) or *Que font les princesses?* (What are the princesses doing?) Note: *faire* to do: present singular *le roi fait*, present plural *les princesses font*.

5. Make three new sentences by joining two actors as sentence subject, as in *Misti et Bobi pleurent*. (Note: When tied to plural subjects, the verb is written with a final *-nt*, but, again, the pronunciation is the same as for the singular: *Misti pleure. Misti et Bobi pleurent.*)

6. Put the question phrase *est-ce que...?* in front or the tag question phrase...*n'est-ce pas?* at the end of those sentences as in *Est-ce que Misti et Bobi pleurent? Misti et Bobi pleurent, n'est-ce pas?*

7. Build sentences with multiple actions, joined by *et* or by *ou* as in *Bobi et Misti chantent et pleurent* or *Bobi et Misti chantent ou pleurent*.

8. Expand your sentences by adding a location phrase (*dans*) and a "with" phrase (*avec*) as in *Le chien et le chat chantent dans la tour avec le roi et la reine.*

9. Make up a few pairs of sentences in which the second sentence of each pair conveys the idea of "also" (*aussi*) or the idea of "but" (*mais*). Example: *Le roi chante et la reine chante aussi. Le roi chante, mais la reine pleure.*

10. Make your sentences negative as in *Le roi ne chante pas et la reine non plus* (neither).

27

Creating Your Own Ministory Plots
Les intrigues de vos propres mini-histoires

You are now urged to create your own ministory plots, to write them out and give them orally. It will be wise to limit yourself to the words you know, supplemented by a selection of a few additional words given in the following lists. An example of a ministory plot is given at the end of this vocabulary list.

Instructions: (1) Write each of these new words on a separate card and put the cards in their appropriate piles. (2) Select certain cards that together can form meaningful statements and arrange them in the order you want. (3) Aim at performing your story plots orally without reading. Aim at smooth-flowing diction. Caution: limit yourself to the words you know, supplemented by a selection of the additional words and phrases given here.

VOCABULARY

Subjects or Agents of Action

singer	*chanteur, chanteuse*
dancer	*danseur, danseuse*
drum player	*tambour*
trombone player	*tromboniste*
violinist	*violoniste*
ballerina	*ballerine*
actress	*actrice*
actor	*acteur*
director	*directeur*
doctor	*médecin*

Action without Impact on Anyone Else (Intransitive Verbs)

dances, is dancing	*danse*
sleeps, is sleeping	*dort* (like *dor-* in *dormitory*)
dies	*meurt*

Action with Impact on Others (Transitive Verbs)

throws	*jette*
defends	*défend*
detests	*déteste*
embraces (kisses)	*embrasse*
helps	*aide*
observes	*observe*

Concrete Objects and Associated Verbs

a rock	*une pierre*
She throws a rock at the violinist.	*Elle jette une pierre au violoniste.*

Places and Associated Verbs

at the opera	*à l'opéra*
She cries at the opera.	*Elle pleure à l'opéra.*
in the dancehall	*dans la salle de danse*
They dance in the dancehall.	*Ils dansent dans la salle de danse.*
in the hospital	*à l'hôpital*
He works at the hospital.	*Il travaille à l'hôpital.*

Time

one day	*un jour*
finally	*enfin*

Sample Beginning of a Ministory Plot

Instructions: Read the ministory and try to understand the main idea. A translation of the story is in the appendix.

1. Il y a une ballerine, une actrice, et un tambour. 2. L'actrice aime le tambour. 3. Le tambour n'aime pas l'actrice. 4. Il déteste l'actrice. 5. Il aime la ballerine. 6. Il ne danse pas avec l'actrice. 7. Il danse avec la ballerine. 8. Il ne chante pas avec l'actrice. 9. Non, le tambour chante avec la ballerine. 10. La ballerine n'aime pas l'actrice. 11. L'actrice n'aime pas la ballerine.

Now create at least three plots of your own. It may help to begin by selecting some of your pictographs and laying them out in front of you, with subjects in one group, action verbs in another, etc. You don't need to create great pieces of fiction, just string statements together in some meaningful order. The more statements you can weave into each story, the better. Write two or more stories on paper, but then tell them without reading. Or better, sit back and relax, letting your mind spin off meaningful strings of statements that form a story line. Strive for unhesitating fluency.

In case you need a few more easy-to-learn, easy-to-use pieces, here are a few extras:

The chef...	*Le chef...*
prepares the dinner.	*prépare le dîner.*
tastes the soup.	*goûte la soupe.*
The driver...	*Le chauffeur...*
enters the house.	*entre dans la maison.*
eats the soup.	*mange la soupe.*

End Tape 1, Side B

Tape 2, Side A

28
▭ *Points, lignes et figures*
Points, Lines, and Figures

▭ PREPARATION FOR SCATTER CHART

Instructions: In the following chapter, you will encounter the following vocabulary items: arrow, right, left, black, white, above, below, between, upward, downward, pointing. See if you can match the French and English from context without using a dictionary.

▭ A. SCATTER CHART

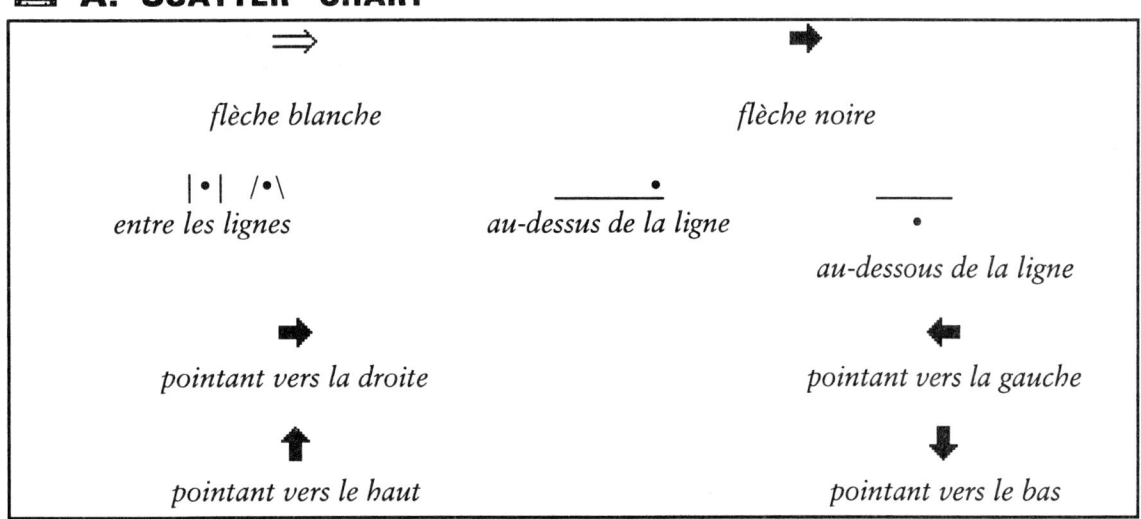

```
    ⇒                              ➡
 flèche blanche                flèche noire

 |•| /•\              ____•____           ____
entre les lignes     au-dessus de la ligne        •
                                          au-dessous de la ligne

    ➡                              ⬅
pointant vers la droite         pointant vers la gauche

    ⬆                              ⬇
pointant vers le haut           pointant vers le bas
```

B. LOOK AND LISTEN

1. ⇒➡   *Voici une flèche blanche et une flèche noire.*

2. ➡/⇒   *La flèche noire est au-dessus de la flèche blanche.*

3. ⇒/➡   *La flèche noire est au-dessous de la flèche blanche.*

4. •/⇒   *La flèche blanche est au-dessous du petit point.*

5. ➡➡/•─ *Une flèche noire est au-dessus d'un point; l'autre est au-dessus d'une ligne.*

6. ⇒ / ⇐   *Une flèche blanche est au-dessus d'une ligne courte; l'autre flèche blanche est au-dessous d'une ligne longue.*

7. ↑___↑   *Une ligne horizontale est entre deux flèches noires.*

8. ➡ | ➡   *Une courte ligne verticale est entre deux flèches noires.*

9. ↑↓   *Une flèche pointant vers le haut, l'autre pointant vers le bas.*

10. ⇒⬅   *La flèche blanche pointant vers la droite, la flèche noire vers la gauche.*

11. ⬅⬅   *Cette flèche pointe vers la gauche. Et cette autre pointe aussi vers la gauche.*

12. ⬅⬅⬅⬅ / ↓↓↓↓   *Ces quatre flèches ne pointent pas vers le haut. Ces quatre non plus.*

🔊 Note: Do not confuse *pointant* (pointing) and *pointent* (plural form of point, "they point"): *Deux flèches pointent vers la droite* means "two arrows point to the right"; *deux flèches pointant vers la droite* means "two arrows pointing to the right."

📼 C. Listen and Look

1. ⇒⬅   2. ⇒⇒↓↓   3. ➡⬅   4. • | •

5. ➡⇒ / • •   6. ⬅ ___ / ___ ➡   7. ⇒⇒ / _____   8. ⇒|⬅

D. Multiple-Choice Frames

🔊 Instructions: Below, you see a series of frames, each with four sections. You'll hear the frame letter and then a sentence referring to what is in one of the four sections (section a, b, c, or d). In the following pause, point to the correct section, and then listen for the answer. Control the pace by stopping and starting the tape. When you are finished, check your answers in the appendix.

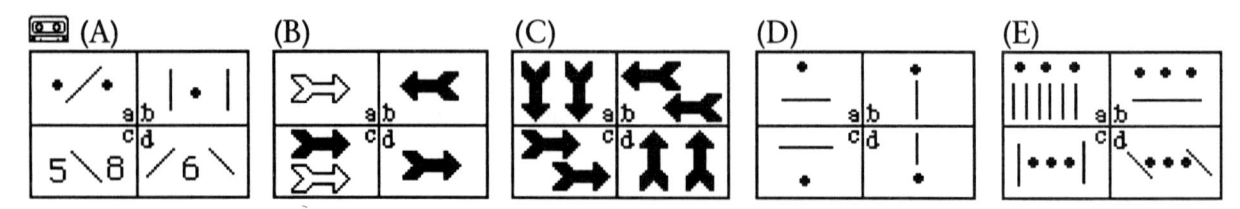

📼 (A) (B) (C) (D) (E)

Stop tape. Read and draw.

88

E. Read and Draw

Instructions: Read the following sentences and draw what is described. You may check your answer in the appendix.

1. *Un point entre deux lignes verticales.*

2. *Une flèche noire pointant vers le bas.*

3. *Une flèche blanche entre deux lignes diagonales.*

4. *Le chiffre quatre au-dessus d'une ligne horizontale et le chiffre cinq au-dessus d'une autre ligne horizontale.*

5. *Deux flèches pointant vers la droite suivies de deux flèches pointant vers la gauche.*

F. Comprehension check

Instructions: Check your comprehension of the twelve sentences in Part B.

1. Here is a white arrow and a black arrow.
2. The black arrow is above the white arrow.
3. The white arrow is above the black arrow.
4. The white arrow is below the small dot.
5. One black arrow is above a dot; the other is above a line.
6. One white arrow is above a short line, the other white arrow is below a long line.
7. A horizontal line is between two black arrows.
8. A short vertical line is between two black arrows.
9. One arrow pointing upward, the other pointing downward.
10. The white arrow points to the right, the black arrow to the left.
11. This arrow points to the left. And this other [one] points also to the left.
12. These four arrows don't point upward. These four also do not.

Challenge: See if you can give the French equivalent of these twelve sentences.

29

Une mère parle à son bébé
French Only
A Mother Talks to Her Baby

Instructions: Listen to and read the following story. Learn words in French about numbers and parts of the body.

One hand. Five fingers.	*Une main. Cinq doigts.*
One, two, three, four, five.	*Un, deux, trois, quatre, cinq.*
Five little fingers, one little hand.	*Cinq petits doigts, une petite main.*
Baby's hand. Baby's fingers.	*La main de bébé. Les doigts de bébé.*
Thumb. Here's your thumb.	*Le pouce. Voici ton pouce.*
Middle finger. Here's your middle finger.	*Le majeur. Voici ton majeur.*
Index finger. Here's your index finger.	*L'index. Voici ton index.*
Two little hands. Ten little fingers.	*Deux petites mains. Dix petits doigts.*
Ten little fingers on two little hands.	*Dix petits doigts sur deux petites mains.*
One, two, three, four, five, six, seven, eight, nine, ten.	*Un, deux, trois, quatre, cinq, six, sept, huit, neuf, dix.*
Baby has little hands.	*Bébé a de petites mains.*
Yes, your hands are little.	*Oui, tes mains sont petites.*
Look how little your hands are.	*Regarde comme tes mains sont petites.*
Mama has big hands.	*Maman a de grandes mains.*
Yes, mama's hands are big.	*Oui, les mains de maman sont grandes.*
Look how big my hands are.	*Regarde comme mes mains sont grandes.*
Baby's little hand is in mama's big hand.	*La petite main de bébé est dans la grande main de maman.*
Look at your hands and look at my hands.	*Regarde tes mains et regarde mes mains.*
Two little hands. Two big hands.	*Deux petites mains. Deux grandes mains.*
One foot. Five toes.	*Un pied. Cinq orteils.*
One, two, three, four, five.	*Un, deux, trois, quatre, cinq.*
Five little toes, one little foot.	*Cinq petits orteils, un petit pied.*
Baby's foot. Baby's toes.	*Le pied de bébé. Les orteils de bébé.*
Big toe. Here is baby's big toe.	*Le gros orteil. Voici le gros orteil de bébé.*
Little toe. Here is baby's little toe.	*Le petit orteil. Voici le petit orteil de bébé.*
Two little feet. Ten little toes.	*Deux petits pieds. Dix petits orteils.*
Ten little toes on two little feet.	*Dix petits orteils sur deux petits pieds.*
One, two, three, four, five, six, seven, eight, nine, ten.	*Un, deux, trois, quatre, cinq, six, sept, huit, neuf, dix.*
Baby has little feet. Mama has big feet.	*Bébé a de petits pieds. Maman a de grands pieds.*
Look at our feet.	*Regarde nos pieds.*
Your feet are little. My feet are big.	*Tes pieds sont petits. Mes pieds sont grands.*
Yes, yours are little; mine are big.	*Oui, les tiens sont petits; les miens sont grands.*
This little foot is yours. This big foot is mine.	*Ce petit pied est le tien. Ce grand pied est le mien.*
Mama has big feet.	*Maman a de grands pieds.*
Look how big my feet are.	*Regarde comme mes pieds sont grands.*
Look at your feet and look at my feet.	*Regarde tes pieds et regarde mes pieds.*
Two little feet. Two big feet.	*Deux petits pieds. Deux grands pieds.*

CULTURE QUESTIONS—SECTION ONE

Instructions: Answer these questions based on your reading. Feel free to check the appendix to find the answers.

1. French ranks with what other language as an international language?

2. What is the French language's nickname?

3. When did France invade Algeria?

4. What is the northern coastal area of Algeria called?

THE ADVENTURE CONTINUES

When you finish the challenge, Gilles checks your work. When you finish, he nods his approval. "Excellent work," he tells you. "You have earned your first clue—flour. Next, seek Jean-Luc at the wharf. He loves to paint."

You thank Gilles for his time and for his help, but before you bid him farewell, you have one more question for him. "Jacqueline said you were from France," you say. "Would you be willing to tell us about your homeland?"

Gilles agrees to your request and briefly summarizes his native culture.

FRANCE CULTURE OVERVIEW

French people, in general, are extremely proud of their culture, heritage, and nation. They are perceived as among the most patriotic people in the world. French people are often private and reserved, but they tend to be more hospitable outside of Paris. France has been a leader in fashion and food for centuries. Paris still sets many trends in European fashion, and French food remains popular all over the world. The French government places so much emphasis on the French language that almost everyone in France speaks the language, despite the variety of nationalities represented in France. In addition to being France's official language, French is the official language of the United Nations.

FACTS AND FIGURES ON FRANCE

- Nearly 90% of France's population belongs to the Catholic church.

- The first French cookbooks were written during the Middle Ages.

- The most popular spectator sports in France are soccer and rugby.

- The most popular participation sports in France are fishing, cycling, tennis, hiking, skiing, and sailing.

- During August, when many people travel, many shops and some factories close.

- Europe's highest mountain, Mt. Blanc, is located in France.

When Gilles finishes his summary, he wishes you luck in your search and bids you farewell. The waiter brings your bill. After paying it, you walk back to the Pétard's home. Zsa-Zsa is preparing dinner and invites you to help. When you agree to do so, she shows you how to make french bread.

RECIPE: *BAGUETTES*—FRENCH BREAD

2 packages active dry yeast

1/2 c warm water

1 T salt

2 c lukewarm water

7 to 7 1/2 c flour, sifted

1 egg white

Soften yeast in warm water (110°F). Combine salt and lukewarm water; beat in 2 cups flour. Add softened yeast. Stir in 4 1/2 to 5 cups flour, or enough to make mderately stiff dough. Turn out dough on lightly floured surface. Knead 10 to 15 minutes, working in remaining flour.

Place in greased bowl. Turn dough once to grease surface. Cover and let rise till double (about 1 hour). Punch down; let rise again till double (30-45 minutes). Turn out dough on floured surface and divide into two portions. Cover; let rest 10 minutes. Roll each portion into 15x12-inch rectangle. Roll up tightly, beginning at long side, sealing well as you roll. Taper ends, if desired.

Place each loaf seam-side down on greased baking sheet sprinkled with cornmeal. Use a sharp knife to slash tops of loaves diagonally every 2 1/2 inches, 1/4 inch deep. Beat egg white till foamy; add 1 tablespoon water. Brush mixture over tops and sides of loaves. Or, for crisp crust, brush just with water. Cover with a damp cloth. Keep the cloth from touching loaves by draping it over inverted glasses. Let rise till double (1 to 1 1/4 hours). Bake at 375°F till light brown, about 20 minutes. Brush again with egg white mixture or water. Bake 15 to 20 minutes or till done. Cool. Makes two loaves.

THE ADVENTURE CONTINUES

After a delicious meal, you and Stump return to your quarters and look up the second point on your map. It corresponds to the wharf that Gilles told you to visit. Evidently you and Stump are on the right track. You work through two more French exercises before you retire for the night.

30

From Word to Discourse
Du mot au discours

Instructions: This activity focuses on the mechanics of sentence formation. You're given a scatter chart from which you must learn to string words into sentences. Samples of well-formed sentences—as well as some ungrammatical ones—are given below for you to study before constructing your own.

SCATTER CHART

	il y a		
sur	*voici*		*ici*
là(-bas)			
est/sont	*est-ce qu(e)...?*	*c'est*	
	n'est-ce pas?		
cette/ces			*une/deux*
des	*tige(s)*		
	l'/la/les		*blanche(s)*
noire(s)	*couchée(s)*		*debout*
toute(s)		*aussi*	
autre(s)	*mais*		
petite(s)	*longue(s)*		
et	*oui*		*non*

Instructions: See if you can match the French words with their equivalent English words. If you can't match all of the words, don't worry! You should be able to get them from the context in the sentences below.

rod	is/are	there is	white	black	there	here
this/these	standing upright	lying down	one/two	some	it is	also
and	yes	no	here is/are	is it that...?	right?	but
other	long	short (=small)	all	the	on	

93

Sample Sentences

Instructions: Carefully study these sentences, including the ungrammatical ones which are starred. Try to determine the patterns and meanings of the patterns in French.

1. There is a rod, a white rod. Here is the white rod. — *Il y a une tige, une tige blanche. Voici la tige blanche.*
2. There is another rod, a black rod. — *Il y a une autre tige, une tige noire.*
3. This rod is black. — *Cette tige est noire.*
4. Is this black rod small? — *Est-ce que cette tige noire est petite?*
5. No, this black rod is long. — *Non, cette tige noire est longue.*
6. A black rod on a white rod. — *Une tige noire sur une tige blanche.*
   *Une noire tige sur une blanche tige.
7. The black rod is on the white rod. — *La tige noire est sur la tige blanche.*
8. It is a small rod. — *C'est une petite tige.*
9. This small rod is here, (standing) upright on the black rod. — *Cette petite tige est ici, debout sur la tige noire.*
10. This other rod is also here, (standing) upright on the black rod. — *Cette autre tige est aussi ici, debout sur la tige noire.*
11. Some white rods are (standing) upright on the black rod. — *Des tiges blanches sont debout sur la tige noire.*
12. The black rod is long. — *La tige noire est longue.*
13. The white rods are small. — *Les tiges blanches sont petites.*
14. All the white rods are (standing) upright. — *Toutes les tiges blanches sont debout.*
15. The black rod is lying there. — *La tige noire est couchée là.*
16. These two white rods are (standing) upright, but these two are lying. — *Ces deux tiges blanches sont debout, mais ces deux sont couchées.*
17. These black rods are long, but these white rods are small, right? — *Ces tiges noires sont longues, mais ces tiges blanches sont petites, n'est-ce pas?*
18. Yes, one is small and the others are long. — *Oui, l'une est petite et les autres sont longues.*
    *Oui, une est petite et des autres sont longues.
19. Are all the black rods long? No, there are long and small rods. — *Est-ce que toutes les tiges noires sont longues? Non, il y a des tiges longues et des petites.*
    *Est-ce que toutes les tiges noires sont longues? Non, voici longues et petites tiges.
20. Are the white rods black? No, the white rods are white, and the black rods are black. — *Est-ce que les tiges blanches sont noires? Non, les tiges blanches sont blanches, et les tiges noires sont noires.*

Instructions: See if you can put these into French. Answers may be found in sentences above.

2. There is another rod, a black rod.
4. Is this black rod small?
5. No, this black rod is long.
7. The black rod is on the white rod.
9. This small rod is here, (standing) upright on the black rod.
15. The black rod is lying there.
17. These black rods are long, but these white rods are small, right?
18. Yes, one is small and the others are long.
19. Are all the black rods long? No, there are long and small rods.
20. Are the white rods black? No, the white rods are white, and the black rods are black.

31

📼 In the Classroom: A French Lesson
French Only
Dans la salle de classe: une leçon de français

📼 Instructions: Listen to and read the following lesson. Work toward full comprehension.

This is a pencil.	📼 *C'est un crayon.*
Paper. This is a sheet of paper.	*Papier. C'est une feuille de papier.*
Say it: pencil, paper: (—,—)	*Dites-le: crayon, papier: (—,—)*
Again: (—,—)	*Encore: (—,—)*
Very good.	*Très bien.*
This pencil is white.	*Ce crayon est blanc.*
It's a white pencil.	*C'est un crayon blanc.*
This paper is white also.	*Ce papier est blanc aussi.*
It's a white paper.	*C'est un papier blanc.*
The pencil and the paper are both white.	*Le crayon et le papier sont tous les deux blancs.*
This paper is yellow.	*Ce papier est jaune.*
This pencil is yellow also.	*Ce crayon est jaune aussi.*
What is this?	*Qu'est-ce que c'est?*
It's a sheet of paper.	*C'est une feuille de papier.*
And this?	*Et ceci?*
Another sheet of paper.	*Une autre feuille de papier.*
What's the difference between them?	*Quelle est la différence entre eux?*
The one is yellow; the other is white.	*L'une est jaune; l'autre est blanche.*
This yellow thing, what is it?	*Cette chose jaune, qu'est-ce que c'est?*
It's a pencil.	*C'est un crayon.*
This white thing, what is it?	*Cette chose blanche, qu'est-ce que c'est?*
It's a sheet of paper.	*C'est une feuille de papier.*
Two more things: a yellow sheet of paper and a white pencil.	*Deux choses de plus: une feuille de papier jaune et un crayon blanc.*
Yes, two yellow things and two white things.	*Oui, deux choses jaunes et deux choses blanches.*
A total of four things: two sheets of paper and two pencils.	*Un total de quatre choses: deux feuilles de papier et deux crayons.*
These two things are white.	*Ces deux choses sont blanches.*
These two things are yellow.	*Ces deux choses sont jaunes.*

📼 THE ADVENTURE CONTINUES

Day Three—0730 hours

Seven Days to Rendezvous

You and Stump are anxious to go to the wharf and find Jean-Luc, but Zsa-Zsa insists that you need to have a more thorough grasp of French vocabulary before you go.

32

Lecture on Geography
French Only
Une leçon de géographie

Instructions: Listen to and read the following geography lesson. Learn geography-related vocabulary in French!

Here is a map of the world.	*Voici une carte du monde.*
North. South. East. West.	*Le nord. Le sud. L'est. L'ouest.*
Here is the north pole, the Arctic Pole.	*Voici le pôle nord, le pôle arctique.*
Here is the south pole, the Antarctic Pole.	*Voici le pôle sud, le pôle antarctique.*
The earth is our spaceship.	*La terre est notre vaisseau spatial.*
It is one of nine planets that revolve around the sun.	*C'est une des neuf planètes qui tournent autour du soleil.*
It is our planet, our home.	*C'est notre planète, notre maison.*
In the world there are two hemispheres:	*Sur la terre, il y a deux hémisphères:*
Here is the northern hemisphere.	*Voici l'hémisphère nord.*
Here is the southern hemisphere.	*Voici l'hémisphère sud.*
The core of the earth is extremely hot.	*Le noyau de la terre est extrêmement chaud.*
Most of the surface of the earth is covered with water.	*La plus grande partie de la surface de la terre est couverte d'eau.*
There are three great oceans:	*Il y a trois grands océans:*
the Pacific Ocean, the Atlantic Ocean, and the Indian Ocean.	*l'océan Pacifique, l'océan Atlantique, et l'océan Indien.*
Here is the Pacific Ocean.	*Voici l'océan Pacifique.*
It is the largest ocean.	*C'est le plus grand océan.*
It is also the deepest.	*C'est également le plus profond.*
Here is the Atlantic Ocean.	*Voici l'océan Atlantique.*
It lies between Europe and North America,	*Il est situé entre l'Europe et l'Amérique du nord,*
also between Africa and South America.	*également entre l'Afrique et l'Amérique du sud.*
Here is the Indian Ocean.	*Voici l'océan Indien.*
It lies wholly in the eastern hemisphere.	*Il est entièrement situé dans l'hémisphère ouest.*
It stretches from Africa to Australia	*Il s'étend de l'Afrique à l'Australie*
and touches Arabia and India.	*et touche l'Arabie et l'Inde.*

Long ago	*Il y a longtemps,*
there was one big land mass,	*il y avait une seule grande masse de terre,*
but now it's divided	*mais maintenant elle est divisée*
into several continents.	*en plusieurs continents.*
The largest land mass or continent is here.	*La plus grande masse de terre ou continent est ici.*
It stretches from Europe to China.	*Elle s'étend de l'Europe à la Chine.*
It is called Eurasia.	*Elle s'appelle l'Eurasie.*

THE ADVENTURE CONTINUES

You and Stump walk to the wharf. You notice an old man sitting on a pier with his sketchbook and watercolors. You approach him, hoping that he is Jean-Luc. You compliment the man on his artwork and ask if he knows anyone named Jean-Luc.

"Je suis Jean-Luc," he tells you. He quickly finishes his watercolor sketch and looks up at you. *"Qui sont vous?"*

You and Stump introduce yourselves and try to explain your search in French. Though your language ability has grown tremendously in the last few days, you find that you lack sufficient French vocabulary to fully explain what you want.

Jean-Luc notices your frustration. "No worries. *Je parle un petit peu d'anglais.* Explain to me what you want in English."

You repeat your explanation in English. Jean-Luc thinks for a moment, then nods. *"Oui, je suis l'homme* whom you seek. I, too, have a challenge. You must complete it if you want your next clue. *Bonne chance!"*

Jean-Luc assigns you a series of French exercises and a few more culture questions. You and Stump get to work, eager to prove your language ability as well as your cultural knowledge.

33
📼 More on Numbers
Au sujet des chiffres et de la quantité

📼 Instructions: Continue learning new numbers in French.

-ANTE NUMBERS

📼 Numbers 30, 40, 50, and 60 are two-part words, the second part of which has the sound "ante":

trente   30
quarante   40
cinquante 50
soixante   60

Think of saying you have one aunt who is 30, named *trente*; one 40, named *quarante*; one 50, named *cinquante*; and one 60, named *soixante*.

Tape off. Review and practice on your own.

📼 Processing aide: 30 <u>tr</u>-aunt 40 <u>car</u>-aunt 50 <u>sank</u>-aunt 60 <u>swass</u>-aunt

Read these numbers:

Decades: *trente, quarante, cinquante, soixante*

Teens: *onze, douze, treize, quatorze, quinze, seize, dix-sept, dix-huit, dix-neuf*

Say these numbers: 30   40   50   60   130   140   150   160

📼 Listen and repeat: 5 50   6 16 60   4 14 40   3 13 30
                                                    150

Point to the number called: 130   140
                                    50   100   30
                                         160   60
                                              40

Tape off. Say those numbers.

📼 TWENTY / *VINGT* - EIGHTY / *QUATRE-VINGTS*

📼 Number 20 is slightly different. It is spelled with five letters (*vingt*) but has the same sound as *vin* "wine". Listen: 20

The predicted form for 80 would be *huit-ante*. That form, however, is not widely used. [It is only used in Switzerland.] In its place, 80 being 4 of 20, they say: *quatre-vingts*.

Point to the number called:

		115	120		
	114	140		116	
144	160		20		80

Tape off. Say those numbers.

Read these numbers: *vingt, trente, quarante, cinquante, soixante, quatre-vingts, mille vingt, cent vingt, mille quatre-vingts, cent quatre-vingts, mille soixante*
teens: *onze, douze, treize, quatorze, quinze, seize, dix-sept, dix-huit, dix-neuf*

SEVENTY / *SOIXANTE-DIX* - NINETY / *QUATRE-VINGT-DIX*

The predicted forms for 70 and 90 would be *septante* and *neuf-ante*. These forms, however, are not widely used. In their place are the following:
90 is 4-20-10: *quatre-vingt-dix*
70 is 60-10: *soixante-dix*

Tape off. Say these numbers:

20	80 [4*20]	90 (4*20 *10)	60	70 [60*10]	
36	45	54	63	20,060	14,400
66	19,616	18,440	17,812	13,333	

Read these numbers: *quarante, quatre-vingts, quatre-vingt-dix, cinquante, soixante, soixante-dix*

Point to the number called:

		70		
	50		40	
90		80		30
	60		190	
		170		

Tape off. Say those numbers.

◉ DECADE SETS

🔊 Listen and observe. The first number in each set is formed differently from the others:

<u>21</u> 22 23 24 25   <u>31</u> 32 33 34   <u>41</u> 42 43 44   <u>51</u> 52 53   <u>61</u> 62 63

Tape off. Say those numbers.

🔊 Notice that within the decade sets (21–29, 31–39, etc.), only the first number has *et*:
21 *vingt et un* ("twenty <u>and</u> one") but 22 *vingt-deux* ("twenty-two")
31 *trente et un* ("thirty <u>and</u> one") but 32 *trente-deux* ("thirty-two")

Read these numbers: *cinquante-cinq, quarante-quatre, soixante-six, trente-trois, vingt-six, trente et un, soixante-dix, quarante et un, cinquante et un, quatre-vingt-un, quatre-vingt-onze, soixante et onze*

REVIEW

1. Practice counting, gradually increasing your speed.

2. Time yourself saying the first string of numbers below from left to right. Then time yourself saying it from right to left. See how much you can improve your time.

3. Do the same with the second and third strings.

1st string
20 40 60 80 70 90 30 44 22 10 33 66 73 13 11 15 14 12 17 19 18 21

⌚ Time on first trial:_____ seconds   ⌚ Time after five trials_____ seconds

2nd string
22   140   166   182   179   199   133   144   122   110   112   116   118   119   121   131   144   155

⌚ Time on first trial:_____ seconds   ⌚ Time after five trials_____ seconds

3rd string
105   1,105   2,203   3,308   4,406   5,504   6,609   7,711   8,812   9,913   10,014   11,015   12,016

⌚ Time on first trial:_____ seconds   ⌚ Time after five trials_____ seconds

Spelling Reference: A Sampling of Numbers 1–10,000

un	*onze*	*vingt et un*	*cinquante et un*	*quatre-vingt-deux*	*deux mille*
deux	*douze*	*vingt-deux*	*cinquante-deux*	*quatre-vingt-dix*	*dix mille*
trois	*treize*	*vingt-trois*	*soixante*	*quatre-vingt-onze*	
quatre	*quatorze*	*trente*	*soixante et un*	*cent*	
cinq	*quinze*	*trente et un*	*soixante-deux*	*deux cents*	
six	*seize*	*trente-deux*	*soixante-dix*	*deux cent un*	
sept	*dix-sept*	*quarante*	*soixante et onze*	*deux cent deux*	
huit	*dix-huit*	*quarante et un*	*soixante-douze*	*mille*	
neuf	*dix-neuf*	*quarante-deux*	*quatre-vingts*	*mille un*	
dix	*vingt*	*cinquante*	*quatre-vingt-un*	*mille deux*	

34

🎞 Thinking *en français*

This module is entirely tape off. As before, you're on your own. Give it your all.

⊙ Instructions: Using pictographs rather than written words, create sentences of your own. You might even try to create a story from the sentences.

PART 1
Pictographs and Words

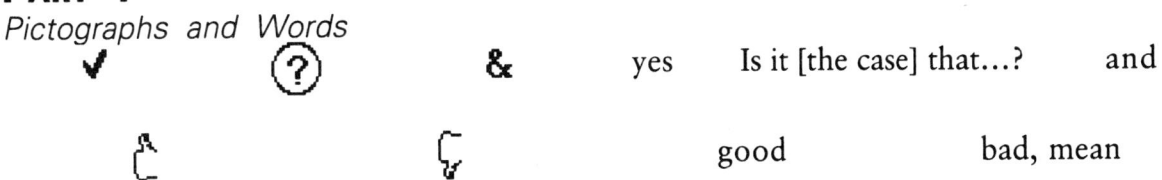

| ✓ | ⊙? | & | yes | Is it [the case] that...? | and |

| ᑕ | ᑐ | | | good | bad, mean |

Sentence Building Blocks—in Words

| OUI |
| EST-CE QUE |

UN CE(T)	BON MÉCHANT	ROI HOMME SERVITEUR	EST	UN	BON MÉCHANT	ROI HOMME SERVITEUR	...et...
	IL		EST		BON MÉCHANT		...qui...

Sentence Building Blocks—in Pictographs

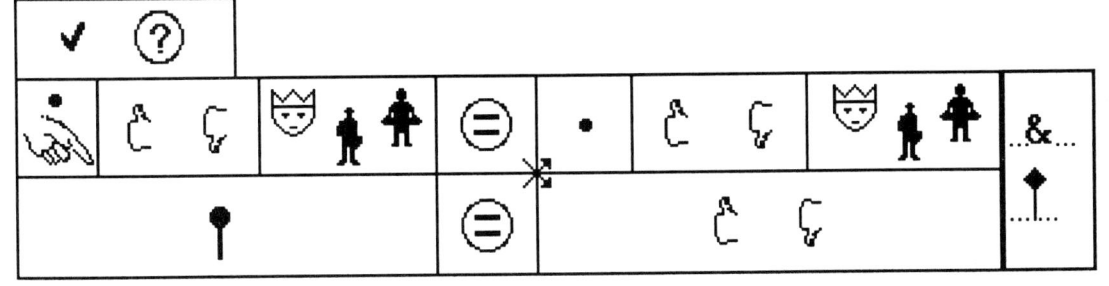

| ✓ ⊙? |
| 👉 ᑕ ᑐ 👑 👤 👥 | = | • | ᑕ ᑐ 👑 👤 👥 | ...&... |
| • | = | ᑕ ᑐ | ...♦... |

*Note: In French, the words *bon* and *bonne* come after the words *homme* and *femme*. This is an exception to the general rule that adjectives precede the nouns they modify.

Sample Sentences
Est-ce que cet homme-ci est un roi?   Oui, il est roi.
⊙? 👉 👤 = • 👑   ✓ ♦ = 👑

101

Est-ce qu'il est un bon roi?   *Oui.*

Est-ce qu'un bon roi est un homme bon?   *Oui, un roi qui est un homme bon est un bon roi.*

Est-ce qu'un roi est un bon serviteur?   *Oui, un roi est un bon serviteur.*

READING ACTIVITY 1

Instructions: Read the ten sentences out loud. If you have any difficulty, check the French equivalent in the appendix.

1.
2.
3.
4.
5.
6.
7.
8.
9.
10.

PART 2

Pictographs and Words

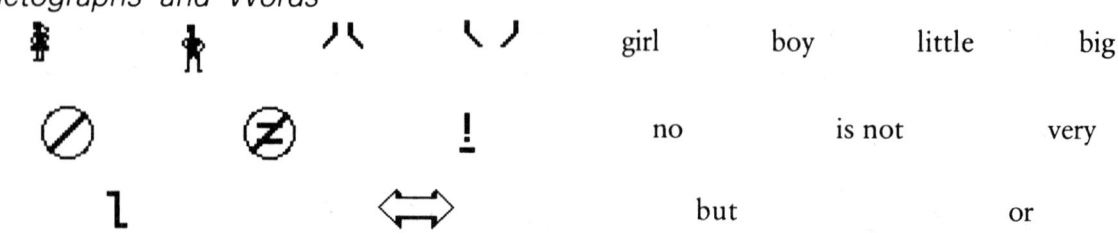

				girl	boy	little	big
⊘	⊜	!		no	is not		very
↥	⇔			but			or

Sentence Building Blocks—in Words

NON							
CE / cette / UN / une	GARÇON / FILLE	N'EST PAS	UN / une	TRES	GRAND / grande / PETIT / petite	GARÇON / FILLE	...ou... / ...mais...
IL ELLE							
QUI QUI?							

Sentence Building Blocks—in Pictographs

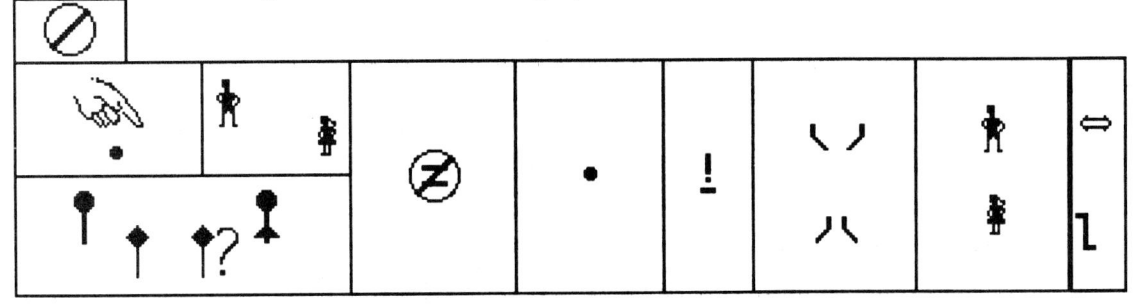

Sample Sentences

Cette fille-ci n'est pas une grande fille.

Et elle n'est pas une petite reine.

Elle n'est pas une petite fille, elle est une grande fille, une très grande fille.

READING ACTIVITY 2

Instructions: Read the nine sentences out loud. If you have any difficulty, check the French equivalent in the appendix.

1.

2.

3. ⊘ ❗ ⊘ · 👑
4. ❗ ⊜ · 👤 & ❗ ⊜ · ❗ 👑
5. · 👤 ⊘ · 👑
6. ❗ ? ⊜ 👉 👤
7. ❓ ❗ ⊜ 👸
8. ❗ ⊜ · 👤 ❗ ⊘ · 👑
9. ❗ ⊜ · ❗ 👑

REVIEW OF PICTOGRAPHS AND WORDS

Instructions: Form sentences from the pictographs in the circle.

Sample Strings

Cet homme-ci est roi.
C'est un bon roi.
Non, il n'est pas un bon roi.
Qui est cette femme-là?
Ce roi-là est un homme.

Elle est une très méchante reine.
Un bon roi est un homme bon.
Oui, c'est un homme.
Est-ce qu'elle est reine?
Est-ce qu'elle est une petite fille?

Est-ce que cet homme-ci est un bon roi?
Un méchant homme n'est pas un bon roi.
Oui, mais elle est reine.

Elle est une femme bonne mais elle n'est pas une bonne reine.
Il est un méchant homme, et il est un très méchant roi.

35

🎧 A Lecture on the Alphabet
French Only
L'alphabet romain

🎧 Instructions: This is an exercise in inferring meaning. Listen to and read this short lecture and try your best to understand the overall meaning of the text. Don't worry if you don't know what every individual word means!

🎧 *L'ALPHABET ROMAIN*

Introduction et Voyelles

Un alphabet est une liste de lettres. Il y a divers alphabets: l'alphabet romain, l'alphabet russe, l'alphabet grec, etc. L'alphabet romain est la liste des lettres qui proviennent du latin. C'est-à-dire, l'alphabet romain est la liste des lettres de l'espagnol, de l'italien, de l'anglais, et de beaucoup d'autres langues. L'arabe, l'hébreu, le russe, et le grec ont leur propre système d'écriture et n'emploient pas l'alphabet romain.

Les lettres d'un alphabet représentent les sons d'une langue.

Les lettres de l'alphabet espagnol représentent les sons de l'espagnol.

Les lettres de l'alphabet anglais représentent les sons de l'anglais.

Les lettres de l'alphabet français représentent les sons du français.

L'alphabet de l'anglais et du français contient vingt-six lettres. De toutes les lettres de l'alphabet, cinq sont des voyelles et vingt-et-une sont des consonnes. Le système phonétique français a cinq voyelles—douze voyelles orales et quatre voyelles nasales. Mais l'alphabet français n'a que cinq lettres pour ces seize sons.

La voyelle <O> apparaît une fois dans non *et deux fois dans* photo. *La voyelle <A> apparaît une fois dans* la, *deux fois dans* papa, *et trois fois dans* Canada.

Écoutez bien les noms de ces cinq voyelles: A E I O U. A *comme dans* la, E *comme dans* le, I *comme dans* police, O *comme dans* lors, U *comme dans* une. *Répétez les noms des cinq voyelles:* A E I O U.

36
🎧 Chatter at a Royal Ball
Bavardages au bal royal

🎧 GETTING READY FOR CONVERSATION

Instructions: Read through this list of vocabulary and see them in use in the conversation.

he does/makes	*il fait*	"they" say/I hear tell	*on dit*
they do/make	*ils font*	{VERB} no more	*ne {VERBE} plus*
he believes	*il croit*	I believe so.	*Je crois que oui.*
he begins	*il commence*	How much does it cost?	*Combien ça coûte?*
true	*vrai*	now	*maintenant*
tonight, this evening	*ce soir*	often	*souvent*
how?	*comment?*	still, yet	*encore*
when?	*quand?*	not yet	*pas encore*
where is he singing?	*où est-ce qu'il chante?*	already	*déjà*
both	*les deux/tous les deux*	he's going to sing	*il va chanter*
doesn't {VERB} yet	*ne {VERBE} pas encore*	where?	*où?*

Instructions: Listen several times to the reading of this dialogue.

🎧 CONVERSATION 4

🎧 Instructions: Recite the English before the French voice speaks on the tape.

- ••: The king that loves to play the drum is singing now, right?
- 🎧 *Le roi qui aime jouer du tambour chante maintenant, n'est-ce pas?*
- •: Yes. He's not playing.
- *Oui. Il ne joue pas.*
- ••: Doesn't he play anymore?
- *Est-ce qu'il ne joue plus?*
- •: Oh, he still plays. He often plays. He's going to play tonight. But he prefers to sing.
- *Oh, il joue encore. Il joue souvent. Il va jouer ce soir. Mais il préfère chanter.*
- ••: Who is it he is singing with?
- *Avec qui est-ce qu'il chante?*
- •: With the queen. Both are singing, and she is playing the drum now.
- *Avec la reine. Tous les deux chantent, et elle joue du tambour maintenant.*
- ••: And the dog and the cat, what are they doing now?
- *Et le chien et le chat, que font-ils maintenant?*
- •: Both are singing with the king and the queen.
- *Les deux chantent avec le roi et la reine.*
- ••: Really? Where? Where are they singing?
- *Vraiment? Où? Où est-ce qu'ils chantent?*
- •: Over there. Listen.
- *Là-bas. Écoute.*
- ••: It's sensational. Imagine!
- *C'est sensationnel. Imagine-toi!*
- •: They like to sing together.
- *Ils aiment chanter ensemble.*
- ••: That's great!
- *C'est formidable!*
- •: They say that the cat has decided to sing with the princess.
- *On dit que le chat a décidé de chanter avec la princesse.*
- ••: When?
- *Quand?*
- •: Now.
- *Maintenant.*
- ••: That's horrible!
- *C'est horrible!*
- •: Listen! They're starting to sing already.
- *Écoute! Ils commencent déjà à chanter.*
- ••: Yukh! How much does this concert cost?
- *Beurk. Combien coûte ce concert?*

37
Focus on the Language 15–23
Concentration sur la langue 15-23

Focus 15

Infinitives ending in [r] (spelled *-r, -re*).

| She likes to see her friends. | *Elle aime voir ses amis.* |
| He hopes to live in Paris. | *Il espère vivre à Paris.* |

1. As stated earlier, most infinitive forms end in the sound "ay", spelled *-er*:

    parler   to speak   *menacer*   to menace, threaten
    décider   to decide   *espérer*   to hope

2. The infinitive form of several verbs ends in the sound [r], spelled *-r* or *-re*:

    voir   to see   *avoir*   to have
    faire   to do, to make   *être*   to be
    vivre   to live   *dire*   to say, to tell

Translate Orally from and into French

He desires to have friends.	*Il désire avoir des amis.*
He hopes to live with friends.	*Il espère vivre avec des amis.*
He desires to see the king.	*Il désire voir le roi.*
She desires to tell the truth.	*Elle désire dire la vérité.*
The dog likes to threaten the cat.	*Le chien aime menacer le chat.*
She prefers to eat with the cat.	*Elle préfère manger avec le chat.*

Focus 16

Future intention: going {to verb} = *va* + {infinitive}.

| She's going to sing. | *Elle va chanter.* |
| They're going to sing. | *Ils vont chanter.* |

A useful way of indicating future intention employs the verb *go* plus an infinitive verb (just as in English). The plural of *il va* "he's going" is *il vont* "they're going."

Translate Orally from and into French

What is he going to do?	*Qu'est-ce qu'il va faire?*
He's going to eat the cheese.	*Il va manger le fromage.*
Who's going to see the queen?	*Qui va voir la reine?*
She's going to live with her.	*Elle va vivre avec elle.*
They're going to tell the truth.	*Ils vont dire la vérité.*
What is the prince going to say?	*Qu'est-ce que va dire le prince?*

Focus 17

Verbs that require a preposition before an infinitive: *décide de chanter*

The dog decides to play.	*Le chien décide de jouer.*
The cat threatens to sing.	*Le chat menace de chanter.*
The duke begins to cry.	*Le duc commence à pleurer.*

Certain verbs require a preposition before an infinitive. The verbs *menacer*, *décider*, *promettre*, and others require the preposition *de* as in the examples above. The verb *commencer* requires the preposition *à*.

Translate Orally from and into French

The cat decides to play with the dog.	*Le chat décide de jouer avec le chien.*
The princess threatens to cry.	*La princesse menace de pleurer.*
She promises to tell the truth.	*Elle promet de dire la vérité.*
The queen begins to talk with the king.	*La reine commence à parler avec le roi.*
She begins to tell the truth.	*Elle commence à dire la vérité.*

Focus 18

Has VERBed.

| The cat has threatened to sing. | *Le chat a menacé de chanter.* |
| The dog has decided to play. | *Le chien a décidé de jouer.* |

Translate Orally from and into French

The princess has threatened to sing.	*La princesse a menacé de chanter.*
The prince has decided to eat the bread.	*Le prince a décidé de manger le pain.*
The prince has eaten the bread.	*Le prince a mangé le pain.*
The king has begun to speak.	*Le roi a commencé à parler.*
They have begun to sing.	*Ils ont commencé à chanter.*
She has decided to begin to sing.	*Elle a décidé de commencer à chanter.*

Focus 19

"Both," "all three," etc., *tous (toutes) les*

There are the duke and duchess.	*Voilà le duc et la duchesse.*
Both are playing.	*Ils jouent tous les deux.*
Here are two queens and a princess.	*Voici deux reines et une princesse.*
All three are crying.	*Elles pleurent toutes les trois.*

Note: *Toute* rather than *tous* is used if the persons are feminine gender.

Translate Orally from and into French

Here is the dog and the cat. Both are talking.	*Voici le chien et le chat. Ils parlent tous les deux.*
Here are the three queens. All three are crying.	*Voici les trois reines. Elles pleurent toutes les trois.*
There are four princes here. All four are singing.	*Il y a quatre princes ici. Ils chantent tous les quatre.*
There are two princesses there. Both desire to talk with you.	*Il y a deux princesses là-bas. Elles désirent toutes les deux parler avec vous.*

Focus 20

"Already" *déjà* and "not yet" *pas encore*.

The king is singing already.	*Le roi chante déjà.*
No, not yet.	*Non, pas encore.*
He is not singing yet.	*Il ne chante pas encore.*

Translate Orally from and into French

The baby talks already.	*L'enfant parle déjà.*
No, he doesn't talk yet.	*Non, il ne parle pas encore.*
But the mother still talks a lot.	*Mais la mère parle encore beaucoup.*

Focus 21

"No more, no longer, not any more" *ne...plus*.

Does the parrot still talk?	*Est-ce que le perroquet parle encore?*
No, it does not talk anymore.	*Non, il ne parle plus.*

Translate Orally from and into French

The queen still sings, right?	*La reine chante encore, n'est-ce pas?*
No, she doesn't sing anymore.	*Non, elle ne chante plus.*
The princess still cries a lot, right?	*La princesse pleure encore beaucoup, n'est-ce pas?*
No, she doesn't cry much anymore.	*Non, elle ne pleure plus beaucoup.*

Focus 22

"He does/makes" *il fait*; "they do/make" *ils font*; "he is" *il est*; "they are" *ils sont*.

What does he do?	*Qu'est-ce qu'il fait?*
What do they do?	*Qu'est-ce qu'ils font?*
The princess is here.	*La princesse est ici.*
The queens are here too.	*Les reines sont ici aussi.*
The dog makes drums.	*Le chien fait des tambours.*
The cats make drums too.	*Les chats font des tambours aussi.*

French speakers pronounce the third person singular and plural forms of regular French verbs identically: *Il joue* and *ils jouent*, *il chante* and *ils chantent* all sound the same despite the difference in spelling. But with a handful of verbs—including *faire* and *être*—there is a difference. These are called irregular forms. (Note that *faire* can mean "make" or "do," as in the last four examples below.)

Translate Orally from and into French

The dog makes drums.	*Le chien fait des tambours.*
The cats make drums too.	*Les chats font des tambours aussi.*
What do kings do?	*Qu'est-ce que les rois font?*
What are the kings doing?	*Qu'est-ce que les rois font?*
What are the kings making?	*Qu'est-ce que les rois font?*

Focus 23

On dit "They say, people say, it is said, I/we hear tell, I/we've heard, I/we've been told," etc.

| People say that the king sings well. | *On dit que le roi chante bien.* |
| They say the cat doesn't sing well. | *On dit que le chat ne chante pas bien.* |

Translate Orally from and into French

I've heard that the prince likes to make drums.	*On dit que le prince aime faire des tambours.*
We hear tell that the cat cries a lot.	*On dit que le chat pleure beaucoup.*
I've been told that the dog doesn't like the cat.	*On dit que le chien n'aime pas le chat.*
It is said that the cat doesn't like the dog anymore.	*On dit que le chat n'aime plus le chien.*
They say the queen cries in the bathroom.	*On dit que la reine pleure dans la salle de bain.*

The impersonal pronoun *on* serves as an impersonal subject in various kinds of sentences. Here are some:

How do you say (how does one say) "cat" in Spanish?	*Comment dit-on "chat" en espagnol?*
French spoken (here).	*On parle français.*
Milk sold here.	*On vend du lait.*
Shall we continue?	*On continue?*
Now what do we do?	*Qu'est-ce qu'on fait maintenant?*
People dance there.	*On y danse.*

Note that where English uses a passive "is spoken," "is sold," French uses an active "one speaks," "one sells." The impersonal *on* can be the equivalent of "you," "they," "we," "I," and even "people" or "there is."

38

📼 *Ma première visite au Québec: première partie*
My First Visit to Québec: Part One

🎞 Instructions: Listen to this diglot-weave story.

📼 As I passed *la frontière*, headed north into *le Canada français*, I was excited by the prospect of *ma première visite au Québec*, but I felt shaky, *un peu incertain* of myself in this new *environnement*.

Having lived in upstate New York for *la* greater *partie de ma vie, et* having long had *un intérêt* in «*nos amis canadiens*» to the *nord*, I had traveled *beaucoup* in *le Canada anglais* but had never yet *visité le Canada français*. I had learned *un peu de français* through the years, *mais* had never had enough *de temps* to *réellement étudier la langue*.

I wanted to kick myself, *mais* now it was *un peu* late—*oui, c'était un peu tard* for that. I was comforted *très peu* by my purchase of *un dictionnaire français/anglais à Montréal. Mais* I determined to practice *mon français* to the *limite. Je* even made *la décision* to write (*je* mean *écrire*) *mon journal en français* as much as *possible*.

Je had no *mission officielle au Canada. Je* was going there *strictement* as *un touriste*, mostly out of *curiosité et un désir* to enjoy *une expérience différente* from usual.

Having been an ice skater, *un patineur sur glace, toute ma vie*—in fact, *un membre du club américain des patineurs sur glace* since *je* was a small *garçon...un petit garçon, je* looked forward to *l'opportunité* to attend *une compétition canadienne le* following *samedi. Un ami français* had given me *un programme* as *un* going-away *cadeau* only a few *jours* before, *et je* had *diligemment* tried to *lire* some of it, using my *dictionnaire français/anglais et comparant les* words *français avec les mots anglais*.

This reading *de texte simple et familier* is *une activité* that *je* can *recommander* to anyone. This is, in my *opinion, l'un des* best ways *d'apprendre une langue*. After some *heures de voyage, je* came to *un petit village et* made *une décision* to stop *et* look around *un peu*.

It was very cold...yes, *il faisait très froid*, just as *je* had expected it *au Canada. Le village de Bois-des-filion* was *absolument tranquille. L'ancien proverbe* came to mind: *Le silence est d'or*. It was 6 P.M., *l'heure du dîner*. Only *un chat blanc* crossed the *rue* in front of *moi. Je* found *mon hôtel* where *je* had made *ma réservation* for *la nuit. Je* felt so tired, *si fatigué*, that *je décidais* to go to bed right away. Since today was Friday, so *demain* would be *samedi, le grand jour de la compétition de patin à glace. L'hôtel était tranquille et je* fell asleep, quickly...*vite*.

Le next *matin, je déjeunais au restaurant de l'hôtel, et* then *je* went for a walk to give my *estomac une chance* to *digérer* that *délicieux déjeuner. Le* sky was *bleu et* without *nuages. L'air* was crisp. *Je* walked around *le village*, looking at *les enfants patinant* on *le lac*, all bundled up in their winter *manteaux*. They looked like *petits Esquimaux* who live in *igloos au pôle nord*.

La compétition was scheduled to start *à deux heures*. Since *je* was *un peu* early, *je* sat in the *audience et* looked at *mon programme*. Then *soudain une radio* came on. *Le commentateur* opened *le programme avec* these *mots*:

Salut amis et bon après-midi.

C'est la radio Canada, un-deux-trois-quatre…

Amis, buvez du Coca-Cola, la boisson la plus rafraîchissante et la plus populaire du monde. Oui, mes amis, buvez du Coca-Cola!

Le Coca-Cola canadien est excellent…magnifique…fantastique…indispensable! Vive le Coca-Cola! Vive le Canada!

He paused *un moment, puis continua*:

Mesdames et Messieurs, bonjour! La compétition va soon *commencer*. All *les participants* have won *des médailles aux Jeux Olympiques*. They're all *excellents. Mesdames et Messieurs, applaudissez s'il vous plaît…*(Clap, clap!)

Les participants s'avancent un by *un* on the rink, *saluent, et* retire. *Finalement la lumière* is dimmed, *de la* soft *musique classique commence, et une magnifique* young lady *s'avance et salue. L'audience applaudit.* She is *si belle avec sa robe bleue et le* shiny golden *ruban* in her hair. In *harmonie avec la belle musique, la* young *fille commence à patiner gracieusement. Je* was *très impressionné* by the *beauté et grâce de la belle patineuse. La musique classique* played softly in the background. *J'étais transporté.* Little by little…*petit à petit, la belle musique classique* subsided. *La patineuse* came to a halt, *le spot de lumière* rested on her as *l'audience* started to *applaudir* heartily. For *le reste de la compétition, je* couldn't get out of my mind *l'image de la belle patineuse en robe bleue avec le* shiny *ruban doré dans les cheveux*.

(To be continued)

39

🔊 The Key of the King's Kingdom
French Only
La clé du royaume du roi

🔊 Instructions: Listen to and read the following story. Then use the diagram to try reciting the story without looking at the text.

Here is a key, a small key.	🔊 *Voici une clé, une petite clé.*
Here is a famous king.	*Voici un roi célèbre.*
And here is the famous king's great kingdom.	*Et voici le grand royaume du roi célèbre.*
In this great kingdom, there is a nice town.	*Dans ce grand royaume, il y a une jolie ville.*
In this nice town, there is a small park.	*Dans cette jolie ville, il y a un petit parc.*
In this small park, there is a white house.	*Dans ce petit parc, il y a une maison blanche.*
In this white house, there is an empty room.	*Dans cette maison blanche, il y a une pièce vide.*
In this empty room, there is a Chinese vase.	*Dans cette pièce vide, il y a un vase chinois.*
In this Chinese vase, there is a pretty blue flower.	*Dans ce vase chinois, il y a une belle fleur bleue.*
The pretty blue flower in the Chinese vase,	*La belle fleur bleue dans le vase chinois,*
the Chinese vase in the empty room,	*le vase chinois dans la pièce vide,*
the empty room in the white house,	*la pièce vide dans la maison blanche,*
the white house in the small park,	*la maison blanche dans le petit parc,*
the small park in the nice town,	*le petit parc dans la jolie ville,*
the nice town in the great kingdom,	*la jolie ville dans le grand royaume,*
and here is the small key	*et voici la petite clé*
of the famous king's great kingdom.	*du grand royaume du roi célèbre.*

Now sit back and take in this delightful piece again, preparing to retell it in your own words.

40
Much Communication with Limited Means
Communiquer avec des moyens limités

Instructions: Learn the following words and their French equivalents.

pour	for, for the purpose of
là	there
travailler	to work, working
manger	to eat, eating
être (mé)content	to be (un)happy
bien	well
mais	but
sans	without
vivre	to live, living
pouvoir	to be able, being able
dormir	to sleep, sleeping
se reposer	to rest, resting
beaucoup	much, a lot
Il faut	One must (you have to, it's necessary to)
C'est stupide.	(It) is stupid.
C'est (im)possible. or *Il est (im)possible.*	It is (im)possible.

Instructions: Now see if you can get the meaning of the following sentences.

1. *Il faut travailler là.*
2. *Il faut beaucoup travailler là.*
3. *Il faut travailler sans se reposer et sans manger.*
4. *Il faut travailler pour manger.*
5. *Il faut bien travailler pour bien vivre.*
6. *Il faut bien travailler pour être content.*
7. *Il faut beaucoup manger pour pouvoir beaucoup travailler.*
8. *Il faut bien dormir pour pouvoir bien travailler.*
9. *Il faut travailler pour pouvoir être content.*
10. *Travailler, c'est vivre.*
11. *Vivre, c'est manger.*
12. *Travailler sans pouvoir dormir, c'est vivre sans pouvoir être content.*
13. *Il est impossible de travailler sans se reposer et sans manger.*
14. *Se reposer sans dormir, c'est possible.*

Instructions: In case you have doubts, here are the same sentences in English. Translate these back into French.

1. One has to work there.
2. You have to work a lot there.
3. It's necessary to work without resting and without eating.
4. You have to work in order to eat.
5. One has to work well in order to live well.
6. It's necessary to work well in order to be happy.
7. You have to eat a lot in order to be able to work a lot.
8. You have to sleep well in order to work well.
9. One has to work in order to be able to be happy.

10. To work is to live (*or* working is living).
11. To live is to eat (*or* living is eating).
12. To work without being able to sleep is to live without being able to be happy.
13. It is impossible to work without resting and without eating.
14. It's possible to rest without sleeping.

Instructions: Create the French equivalents of the following sentences.

1. Eating is living.
2. Sleeping is impossible there
   (*or* it is impossible to sleep there).
3. Working without being happy is impossible there
   (*or* it is impossible to work there without being happy).
4. It is stupid to eat a lot in order to sleep well
   (*or* eating a lot in order to sleep well is stupid).
5. It is impossible to sleep without resting, but it is possible to rest without sleeping.
6. It is possible to work without rest, but it is stupid.

41
Focus on the Language 24–28
Concentration sur la langue 24-28

Focus 24

Commencer à + infinitive, "to begin to" + infinitive.

He decides to eat the cheese.	*Il décide de manger le fromage.*
He begins to eat the cheese.	*Il commence à manger le fromage.*
He has begun to eat the cheese.	*Il a commencé à manger le fromage.*

As explained before, not all verbs can directly precede an infinitive. Many must have a special particle placed between, as in the examples. With some verbs, as you know (*décider, menacer*, etc.) the required particle is *de*; with *commencer* (and some others) it is *à*.

Translate Orally from and into French

He begins to sing.	*Il commence à chanter.*
He has begun to sing.	*Il a commencé à chanter.*
He threatens to eat the cheese.	*Il menace de manger le fromage.*
He has begun to threaten to eat the cheese.	*Il a commencé à menacer de manger le fromage.*
She's decided to begin to talk with the king.	*Elle a décidé de commencer à parler avec le roi.*

Focus 25

(Avoir) a : ont. (Aller) va : vont. (Faire) fait : font.

He has some dogs.	*Il a des chiens.*
They have cats.	*Ils ont des chats.*
She desires to have cats.	*Elle désire avoir des chats.*
He goes with the dog.	*Il va avec le chien.*
They go with the cats.	*Ils vont avec les chats.*
They desire to go with the cat.	*Ils désirent aller avec le chat.*
He makes drums.	*Il fait des tambours.*
They make drums.	*Ils font des tambours.*
They desire to make drums.	*Ils désirent faire des tambours.*

Avoir "to have," *aller* "to go," and *faire* "to do or make" are irregular verbs.
The plural of *a* "has" is *ont* "have";
the plural of *va* "goes" is *vont* "go";
the plural of *fait* "makes" or "does" is *font* "do."
The plural forms rhyme: *ont, vont,* and *font*. Also *a* and *va* rhyme. *Fait* rhymes with *sait* "knows."

Translate Orally from and into French

The prince has the drum.	*Le prince a le tambour.*
The princes have the drums.	*Les princes ont les tambours.*

The dukes make drums.	*Les ducs font des tambours.*
She doesn't have the cat.	*Elle n'a pas le chat.*
They don't have the cat.	*Ils n'ont pas le chat.*
He wants to have cats.	*Il désire avoir des chats.*
The duke goes with the duchess.	*Le duc va avec la duchesse.*
They go together.	*Ils vont ensemble.*
The prince desires to go with the dog.	*Le prince désire aller avec le chien.*

Focus 26

Subject-verb inversion and "the T-buffer."

He speaks English.	*Il parle anglais.*
Does he speak French?	*Parle-t-il français?*
He has some dogs.	*Il a des chiens.*
Has he any cats?	*A-t-il des chats?*

In *statements*, the normal order of things is subject-verb: *Robert chante.* In *questions*, this may be reversed. For example: *Robert, chante-t-il?* The -t- is inserted before a vowel of the initial pronoun. We call it "the T-buffer." If the verb ends in the letter *t*, no "t-buffer" is needed: *Le duc, que fai<u>t</u>-il? Robert et René, chanten<u>t</u>-ils?*

Translate Orally from and into French

The duke, has he a dog?	*Le duc, a-t-il un chien?*
Does the princess have a cat?	*La princesse, a-t-elle un chat?*
The duchess who is speaking with the prince, has she a cat?	*La duchesse qui parle avec le prince, a-t-elle un chat?*
Does the duke who is singing have a dog?	*Le duc qui chante, a-t-il un chien?*
Does the king speak French?	*Le roi, parle-t-il français?*
Does the queen sing <u>in</u> French?	*La reine, chante-t-elle <u>en</u> français?*
Do the princes have dogs?	*Les princes, ont-ils des chiens?*

Focus 27

Why, where, when, how, what questions and "the T-buffer."

Why does she cry?	*Pourquoi pleure-t-elle?*
How does she play?	*Comment joue-t-elle?*
Where is he going?	*Où va-t-il?*
When is he going?	*Quand va-t-il?*
How much does he have?	*Combien a-t-il?*
What is he going to do?	*Que va-t-il faire?*

Translate Orally from and into French

What does the prince eat?	*Le prince, que mange-t-il?*
What will he eat?	*Que va-t-il manger?*
How much does he eat?	*Combien mange-t-il?*
Why does he sing?	*Pourquoi chante-t-il?*
With whom does he speak?	*Avec qui parle-t-il?*
Where does the king prefer to sing?	*Le roi, où préfère-t-il chanter?*
When does the duke desire to sing?	*Le duc, quand désire-t-il chanter?*

Focus 28

Alternative forms of questions: (a) *Où chante-t-il?* (b) *Où est-ce qu'il chante?* French speakers generally use the second form—the longer form—more often.

a.	Where does he sing?	*Où chante-t-il?*
b.	Where is it that he sings?	*Où est-ce qu'il chante?*
a.	What does he sing?	*Que chante-t-il?*
b.	What is it that he sings?	*Qu'est-ce qu'il chante?*
a.	What does he do?	*Que fait-il?*
b.	What is it he does?	*Qu'est-ce qu'il fait?*
a.	When does he make drums?	*Quand fait-il des tambours?*
b.	When is it he makes drums?	*Quand est-ce qu'il fait des tambours?*

You know two ways of forming a yes-or-no question:

	Formation of Question	Statement	Question
1.	Putting the phrase *est-ce que* in front	*Le roi chante.*	*Est-ce que le roi chante?*
2.	Subject-verb inversion	*Le roi chante.*	*Le roi, chante-t-il?*

As you have seen, you can put question words such as *où* "where," *que* "what," *pourquoi* "why," *quand* "when," *comment* "how," *combien* "how much," etc. in front of *est-ce que* to form questions. Alternatively, you can make questions in the form of the *b* sentences in the chart above.

Translate Orally from and into French

Where is it that he likes to sing?	*Où est-ce qu'il aime chanter?*
When is it that he likes to sing?	*Quand est-ce qu'il aime chanter?*
How much does he sing?	*Combien chante-t-il?*
When is it that the princess cries?	*La princesse, quand est-ce qu'elle pleure?*
What is the king doing?	*Que fait le roi?*
And the duke, what is he doing?	*Et le duc, que fait-il?*
What is he going to do tonight?	*Que va-t-il faire ce soir?*
And the duchess, what is she going to do?	*Et la duchesse, que va-t-elle faire?*
When is she going to begin to make drums?	*Quand va-t-elle commencer à faire des tambours?*
What is it that kings do?	*Qu'est-ce que font les rois?*
What do kings do?	*Les rois, que font-ils?*

Change the Form of the Question

Instructions: Change the given question form to one or more alternative question forms. You can check your answers in the appendix.

1. What does the king sing?
2. When does the king sing?
3. Does the princess cry a lot?
4. Where does she cry?
5. Why does she cry?
6. Doesn't she sing?

7. What does the prince do?

CULTURE QUESTIONS—SECTION TWO

Instructions: Answer these questions based on your reading. Feel free to check the appendix to find the answers.

1. What is Algeria's official language?

2. What are Belgium's two official languages?

3. In what language do most schools in Québec conduct classes?

4. Name at least three popular sports in Canada.

THE ADVENTURE CONTINUES

When you finish, Jean-Luc carefully checks your work. You make small talk while he checks, and you ask him where he is from.

He gives you a funny look. "I am from this island," he tells you. "Where else would I come from?"

You thank Jean-Luc for taking the time to speak with you. *"Pas de quoi,"* he tells you. "Your next clue is milk. Next, find Samuel Bernier. He works at the private school. I hope you find what you seek."

With that, Jean-Luc returns to his painting. You and Stump watch him paint for a moment and then politely excuse yourselves. You pull out the map and look up the third point marked on it. You think you can figure out how to reach it, but Stump reminds you that schools have probably dismissed for the day. You and Stump wander back to the Pétard's residence. You are thrilled with the progress you are making with your language skills and cultural understanding, but you feel a little dismayed at the time it takes you to learn each clue. The submarine will arrive to pick you up in only seven days.

When you and Stump reach the Pétard residence, you go to the computer room in the basement and email the submarine captain. He encourages you and seems pleased with your progress. He does not, however, tell you what you were sent to find.

For dinner that evening, Jacqueline prepares a pea soup recipe that she learned while studying in Québec.

RECIPE: SPLIT PEA SOUP

2 1/4 c green split peas

1 meaty ham bone (about 1 1/2 lbs)

1 large onion, finely chopped

1/4 t marjoram, crushed

1 t salt

1/2 t pepper

1/4 t thyme

1/4 t savory flakes

1 1/4 c diced celery

1 1/2 c diced carrots

Cover peas with 2 quarts cold water. Simmer gently for 2 minutes. Remove from heat. Cover and let stand 1 hour. Add ham bone, onion, marjoram, salt, pepper, thyme, and savory flakes. Bring mix to boil. Reduce heat. Cover and simmer 1 1/2 hours. Stir occasionally. Remove bone from soup. Remove meat from bone. Dice meat and return to soup. Add vegetables and cook slowly, uncovered, 30 to 40 minutes. Makes 6 to 8 servings.

THE ADVENTURE CONTINUES

After dinner, you and Stump return to your quarters. You work through more vocabulary-building exercises before you fall asleep.

42
Stringing Together Your Own Narratives
Regrouper vos propres histoires

Instructions: (1) Study the words in the scatter chart below. (2) Read the practice sentences. (3) Translate the sentences of the sample story plot. (4) Refer to the chart, and use only those words to compose narratives of your own invention.

SCATTER CHART

une pharmacie   *dame*
la pharmacienne
jeune fille   *amie*
à   *la*
achète   *dans*   *une*
vend   *va*   *vient*   *dit*
une bouteille de   *et*   *mais*
okay   *oui*   *non*
elle   *limonade*
goûte   *orangeade*
apporte   *porte*
la femme   *est bonne*   *n'est pas bonne*

English Equivalent

a pharmacy   lady
the pharmacist (f)
girl(f)   friend (f)
to   the
buys   in   a
sells (or <u>vends</u>)   goes   comes   says
a bottle of   and   but
okay   yes   no
she   lemon soda (f)
tastes   orangeade (f)
brings   takes, carries
the woman   is good   is not good

Sample Sentences

A girl comes to a pharmacy.	*Une jeune fille vient à une pharmacie.*
She buys a bottle of lemon soda.	*Elle achète une bouteille de limonade.*
She tastes the lemon soda.	*Elle goûte la limonade.*
She says, "The lemon soda is not good."	*Elle dit, «La limonade n'est pas bonne.»*

Sample Story Plot

Instructions: Give the French equivalent of the following story. Check your answer in the appendix.

1. A lady goes to the pharmacy. 2. She buys a bottle of orangeade. 3. She takes the bottle to a friend, a girl. 4. The girl goes to the pharmacy. 5. She buys a bottle of lemon soda. 6. She brings the bottle to the lady. 7. The lemon soda is good. 8. The orangeade is not good. 9. The girl takes the bottle of orangeade to the pharmacy and says, "The bottle is not good." 10. The woman in the pharmacy says, "The bottle is good." 11. The young girl says, "No, the orangeade is not good. The bottle is good, but the orangeade in the bottle is not good." 12. The pharmacist says, "Okay, the orangeade in the bottle is not good." 13. The girl says, "Okay," and buys a bottle of lemon soda. 14. She says, "The lemon soda is good." 15. "Yes," says the pharmacist, "the lemon soda is good."

Challenge

Instructions: Compose (orally or in writing) ten or more sentences using only the words in the scatter chart. Use the sentences in the sample story plot as a model but not verbatim.

End Tape 2, Side A

Tape 2, Side B

43

Points, lignes et figures
Points, Lines, and Figures

Instructions: As explained before, this learning activity is designed to help you push the envelope of listening comprehension and develop critical skills in inferring meaning. Look for patterns of sentence formation.

A. SCATTER CHART

∩ ⊃	———	< ∑
lignes courbes	*ligne droite*	*lignes crochues*
\\|| ≡	⊥ T + ×	a b c x y z
lignes parallèles	*lignes perpendiculaires*	*lettres*

B. LISTEN AND LOOK

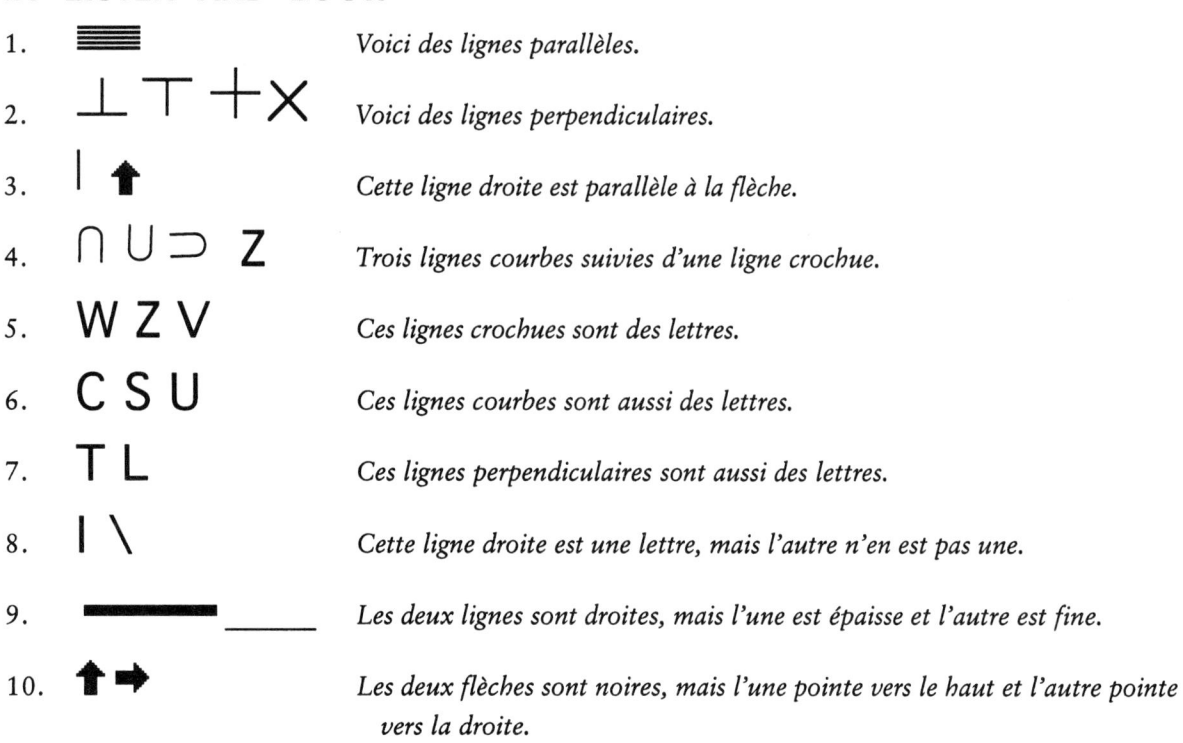

1. ≡ Voici des lignes parallèles.
2. ⊥ T + × Voici des lignes perpendiculaires.
3. | ↑ Cette ligne droite est parallèle à la flèche.
4. ∩ ∪ ⊃ Z Trois lignes courbes suivies d'une ligne crochue.
5. W Z V Ces lignes crochues sont des lettres.
6. C S U Ces lignes courbes sont aussi des lettres.
7. T L Ces lignes perpendiculaires sont aussi des lettres.
8. | \ Cette ligne droite est une lettre, mais l'autre n'en est pas une.
9. ▬▬ ___ Les deux lignes sont droites, mais l'une est épaisse et l'autre est fine.
10. ↑ ➡ Les deux flèches sont noires, mais l'une pointe vers le haut et l'autre pointe vers la droite.

11. | | *Est-ce que ces deux lignes sont verticales? Oui. Ces deux lignes sont verticales. Elles sont parallèles.*

12. C | *Est-ce que ces deux lignes sont parallèles? Non. L'une est droite et l'autre est courbe.*

C. Look and Listen

1. | | ≡
2. ⊥ T + X
3. | ↑
4. ∩ U ⊃ Z
5. W Z V
6. C S U
7. T L
8. | \
9. ▬ ▬
10. → ↓ ←

D. Multiple-Choice Frames

Instructions: Below, you see a series of frames, each with four sections. You'll hear the frame letter and then a sentence referring to what is in one of the four sections (section a, b, c, or d). In the following pause, point to the correct section, and then listen for the answer. Control the pace by stopping and starting the tape. When you are finished, check your answers in the appendix.

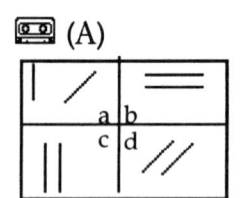

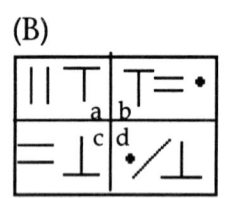

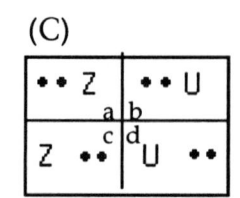

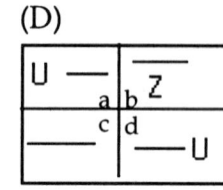

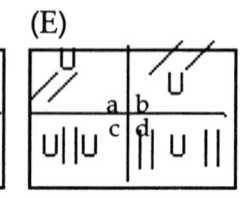

(A) (B) (C) (D) (E)

E. Listen and Draw

Instructions: Listen to the descriptions on tape and draw what is described. Stop the tape if the pace is too fast. When you are finished, check your answers in the appendix.

1.　　　　　2.　　　　　3.

F. Reading Comprehension

Instructions: Read the following sentences aiming to understand the meaning. You can check your comprehension in the appendix.

1. *Une ligne droite et une ligne courbe ne peuvent pas être parallèles, mais deux lignes courbes peuvent être parallèles, n'est-ce pas?*
2. *Ces deux lignes ne sont pas parallèles, parce que l'une est droite et l'autre est courbe.*
3. *Les lignes verticales sont parallèles. Les lignes horizontales sont aussi parallèles. Les lignes diagonales peuvent être parallèles.*
4. *Certaines lignes perpendiculaires peuvent former les lettres: L, T, E, F, H.*
5. *Certaines lignes courbes peuvent aussi former les lettres: C, S, J, U.*
6. *Les lignes perpendiculaires peuvent être épaisses ou fines, mais elles ne peuvent pas être courbes, n'est-ce pas?*

If you want a challenge, you may wish to go back to part B, cover the French, look only at the items pictured, and make statements about them similar to those made on the tape.

44

📼 Story Time: The Keys of Rome
French Only
Les clés de Rome

📼 **Instructions:** Listen to and read this short story. Then look at the diagram and try to recite the story without looking at the text.

Here are the keys of Rome.	📼 *Voici les clés de Rome.*
Take them.	*Prends-les.*
In Rome there is a plaza.	*À Rome il y a une place.*
In the plaza there is a street.	*Dans la place il y a une rue.*
In the street there is a house.	*Dans la rue il y a une maison.*
In the house there is a bed.	*Dans la maison il y a un lit.*
In the bed there is a lady.	*Dans le lit il y a une dame.*
At the lady's feet there is a parrot.	*Aux pieds de la dame il y a un perroquet.*
And the parrot says:	*Et le perroquet dit:*
"DON'T TELL LIES!"	*«NE MENS PAS!»*
The lady isn't in the bed.	*La dame n'est pas dans le lit.*
The bed isn't in the house.	*Le lit n'est pas dans la maison.*
The house isn't in the street.	*La maison n'est pas dans la rue.*
The street isn't in the plaza.	*La rue n'est pas dans la place.*
The plaza isn't in Rome.	*La place n'est pas à Rome.*
And the keys are not the keys of Rome.	*Et ces clés ne sont pas les clés de Rome.*

📼 THE ADVENTURE CONTINUES

Day Four—0900 hours

Six Days to Rendezvous

You speak with Jacqueline to confirm that the third point marked on the map is a private school. She tells you that it is and gives you directions. With Jacqueline's help, you find the school without problems. You ask the secretary if you can speak with Samuel Bernier. She guides you to the right room but warns you that he is teaching a class right now. You will have to wait to meet with him. You and Stump work through two more French activities while you wait for Samuel.

45

A Geography Lesson
French Only
Une leçon de géographie

Instructions: Listen to and read the following geography lesson. Learn how the continents are said in French!

This continent here is Africa.	*Ce continent-ci est l'Afrique.*
Africa is very large, but it's not half as large as Eurasia.	*L'Afrique est très grande, mais elle ne fait pas la moitié de l'Eurasie.*
In the northern part of Africa is Egypt.	*Au nord de l'Afrique se trouve l'Égypte.*
A large river called the Nile flows through Egypt.	*Une grande rivière, qui s'appelle le Nil, coule à travers l'Égypte.*
The great Egyptian civilization developed here over six thousand years ago.	*La grande civilisation égyptienne s'y est développée il y a plus de six mille ans.*
Here you see another great continent.	*Ici vous voyez un autre grand continent.*
This is South America.	*C'est l'Amérique du Sud.*
Here is found another great river.	*On y trouve une autre grande rivière.*
It is the largest river in the world.	*C'est la plus grande rivière du monde.*
It is called the Amazon River.	*Elle s'appelle l'Amazone.*
It flows east through Brazil.	*Elle coule vers l'est à travers le Brésil.*
Brazil is a very large country.	*Le Brésil est un très grand pays.*
It's the largest country in South America.	*C'est le plus grand pays de l'Amérique du Sud.*
It is as large as the continental United States.	*Il est aussi grand que les États-Unis continentaux.*
It is almost as large as China.	*Il est presque aussi grand que la Chine.*
But its population is relatively small.	*Mais sa population est relativement peu nombreuse.*
The greater part of Brazil is covered with forest.	*La plus grande partie du Brésil est recouverte par une forêt.*
And in the forest live many varieties of animals.	*Et dans la forêt vivent une grande variété d'animaux.*
There are also many snakes and reptiles.	*Il y a aussi beaucoup de serpents et de reptiles.*
Not many people live in the forest.	*Il n'y a pas beaucoup de gens qui vivent dans la forêt.*
The large cities of Brazil are on the coast.	*Les grandes villes du Brésil sont sur la côte.*
Here is Sao Paulo, Brazil's largest city and one of the largest cities in the world.	*Voici Sao Paulo, la plus grande ville du Brésil, et l'une des plus grandes villes du monde.*
And here is Rio de Janeiro, one of the most beautiful cities in the world.	*Et voici Rio de Janeiro, une des plus belles villes du monde.*
In the western part of South America is found a great mountain chain.	*Dans la région ouest de l'Amérique du Sud se trouve une grande chaîne de montagnes.*
There are many peaks above five thousand meters.	*Il y a beaucoup de sommets au dessus de cinq mille mètres.*
In those mountains there is much gold and silver.	*Dans ces montagnes, il y a beaucoup d'or et d'argent.*
There is also much tin and iron.	*Il y a aussi beaucoup d'aluminium et de fer.*
In ancient times a civilization developed in this area.	*Dans les temps anciens, une civilisation s'est développée dans cette région.*

46

A Mother Talks to Her Baby
French Only
Une mère parle à son bébé

Instructions: Listen to and read the following text. Learn new vocabulary in French.

Here is your little girl dolly. Her name is Ann.	*Voici ta petite poupée. Elle s'appelle Anne.*
Ann has hands and feet.	*Anne a des mains et des pieds.*
Her hands and feet are like yours.	*Ses mains et ses pieds sont comme les tiens.*
But they are very little.	*Mais ils sont très petits.*
Look how little they are.	*Regarde comme ils sont petits.*
Two tiny little hands.	*Deux petites mains minuscules.*
Here is your little boy dolly.	*Voici ton petit poupon.*
His name is Pinocchio. He is Ann's big brother.	*Il s'appelle Pinocchio. C'est le grand frère d'Anne.*
Does Pinocchio have hands and feet?	*Est-ce que Pinocchio a des mains et des pieds?*
He has hands and feet like Ann's.	*Il a des mains et des pieds comme ceux d'Anne.*
He has hands and feet just like yours.	*Il a des mains et des pieds exactement comme toi.*
Look, his hands and feet are like yours.	*Regarde, ses mains et ses pieds sont comme les tiens.*
Does Pinocchio have a nose?	*Est-ce que Pinocchio a un nez?*
Yes, look at his nose. He has a long nose.	*Oui, regarde son nez. Il a un long nez.*
Is his nose like Ann's nose?	*Est-ce que son nez est comme celui d'Anne?*
No, Pinocchio's nose is long.	*Non, le nez de Pinocchio est long.*
Look how long his nose is.	*Regarde comme son nez est long.*
Where is your nose?	*Où est ton nez?*
Here it is. Here is your nose.	*Le voilà. Voilà ton nez.*
Is it long like Pinocchio's?	*Est-ce qu'il est long comme celui de Pinocchio?*
No, it's not a long nose.	*Non, ce n'est pas un long nez.*
You don't have a long nose like Pinocchio.	*Tu n'as pas un long nez comme Pinocchio.*
You have a little nose.	*Tu as un petit nez.*
Look at Ann's face.	*Regarde le visage d'Anne.*
She has a pretty face, doesn't she?	*Elle a un joli visage, n'est-ce pas?*
Where are Ann's eyes? Here are her eyes.	*Où sont les yeux d'Anne? Voici ses yeux.*
Her eyes are pretty, aren't they?	*Ses yeux sont jolis, n'est-ce pas?*
Two pretty eyes. Ann is a pretty dolly.	*Deux jolis yeux. Anne est une jolie poupée.*
Where are Pinocchio's ears?	*Où sont les oreilles de Pinocchio?*
Here they are. Here are his ears.	*Les voilà. Voilà ses oreilles.*
He has two ears and two eyes.	*Il a deux yeux et deux oreilles.*
How many eyes do you have?	*Combien d'yeux as-tu?*
You have two eyes, of course.	*Tu as deux yeux, bien sûr.*
And how many ears? Two.	*Et combien d'oreilles? Deux.*
You have two ears and two eyes.	*Tu as deux oreilles et deux yeux.*
Two ears to hear with. Two eyes to see with.	*Deux oreilles pour entendre. Deux yeux pour voir.*

◉ THE ADVENTURE CONTINUES

About twenty young children file out of Samuel's classroom. Samuel follows them, rubbing chalk dust off his fingertips. He smiles pleasantly and asks how he can help you. You and Stump explain your search as well as you can.

"Ah!" Samuel exclaims. "*Oui!* I have your next clue. Please, come with me."

Samuel leads you to the teachers' lounge. "Like those before me, I have a challenge you must complete to receive your clue."

You know exactly what to expect. "Let me guess—more French exercises," you comment.

Samuel nods. "More culture questions, as well," he tells you. He gives you your assignment. Confident that you can complete it promptly, you and Stump get to work.

47

A French Lesson in a Classroom
French Only
Une leçon de français dans la salle de classe

Instructions: Listen to and read the following lecture. Work toward full comprehension.

Here I have the sheet of white paper.	*Ici, j'ai la feuille de papier blanc.*
And here I have the white pencil.	*Et ici, j'ai le crayon blanc.*
Here I have the sheet of yellow paper.	*Ici, j'ai la feuille de papier jaune.*
And here I have the yellow pencil.	*Et ici, j'ai le crayon jaune.*
So, I have four things: two sheets of paper and two pencils. I have two white things and two yellow things, right?	*Alors, j'ai quatre choses: deux feuilles de papier et deux crayons. J'ai deux choses blanches et deux choses jaunes, n'est-ce pas?*
Ah, but here I also have a red thing.	*Ah, mais ici j'ai aussi une chose rouge.*
Who has some yellow paper?	*Qui a du papier jaune?*
You have some. You don't have any.	*Vous en avez. Vous n'en avez pas.*
Who has some yellow pencils?	*Qui a des crayons jaunes?*
You have a lot of them.	*Vous en avez beaucoup.*
But you don't have any of them.	*Mais vous n'en avez aucun.*
What do you have there? A red pencil?	*Qu'avez-vous là? Un crayon rouge?*
No. You have a yellow pencil and some white paper.	*Non. Vous avez un crayon jaune et du papier blanc.*
How many sheets do you have? Three?	*Combien de feuilles avez-vous? Trois?*
What else? What else do you have?	*Quoi d'autre? Qu'avez-vous d'autre?*
Another pencil. You have another pencil.	*Un autre crayon. Vous avez un autre crayon.*
It's a black pencil. You have a black pencil.	*C'est un crayon noir. Vous avez un crayon noir.*
I have a yellow pencil and a white pencil, and you have a black pencil.	*J'ai un crayon jaune et un crayon blanc, et vous avez un crayon noir.*
What else do you have?	*Qu'avez vous d'autre?*
You have a sheet of red paper.	*Vous avez une feuille de papier rouge.*
Look, I don't have red paper.	*Regardez, je n'ai pas de papier rouge.*
Not even one sheet.	*Pas même une feuille.*
But you don't have yellow paper.	*Mais vous n'avez pas de papier jaune.*
Do you have white paper?	*Avez-vous du papier blanc?*
Yes, look, you have some.	*Oui, regardez, vous en avez.*
Do you have pencils?	*Avez-vous des crayons?*
Yes, you have a lot of them.	*Oui, vous en avez beaucoup.*
Do you have a white pencil?	*Avez-vous un crayon blanc?*
No, you don't have a white pencil.	*Non, vous n'avez pas de crayon blanc.*
But you have a yellow pencil.	*Mais vous avez un crayon jaune.*
How about Robert?	*Et Robert?*
Does he have a sheet of yellow paper?	*A-t-il une feuille de papier jaune?*
No, he doesn't have yellow paper.	*Non, il n'a pas de papier jaune.*
He doesn't have any. Not even one sheet.	*Il n'en a pas. Pas même une feuille.*
Do you have some?	*En avez-vous?*

48
🎧 Points, lignes et figures
Points, Lines, and Figures

A. Scatter Chart

△	△○□☆	□	☆	✚	○
triangle	*figures*	*carré*	*étoile*	*croix*	*cercle*

B. Look, Listen, and Read

1. ✚ Qu'est-ce que c'est? C'est une croix.

2. ✚ ✚ ☆ ☆ ☆ Qu'est-ce que c'est? Ce sont des croix et des étoiles.

3. ☆ ☆ □ □ □ Et qu'est-ce que c'est? Ce sont des figures: des étoiles et des carrés.

4. ○○△△ Voici d'autres figures. Ce sont des cercles et des triangles.

5. ○○△△□□☆☆ Les cercles, les triangles, les carrés, et les étoiles sont toutes des figures.

6. ○ Quel genre de figure est-ce? C'est un cercle. C'est aussi la lettre o.

7. ▬▬▬ Quel genre de ligne est-ce? C'est une ligne horizontale, longue, et épaisse.

8. W Quel genre de ligne est-ce? C'est une ligne crochue. Et c'est une lettre.

9. □ □ Ces figures sont-elles des triangles ou des carrés? Ce sont des carrés.

10. △▽△▽ Toutes ces figures sont des triangles, deux pointant vers le haut et deux pointant vers le bas.

11. ▫□ △□ △▫▫ Voici des carrés et des triangles. Les carrés sont gros ou petits, mais les triangles sont tous gros.

12. ___ ___ ||| \\ // Qu'est-ce que c'est? Ce sont toutes des lignes droites: des lignes horizontales, verticales, et diagonales.

C. Look and Listen

1. ✚
2. ✚ ✚ ☆ ☆ ☆
3. ☆ ☆ □ □ □
4. ○○△△
5. ○○△△□□☆☆
6. ○
7. ▬▬▬
8. W
9. □ □

10. △▽△▽   11. ▫▢ △▢ △▫▫   12. ___ ___ ||| \\\ //

D. Multiple-Choice Frames

Instructions: Below, you see a series of frames, each with four sections. You'll hear the frame letter and then a sentence referring to what is in one of the four sections (sections a, b, c, or d). In the following pause, point to the correct section, and then listen for the answer. Control the pace by stopping and starting the tape. When you are finished, check your answers in the appendix.

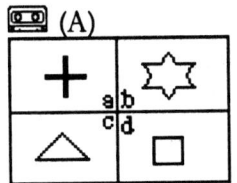

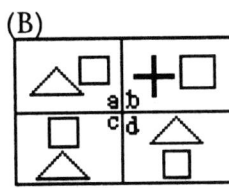

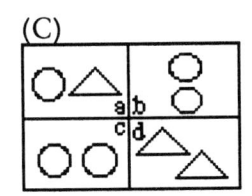

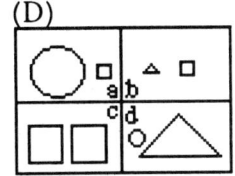

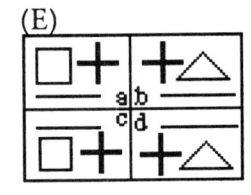

(A)   (B)   (C)   (D)   (E)

E. Listen and Draw

Instructions: Listen to the descriptions on tape and draw what is described. Stop the tape if the pace is too fast. When you are finished, check your answers in the appendix.

1.   2.   3.

4.   5.

F. Reading Comprehension

Instructions: Read the following sentences aiming to understand the meaning. Check your comprehension in the appendix.

1. *Quelle lettre est-ce? Est-ce un D ou un O? C'est un D.*
2. *Quel genre de figure est-ce? Est-ce un cercle ou un carré?*
3. *Tous ces triangles pointent vers le haut, et toutes ces flèches pointent vers le bas. Il y a autant de triangles que de flèches (autant de...que = as many...as).*
4. *Ces deux figures sont entre deux lignes verticales, courtes et épaisses.*
5. *Est-ce que les cercles, les carrés, les points, et les lignes sont des figures? Les cercles et les carrés le sont, les points et les lignes ne le sont pas.*
6. *Ces figures sont formées de lignes.*

49
🎞️ Thinking *en français*

Tape off. You're on your own. Give it your best.

▣ PART 1
Pictographs and Words

Instructions: Review earlier chapters for other pictographs and descriptions.

				what?	wolf	dog	or
				que?	*loup*	*chien*	*ou*
			:	it	the	know(s)	that (+ clause)
				c'est	*le, la*	*sait*	*que*
				love(s)	hate(s)	has/have
				aime	*déteste*	*a/ont*

Sample Sentences

Qu'est-ce que c'est?

C'est un chien.

C'est un grand chien et un bon chien.

Ce n'est pas un chien.

Est-ce que c'est un loup ou un chien?

C'est un grand méchant loup.

Le loup déteste le chien, mais le chien aime le loup.

Le loup sait que le chien déteste la reine.

La reine sait que le roi a un chien et que le chien aime le roi.

Nine Sentences to Read Out Loud 1

Illustrations: See the appendix to check your French rendition of these icons.

1.
2.
3.
4.
5.
6.
7.
8.
9.

PART 2
Pictographs and Words

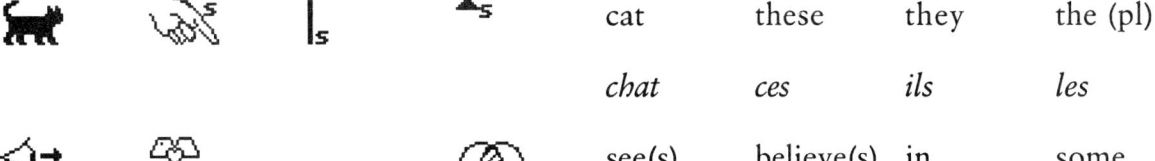

cat	these	they	the (pl)
chat	*ces*	*ils*	*les*
see(s)	believe(s)	in	some
voit (sg) or *voient* (pl)	*croit* (sg) or *croient* (pl)	*dans*	*des* or *certains*
forest			
forêt			

135

Sample Sentences

Que sont-ils?

Ce sont des chiens et des chats.

Le loup déteste ces chats.

Et ils détestent le loup.

Est-ce que le loup est dans la forêt?

Ces chats croient que le loup est dans la forêt.

Ils croient qu'ils voient le loup dans la forêt.

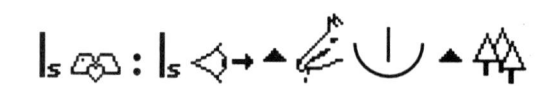

Ces chiens sont grands.

Les grands chiens voient des petits chats ou des petits chiens.

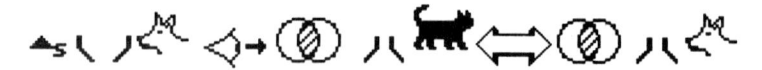

Nine Sentences to Read Out Loud 2

Illustrations: Read these sentences repeatedly until fluency is attained.

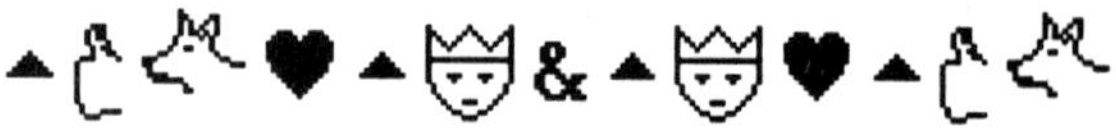

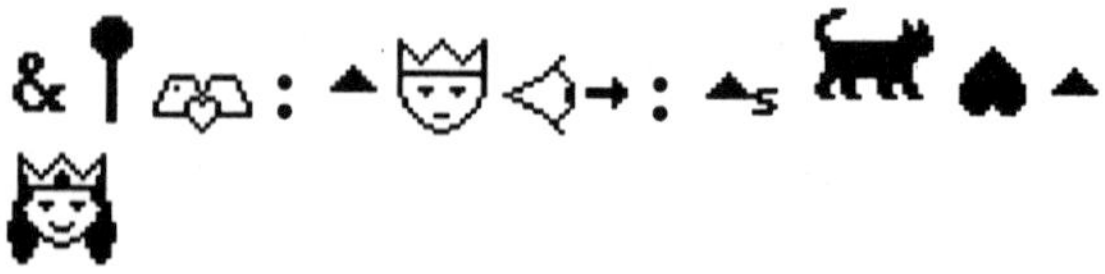

50

Ma première visite au Québec: deuxième partie
My First Visit to Québec: Part Two

Instructions: Continue listening to this diglot-weave story.

La compétition had lasted all *après-midi*. It was now *six heures, l'heure du dîner. Je* was famished…I mean, *j'avais faim*. Haunted by *le souvenir de la belle jeune fille, je* returned to *le restaurant de l'hôtel. Je* was so busy keeping *l'image de la patineuse* that at first *je* didn't notice *le vase de fleurs au milieu de la table*.

Soudain I heard *une voix* behind *moi* which asked, «*Un menu, Monsieur?*»

It was *réellement la voix d'un ange* from heaven. *J'ai* looked, *et* to my *grande surprise* the waitress *ressemblait beaucoup à la belle patineuse, à la princesse enchanteresse*.

«*Non merci*», *je répondis*. «*Un steak* with *frites, s'il vous plaît.*»

«*Une bouteille de vin ou de jus de fruit?*»

«*Oui, un jus d'orange, s'il vous plaît, mademoiselle.*»

«*Pardonnez-moi, Monsieur, mais nous n'avons plus de jus d'orange. Mais nous avons du jus d'abricot.*»

«*Très bien, je préfère le jus d'abricot.*»

«*Bien, un steak avec frites et un jus d'abricot. C'est tout?*»

«*Oui, c'est tout.*»

Besides being *très belle, la demoiselle* was *très sympatique. Elle était jeune*, maybe *18 ans. Je* thought back on *la compétition et* wondered if *la jeune fille était la belle patineuse de cet après-midi. Je* looked at *les belles fleurs dans le vase sur la table, les roses rouges et blanches*. Then *je* noticed *que* on the walls of *le restaurant* there were dozens…*douzaines de photos de personnages* famous, *par exemple, des présidents de la république, des chefs de gouvernement (sénateurs, ministres, et autres), des footballeurs, et d'autre athlètes, des révolutionnaires, des personnages du cinéma et du théâtre*.

Très intéressant, je thought, *et très rare que tant de personnages célèbres* had *visité ce restaurant*. Just then *la demoiselle* came *avec mon ordre, et* again *je* heard *la voix de l'ange*:

«*Monsieur, votre steak avec frites et votre verre de jus d'abricot.*»

«*Merci, mademoiselle. Mmm, c'est délicieux. La nourriture est délicieuse.*»

«*De la musique, Monsieur?*»

«Comment?»

«Vous voulez de la musique?»

«Oh oui.»

«Quel genre de musique préférez-vous?»

«J'aime beaucoup la musique classique, surtout la musique de Chopin.»

Je expected her to tell *moi* that she only had *de la musique canadienne, mais* instead she smiled *et* sat down at *le piano. Je* listened *comme en transe* as *la princesse enchanteresse* played *le célèbre Impromptu de Chopin, mon morceau favori. Et jamais* had *je* heard it played *aussi expressivement et expertement.*

Finalement je dared to ask her *la question.* Who could she be? *Qui était cette princesse enchanteresse? Était-elle la belle patineuse? Je* wanted to know more about her, but *mon français* was *extrêmement limité.*

51

🎙 A Lecture on the Alphabet
French Only
L'alphabet romain

🎙 Instructions: Listen to and read this lecture on the alphabet. Try to understand the general meaning; don't worry about the details.

🎙 CONSONNES

La prononciation des consonnes est la suivante:

b	c	d	f	g	h	j	k	l	m	n
be	ce	de	ef	ge	ash	jee	ka	el	em	en

p	q	r	s	t	v	w	x	y	z
pe	qu	er	es	te	ve	double ve	ix	i-grec	zed

La première lettre de l'alphabet n'est pas une consonne, c'est une voyelle, la voyelle A. A n'est pas une consonne, ni en anglais ni en français. A est toujours une voyelle.

La dernière lettre de l'alphabet n'est pas une voyelle mais une consonne, la consonne Z. Z n'est pas une voyelle, ni en anglais ni en français. Z est toujours une consonne.

En d'autres termes, A, la première lettre de l'alphabet romain est une voyelle, et Z, la dernière lettre de l'alphabet romain est une consonne.

Après la lettre A vient la lettre B, et après B vient C. Avant la lettre F vient la lettre E, et avant E vient D. Quelle lettre vient avant H? G. Quelle lettre vient entre I et K? La lettre J vient entre I et K. Et X vient entre W et Y, n'est-ce pas?

Dans l'alphabet français, la lettre M vient avant la lettre N. Ces consonnes nasales sont les seules dans l'alphabet. Combien de consonnes nasales y a-t-il dans l'alphabet? Deux. Lesquelles? Le M et le N. Laquelle vient la première dans l'alphabet? La lettre M vient en premier. De ces 3 lettres M, N, O, laquelle est une voyelle? O.

52

From Word to Discourse
Du mot au discours

Instructions: This activity focuses on the mechanics of sentence formation. You're given a scatter chart from which you must learn to string words into sentences. Samples of well-formed sentences—as well as some ungrammatical ones—are given below for your to study before constructing your own. Most of these words should be a review for you.

SCATTER CHART

```
                            il y a
              sur        prenez          mettez              donnez
  moi    lui
              voici    ici                              là(-bas)
                         est / sont    est-ce qu(e)...?
     c'est   n'est-ce pas?
                              cette/ces      la          des
           une/deux
                            tige(s)
                   blanche(s)              noire(s)
  couchée(s)   debout
                      elle(s)      l'/la/les
                 toute(s)          aussi           non plus
                   autre(s)          mais
                                          petite(s)     longue(s)
           oui   non              ne, n'... pas
```

Partial Word List

Instructions: See if you can match the French words with their equivalent English words. If you can't match all of the words, don't worry! You should be able to get them from the context in the sentences below.

take	put	give	him	me	rod	is/are
there	white	black	here	this/these	one/two	standing upright
also	not	either	other	long	some	short (=small)
on	here is	is it that..?	it/she/they	but	yes	no
the	it	lying down	there is	it is	all	

Sample Sentences

Instructions: Read through these sentences. The starred sentences are ungrammatical.

140

Give me the small black rod.	*Donnez-moi la petite tige noire.*
Give him the long white rod.	*Donnez-lui la longue tige blanche.*
Take this rod and give it to me.	*Prenez cette tige et donnez-la moi.*
Take the white rod and put it here.	*Prenez la tige blanche et mettez-la ici.*
Take the black rod and put it there.	*Prenez la tige noire et mettez-la là-bas.*
Take all the rods and put them here.	*Prenez toutes les tiges et mettez-les ici.*
This white rod is not long.	*Cette tige blanche n'est pas longue.*
	*Cette tige blanche est non longue.
Aren't these black rods small?	*Est-ce que ces tiges noires ne sont pas petites?*
No, these black rods are not small.	*Non, ces tiges noires ne sont pas petites.*
These black rods are not long either.	*Ces tiges noires ne sont pas longues non plus.*
This rod is long, but it is not black.	*Cette tige est longue, mais elle n'est pas noire.*
That long rod is not standing upright.	*Cette longue tige n'est pas debout.*
It is lying down.	*Elle est couchée.*
These white rods are not lying down.	*Ces tiges blanches ne sont pas couchées.*
They are (standing) upright.	*Elles sont debout.*
Don't give me the black rod.	*Ne me donnez pas la tige noire.*
Give me the white one.	*Donnez-moi la blanche.*
Don't put the black one on the white one.	*Ne mettez pas la noire sur la blanche.*
	*Ne pas mettez la noire une sur la blanche une.
Don't take this white rod.	*Ne prenez pas cette tige blanche.*
Don't take that black rod either.	*Ne prenez pas cette tige noire non plus.*
	*Ne pas prenez cette noire tige aussi.
Here is the small white rod.	*Voici la petite tige blanche.*
Take it, but don't put it on the black rods.	*Prenez-la, mais ne la mettez pas sur les tiges noires.*
Take the other two white rods.	*Prenez les deux autres tiges blanches.*
	*Prenez les autres deux tiges blanches.
Don't give him these rods.	*Ne lui donnez pas ces tiges.*
	*Ne donnez pas lui ces tiges.

Translation Exercise

Instructions: Can you give the French equivalent for the following? Check your answers in the appendix.

1. Give him the long white rod.
2. Take all the rods and put them here.
3. These black rods are not small?
4. These black rods are not long either.
5. These white rods are not standing, they are lying.
6. Don't give me the black rod, give me the white one.
7. Don't take that black rod either.
8. Here is the small white rod.
9. Take it, but don't put it on the black rods.
10. Take the other two small white rods and put them there.

53
More on Numbers
Plus au sujet des chiffres

Instructions: Practice saying each number in English and French, then say all the numbers consecutively in French. Write each number on a slip of paper, shuffle the papers, and practice saying the numbers until you're comfortable with them.

Cardinals	Ordinals	Cardinals	Ordinals
one	first	*un*	*premier (m), première (f)*
two	second	*deux*	*deuxième* (also +*second*)
three	third	*trois*	*troisième*
four	fourth	*quatre*	*quatrième*
five	fifth	*cinq*	*cinquième*
six	sixth	*six*	*sixième*
seven	seventh	*sept*	*septième*
eight	eighth	*huit*	*huitième*
nine	ninth	*neuf*	*neuvième*
ten	tenth	*dix*	*dixième*
eleven	eleventh	*onze*	*onzième*
twelve	twelfth	*douze*	*douzième*
thirteen	thirteenth	*treize*	*treizième*
fourteen	fourteenth	*quatorze*	*quatorzième*
fifteen	fifteenth	*quinze*	*quinzième*
sixteen	sixteenth	*seize*	*seizième*
seventeen	seventeenth	*dix-sept*	*dix-septième*
eighteen	eighteenth	*dix-huit*	*dix-huitième*
nineteen	nineteenth	*dix-neuf*	*dix-neuvième*
twenty	twentieth	*vingt*	*vingtième*
twenty-one	twenty-first	*vingt et un*	*vingt et unième*
twenty-two	twenty-second	*vingt-deux*	*vingt-deuxième*
thirty	thirtieth	*trente*	*trentième*
forty	fortieth	*quarante*	*quarantième*
fifty	fiftieth	*cinquante*	*cinquantième*
sixty	sixtieth	*soixante*	*soixantième*
seventy	seventieth	*soixante-dix*	*soixante-dixième*
eighty	eightieth	*quatre-vingts*	*quatre-vingtième*
ninety	ninetieth	*quatre-vingt-dix*	*quatre-vingt-dixième*
hundred	hundredth	*cent*	*centième*
hundred and one	hundred and first	*cent un*	*cent et unième*
thousand	thousandth	*mille*	*millième*

54
Focus on the Language 29–33
Concentration sur la langue 29-33

FOCUS 29
"As, like" *comme*.

He sings like a dog.	*Il chante comme un chien.*
It's like me, not like him.	*C'est comme moi, pas comme lui.*
As I (have) said...	*Comme je l'ai dit...*

Translate Orally from and into French
He cries like a cat. — *Il pleure comme un chat.*
She plays like him. — *Elle joue comme lui.*
As I said, both sing like dogs. — *Comme je l'ai dit, ils chantent tous les deux comme des chiens.*

It's true, as I said. — *C'est vrai, comme je l'ai dit.*

FOCUS 30
"If, whether" *si*.

If the king sings, the queen plays.	*Si le roi chante, la reine joue.*
When the king sings, the queen plays.	*Quand le roi chante, la reine joue.*
I don't know if the cat cries.	*Je ne sais pas si le chat pleure.*
I don't know whether it's true or not.	*Je ne sais pas si c'est vrai ou non.*

Translate Orally from and into French
If he's going to sing, she's going to cry. — *S'il va chanter, elle va pleurer.*
If he goes to church, she goes with him. — *S'il va à l'église, elle va avec lui.*
If she has a drum, she will play with you. — *Si elle a un tambour, elle jouera avec vous.*
I don't know if he has a drum or a piano. — *Je ne sais pas s'il a un tambour ou un piano.*

FOCUS 31
"In" *dans, en, à*.

In the castle.	*Dans le château.*
In Russian or in Chinese?	*En russe ou en chinois?*
He's in Paris, in the school.	*Il est à Paris, à l'école.*

For now, accept the fact that *dans, en,* and *à*, though not interchangeable, are close in meaning and that each is sometimes the translation equivalent of *in*. Note: "in Africa" *en Afrique*; "in Peking" *à Pékin*.

Translate Orally from and into French
The king is in Paris; the queen is in Peking. — *Le roi est à Paris; la reine est à Pékin.*
He is speaking in French; she, in English. — *Il parle en français; elle, en anglais.*
He speaks French and English. — *Il parle français et anglais.*

143

She sings in the castle.   *Elle chante dans le château.*

FOCUS 32

"Only" (= "nothing but") *ne (verbe) que.*

He has only one drum.	*Il n'a qu'un tambour.*
(literal) He doesn't have but one drum.	*Il n'a qu'un tambour.*
She drinks only milk.	*Elle ne boit que du lait.*
She drinks only a little.	*Elle ne boit qu'un peu.*

When "only" can be rendered "but," "not but," or "nothing but," it is rendered by *ne {verbe} que.*

Translate Orally from and into French

She sings only in the tower.	*Elle ne chante que dans la tour.*
And she sings only a little in the tower.	*Et elle ne chante qu'un peu dans la tour.*
She sings only with the prince.	*Elle ne chante qu'avec le prince.*
She doesn't sing anything but funeral chants.	*Elle ne chante que des chants funèbres.*
She has only two cats.	*Elle n'a que deux chats.*
He doesn't have but one cat.	*Il n'a qu'un chat.*
The prince has but one dog.	*Le prince n'a qu'un chien.*
The king does nothing but sing.	*Le roi ne fait que chanter.*

FOCUS 33

Negators *jamais* and *rien.*

She never drinks.	*Elle ne boit jamais.*
He drinks nothing.	*Il ne boit rien.*
He never drinks it.	*Il n'en boit jamais.*
One never knows.	*On ne sait jamais.*
He drinks none of it.	*Il n'en boit rien.*
I know nothing about it.	*Je n'en sais rien.*

Note: Negative words such as *jamais* and *rien* are like *pas* and usually follow the verb. They replace *pas*. Like *pas*, both *jamais* and *rien* can stand alone: *Jamais!* "Never!" *Rien.* "Nothing."

Translate Orally from and into French

He doesn't drink milk.	*Il ne boit pas de lait.*
He never drinks milk. Never.	*Il ne boit jamais de lait. Jamais.*
He doesn't sing anything. Not anything.	*Il ne chante rien. Rien.*
She never sings at school.	*Elle ne chante jamais à l'école.*
That's nothing.	*Ce n'est rien.*
I don't know.	*Je ne sais pas.*

55
Stringing Together Your Own Narratives
Regrouper vos propres histoires

Instructions: (1) Study the words in the scatter chart below. (2) Read the practice sentences. (3) Translate the sentences of the sample story plot. (4) Refer to the scatter chart and use only those words to compose narratives of your own invention.

SCATTER CHART

(dans le) marché			*(au) marché*	
frère		*sœur*		
	vendeur			
son, sa			*(il, elle) vend*	
à	*le*	*(il, elle) achète*		
(il, elle) donne			*(il, elle) dit*	
alors	*un*	*il*	*elle*	
un autre	*(il, elle) demande si*			
(il, elle) vient				
		(il, elle) répond que		
(il, elle) apporte		*(il, elle) va*		
kilo de bonbons			*et*	
delicieux!		*non*	*oui*	
(un) bonbon	*(les) bonbons*			
(il, elle) goûte		*(des) bonbons*		
(il, elle) prend		*(il, elle) mange*		
(ils) sont (très) bons				
(ils) ne sont pas (très) bons				

145

English Equivalent

```
          (in the) market                              (to the) market
              brother                                        sister
                            vendor
        his, her                                         (he, she) sells
      to (a person)                    the               (he, she) buys
    (he, she) gives                                      (he, she) says
           then                        a          he         she
        another                            (he, she) asks if
                         (he, she) comes
                                                  (he, she) answers that
  (he, she) takes, carries                         (he, she) goes
         kilogram of candies                                        and
        tasty, delicious!                              no        yes
    (a) piece of candy    (the) candies
             (he, she) tastes                      (some) sweets, candy
         (he, she) takes, picks up                    (he, she) eats
                    (they) are (very) good
        (they) are not (very) good
```

Sample Sentences

Jacques comes to the market.	*Jacques vient au marché.*
He buys a kilogram of candies.	*Il achète un kilo de bonbons.*
He tastes a piece of candy.	*Il goûte un bonbon.*
He says, "The candies are not tasty."	*Il dit: «Les bonbons ne sont pas délicieux.»*
He sells the candies.	*Il vend les bonbons.*

Sample Story Plot

Instructions: Give the French equivalent of these sentences. Check your answers in the appendix.

1. A vendor sells candies in the market. 2. Pierre comes to the market. 3. Pierre asks if the candies are good. 4. The vendor answers that the candies are very good. 5. He gives a piece of candy to Pierre. 6. Pierre takes (*prend*) the piece of candy. 7. He tastes the candy, and he says, "Mmm, yes, the candies are very good." 8. The vendor sells a kilo of the candies to Pierre. 9. Then Pierre takes (*apporte*) the candies to his brother. 10. He gives a piece of candy to his brother. 11. The brother takes the candy. 12. He tastes the candy and says, "Mmm, the candies are very good." 13. He eats and eats. He eats the kilo of candy. 14. Pierre asks if the candies are good. 15. His brother answers, "No, the candies are not very good." 16. Then the brother goes to the market. 17. He buys a kilo of candies. 18. He takes (*apporte*) the candies to his sister Michelle. 19. Michelle takes the candies. 20. She eats the candies. 21. Then she says, "The candies are very good."

56
Easy Words to Learn and Important Words to Know
Mots faciles à apprendre et mots importants à savoir

Instructions: Learn the following vocabulary words.

sir, gentleman, Mr.	*Monsieur*	a lady	*une dame*
a man	*un homme*	Mrs. ("my lady")	*Madame*
a child	*un enfant*	uncle/aunt	*oncle/tante*
boy/girl	*garçon/fille*	nephew/niece	*neveu/nièce*
son/daughter	*fils/fille*	cousin (m)/cousin (f)	*cousin/cousine*
father/mother	*père/mère*	fiancé/fiancée	*fiancé/fiancée*
grandfather	*grand-père*	widower/widow	*veuf/veuve*
grandmother	*grand-mère*	brother/sister	*frère/sœur*
grandparents	*grand-parents*	husband/wife	*mari/femme*
grandson	*petit-fils*	father-/mother-in-law	*beau-père/belle-mère*
granddaughter	*petite-fille*	son-/daughter-in-law	*beau-fils/belle-fille*
grandchildren	*petits-enfants*	brother-/sister-in-law	*beau-frère/belle-sœur*

Instructions: Now study the following sentences.

Who is she? Is she your sister?	*Qui est-ce? Est-ce ta sœur?*
She is my aunt.	*C'est ma tante.*
Two children: one boy, one girl.	*Deux enfants: un garçon, une fille.*
My brother is a widower.	*Mon frère est veuf.*
Is his wife a widow?	*Est-ce que sa femme est veuve?*
No, she is not a widow.	*Non, elle n'est pas veuve.*
Mr. Smith and Amy are my friends.	*Monsieur Smith et Amy sont mes amis.*
She is the daughter of my brother; that is to say, she is my niece.	*Elle est la fille de mon frère; c'est à dire, elle est ma nièce.*
Roland is my nephew, the son of my brother.	*Roland est mon neveu, le fils de mon frère.*
Your nephew is the son of your brother or sister.	*Ton neveu est le fils de ton frère ou ta sœur.*
Mrs. Laroche is my teacher.	*Madame Laroche est mon professeur.*
Mr. Laroche is my teacher.	*Monsieur Laroche est mon professeur.*
My son and your daughter are engaged.	*Mon fils et ta fille sont fiancés.*
Your grandfather is the father of your mother or your father.	*Ton grand-père est le père de ta mère ou de ton père.*

FREE PRACTICE
Exercise A

Translate some of the above sentences from English to French until you have a feel for the material. Try giving definitions of your grandchild, cousin, niece, brother-in-law, etc.

Exercise B

Cover the English side and look only at the French sentences. See if you can give the English equivalent of each.

Exercise C

Cover the French side and look only at the English sentences. See if you can visualize the French equivalent of each.

Exercise D

Think of your own relatives and, using the kinds of things you have learned, tell some things about them that are true—including negatives like "My brother is not a widower."

Exercise E

Write the French equivalent of the following.

A son. A daughter.	The grandson. The granddaughter.
Boys and girls.	A mother and one girl.
One brother and two sisters.	Husband. Wife. Husband and wife.
Grandpa. Grandma. Grandparents.	Uncles. Aunts. Aunts and uncles.
Nephews. Nieces. Nieces and nephews.	Cousins (m) and cousins (f).

Exercise F

Write out one or more "definitions" using the terms below. Voice one or more of these "definitions."

Example: *mon fils David*:   1) *est le petit-fils de mon grand-père.*
2) *est le frère de ma fille Cassandra.*

mon père	*ma mère*
mon frère (NAME)	*ma sœur* (NAME)
mon oncle (NAME)	*ma tante* (NAME)
mon cousin (NAME)	*ma cousine* (NAME)
ma nièce (NAME)	*mon neveu* (NAME)
mon petit-fils (NAME)	*ma petite-fille* (NAME)

CULTURE QUESTIONS—SECTION THREE

Instructions: Answer these questions based on your reading. Feel free to check the appendix to find the answers.

1. What is Algeria's state religion?

2. Name four foods for which Belgium is famous.

3. What name do French-speaking people in Québec have for themselves?

4. What is Québec's dominant religion?

5. What are the two most popular spectator sports in France?

THE ADVENTURE CONTINUES

You and Stump finish Samuel's challenge about an hour after school lets out. Samuel checks your work carefully. "Very good!" he compliments you. "I can see you have put much effort into learning my language."

You acknowledge Samuel's compliment and ask him where he learned English. "I studied in England—not that far from my native Luxembourg," he tells you with a grin. "It always pays to know a foreign language."

"I didn't know you were from Luxembourg," Stump exclaims.

"Would you mind taking time to tell us about your homeland?" you ask.

Samuel nods and shifts to a more comfortable position in his chair. "There is no rush," he tells you. "Would you like a brief summary or all the details?"

You request a brief summary. Samuel nods and begins.

LUXEMBOURG CULTURE OVERVIEW

Though the people of Luxembourg come from several ethnic groups and speak several different languages, they maintain a strong national pride. Luxembourg's customs and traditions have been influenced by Belgium, Germany, and France. However, there are differences. For example, the pace of life in Luxembourg tends to be much less hurried than that in other European countries. Luxembourg's national motto is: "We wish to remain what we are." Nearly 90 percent of Luxembourgians are Roman Catholic.

FACTS AND FIGURES ON LUXEMBOURG

- Luxembourg's population is about 416,000. It is growing by 1% annually.

- Luxembourg's official languages are Luxembourgish, French, and German.

- Cycling and hiking are favorite activities in Luxembourg.

- Part of the famous *Tour de France* bicycle race passes through Luxembourg.

- The Moselle River forms Luxembourg's southern border.

- Luxembourg is officially called the Grand Duchy of Luxembourg.

- Rubber, chemicals, and steel are important exports, but nearly half of Luxembourg's work force has services-related jobs.

- Luxembourg is ruled through constitutional monarchy—the Grand Duke, a unicameral legislature, and a prime minister.

THE ADVENTURE CONTINUES

Samuel finishes his summary. Before you leave, he gives you your next clue. "Sugar. Next, speak with the owner of *L'hermitage*."

You thank Samuel for his time. Then you and Stump return to the Pétard residence. You savor a delicious dinner and then go to your quarters to study some more French. You are pleased with your progress in learning the language and the culture, and you are anxious to continue your studies.

End Tape 2, Side B

57
📼 Focus on Action
Concentration sur l'action

Tape off. Read the explanation. Learn the pictographs on the scatter chart, then take the self-quiz.

🎧 Instructions: In this activity, pictographs represent various actions. In the scatter chart below you are given pictographs and the English and French equivalent. Study them.

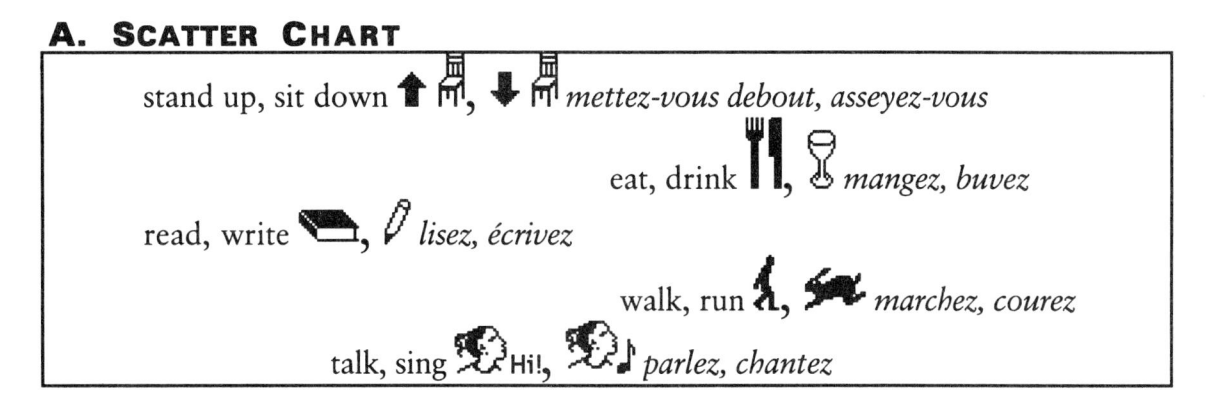

A. SCATTER CHART

stand up, sit down ⬆🪑, ⬇🪑 *mettez-vous debout, asseyez-vous*

eat, drink 🍴, 🍷 *mangez, buvez*

read, write 📖, ✏ *lisez, écrivez*

walk, run 🚶, 🐇 *marchez, courez*

talk, sing 🗣Hi!, 🗣♪ *parlez, chantez*

B. SELF-QUIZ

Instructions: Can you "read" these pictographs in French?

📼 C. MULTIPLE-CHOICE FRAMES

Instructions: Listen and identify which sector of the frame contains the depicted action or actions called on the tape. Then listen for the confirmatory response. [The script is in the appendix.]

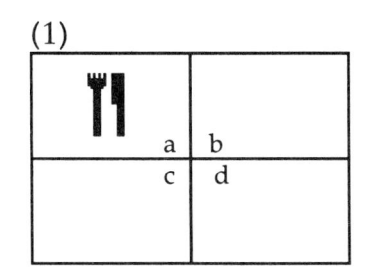

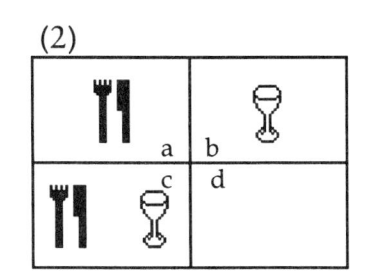

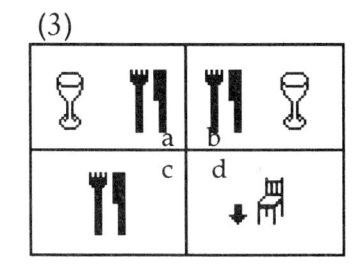

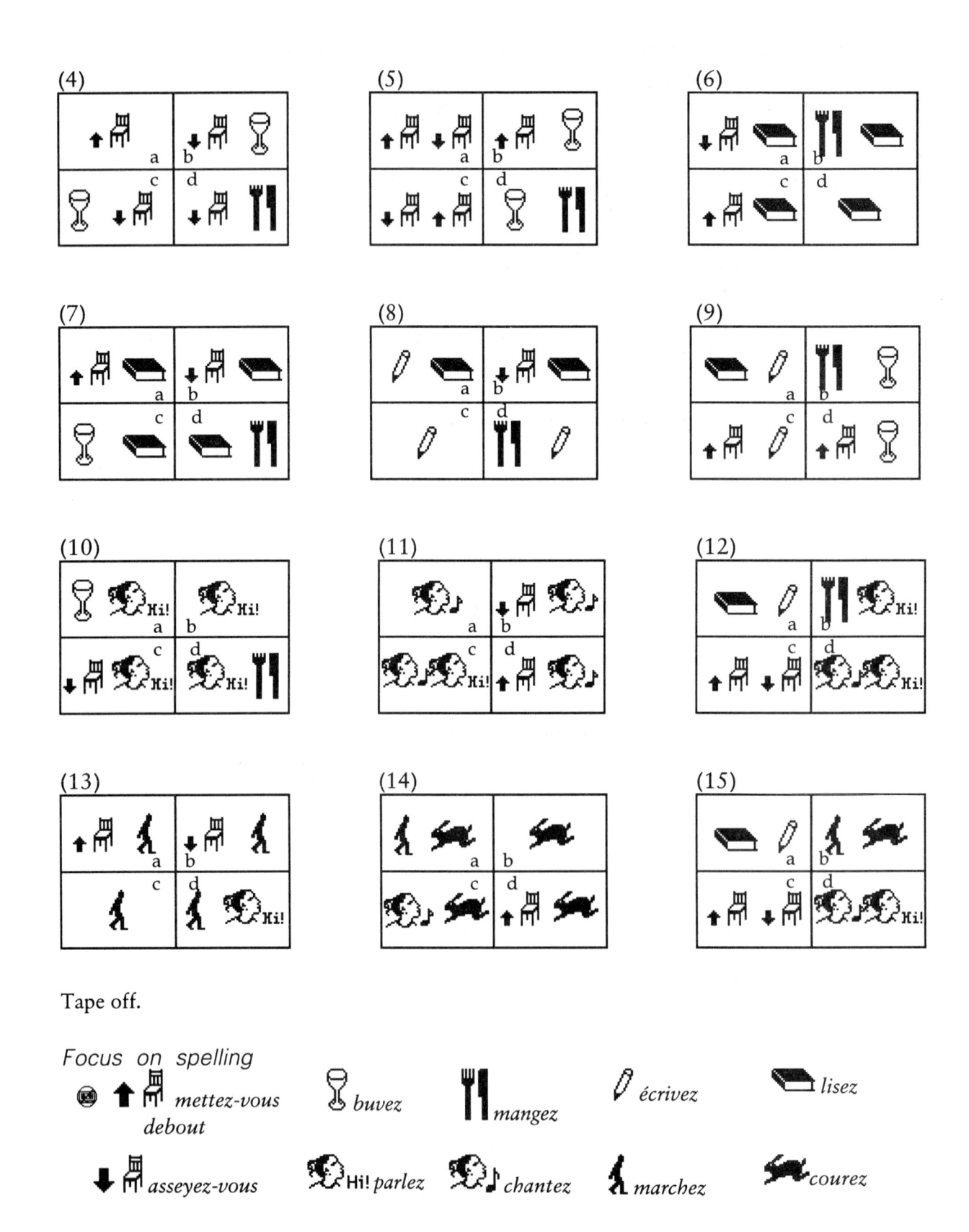

Tape off.

Focus on spelling

🔊 ⬆🪑 *mettez-vous debout* 🍷 *buvez* 🍴 *mangez* ✏ *écrivez* 📕 *lisez*

⬇🪑 *asseyez-vous* 💬Hi! *parlez* 💬♪ *chantez* 🚶 *marchez* 🐇 *courez*

152

D. Listen and Anticipate the Response

Instructions: You'll hear, for example, "What is this man doing?" «*Que fait cet homme?*» followed by a short pause while you anticipate the response: "He is eating." «*Il mange.*»
[The script is in the appendix.]

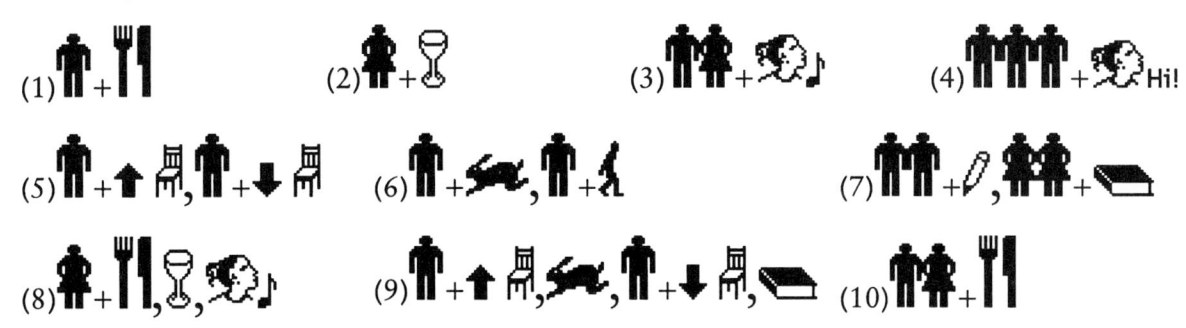

(1) 🧍+🍴 (2) 👩+🥛 (3) 👫+💬 (4) 👨‍👨‍👦+💬 Hi!

(5) 🧍+⬆️🪑, 🧍+⬇️🪑 (6) 🧍+🐇, 🧍+🚶 (7) 👬+✏️, 👫+📖

(8) 👩+🍴🥛💬 (9) 🧍+⬆️🪑🐇, 🧍+⬇️🪑📖 (10) 👫+🍴

E. Act Out or Pantomime What You Hear

Instructions: Pantomime what is called out on the tape. The script is in the appendix.

Tape off.

F. Read and perform the actions

Mangez.	Marchez.	Asseyez-vous.	Asseyez-vous et mangez.
Buvez.	Courez.	Mettez-vous debout.	Mettez-vous debout et parlez.
Lisez.	Parlez.	Asseyez-vous et lisez.	Asseyez-vous, buvez, mangez, et parlez.
Écrivez.	Chantez.	Mettez-vous debout et chantez.	Mettez-vous debout, écrivez, lisez, chantez, parlez et asseyez-vous.

G. Review

Instructions: Look back at the set of pictographs. How many of them can you say in French?

58
🎞 Thinking *en français*
Du pictogramme au discours

You're on your own. Tape off.

🎞 Instructions: Make an effort to learn these new pictographs.

PART 1
Pictographs and Words

→1	→2	→2ₛ	the one	the other	the others
			l'un	l'autre	les autres
⊘	✝	👄	all	also	say(s)
			tous	aussi	dit

Sample Sentences

Que sont-ils?   L'un est un gros chien; l'autre est un loup.

L'un est un loup; les autres sont des chiens.

Certains grands chiens sont bons mais ce grand chien est méchant.

Six Sentences to Read Out Loud 1

1.
2.
3.

4. [pictographs]

5. [pictographs]

6. [pictographs]

PART 2
Pictographs and Words

				where?	where	there	here
				où?	*où*	*là*	*ici*
				was/were	behind	also	
				était	*derrière*	*aussi*	
				with	those	house	
				avec	*ces*	*maison*	

Sample Sentences

Où était le chat?

[pictographs]

Était-il dans la maison avec le chien?

[pictographs]

Non, il était derrière la maison.

[pictographs]

Et dans la forêt?

[pictographs]

Le loup était là.

[pictographs]

Et le chien était là aussi.

[pictographs]

Le chien était là où le loup était.

[pictographs]

Le loup était ici où le chien est.

[pictographs]

Sont-ils là ou sont-ils ici?

[pictographs]

Ils sont tous ici.

Ces chiens sont grands.

Ces chiens sont petits.

Le chat était dans la maison.

Le chien et le loup étaient là aussi.

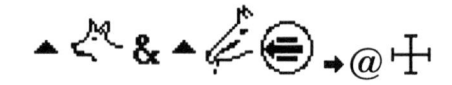

Six Sentences to Read Out Loud 2

1.
2.
3.
4.
5.
6.

59

Une leçon de géographie
French Only
A Geography Lesson

Instructions: Listen to and read the following geography lesson. Learn geography-related vocabulary.

Between South America and North America lies Central America.	*Entre l'Amérique du sud et l'Amérique du nord se trouve l'Amérique centrale.*
Panama is here.	*Panama se trouve là.*
In Panama there is a canal	*À Panama il y a un canal*
that links the Atlantic and Pacific Oceans.	*qui joint l'océan Atlantique à l'océan Pacifique.*
The canal is a bridge between east and west.	*Le canal est un pont entre l'est et l'ouest.*
Farther north lies Mexico.	*Plus au nord se trouve le Mexique.*
Its capital is Mexico City.	*Sa capitale est Mexico.*
It is destined to become	*Elle est destinée à devenir*
the world's largest city.	*la plus grande ville du monde.*
North of Mexico is the United States.	*Au nord du Mexique se trouvent les États-Unis.*
The U.S. lies between the Pacific and the Atlantic Oceans.	*Les États-Unis s'étendent entre l'océan Pacifique et l'océan Atlantique.*
The east coast touches the Atlantic.	*La côte est touche l'Atlantique.*
The west coast touches the Pacific.	*La côte ouest touche le Pacifique.*
The south coast touches the Gulf of Mexico.	*La côte sud touche le Golfe du Mexique.*
The capital, Washington,	*La capitale, Washington,*
is on the east coast.	*se trouve sur la côte est.*
The largest city, New York, is there too.	*La plus grande ville, New York, s'y trouve aussi.*
On the west coast is California.	*Sur la côte ouest se trouve la Californie.*
San Francisco is here, in California.	*San Francisco est ici, en Californie.*
Los Angeles is here.	*Los Angeles est ici.*
In San Francisco and Los Angeles	*À San Francisco et à Los Angeles*
there are many people who speak Spanish.	*il y a beaucoup de gens qui parlent espagnol.*
The state of Utah	*L'état d'Utah*

is one of fifty states in the USA.	est l'un des cinquante états des États-Unis.
It is neither the biggest nor the smallest state.	Ce n'est ni le plus grand ni le plus petit état.
It is located in the western part,	Il se trouve dans la partie ouest,
but it is far from the west coast.	mais il est loin de la côte ouest.
Utah is famous for its great salt lake.	L'Utah est connu pour son grand lac salé
and also for its beautiful pàrks.	et aussi pour ses beaux parcs.
Here is Hawaii.	Voici Hawaï.
Hawaii is a string of islands in the Pacific Ocean.	Hawaï est un chapelet d'îles dans l'océan Pacifique.
Hawaii is very beautiful.	Hawaï est très beau.
The island is covered with flowers.	L'île est couverte de fleurs.
It is always warm there.	Il y fait toujours chaud.
Here is Alaska.	Voici l'Alaska.
It is the largest state.	C'est le plus grand état.
Alaska is covered with forests.	L'Alaska est couvert de forêts.
And in winter, of course,	Et en hiver, bien évidemment,
it is covered with snow.	l'Alaska est recouvert de neige.
In winter Alaska is extremely cold.	En hiver, il fait extrêmement froid en Alaska.

60
Proverbes
Proverbs

Instructions: Read the following proverbs and see how many you understand. The translations are in chapter 128.

Tout ce qui brille n'est pas d'or.

    Tout est bien qui finit bien.

        Mieux vaut tard que jamais.

            Qui se ressemble s'assemble.

            Rira bien qui rira le dernier.

                Aide-toi, le ciel t'aidera.

                    L'homme propose mais Dieu dispose.

                      Pas de nouvelles, bonnes nouvelles.

                    Qui ne risque rien n'a rien.

            On ne doit pas dire du mal de ses voisins.

            Usage rend maître.

              La parole est d'argent, mais le silence est d'or.

        Dis-moi ce qu'il mange et je te dirai ce qu'il est.

        Les murs ont des oreilles.

    Vouloir, c'est pouvoir.

Il n'y a pas de fumée sans feu.

61

📼 *Une leçon de français*
A French Lesson

📼 Instructions: Listen to and read the following lesson. How many French vocabulary words are new to you?

📼 Take your pencil. Take it.	*Prenez votre crayon. Prenez-le.*
Put your pencil here. Put it here.	*Mettez votre crayon ici. Mettez-le ici.*
Take your white paper. Take it.	*Prenez votre papier blanc. Prenez-le.*
Put your paper here. Put it here.	*Mettez votre papier ici. Mettez-le ici.*
Take my red pencil. Take it.	*Prenez mon crayon rouge. Prenez-le.*
Put my pencil here. Put it here.	*Mettez mon crayon ici. Mettez-le ici.*
Take my red paper. Take it.	*Prenez mon papier rouge. Prenez-le.*
Put my paper here.	*Mettez mon papier ici.*
Excellent!	*Excellent!*
Here there is a pencil.	*Ici il y a un crayon.*
And here there are two pencils.	*Et ici il y a deux crayons.*
How many pencils? Two.	*Combien de crayons? Deux.*
Put this one in the box.	*Mettez celui-ci dans la boîte.*
Put it in.	*Mettez-l'y.*
Put these in the box too.	*Mettez ceux-ci dans la boîte aussi.*
Put them in.	*Mettez-les y.*
Take a paper and put it in this box.	*Prenez un papier et mettez-le dans cette boîte.*
Take another paper and put it in the same box.	*Prenez un autre papier et mettez-le dans la même boîte.*
Take two pencils and put them in this sack.	*Prenez deux crayons et mettez-les dans cette bourse.*
Take another pencil and put it in the same sack.	*Prenez un autre crayon et mettez-le dans la même bourse.*
In the sack there is a pencil.	*Dans la bourse il y a un crayon.*
Take it out.	*Sortez-le.*
Take one pencil from the sack and put it in the box.	*Sortez un crayon de la bourse et mettez-le dans la boîte.*
Take one paper from the box and put it in the sack.	*Sortez un papier de la boîte et mettez-le dans la bourse.*
Take the red paper out and put it in the box.	*Sortez le papier rouge et mettez-le dans la boîte.*
Pick up the box. Pick it up.	*Prenez la boîte. Prenez-la.*
Give it to me.	*Donnez-la moi.*
Pick up the pencil. Pick it up.	*Prenez le crayon. Prenez-le.*
Give it to me.	*Donnez-le moi.*
Pick up your pencils. Pick them up.	*Prenez vos crayons. Prenez-les.*
Give them to me.	*Donnez-les moi.*
Pick up the sack. Pick it up.	*Prenez la bourse. Prenez-la.*
Give it to me.	*Donnez-la moi.*
Pick up the sheets. Pick them up.	*Prenez les feuilles. Prenez-les.*
Give them to me.	*Donnez-les moi.*
Yes, give them to me, please.	*Oui, donnez-les moi, s'il vous plaît.*

62

Une mère parle à son enfant
French Only
A Mother Talks to Her Child

Instructions: Listen and read the following text. Come up with a list of ten French words you have not heard of before. Then do your best to learn them!

This man's name is James. James has a long, black beard. But he doesn't have hair on the top of his head. You have hair on the top of your head, don't you? Mama has hair on the top of her head too.	*Le nom de cet homme est Jacques.* *Jacques a une longue barbe noire.* *Mais il n'a pas de cheveux* *au sommet de sa tête.* *Tu as des cheveux* *au sommet de la tête, n'est-ce pas?* *Maman a aussi des cheveux au sommet* *de la tête.*
This is a baby, a little baby boy. He has a mouth, but he doesn't have teeth yet. He doesn't have hair on his head yet, does he? No, some babies don't have hair. Does this little baby have a beard? No, babies don't have a beard. Mama doesn't have a beard either, does she? No, mamas don't have a beard.	*Ceci est un bébé, un petit bébé garçon.* *Il a une bouche,* *mais il n'a pas encore de dents.* *Il n'a pas encore de cheveux* *sur la tête, n'est-ce pas?* *Non, certains bébés n'ont pas de cheveux.* *Est-ce que ce petit bébé a une barbe?* *Non, les bébés n'ont pas de barbe.* *Maman n'a pas de barbe non plus,* *n'est-ce pas?* *Non, les mamans n'ont pas de barbe.*
This man is called Smee. Smee is a pirate. Poor Smee! He has only one eye. Only one ear. And only one leg. He doesn't have a pretty face. Worse yet, he doesn't have friends.	*Cet homme s'appelle Smie.* *Smie est un pirate.* *Pauvre Smie!* *Il n'a qu'un oeil.* *Qu'une oreille.* *Et qu'une jambe.* *Il n'a pas un joli visage.* *Et pire encore, il n'a pas d'amis.*
Here is another pirate, a famous pirate. It is Captain Hook. He has only one arm: his right arm. Do you know why he has only one arm? It's because a crocodile ate his other arm.	*Voici un autre pirate, un pirate célèbre.* *C'est Capitaine Crochet.* *Il n'a qu'un bras: le bras droit.* *Sais-tu pourquoi il n'a qu'un bras?* *C'est parce qu'un crocodile a mangé l'autre.*
Does Captain Hook have friends? No, he doesn't have any friends. But he still has his head. He still has his eyes and his ears. He can see with his eyes. He can hear with his ears.	*Est-ce que Capitaine Crochet a des amis?* *Non, il n'a pas d'amis.* *Mais il a toujours sa tête.* *Il a toujours ses yeux et ses oreilles.* *Il peut voir par ses yeux.* *Il peut entendre par ses oreilles.*
Here is a person without eyes.	*Voici une personne sans yeux.*

He is blind, poor fellow.	*Il est aveugle, le pauvre.*
He can't see. He can't see anything.	*Il ne peut pas voir. Il ne peut rien voir.*
Without eyes you can't see anything.	*Sans yeux tu ne peux rien voir.*
Do you know a person who is blind?	*Connais-tu quelqu'un d'aveugle?*
Do you know a person with only one eye?	*Connais-tu quelqu'un qui n'a qu'un oeil?*
Here is an ugly giant, a monster.	*Voici un vilain géant, un monstre.*
He was born with only one eye.	*Il est né avec un seul oeil.*
At least he can see.	*Au moins il peut voir.*
He is not blind.	*Il n'est pas aveugle.*
But he doesn't have any friends.	*Mais il n'a pas d'amis.*
Why doesn't he have any friends?	*Pourquoi n'a-t-il pas d'amis?*
Because people don't like monsters	*Parce que les gens n'aiment pas les monstres*
with only one eye in the middle	*qui n'ont qu'un oeil au milieu*
of their forehead.	*de leur front.*
They are afraid of them.	*Ils ont peur d'eux.*
Here is another giant.	*Voici un autre géant.*
He is a bad giant.	*C'est un mauvais géant.*
He is mean.	*Il est méchant.*
His name is Grosso.	*Il s'appelle Grosso.*
Grosso is very tall and very strong.	*Grosso est très grand et très fort.*
He is as tall as a giraffe	*Il est aussi grand qu'une girafe*
and as strong as an elephant.	*et aussi fort qu'un éléphant.*
But his heart is very small	*Mais son coeur est très petit*
and full of hate.	*et plein de haine.*
He doesn't like anyone.	*Il n'aime personne.*
Not even his mother.	*Pas même sa mère.*
He hates everyone.	*Il déteste tout le monde.*
I think he even hates himself.	*Je crois qu'il se déteste lui-même.*
Do you like Grosso?	*Aimes-tu Grosso?*
Is he your friend?	*Est-il ton ami?*
I think he needs a friend.	*Je crois qu'il a besoin d'un ami.*
Won't you be his friend?	*Ne seras-tu pas son ami?*
Poor Grosso!	*Pauvre Grosso!*
Are you afraid of Grosso?	*As-tu peur de Grosso?*
Don't you want to be his friend?	*Ne veux-tu pas être son ami?*
Do you want to have a giant for your friend?	*Veux-tu avoir un géant pour ami?*
Are you a giant?	*Es-tu un géant?*

🎬 THE ADVENTURE CONTINUES

Day Five—0830 hours

Five Days to Rendezvous

Over breakfast the next morning, you and Stump puzzle over Samuel's clue.

"*L'hermitage*—that means 'the hermitage.' Hmmm," Stump thinks aloud. "I wonder what he meant by that."

"*L'hermitage* is a very classy restaurant next door to the island's resort hotel," Jacqueline explains. "I've only been there once."

"I will make reservations for you," Zsa-Zsa offers.

Zsa-Zsa calls the restaurant. They are already booked for this evening, but they can fit you in tomorrow at lunch. Zsa-Zsa makes reservations for that time and gives you directions to the restaurant. She suggests that you and Stump spend the rest of the day reviewing and studying. You and Stump complete seven French exercises by mid-afternoon.

63

Child Talk 1
Des questions posées par un enfant

Instructions: Listen to this fun conversation. Try to retell it!

Mama, where do giraffes live?	*Maman, où est-ce que vivent les girafes?*
Giraffes live in Africa.	*Les girafes vivent en Afrique.*
Do I live in Africa?	*Est-ce que je vis en Afrique?*
No, you don't live in Africa.	*Non, tu ne vis pas en Afrique.*
You and Daddy, do you live in Africa?	*Toi et Papa, vivez-vous en Afrique?*
No, we don't live in Africa.	*Non, nous ne vivons pas en Afrique.*
Why not?	*Pourquoi pas?*
Because we're not giraffes.	*Parce que nous ne sommes pas des girafes.*

64

Chatter at a Royal Ball
Bavardages au bal royal

GETTING READY FOR CONVERSATION

Instructions: Familiarize yourself with these new words. Then see them being used in the conversation below.

there is/are	*il y a*	which one?	*lequel?*
to ask	*demander*	which ones?	*lesquels?*
to live	*vivre*	here it is	*le voici*
to dwell	*habiter*	here they are	*les voici*
what is more...	*qui plus est...*	this one	*ceci, celui-ci*
naturally, of course	*naturellement*	that one	*ça, cela, celui-là*
truly, really	*vraiment*	scandalous	*scandaleux*

CONVERSATION

In this story there's a castle.	*Dans cette histoire il y a un château.*
Here it is.	*Le voici.*
There is also a king and a queen.	*Il y a aussi un roi et une reine.*
Here they are.	*Les voici.*
They live together. They live in the castle.	*Ils vivent ensemble. Ils habitent dans le château.*
Who lives in the castle with them, you ask?	*Tu demandes qui vit dans le château avec eux?*
A beautiful princess and a handsome prince, of course.	*Une belle princesse et un beau prince, naturellement.*
Oh yes, there's also a dog and a cat.	*Oh oui, il y a aussi un chien et un chat.*
The dog does nothing but play with the cat.	*Le chien ne fait que jouer avec le chat.*

65

Focus on the Language 34-39
Concentration sur la langue 34-39

FOCUS 34

Dire "to say" *dit:disent*. *Lire* "to read": *lit:lisent*. *Vivre* "to live" *vit:vivent*.

He says that the king yet lives.	*Il dit que le roi vit encore.*
They read together often.	*Ils lisent souvent ensemble.*
The dukes say he reads a lot.	*Les ducs disent qu'il lit beaucoup.*
It is said they live without drinking.	*On dit qu'ils vivent sans boire.*

Vivre, *lire*, and *dire* share the rhyme: *vit*, *lit* and *dit* (pronounced [vi], [li], [di]). The respective plurals are *vivent* [viv], *lisent* [liz], and *disent* [diz].

Note: In English we can say either "He says that she lives here" or "he says she lives here." In French, however, *que* cannot be left out: «*Il dit qu'elle vit ici*», NOT «*Il dit elle vit ici.*»

The verb *habiter* rather than *vivre* is usually used to mean living at a place: «*Il habite à l'école*» "He lives at the school" is more common than «*Il vit à l'école.*»

Translate Orally from and into French.

They live like kings.	*Ils vivent comme des rois.*
It is true that he reads a lot.	*C'est vrai qu'il lit beaucoup.*
They read together often.	*Ils lisent souvent ensemble.*
He says that she lives without eating.	*Il dit qu'elle vit sans manger.*

FOCUS 35

"Only, alone" *seul(e)(s)*.

Only the king knows.	*Seul le roi sait.*
Only the queen knows.	*Seule la reine sait.*
He lives alone.	*Il vit seul.*
She lives alone.	*Elle vit seule.*
They like to play alone.	*Ils aiment jouer seuls.*
They (f) like to play alone.	*Elles aiment jouer seules.*

When *seul* means "alone" it is rendered by *seul(e)(s)*. *Seul, seule, seuls, seules* are pronounced the same with the exception that before vowel-initial words, the final <s> of *seuls* and *seules* is [z].

Translate Orally from and into French

Only the king goes to church.	*Seul le roi va à l'église.*
Only the queen plays at school.	*Seule la reine joue à l'école.*
The prince lives alone.	*Le prince vit seul.*
The king and queen live alone.	*Le roi et la reine vivent seuls.*
It is said that she lives alone.	*On dit qu'elle vit seule.*
The princes say she lives alone.	*Les princes disent qu'elle vit seule.*
They sing alone from time to time.	*Ils chantent seuls de temps en temps.*
The queens don't like to sing alone.	*Les reines n'aiment pas chanter seules.*

FOCUS 36

How to ask which one(s): *lequel, laquelle, lesquels, lesquelles*.

1.	Which king sings?	*Quel roi chante?*
2.	Which queen sings?	*Quelle reine chante?*
3.	Which dukes sing?	*Quels ducs chantent?*
4.	Which duchesses sing?	*Quelles duchesses chantent?*
5.	Which one (m) sings?	*Lequel chante?*
6.	Which one (f) sings?	*Laquelle chante?*
7.	Which ones (m) sing?	*Lesquels chantent?*
8.	Which ones (f) sing?	*Lesquelles chantent?*

Note: *Quel, quelle,* and *quels* cannot stand alone. They are always linked to a following noun, as you see in 1–4 above. To express "which one(s)" the French say "the-which": *lequel, laquelle* or *lesquels, lesquelles* as in 5–8 above. Which of these to select depends of course on the gender and number of the noun referred to.

Translate Orally from and into French

There are two kings. Which one sings?	*Il y a deux rois. Lequel chante?*
There are two queens. Which one plays?	*Il y a deux reines. Laquelle joue?*
There are three dukes. Which ones dance?	*Il y a trois ducs. Lesquels dansent?*
There are three queens. Which ones dance?	*Il y a trois reines. Lesquelles dansent?*

FOCUS 37

"Here" *ici* and "there" *là* and some combinations.

He is here, she is there.	*Il est ici, elle est là.*
This one here is the king.	*Celui-ci est le roi.*
That one there is the duke.	*Celui-là est le duc.*
This queen here plays.	*Cette reine-ci joue.*
That queen there sings.	*Cette reine-là chante.*
There is the duke.	*Voilà le duc.*
Here is the king.	*Voici le roi.*

Ici and *là* are high-frequency words, and they combine with stems to express relative proximity to speaker (*voici, cette reine-ci, celui-ci*) or non-proximity to speaker (*voilà, cette reine-là, celui-là*). *Voici* and *voilà* are made up of *voi* "see" with *ici* "here" or *la* "there."

Distinguish between the "existential" *il y a* "there is" or "there are" as in: *Il y a un roi dans la tour* "There is a king in the tower" and *Voilà le roi dans la tour!* "Behold the king there in the tower!" Obviously *voilà* "there is" is the counterpart of *voici* "here is."

Translate Orally from and into French

Who's there? The prince.	*Qui est là? Le prince.*
Who's here? The princess is here.	*Qui est ici? La princesse est ici.*
Here is the tower.	*Voici la tour.*
There is the drum.	*Voilà le tambour.*
This one here is the king; that one there is the duke.	*Celui-ci est le roi, celui-là est le duc.*
This one here is the queen; that one there is the duchess.	*Celle-ci est la reine, celle-là est la duchesse.*

FOCUS 38

Here it is. *Le voici.*

Here it is!	*Le voici!*
There they are!	*Les voilà!*
There it is!	*Le voilà!*

Translate Orally from and into French

Where is the drum? Here it is.	*Où est le tambour? Le voici.*
Where are the drums? Here they are.	*Où sont les tambours? Les voici.*
Where are the castles? Here they are.	*Où sont les châteaux? Les voilà.*
Where is the princess? Here she is.	*Où est la princesse? La voici.*

FOCUS 39

"Stand-alone" personal pronouns *lui* and *eux*

What is he doing?		*Qu'est-ce qu'il fait?*
He is singing.		*Il chante.*
	NOT:	**Lui chante.*
What are they doing?		*Qu'est-ce qu'ils font?*
They're playing.		*Ils jouent.*
	NOT:	**Eux jouent.*
Who's singing?		*Qui chante?*
Her. It's her. SHE is.		*Elle. C'est elle. Elle, elle chante.*
Him. It's him. HE is.		*Lui. C'est lui. Lui, il chante.*
	NOT:	**Il. C'est il. Lui chante.*
Who's playing?		*Qui joue?*
Them (f). It's them. They are.		*Elles. Ce sont elles. Elles, elles jouent.*
Them (m). It's them. They are.		*Eux. Ce sont eux. Eux, ils jouent.*
	NOT:	**Ils. Ce sont ils. Eux jouent.*
Who is he singing with?		*Avec qui chante-t-il?*
With him. With them (m).		*Avec lui. Avec eux.*
	NOT:	**Avec il. Avec ils.*

Note how the masculine pronouns *il* and *ils* are used in examples 1–2, but *lui* and *eux,* are used in examples 3–5. The selection depends on whether the pronoun deals with known (old) or unknown (new) information.

Lui and *eux* are "stand-alone" pronouns. A question can be answered with *lui* alone but not with *il* alone; with *eux* alone but not with *ils*. To highlight "he" in "He sings" we raise our voice, but French does not use voice highlighting in such cases; rather it uses *lui*, the emphatic counterpart of *il*. Likewise with *ils* and *eux*. *Elle* and *elles*, on the other hand, can stand alone. French uses the disjunctive pronoun followed by the subject pronoun, pausing in-between, thus:

> *Lui, il chante.*
> *Elle, elle chante.*
> *Eux, ils chantent.*
> *Elles, elles chantent.*

After prepositions such as *avec, pour,* etc. the forms *lui* and *eux* are used.

Translate Orally from and into French

Who is there? It's him.	*Qui est là? C'est lui.*
If it's him, that's terrible!	*Si c'est lui, c'est terrible!*
Who is the king? The one who sings.	*Qui est le roi? Celui qui chante.*
Who sings there? Not him (but) her.	*Qui chante là? Pas lui, elle.*
It's him that is singing.	*C'est lui qui chante.*
It's them (m) that are singing.	*Ce sont eux qui chantent.*
The king plays with him and her.	*Le roi joue avec lui et avec elle.*
The duke sings with them.	*Le duc chante avec eux.*

66
Review
Révision

Instructions: Take a while to look over the sentences below. Read the French sentence out loud, then look away and repeat it, thinking of its meaning. Then cover the French and see if you can quickly render the English into French.

GROUP A

He already sings.	*Il chante déjà.*
He's already singing and dancing.	*Il chante et danse déjà.*
Who sings and who dances now?	*Qui chante et qui danse maintenant?*
She sings and he dances now.	*Elle chante et il danse maintenant.*
That princess doesn't sing.	*Cette princesse ne chante pas.*
This one does.	*Celle-ci, oui.*
That prince no longer sings.	*Ce prince ne chante plus.*
This one does.	*Celui-ci, oui.*
Who's dancing? Him and her.	*Qui danse? Lui et elle.*
No, he is dancing but she isn't.	*Non, lui, il danse, mais elle, non.*
She doesn't dance any more.	*Elle ne danse plus.*

GROUP B

They are not dancing.	*Ils ne dansent pas.*
They don't dance.	*Ils ne dansent pas.*
They don't dance.	*Eux, ils ne dansent pas.*
And they don't sing either.	*Et ils ne chantent pas non plus.*
They're not playing but singing.	*Ils ne jouent pas mais ils chantent.*
Now the queen is singing a little, but not much.	*Maintenant la reine chante un peu, mais pas beaucoup.*
The king used to play a little.	*Le roi jouait un peu.*
They both play a little.	*Tous les deux jouent un peu.*

GROUP C

The prince and princess sing.	*Le prince et la princesse chantent.*
Yes, both sing already.	*Oui, tous les deux chantent déjà.*
The prince sings a lot.	*Le prince chante beaucoup.*
The princess doesn't sing much.	*La princesse ne chante pas beaucoup.*
She doesn't sing but a little.	*Elle ne chante qu'un peu.*
Does he still sing a lot? Yes!	*Chante-t-il encore beaucoup? Oui!*
But the king doesn't know it yet.	*Mais le roi ne le sait pas encore.*
He knows the dog doesn't sing.	*Il sait que le chien ne chante pas.*
That is to say, he doesn't sing.	*C'est-à-dire qu'il ne chante pas.*

GROUP D

The king no longer speaks French.	*Le roi ne parle plus français.*
He used to speak French often.	*Il parlait souvent français.*
He still speaks French a little.	*Il parle encore un peu français.*
The princess doesn't speak French yet.	*La princesse ne parle pas encore français.*
But she still speaks Chinese.	*Mais elle parle encore chinois.*
The prince still swears that he's going to eat.	*Le prince jure encore qu'il va manger.*
She still thinks that the prince is going to eat.	*Elle pense encore que le prince va manger.*

67

Test Your Performance
Testez vos compétences

Instructions: Cover the French column and translate orally from English into French.

GROUP A

This king doesn't sing.	*Ce roi ne chante pas.*
He doesn't dance either.	*Il ne danse pas non plus.*
Not yet. Imagine!	*Pas encore. Imagine-toi!*
This queen isn't crying.	*Cette reine ne pleure pas.*
The princess (is) not either.	*La princesse non plus.*
The prince and princess sing.	*Le prince et la princesse chantent.*
The prince also dances.	*Le prince danse aussi.*
But the princess doesn't dance.	*Mais la princesse ne danse pas.*
That is to say, she doesn't dance yet.	*C'est-à-dire qu'elle ne danse pas encore.*

GROUP B

This king does not sing yet.	*Ce roi ne chante pas encore.*
That's true. Not yet.	*C'est vrai. Pas encore.*
This queen doesn't either.	*Cette reine non plus.*
The king doesn't dance either.	*Le roi ne danse pas non plus.*
It's well that the king and queen don't sing.	*C'est bien que le roi et la reine ne chantent pas.*
This prince still sings a lot.	*Ce prince chante encore beaucoup.*
Is it true? Yes, it's true.	*C'est vrai? Oui, c'est vrai.*
Not true…that's not true.	*Pas vrai…ce n'est pas vrai.*
It's absolutely incredible!	*C'est absolument incroyable!*

GROUP C

The prince already sings.	*Le prince chante déjà.*
He no longer plays.	*Il ne joue plus.*
Does the king no longer play?	*Est-ce que le roi ne joue plus?*
He no longer plays in the tower.	*Il ne joue plus dans la tour.*
They no longer cry in the bar.	*Ils ne pleurent plus dans le bar.*
Does the prince cry in the bar?	*Le prince pleure-t-il dans le bar?*
Who knows?	*Qui sait?*

GROUP D

Who already sings?	*Qui chante déjà?*
This princess already sings.	*Cette princesse chante déjà.*
This prince and this princess already sing?	*Ce prince et cette princesse chantent déjà.*
This queen doesn't sing; this king doesn't either.	*Cette reine ne chante pas; ce roi non plus.*
What do they do?	*Que font-ils?*
What do they do?	*Qu'est-ce qu'ils font?*
How's that?…Pardon?	*Comment?…Pardon?*
They sing in the tower now and then.	*Ils chantent dans la tour de temps en temps.*

GROUP E

He swears that Bobi sings.	*Il jure que Bobi chante.*
But he swears he doesn't dance.	*Mais il jure qu'il ne danse pas.*

He says that Misti dances.	*Il dit que Misti danse.*
She says that Misti doesn't dance.	*Elle dit que Misti ne danse pas.*
She thinks Bobi dances a lot.	*Elle croit que Bobi danse beaucoup.*
I believe that Misti sings a lot.	*Je crois que Misti chante beaucoup.*
They know Misti sings a lot.	*Ils savent que Misti chante beaucoup.*
I know he doesn't dance much.	*Je sais qu'il ne danse pas beaucoup.*
I think that Bobi doesn't sing.	*Je crois que Bobi ne chante pas.*
I know that he doesn't dance.	*Je sais qu'il ne danse pas.*
He says that if the princess sings, it's shocking.	*Il dit que si la princesse chante, c'est choquant.*
For sure, it's very shocking!	*C'est sûr, c'est très choquant!*

GROUP F

It's true that Bobi doesn't sing.	*Il est vrai que Bobi ne chante pas.*
I think it's true that he dances.	*Je crois que c'est vrai, qu'il danse.*
If it's true, it's a pity.	*Si c'est vrai, c'est dommage!*
It's good he doesn't sing anymore.	*C'est bien qu'il ne chante plus.*
He swears that Bobi says that Misti sings from time to time.	*Il jure que Bobi dit que Misti chante de temps en temps.*
He says that Bobi swears that Misti still sings.	*Il dit que Bobi jure que Misti chante encore.*
It's terrible that he still sings.	*C'est terrible qu'il chante encore.*
If it's true, it's shocking!	*Si c'est vrai, c'est choquant!*
That is to say, it's terrible!	*C'est-à-dire que c'est terrible!*
Of course it's terrible!	*Bien sûr que c'est terrible!*

GROUP G

The king that used to play now sings.	*Le roi qui jouait chante maintenant.*
The king that played funeral chants on the drum is now singing.	*Le roi qui jouait des chants funèbres au tambour chante maintenant.*
The queen is singing too, right?	*La reine chante aussi, n'est-ce pas?*
Both cry from time to time.	*Les deux pleurent de temps en temps.*
They don't cry in the tower.	*Ils ne pleurent pas dans la tour.*
They cry in the bathroom.	*Ils pleurent dans la salle de bain.*
All four of them cry a little.	*Tous les quatre pleurent un peu.*
All four of them curse from time to time.	*Tous les quatre jurent de temps en temps.*
Both of them speak Chinese a lot.	*Tous les deux parlent beaucoup chinois.*
The Chinese speak French from time to time, right?	*Les Chinois parlent français de temps en temps, n'est-ce pas?*
That is to say, they speak a little French.	*C'est-à-dire qu'ils parlent un peu français.*

GROUP H

What is it he's doing?	*Qu'est-ce qu'il fait?*
He's playing.	*Il joue.*
Who is playing?	*Qui joue?*
Him. It's him that's playing.	*Lui. C'est lui qui joue.*
<u>He's</u> playing.	*<u>Lui</u>, il joue.*
What is it they're doing?	*Qu'est-ce qu'ils font?*
They are singing.	*Ils chantent.*
It's them that are singing.	*Ce sont eux qui chantent.*
<u>They</u> are singing.	*<u>Eux</u>, ils chantent.*
Who is singing now?	*Qui chante maintenant?*
Her. It's her that's singing.	*Elle. C'est elle qui chante.*
Not her, it's him!	*Pas elle, c'est lui!*
It's him that's crying.	*C'est lui qui pleure.*
It's her that's singing.	*C'est elle qui chante.*

It's them playing.	*Ce sont eux qui jouent.*
It's not them.	*Ce ne sont pas eux.*
It's not him either.	*Ce n'est pas lui non plus.*
The dukes don't play anymore.	*Les ducs ne jouent plus.*

68

Wrap-up Activities
Creating and Telling Stories
Activités récapitulatives

READ AND RESPOND TO QUESTIONS
Résumé

Il y a un roi. Le roi jouait au tambour. Il jouait des chants funèbres au tambour dans la tour. Mais maintenant il ne joue pas du tambour. Maintenant il chante. Il chante avec la reine. Il chante des chants funèbres avec la reine dans la tour. Le roi chante mieux. Oui, il chante mieux qu'elle...mieux que la reine. La reine chante assez bien, mais pas aussi bien que le roi. Mais elle joue bien du tambour.

Il y a aussi un chien et un chat qui chantent avec le roi et la reine, n'est-ce pas? Oui, et tous les quatre chantent maintenant. Le chat et le chien chantent maintenant avec le roi et la reine dans la tour. Imaginez-vous! Un chien et un chat qui chantent avec un roi et une reine. Tous les quatre chantent des chants funèbres dans la tour. Le chien et le chat ne chantent pas très bien. Incroyable, n'est-ce pas? Absolument incroyable!

La reine est maintenant dans la tour avec le roi. Ils chantent ensemble. Ils chantent des chants funèbres. Il semble qu'ils ne chantent que des chants funèbres. Ils aiment chanter des chants funèbres ensemble. La reine joue au tambour. Elle joue bien. Elle joue mieux que le roi. Mais elle ne chante pas mieux que le roi. Intéressant, n'est-ce pas? Très intéressant.

Some Explanations

Why does the king sing?	*Pourquoi le roi chante-t-il?*
The king sings because he loves the queen.	*Le roi chante parce qu'il aime la reine.*
Why does the queen sing?	*Pourquoi la reine chante-t-elle?*
The queen sings because she loves the king.	*La reine chante parce qu'elle aime le roi.*
Why does the king love the queen?	*Pourquoi le roi aime-t-il la reine?*
It's because she likes to sing with him.	*C'est parce qu'elle aime chanter avec lui.*
And why does the queen love the king?	*Et pourquoi la reine aime-t-elle le roi?*
It's because he likes to sing with her.	*C'est parce qu'il aime chanter avec elle.*
When does the king sing?	*Quand est-ce que le roi chante?*
The king sings when the queen is content.	*Le roi chante quand la reine est contente.*
When does the queen sing?	*Quand est-ce que la reine chante?*
The queen sings when the king is content.	*La reine chante quand le roi est content.*
They sing together when they both are content.	*Ils chantent ensemble quand ils sont tous les deux contents.*
And when are they content?	*Et quand sont-ils contents?*
They are content when they sing together.	*Ils sont contents quand ils chantent ensemble.*

QUESTIONS ON THE TEXT

Instructions: Try to answer the questions based on the text. Feel free to review the text if you need help!

1. *Qui est-ce?* 😺 *Est-ce le prince ou le roi?*
2. *Que fait le prince?*
3. *Est-ce que le chien et le chat chantent ensemble?*
4. *Avec qui chantent-ils? Avec la princesse et le prince?*
5. *Où chantent-ils avec le roi et la reine? Dans la salle de bain?*
6. *Est-ce que le roi et la reine chantent bien ensemble?*
7. *Est-ce que le chien et le chat chantent bien ensemble?*
8. *Qui chante mieux, le chat ou le chien?*
9. *Quelle sorte de chants chantent-ils avec le roi et la reine?*

69
Generating Sentences for Oral Practice
Formuler des phrases pour s'exprimer oralement

Instructions: Use these lists of words to make stories and sentences of your own.

WORDS YOU KNOW
Functions and some expressions to fill them

Actor-Nouns
roi, reine, prince, princesse, duc, duchesse, chien, chat, Bobi, Misti, chanteur, chanteuse, ballerine, danseur, danseuse, tromboniste, joueur de tambour, violoniste, acteur, actrice, directeur

Pronouns
il-lui, ils-eux, elle, elles, les deux, tous les quatre

Adjectives
beau-belle, content-contente

Places
le bar, la tour, la salle de bain, la salle de danse, ici, là, là-bas

Attestation Preface
il sait que; il pense que; il jure que; il dit que; il lit que; il observe que

Verb Stems
fum-, parl-, chant-, jou-, pleur-, prépar-, attaqu-, fabriqu-, insult-

Endings
{present} -e, -ent (silent); {past} -ait, -aient (pronounced [e])

Info-Question Words
Que? Qui? Quel(le)? Où? Comment? Pourquoi?

Yes-No Question-Markers
Est-ce que...? N'est-ce pas?

Location Prepositions
dans, à, avec

Quantity
beaucoup, un peu, assez

Temporal
maintenant, encore, déjà

Manner, Etc.

bien, mal, ensemble

Rejoinders

finalement, c'est tout, bien sûr, vraiment, c'est vrai, c'est la vérité, formidable, terrible, d'accord, je crois que oui, comme c'est étrange!, exactement, probablement, quel dommage, imagine-toi!

Conjunctions and Related Words

et, ou, mais, aussi, non plus

Quickly draw on a slip of paper or a small card a pictograph (or a written word) to represent each of the above vocabulary words. Then arrange your cards into piles according to the function categories above.

SENTENCE-CONSTRUCTION EXERCISES

1. Take three actor-nouns and three action-words from your piles. By adding the proper grammatical details, make up three quick sentences on the model of *Le chien danse*. (Strive to say your sentences rapidly and without hesitation once they are launched.)

   1a. Put the question phrase *Est-ce que…?* in front of those sentences, asking, for example, *Est-ce que le roi pleure?*

   1b. Put the tag question *n'est-ce pas?* at the end of your sentences, as in *Le roi pleure, n'est-ce pas?* "The king is crying, right?"

   1c. To such statements, add a "preface" construction: *Il sait que le chien chante* "He knows that the dog sings," *Il pense que le chat parle.* "He thinks that the cat talks." *Il observe que le roi joue.* "He observes that the king plays." *Il jure que le chien boit du lait.* "He swears the dog drinks milk."

2. Compose some plural sentences on the model *Les chiens chantent*. (Don't forget the plural-marker *-nt* on the action verb.) Look up and say each statement without hesitation once the sentence is launched.

3. Turn these sentences into yes-no questions by reversing the noun and the verb on the model of *Le chien, danse-t-il?* Aim for high-speed delivery.

4. Form some who-, which- or with whom-questions as in: *Qui chante? Quel roi chante? Avec qui chante-t-il? Lequel joue? Lesquelles pleurent?*

5. Turn the sentences into what-questions as in: *Qu'est-ce que la princesse chante?*

6. Change the sentences to what-action-questions as in: *Que fait le chien?* or *Que font les chiens?*

7. Make new sentences by conjoining two actors, on the model *Le prince et la princesse chantent*.

8. Expand your sentences by adding modifiers like *encore, déjà, aussi, maintenant, non plus,* on the model *Le chien chante encore beaucoup.*

SAMPLE SENTENCE PATTERNS

Instructions: Here are some easy-to-learn patterns to weave into stories. Try to make some stories of your own.

The court poet...
    composes a poem.
    reads his poem to the queen.

The pretty secretary...
    listens and observes with interest.
    works with enthusiasm.

The gardener...
    has an idea, a plan.
    hides the flowers in the garden.

The impartial judge...
    studies the case.
    pardons the gardener.

The court magician...
    invents a formula.
    insists that the formula is good.

The chambermaid...
    considers the situation.
    observes the magician.

The inspector...
    finds the thief.
    arrests the thief.

The viceroy...
    is the vice-president.
    continues to chase cats.

The innocent child...
    responds to the question.
    declares the truth.

The lawyer (advocate)...
    contests the decision.
    presents incontestible evidence.

The police officer...
    supposes the poet is culpable.
    speaks with the chief by phone.

The young engineer...
    explains the problem.
    resolves the problem.

The driver...
    usually drives the car.
    drives the plane.

Le poète de la cour...
    compose un poème.
    lit son poème à la reine.

La jolie secrétaire...
    écoute et observe avec intérêt.
    travaille avec enthousiasme.

Le jardinier...
    a une idée, un plan.
    cache les fleurs dans le jardin.

Le juge impartial...
    étudie le cas.
    pardonne le jardinier.

Le magicien de la cour...
    invente une formule.
    insiste que la formule est bonne.

La femme de chambre...
    considère la situation.
    observe le magicien.

L'inspecteur...
    trouve le voleur.
    arrête le voleur.

Le vice-roi...
    est le vice-président.
    continue à chasser des chats.

Un enfant innocent...
    répond à la question.
    déclare la vérité.

L'avocat...
    conteste la décision.
    présente une évidence incontestable.

L'agent de police...
    suppose que le poète est coupable.
    parle avec le chef par téléphone.

Le jeune ingénieur...
    explique le problème.
    résoud le problème.

Le chauffeur...
    conduit d'ordinaire la voiture.
    conduit l'avion.

ABOUT THE STRUCTURE OF STORIES

Stories generally follow a more or less predictable story line that consists of several parts:

1. Introduction or setting the story and its character(s) in time and place: "Once there was a king who lived in a tower."

2. Further characterization: "This king was wicked but he had a wife who was kind."

3. Rise in suspense or anticipation of conflict: "She liked to play the drums, but he didn't like to hear her music."

4. Conflict: "He said to her, 'Don't play the drums or I'll throw them off the tower.' But she played anyway."

5. Climax: "When he went to throw the drums off, he slipped and hurt his back."

6. Conclusion or resolution of conflict: "While he was in bed, his only entertainment was to listen to his wife play the drums!"

SAMPLE STORY PLOTS

Instructions: Observe this structure in the following story plots. Look in the appendix to find a translation of the story plots.

Sample Plot One

1. Dans cette histoire il y a un chat et un chien. 2. Les deux chantent dans la salle de bain. 3. Mais le chien n'est pas content. 4. Pourquoi le chien n'est-il pas content? 5. Parce qu'il déteste le chat. 6. Et pourquoi le chien déteste-t-il le chat? 7. C'est parce que le chat chante mieux. 8. Qu'est-ce que le chien jure de faire? 9. Il jure qu'il va attaquer le chat. 10. Oui, il jure qu'un jour il va attacquer le chat. 11. Et finalement, un jour il attaque le chat! 12. Très choquant, n'est-ce pas? 13. C'est tout.

Sample Plot Two

1. Dans cette histoire il y a un palais. 2. Le roi est dans le palais. 3. Le roi a un trésor. 4. Le roi a des bijoux. 5. Il aime les bijoux. 6. C'est un secret où il cache les bijoux. 7. Mais la belle secrétaire connaît le secret. 8. La duchesse sait aussi où le roi cache les bijoux. 9. Dans cette histoire, il y a aussi un voleur. 10. Ce voleur est aussi dans le palais. 11. Il ne sait pas où sont les bijoux. 12. Mais il pense qu'ils sont dans la salle de bain. 13. Il entre dans la salle de bain. 14. Il cherche et cherche, mais il ne trouve pas les bijoux. 15. Il pense que les bijoux sont dans la tour. 16. Il monte dans la tour. 17. Il cherche et cherche, mais il ne trouve pas les bijoux. 18. Il pense maintenant que les bijoux sont dans la chambre de la reine. 19. Il entre dans la chambre de la reine. 20. Il cherche et cherche, et finalement trouve les bijoux.

GENERATING YOUR OWN STORIES

Here is a sentence-generation chart you can use to practice generating some typical story beginnings.

Il y avait   un   prince   qui   était   pauvre.

There was	a	prince	who	was	poor.
Il y avait	*des*	*ducs*	*qui*	*étaient*	*riches.*
There were	some	dukes	who	were	rich.

Practice generating some story beginnings from the chart. Most important is to understand what your sentence creations mean, but of course you should give attention to certain details of grammatical propriety. Match singular nouns with singular verb-forms and plural nouns with plural verb-forms. Also keep the tense consistent: present with present, past with past.

Now create your own mini-story plots. Plan them out, using words you have used before plus new expressions taken from the material in this and previous lessons. Write some stories out and practice presenting them orally (without reading). *Do not start by writing out a story in English and then trying to find words and structures to translate it.* Do not try to go beyond the words supplied in this book. Practice telling your stories until you can tell them fluently from only an outline or from pictographs you have drawn on cards. Fluency is your aim, hesitation your enemy.

THE ADVENTURE CONTINUES

Just as you finish the seventh exercise, you notice delicious smells wafting into your room from the kitchen. You and Stump wander to the kitchen and find Zsa-Zsa teaching Jacqueline how to make French pastries.

After a wonderful dinner, you and Stump return to your rooms for more study.

70

🔊 *L'alphabet romain* (continued)
French Only
Une leçon au sujet de l'alphabet

🔊 Instructions: Listen to and read the following text. Try your best to understand the general meaning; don't worry about understanding every detail.

🔊 *<D> plus <E> plus <S> forment le mot DES. La première lettre de DES est <D>, <E> est la seconde, et <S> est la troisième et dernière lettre.*

Est-ce que <Y> est toujours une consonne? Non, pas toujours. Ordinairement <Y> sert de consonne. Dans les mots YEN et YANKEE par exemple, <Y> sert de consonne. Mais dans le mot Y (il y a), <Y> est une voyelle.

Les lettres <K> et <W> ne sont pas des lettres ordinaires en français. Ces lettres (<K> et <W>) ne se présentent pas dans les mots d'origine française. Les mots KIWI et WAGON ne sont pas d'origine française.

Voici l'alphabet dans son entier. Regardez:

A	B	C	D	E	F	G	H	I	J	K	L	M
a	b	c	d	e	f	g	h	i	j	k	l	m

N	O	P	Q	R	S	T	U	V	W	X	Y	Z
n	o	p	q	r	s	t	u	v	w	x	y	z

Remarquez que chaque lettre contient deux formes, la forme majuscule et la forme minuscule. Les lettres majuscules sont plus grandes que les lettres minuscules.

Les lettres majuscules sont placées en position initiale pour tous les noms propres (noms de personnes, de lieu) et en position initiale de phrase. Par exemple, mon nom s'écrit ainsi: Nathalie. Remarquez que le <N> initial s'écrit en majuscule, mais les autres lettres s'écrivent en minuscule.

Toutes les lettres, soit majuscules soit minuscules, peuvent s'écrire en lettres capitales ou en lettres cursives. Par exemple, voici un nom écrit en lettres capitales: ROBERT et le voici en lettres cursives: Robert

L'art d'écrire en formant de belles lettres s'appelle la calligraphie.

71

Child Talk 2
Des questions posées par un enfant

Instructions: Listen to and read the following conversation. Try to retell it!

Mama, what language do Germans speak?	*Maman, quelle langue les Allemands parlent-ils?*
Germans speak German.	*Les Allemands parlent allemand.*
Do I speak German?	*Est-ce que je parle allemand?*
No, you don't speak German.	*Non, tu ne parles pas allemand.*
You and Daddy, do you speak German?	*Toi et Papa, est-ce que vous parlez allemand?*
No, we don't speak German.	*Non, nous ne parlons pas allemand.*
Why not?	*Pourquoi pas?*
Because we're not Germans.	*Parce que nous ne sommes pas allemands.*

72

📼 A Surprising Discovery
French Only
Une découverte surprenante

🎧 Instructions: Listen to this story. How many words are new to you? Make an effort to learn them!

One night when I was small,
I looked through a keyhole
and here is what I saw:
   I saw a table,
   I saw a chair,
   I saw a cushion,
   and I saw a candle.

The table was on the floor,
the chair was on the table,
the cushion was on the chair,
and the candle lit up the room.

I blinked my eyes and looked again,
and here is what I saw:
   I saw a candle,
   I saw a cushion,
   I saw a chair,
   and I saw a table.
The cushion was under the candle,
the chair was under the cushion,
the table was under the chair,
the floor was under the table, and you know,
the same candle lit up the room.

📼 *Un soir quand j'étais petite,
j'ai regardé par le trou d'une serrure,
Et voici ce que j'ai vu:
   j'ai vu une table,
   j'ai vu une chaise,
   j'ai vu un coussin,
   et j'ai vu une bougie.*

*La table était sur le plancher,
la chaise était sur la table,
le coussin était sur la chaise,
et la bougie illuminait la pièce.*

*J'ai cligné des yeux et regardé à nouveau,
et voici ce que j'ai vu:
   j'ai vu une bougie,
   j'ai vu un coussin,
   j'ai vu une chaise,
   et j'ai vu une table.
Le coussin était sous la bougie,
la chaise était sous le coussin,
la table était sous la chaise,
le plancher était sous la table, et vous savez,
la même bougie illuminait la pièce.*

73
Une leçon de géographie
French Only
A Geography Lesson

Instructions: Listen to and read the following geography lesson. Learn how many countries are said in French!

Here is Canada,	Voici le Canada,
north of the U.S.	au nord des États-Unis.
And here, on the other side of the Atlantic, is Europe.	Et ici, de l'autre côté de l'Atlantique, se trouve l'Europe.
In Western Europe are found	En Europe de l'ouest se trouvent
England, The Netherlands,	l'Angleterre, les Pays-Bas,
France, Spain, and Germany,	la France, l'Espagne, et l'Allemagne,
as well as Denmark, Norway,	ainsi que le Danemark, la Norvège,
Sweden, Finland, Switzerland,	la Suède, la Finlande, la Suisse,
Italy, and Greece.	l'Italie, et la Grèce.
In Eastern Europe are found	En Europe de l'est se trouvent
Poland, Czechoslovakia, Hungary,	la Pologne, la Tchécoslovaquie, la Hongrie,
Bulgaria, Yugoslavia, and Romania.	la Bulgarie, la Yougoslavie et la Roumanie.
Oh, and of course, part of what was formerly the USSR.	Oh, et bien sûr, une partie de ce qui était anciennement l'URSS.
The Soviet Union, or Russia as it was called,	L'Union Soviétique, ou la Russie comme on l'appelait,
stretches from Europe to Asia as far as Japan.	s'étend de l'Europe à l'Asie jusqu'au Japon.
North of Russia is the Arctic Ocean.	Au nord de la Russie se trouve l'océan Arctique.
And countries which border Russia on the south include:	Et les pays qui font frontière avec la Russie au sud sont:
Turkey, Iran,	la Turquie, l'Iran,

Pakistan, Mongolia, and China.

Here is China.
China is famous for many things.
First and foremost,
it is the most populous nation in the world,
having almost one-fourth
of the entire world's population.
And here is India.
It is the second most populous nation in the world.

le Pakistan, la Mongolie, et la Chine.

Voici la Chine.
La Chine est réputée pour beaucoup de choses.
D'abord et avant tout,
c'est la nation la plus peuplée au monde,
comprenant près d'un quart
de la population mondiale totale.
Et ici se trouve l'Inde.
C'est la deuxième nation la plus peuplée au monde.

74
📼 Storytime: The Three Little Pigs
Les trois petits cochons

📼 Instructions: Listen to and read this familiar story. Circle all the French words you've never heard before. Some memory aids have been provided for you.

📼 Three little pigs.	*Trois petits cochons.* (associate with "cushions")
Brothers.	*Frères.*
Three houses.	*Trois maisons.*
A house of straw.	*Une maison en paille.* (assoc: "pie")
A house of sticks.	*Une maison en planches.* (assoc: "planks")
A house of bricks.	*Une maison en briques.*
A wolf.	*Un loup.*
He comes hungry.	*Il vient affamé.* (assoc: "famished")
He comes to the house of straw.	*Il vient à la maison en paille.*
He blows.	*Il souffle.*
The house of straw falls.	*La maison en paille tombe.* (assoc: "tumbles")
But the little pig escapes.	*Mais le petit cochon s'échappe.*
The wolf comes another time.	*Le loup vient une fois de plus.*
He comes to the house of sticks.	*Il vient à la maison en planches.*
He comes very hungry.	*Il vient très affamé.*
He blows.	*Il souffle.*
The house of sticks falls.	*La maison en planches tombe.*
But the little pig escapes.	*Mais le petit cochon s'échappe.*

The wolf comes another time.	*Le loup vient une fois de plus.*
He comes to the house of bricks.	*Il vient à la maison en briques.*
He is VERY hungry.	*Il est TRÈS affamé.*
He blows.	*Il souffle.*
He blows another time.	*Il souffle une fois de plus.*
But the house of bricks doesn't fall.	*Mais la maison en briques ne tombe pas.*
And the wolf leaves	*Et le loup part*
VERY, VERY hungry.	*TRÈS TRÈS affamé.*

THE ADVENTURE CONTINUES

Day Six—0900 hours

Four Days to Rendezvous

You wake up early the next morning and dress nicely for your lunch at *L'hermitage*. Before walking to the restaurant, you and Stump work through four more French activities.

75

📼 *Ma première visite au Québec: troisième partie*
My First Visit to Québec: Part Three

📼 Instructions: Continue listening to this diglot-weave story.

📼 When she had *fini de* playing *l'impromptu, je* asked hopefully:

—*Parlez-vous anglais, mademoiselle?*

—*Non, Monsieur, lamentablement. Seulement le français.*

—*Quel dommage! Votre nom?*

—*Camille Ferrand, Monsieur, à votre service.*

—*Camille Ferrand…vous participiez à la compétition cet après-midi?*

—*Oui, Monsieur, vous étiez dans* the audience?

—*Oui, j'étais dans l'assistance.* Oh, *vous patinez si merveilleusement bien. Je* found *vous très gracieuse et élégante.* Where are you from…*D'où venez-vous?*

—*De la capitale, de la ville de Québec. Je viens ici pour participer aux compétitions de patin à glace. Et vous, Monsieur, d'où venez-vous? Est-ce votre première visite au Canada?*

—*Je viens de l'état de New-York. Et oui, c'est la première fois que je viens au Canada.*

—*Vous comprenez et parlez très bien. Vous savez beaucoup de français.*

—*Non, pas beaucoup. En réalité très peu. Le français est difficile pour moi. Je suis un idiot.*

—*Non, non, Monsieur. Vous n'êtes pas un idiot. Je ne parle pas anglais, mais je ne suis pas une idiote.*

—*Oui, c'est vrai, vous n'êtes pas une idiote, vous êtes une demoiselle très belle et très talentueuse.*

Je thought to myself: *Quel dommage!* Yes, what a pity! Here *je suis* on *ma première visite au Canada. C'est ma première occasion de parler avec une demoiselle canadienne (une princesse enchanteresse), et je* was at a loss for *mots pour m'exprimer.*

Not wanting her to go away, *je* asked *une question stupide*:

—Could you tell *moi l'histoire de votre vie?*

—*Bien, Monsieur, maintenant je travaille, mais demain après-midi, après la pratique à la patinoire, nous pourrons parler.*

L'histoire continue: After *une belle nuit*, full of sweet *rêves de la princesse enchanteresse, je* woke up early, got ready *et* went to *déjeuner au restaurant de l'hôtel. Je* knew that *ma belle patineuse/serveuse* wouldn't be there. She only *travaille le soir, à l'heure du dîner. Je* ate *une orange, deux croissants et* drank *une tasse de chocolat chaud.* Warmed up *et* happy, *je* went for *une promenade. Le ciel était bleu et clair. Il faisait froid. Je* took *un autobus pour Québec pour visiter la ville et prendre des photos. Québec est une grande ville. Dans la ville il y a un grand parc. Dans le parc il y a un grand lac. Sur le lac il y a des patineurs. Je* sat *et les observais* for a *longtemps. Je* wanted to *patiner* with them, *mais je n'avais pas mes patins à glace. Le temps passa et c'était* soon *l'heure de la pratique. Je* returned to *Bois-des-filion pour* attend *la pratique à la patinoire et* to meet *Camille, la belle patineuse de la compétition.*

Around *deux heures,* she came in, dressed *de la même robe bleue avec le* shiny *ruban doré dans les cheveux. Capturé par son charme, je* couldn't hear *la musique* or see *les autres patineurs. Je* could only see her.

La pratique came *et* went in *un flash.* Soon *les patineurs* left *la patinoire et Camille* was alone. *Je* walked down the stairs *un peu incertain.* She greeted me with a bright *sourire et* said:

—*Bonjour Monsieur, comment allez-vous?*

—*Bien, merci, et vous?*

—*Très bien. Comment avez-vous trouvé la pratique?*

—*Comment?*

—*Avez-vous aimé la pratique?*

—*Oh oui, mademoiselle. Vous étiez magnifique!*

Her *visage* turned *rouge.*

—*Je* meant to say, *vous all…tous étiez magnifiques!*

—*Merci du compliment. Vous êtes bien aimable.*

—*Travaillez-vous ce soir?*

—*Oui, Monsieur. Mais je finis à sept heures.*

—Would you like to go *danser après le travail? Je* must leave tomorrow…*demain, très* early *et je* would like to see you again before *je* leave.

—*Oui Monsieur, j'aimerais beaucoup* to go *danser avec vous ce soir.*

—Don't call me *Monsieur, appelez-moi Tom.*

—*O.K., Monsieur Tom!*

—*Vous êtes comique.* See you *ce soir.*

À neuf heures, je went to *le restaurant, mais la belle princesse enchanteresse* wasn't there. Where could she be, *je* wondered. *Je* waited *et* waited *mais* no *Camille* came. *Je* didn't know what to *penser. Mon train* was to leave at *cinq heures demain matin.* What could *je* do?

À onze heures, les last *clients* were leaving. *Le restaurant* was going to close *et la patineuse* had not come. *Je* knew *son nom et* that she lived *à Québec, mais je* knew *que je* could never ever find her.

Finalement, à onze heures dix, un Monsieur came to me *et* told me that *le restaurant* was closing *maintenant et* that *je* should go home. *Je* felt *dévasté.*

Why hadn't she come? Why did she act so kind if she meant to stand me up? Maybe it is a *coutume canadienne. Le Monsieur,* seeing *ma confusion* asked shyly:

—*Êtes-vous Monsieur Tom?*

—*Oui!*

—*Attendiez-vous Camille Ferrand?*

—*Oui,* where is she?

—*Elle est venue ici à sept heures, mais vous n'étiez pas là.*

—*Je* thought *que* we had *rendez-vous à neuf heures.*

—*Oh non Monsieur. Elle devait rentrer à Québec par le train de neuf heures. Elle est partie en pensant que c'était peut-être une coutume américaine de poser des lapins aux filles.*

The man left, chuckling. I hadn't understood all that he said but I knew Camille had come at seven and not nine. I wanted to kick myself for not having spent time learning numbers better and missing out on such an opportunity. I sadly promised myself this would <u>never</u> happen again, *jamais!*

End Tape 3, Side A

76

Focus on Action
Concentration sur l'action

Tape off. Do parts A and B on your own. When you're ready to proceed, turn the tape on.

A. SCATTER CHART

Instructions: Familiarize yourself with these pictographs and their meaning.

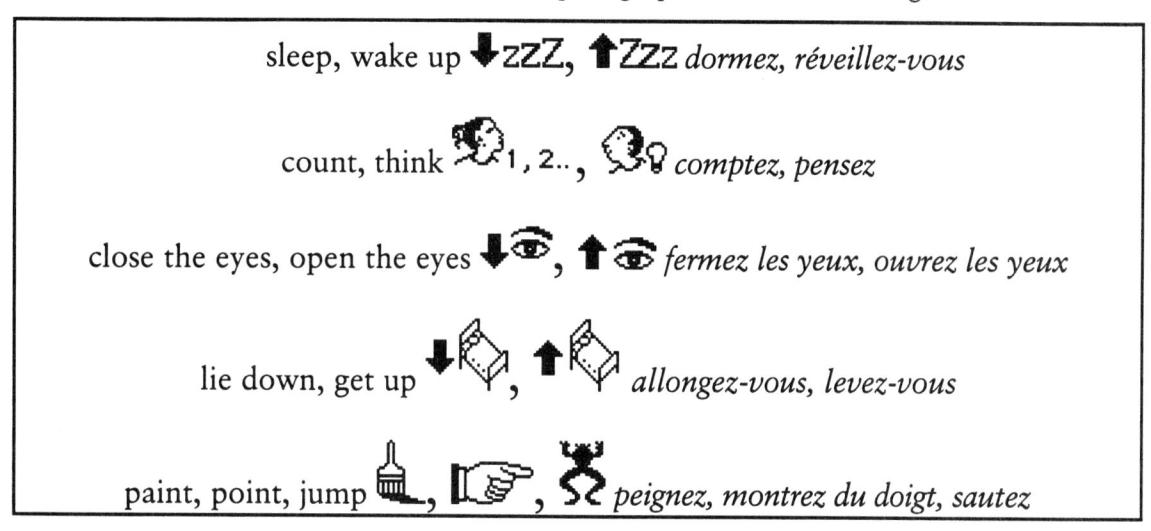

- sleep, wake up ↓zzZ, ↑Zzz *dormez, réveillez-vous*
- count, think 🗣1, 2.., 🗣 *comptez, pensez*
- close the eyes, open the eyes ↓👁, ↑👁 *fermez les yeux, ouvrez les yeux*
- lie down, get up ↓🛏, ↑🛏 *allongez-vous, levez-vous*
- paint, point, jump 🖌, ☞, 🤸 *peignez, montrez du doigt, sautez*

B. SELF-QUIZ

Instructions: Can you interpret these pictographs in French?

Review pictographs

C. Multiple-choice Frames

Instructions: Listen and identify which sector of the frame contains the depicted action(s). [The script is in the appendix.]

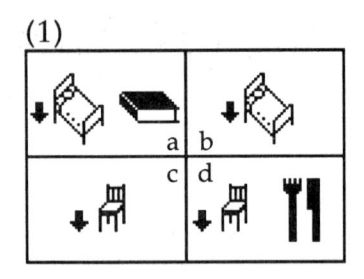

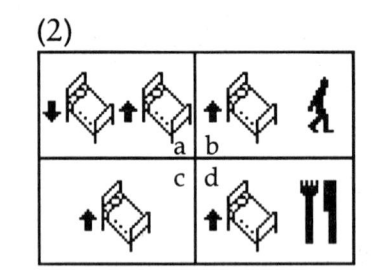

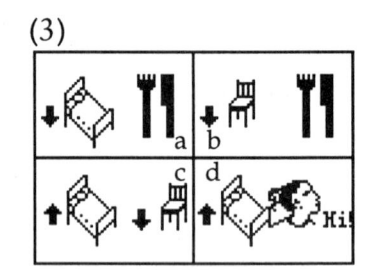

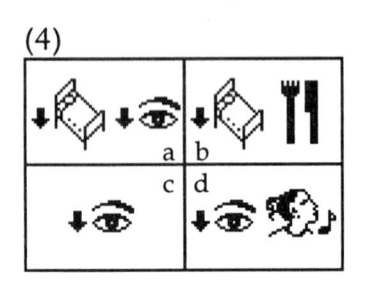

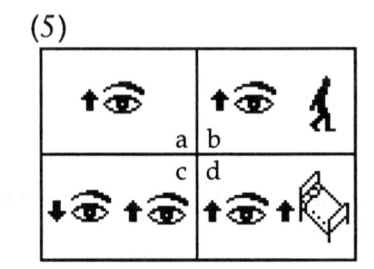

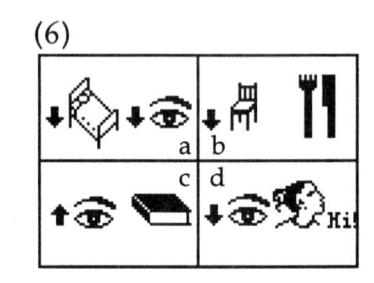

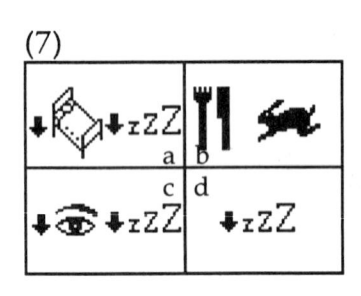

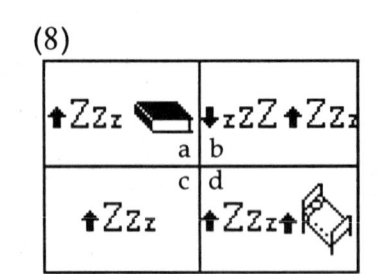

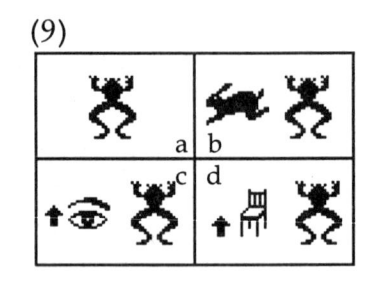

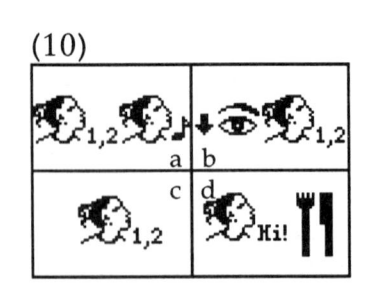

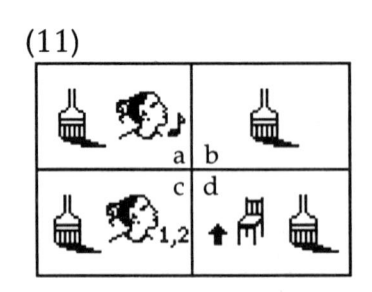

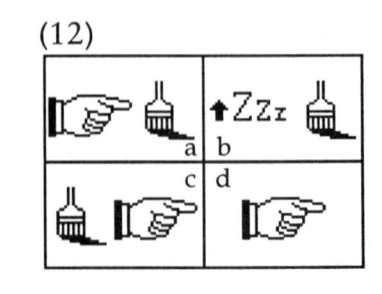

🔊 Focus on Spelling

🧟 *sautez*   🖌️ *peignez*   👉 *montrez du doigt*   🛏️↓ *allongez-vous*

🛏️↑ *levez-vous*   👁️↓ *fermez les yeux*   👁️↑ *ouvrez les yeux*   💭 1, 2.. *comptez*

💭 *pensez*   ↓zZZ *dormez*   ↑Zzz *réveillez-vous*

📼 D. Listen and Anticipate the Response

(1) 👨 + 🖌️   (2) 👩 + 👉

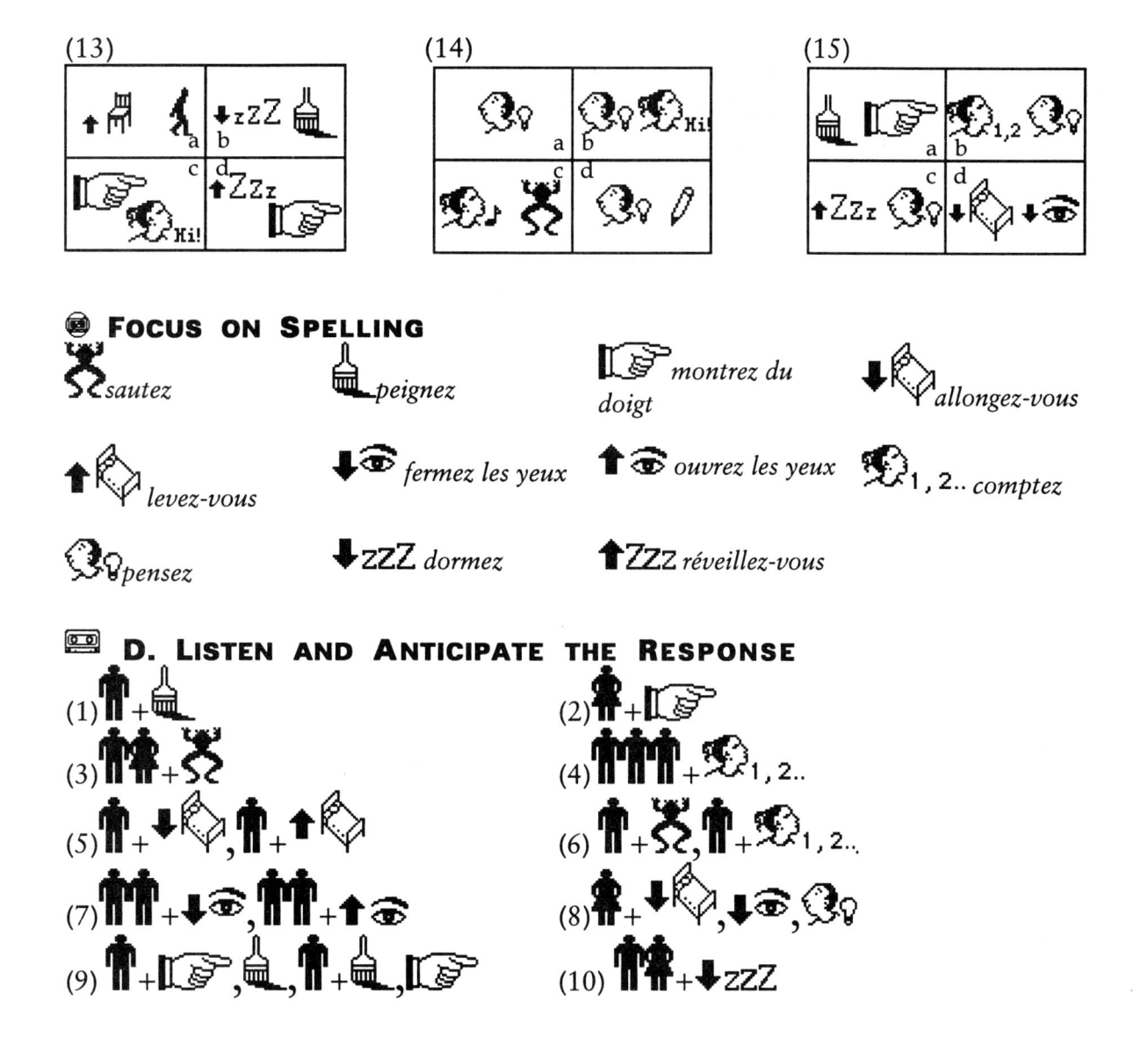

(3) 👨👩 + 🧟   (4) 👨👨👨 + 💭 1, 2..

(5) 👨 + 🛏️↓, 👨 + 🛏️↑   (6) 👨 + 🧟, 👨 + 💭 1, 2..

(7) 👨👨 + 👁️↓, 👨👨 + 👁️↑   (8) 👩 + 🛏️↓, 👁️↓, 💭

(9) 👨 + 👉, 🖌️, 👨 + 🖌️, 👉   (10) 👨👩 + ↓zZZ

Questions and Responses Tied to Pictographs

Instructions: Cover the question and response column. See if you can formulate a question asking what the people are doing in the present tense, future, and past progressive ("was [VERB]ing"). Then answer the question. Check the question and response columns to see if you are correct.

	Pictograph	Question	Response
1.	👨 + 🖌️	*Que fait cet homme?* *Que va faire cet homme?* *Que faisait cet homme?*	*Il peint.* *Il va peindre.* *Il peignait.*
2.	👩 + 👉	*Que fait cette femme?* *Que va faire cette femme?* *Que faisait cette femme?*	*Elle montre du doigt.* *Elle va montrer du doigt.* *Elle montrait du doigt.*
3.	👨👩 + 🧟	*Que font ces gens?* *Que vont faire ces gens?* *Que faisaient ces gens?*	*Les deux sautent.* *Les deux vont sauter.* *Les deux sautaient.*

4.		*Que font ces gens?*	*Ils comptent tous.*
		Que vont faire ces gens?	*Ils vont tous compter.*
		Que faisaient ces gens?	*Ils comptaient tous.*
5.		*Que font ces gens?*	*L'un s'allonge et l'autre se lève.*
		Que vont faire ces gens?	*L'un va s'allonger et l'autre va se lever.*
		Que faisaient ces gens?	*L'un s'allongeait et l'autre se levait.*
6.		*Que font ces gens?*	*L'un saute et l'autre compte.*
		Que vont faire ces gens?	*L'un va sauter et l'autre va compter.*
		Que faisaient ces gens?	*L'un sautait et l'autre comptait.*
7.		*Que font ces gens?*	*Deux ferment les yeux et deux ouvrent les yeux.*
		Que vont faire ces gens?	*Deux vont fermer les yeux et deux vont ouvrir les yeux.*
		Que faisaient ces gens?	*Deux fermaient les yeux et deux ouvraient les yeux.*
8.		*Que fait cette femme?*	*Elle s'allonge, ferme les yeux, et pense.*
		Que va faire cette femme?	*Elle va s'allonger, fermer les yeux et penser.*
		Que faisait cette femme?	*Elle s'allongeait, fermait les yeux et pensait.*
9.		*Que font ces gens?*	*L'un montre du doigt et peint et l'autre peint et montre du doigt.*
		Que vont faire ces gens?	*L'un va montrer du doigt et peindre et l'autre va peindre et montrer du doigt.*
		Que faisaient ces gens?	*L'un montrait du doigt et peignait et l'autre peignait et montrait du doigt.*
10.		*Que font ces gens?*	*Ils dorment ensemble.*
		Que vont faire ces gens?	*Les deux vont dormir.*
		Que faisaient ces gens?	*Les deux dormaient.*

E. ACT OUT OR PANTOMIME WHAT YOU HEAR

Instructions: Pantomime what is called out on the tape. The script is in the appendix.

F. READ AND PERFORM THE ACTION

Mangez.   *Sautez.*   *Chantez.*   *Pensez.*   *Réveillez-vous.*   *Asseyez-vous.*
Buvez.   *Marchez.*   *Dormez.*   *Peignez.*   *Ouvrez les yeux.*

Lisez.	*Courez.*	*Levez-vous.*	*Allongez-vous.*	*Montrez du doigt.*
Écrivez.	*Parlez.*	*Comptez.*	*Fermez les yeux.*	*Mettez-vous debout.*

G. Review

Instructions: How many of these can you say in French?

77

🎧 *Une leçon de géographie*
French Only
A Geography Lesson

🎧 Instructions: Listen to and read this geography lesson. Circle all the words you've heard before.

This picture represents the solar system.	🎧 *Ce dessin représente le système solaire.*
In orbit around the sun, there are nine planets.	*En orbite autour du soleil il y a neuf planètes.*
We live on one of those planets, the third from the sun.	*Nous vivons sur l'une de ces planètes, la troisième du soleil.*
We call our planet: Earth.	*Nous appelons notre planète: Terre.*
Like all the other planets, our earth is a satellite of the sun.	*Comme toutes les autres planètes, notre terre est un satellite du soleil.*
It orbits the sun once every year.	*Elle orbite autour du soleil une fois par an.*
The earth has its own satellite.	*La terre a son propre satellite.*
It is called the moon.	*Il s'appelle la lune.*
The moon orbits the earth about once every month, or rather about once every twenty-eight days.	*La lune orbite autour de la terre environ une fois par mois, ou plutôt environ une fois tous les vingt-huit jours.*
The earth has two poles, the north pole and the south pole, delimited by two circles, Arctic and Antarctic.	*La terre a deux pôles, le pôle nord et le pôle sud, délimités par deux cercles polaires, nord et sud.*
The earth is divided into two hemispheres: the northern and the southern hemisphere.	*La terre est divisée en deux hémisphères: l'hémisphère nord et l'hémisphère sud.*
The two hemispheres are separated by a line called the equator.	*Les deux hémisphères sont séparés par une ligne appelée l'Équateur.*
The hemisphere north of the equator is the northern hemisphere.	*L'hémisphère au nord de l'Équateur est l'hémisphère nord.*
The hemisphere south of the equator is of course the southern hemisphere.	*L'hémispère au sud de l'Équateur est bien sûr l'hémisphère sud.*
In the northern hemisphere there are three continents: North America, Europe, and Asia.	*Dans l'hémisphère nord se trouvent trois continents: l'Amérique du Nord, l'Europe, et l'Asie.*
In the southern hemisphere there are four continents: South America, Africa, Australia, and Antarctica.	*Dans l'hémisphère sud se trouvent quatre continents: l'Amérique du Sud, l'Afrique, l'Australie, et l'Antarctique.*

78

📼 A Dream about a Little Girl
Un rêve à propos d'une petite fille

🔘 Instructions: Listen to and read the following story. Work toward full comprehension.

📼 This I saw in a dream:	*Ceci, je l'ai vu dans un rêve:*
a little girl walking down the street came to my house.	*une petite fille, marchant dans la rue, est venue chez moi.*
She came up to the door, opened it, and went in.	*Elle est arrivée à la porte, l'a ouverte et est entrée.*
She entered the kitchen, went up to the table,	*Elle est entrée dans la cuisine, est allée vers la table,*
sat on a chair, put her hands on the table,	*s'est assise sur une chaise, a mis les mains sur la table,*
laid her head in her hands, and cried and cried.	*a mis sa tête dans ses mains, et a pleuré et pleuré.*
And as I looked at her, I also cried.	*Et en la regardant, j'ai pleuré aussi.*
Then she stood up,	*Puis elle s'est levée,*
wiped her tears,	*a essuyé ses larmes,*
went to the door,	*est allée vers la porte,*
opened it, and went out.	*l'a ouverte, et est sortie.*
I watched her go down the street.	*Je l'ai regardée descendre la rue.*
Why she was crying I'd like to know.	*Pourquoi elle pleurait, j'aimerais le savoir.*
Perhaps she had lost a kitten?	*Peut-être avait-elle perdu un chaton?*
Perhaps she had lost a friend?	*Peut-être avait-elle perdu un ami?*
Only she knows.	*Elle seule le sait.*
I think I'll never find out.	*Je crois que je ne le saurai jamais.*

🔘 THE ADVENTURE CONTINUES

You and Stump walk to *L'hermitage* and arrive right on time. An attractive middle-aged woman with a wide, friendly smile seats you at a secluded table and presents you with menus. You ask for her recommendations. She points out the specialty of the house, and you and Stump accept her recommendation. Before the waitress leaves your table, you ask if you can speak with the owner of the restaurant. The woman raises her eyebrows.

"Je suis Isabelle Depardieu," she tells you. "I own *L'hermitage*. How may I help you this afternoon?"

You explain your search and tell Isabelle that Samuel told you to speak with her.

"Hmmm," Isabelle says, pursing her lips. "Yes, I can help you. I will place your orders, and then *on peut parler*—we can talk."

Isabelle bustles toward the kitchen, smiling and greeting customers as she goes. She returns a few minutes later carrying your appetizers.

"Here you go—the best in the house," she tells you. She sets the food on your table with great finesse. "As Samuel hinted, I have your next clue," she continues, "but I cannot give you this clue until you pass my challenge."

She assigns you another series of French exercises and a brief series of culture questions. Then she excuses herself to see to another table. You and Stump attack the wonderful food and the French exercises with equal zeal.

79

🔊 *Dans la salle de classe: une leçon de français*
In the Class: A French Lesson

🔊 Instructions: Listen to and read the following lesson. Translate the English column into French when you feel ready.

🔊 This is my pencil. It's mine.	*C'est mon crayon. C'est le mien.*
It is not yours.	*Ce n'est pas le vôtre.*
Do you have a pencil too?	*Avez-vous aussi un crayon?*
Yes, you have a red pencil.	*Oui, vous avez un crayon rouge.*
This is my pencil. This is your pencil.	*Ceci est mon crayon. Ceci est votre crayon.*

This pencil is mine.	*Ce crayon est le mien.*
That one is yours.	*Celui-là est le vôtre.*
That paper is yours.	*Ce papier est le vôtre.*
Your paper is here.	*Votre papier est ici.*
My paper is here.	*Mon papier est ici.*
Where is the yellow paper?	*Où est le papier jaune?*
It's there.	*Il est là.*

Your pencil is long.	*Votre crayon est long.*
Your paper is long too.	*Votre papier est long aussi.*
But this pencil is short.	*Mais ce crayon est petit.*
Is it yours?	*Est-ce le vôtre?*
That paper is small.	*Ce papier est petit.*
Is it mine?	*Est-ce le mien?*
Is this pencil yours or mine?	*Est-ce que ce crayon est le vôtre ou le mien?*
I believe it's yours.	*Je crois que c'est le vôtre.*
Give me your paper.	*Donnez-moi votre papier.*
Give me a pencil.	*Donnez-moi un crayon.*
Thank you.	*Merci.*

80

Chatter at a Royal Ball
Bavardages au bal royal

GETTING READY FOR CONVERSATION

Instructions: Learn the following new words in French. Then see them used in sentences in the conversation below.

to eat butter	*manger du beurre*	his/her son	*son fils*
He eats a lot <u>of it</u>.	*Il <u>en</u> mange beaucoup.*	his/her daughter	*sa fille*
to delude, deceive	*tromper*	her/his cats	*ses chats*
to deceive oneself	*se tromper*	everywhere	*partout*
to ask	*demander*	at least	*au moins*
to wonder	*se demander*	each day	*chaque jour/tous les jours*
to cover	*couvrir*	usually	*d'habitude/d'ordinaire*
covered with	*couvert de*	he himself	*lui-même*
he always went	*il allait toujours*	fat	*gros, grosse*
happy	*heureux (heureuse)*	then, well then, so	*alors*
unfortunately	*malheureusement*	some cream (from milk)	*de la crème de lait*

fortunately	*heureusement*
If I'm not mistaken (or If I don't deceive myself).	*Si je ne me trompe pas.*
Everyone knows <u>it</u>.	*Tout le monde <u>le</u> sait.*
How disgusting!	*Que c'est dégoûtant!*
It's always the same thing.	*C'est toujours la même chose.*
I wonder ("ask myself") why.	*Je me demande pourquoi.*
He drinks a lot <u>of it</u>.	*Il <u>en</u> boit beaucoup.*
I know nothing <u>about it</u>.	*Je n'<u>en</u> sais rien.*
Cats are the same everywhere.	*Les chats sont partout les mêmes.*

CONVERSATION

••: Who's that fat lady talking with? — *Avec qui parle la grosse dame?*
•: With her cats...and with her son, the fat duke. — *Avec ses chats...et avec son *mari, le gros duc.*
••: Oh, it's the same duke who always went to church. — *Oh, c'est le même duc qui allait toujours à l'église.*
•: He himself. — *Lui-même.*
••: What are they drinking? — *Qu'est-ce qu'ils boivent?*
•: If I'm not mistaken, they're drinking cream. They drink a lot of it. — *Si je ne me trompe pas, ils boivent de la crème de lait. Ils en boivent beaucoup.*
••: Well then, of course they're fat! — *Alors, bien sûr qu'ils sont gros!*
•: What is the duke eating? — *Le duc, qu'est-ce qu'il mange?*
••: Butter covered with chocolate. — *Du beurre couvert de chocolat.*
•: How disgusting! Does he eat a lot of it? — *Que c'est dégoûtant! Est-ce qu'il en mange beaucoup?*
••: They say he eats a lot of it...at least a kilogram every day. — *On dit qu'il en mange beaucoup...au moins un kilo chaque jour.*
•: It's not true! — *Ce n'est pas vrai!*

••:	Unfortunately it's the truth. Everybody knows it.	Malheureusement, c'est la vérité. Tout le monde le sait.
•:	Heavens!	Ciel!
••:	And the cats, what are they drinking?	Et les chats, qu'est-ce qu'ils boivent?
•:	Milk, no doubt. Ordinarily cats don't drink orange juice.	Du lait, sans doute. D'ordinaire les chats ne boivent pas de jus d'orange.
••:	I wonder why.	Je me demande pourquoi.
•:	Who knows? I know nothing <u>about that</u>. Cats are the same everywhere.	Qui sait? Je n'<u>en</u> sais rien. Les chats sont partout les mêmes.

*Note: *mari* should read *fils* on the tape instead.

(Listen to the conversation again in French only.)

◉ TASK

Use your hands as puppets and dramatize the dialogue, <u>looking only at the English</u>. Aim for "Frenchiness" and fluency.

A servant answers her small child's questions

•:	Mama, why is it that the duke and duchess are so fat?	Maman, pourquoi est-ce que le duc et la duchesse sont si gros?
••:	It's because they eat a lot of butter.	C'est parce qu'ils mangent beaucoup de beurre.
•:	Why do they eat a lot of butter?	Pourquoi est-ce qu'ils mangent beaucoup de beurre?
••:	It's because they like to eat it.	C'est parce qu'ils aiment en manger.
•:	And you, do you like to eat butter?	Et toi, est-ce que tu aimes manger du beurre?
••:	No, daughter, I don't like to eat butter.	Non, ma fille, je n'aime pas manger de beurre.
•:	Why not?	Pourquoi pas?
••:	Because I don't want to be fat.	Parce que je ne veux pas être grosse.

81

Focus on the Language 40–44
Concentration sur la langue 40-44

FOCUS 40

Adjective-Noun Gender agreement review: *gros, grosse, bon, bonne.*

1.	The duke is fat (good).	*Le duc est gros (bon).*
	The fat (good) duke is here.	*Le gros (bon) duc est ici.*
2.	The duchess is fat (good).	*La duchesse est grosse (bonne).*
	The fat (good) duchess is here.	*La grosse (bonne) duchesse est ici.*

Nouns have inherent masculine or feminine gender, but words that modify nouns (such as *le* and *la*, *ce* and *cette*) do not. Many have one form when they go with a masculine noun and another when they go with a feminine noun. Such words reflect the gender of the noun they modify. Adjectives such as "fat, good, big, first," which limit or describe a noun must similarly reflect the gender of the noun they modify.

Often the difference between the masculine and feminine forms of such words parallels that between *gros* and *grosse*, *bon* and *bonne*, the feminine form having a final *e* and the preceding consonant being doubled. But two-syllable adjectives don't double the consonant: *petit* (m) and *petite* (f), *content* (m) and *contente* (f). Some differ more radically: *beau* (m) and *belle* (f).

Translate Orally from and into French

The fat son sings.	*Le gros fils chante.*
The fat daughter plays.	*La grosse fille joue.*
The father is fat.	*Le père est gros.*
The mother is not fat.	*La mère n'est pas grosse.*
He is good and she is good.	*Il est bon et elle est bonne.*
The handsome duke doesn't ever dance.	*Le beau duc ne danse jamais.*
The beautiful duchesse doesn't either.	*La belle duchesse non plus.*
The good king is content.	*Le bon roi est content.*
And the good queen is content too.	*Et la bonne reine est contente aussi.*

FOCUS 40A

Possessive pronouns: *sa* with feminine, *ses* with plural.

1a.	He and the daughter.	*Lui et la fille.*
1b.	He and <u>his</u> daughter.	*Lui et <u>sa</u> fille.*
1c.	She and <u>her</u> daughter.	*Elle et <u>sa</u> fille.*
2a.	He and the daughters.	*Lui et les filles.*
2b.	He and <u>his</u> daughters.	*Lui et <u>ses</u> filles.*

Possessive pronouns (his, her, my, etc.) in French reflect the gender of a singular thing possessed. If what is possessed is of feminine gender (*la reine, la tour*) the pronoun has the feminine form *sa* (in 1b, 1c). If what is possessed is plural, the possessive pronoun has the plural form *ses* (in 2b). You can see the parallel of *sa*, *ses* with *la*, *les*. Notice that *sa* translates both "his" and "her." *Ses* and *ces* "these" are both pronounced [se].

Translate Orally from and into French

The duke and his wife.	*Le duc et sa femme.*
The duke and his daughter.	*Le duc et sa fille.*
The king and his daughters.	*Le roi et ses filles.*
The duke and his mother.	*Le duc et sa mère.*
The duke and his grandmother.	*Le duc et sa grand-mère.*
The duke and his sister.	*Le duc et sa sœur.*
The queen and her sisters.	*La reine et ses sœurs.*
The duchess and her daughter.	*La duchesse et sa fille.*

FOCUS 40B

Possessive pronouns: *son* with masculine, *ses* with plural.

1a.	He and the son.	*Lui et le fils.*
1b.	He and <u>his</u> son.	*Lui et <u>son</u> fils.*
1c.	She and <u>her</u> son.	*Elle et <u>son</u> fils.*
2a.	He and the sons.	*Lui et les fils.*
2b.	He and <u>his</u> sons.	*Lui et <u>ses</u> fils.*

Where the thing possessed is of masculine gender (*le roi, le tambour*), the pronoun has the masculine form *son* (in 1b, 1c). Note that *son* translates both "his" and "her."

Translate Orally from and into French

The duke and his son.	*Le duc et son fils.*
The duke and his wife.	*Le duc et sa femme.*
The duke and his wives.	*Le duc et ses femmes.*
The duchess and her son.	*La duchesse et son fils.*
The duchess and her daughter.	*La duchesse et sa fille.*
The queen and her brothers.	*La reine et ses frères.*

FOCUS 41

Possessive pronouns: *ma, mes, mon* "my."

1.	She's my daughter.	*Elle est ma fille.*
2.	They are my sons and daughters.	*Ils sont mes fils et mes filles.*
3.	He is my son.	*Il est mon fils.*

Whereas English has only the one form "my," French has three forms: *ma, mes* and *mon*. You can see the parallel between *ma:sa*; *mes:ses*; and *mon:son*.

Translate Orally from and into French

He is my brother.	*Il est mon frère* (or *C'est mon frère*).
His name is Pierre.	*Son nom est Pierre.*
My name is Richard.	*Mon nom est Richard.*
She is my sister.	*Elle est ma sœur* (or *C'est ma sœur*).
Her name is Marie.	*Son nom est Marie.*
The duke and his wife.	*Le duc et sa femme.*

They are my children. *Ils sont mes enfants* (or *Ce sont mes enfants*).

Focus 42

Three uses of *même* "same."

It's the same king.	*C'est le même roi.*
It's the same thing.	*C'est la même chose.*
He himself does it.	*Il le fait lui-même.*
I myself do it.	*Je le fais moi-même.*
They themselves do it.	*Ils le font eux-mêmes.*
The king himself does it.	*Le roi lui-même le fait.*
Even if the king does it.	*Même si le roi le fait.*
Even the king does it.	*Même le roi le fait.*

Note the use of *même* with the "stand-alone" pronouns.

he himself	LUI-*même*	(NOT *il même*)
they themselves	EUX-*mêmes*	(NOT *ils même*)
I myself	MOI-*même*	(NOT *je même*)

Translate Orally from and into French

It's the same queen.	*C'est la même reine.*
The queen herself says it.	*La reine elle-même le dit.*
I myself say it.	*Je le dis moi-même.*
It's the same thing.	*C'est la même chose.*
I myself go to church.	*Je vais à l'église moi-même.*
They themselves go to church.	*Ils vont à l'église eux-mêmes.*
Even the queen goes to church.	*Même la reine va à l'église.*

Focus 43

"To wonder, to be mistaken" *se demander, se tromper.*

I wonder. (I ask myself.)	*Je me demande.*
He wonders.	*Il se demande.*
They wonder.	*Ils se demandent.*
I am mistaken. (I deceive myself.)	*Je me trompe.*
He is mistaken.	*Il se trompe.*

Translate Orally from and into French

I wonder if she loves the prince.	*Je me demande si elle aime le prince.*
I wonder if she remembers me.	*Je me demande si elle se souvient de moi.*
If I am not mistaken, he is a duke.	*Si je ne me trompe pas, il est duc.*
Unfortunately, they are mistaken.	*Malheureusement, ils se trompent.*

Focus 44

Generic class: (All) the Americans, the rich, etc.

The Chinese are smart.	*Les chinois sont intelligents.*
Americans are rich.	*Les américains sont riches.*
Elephants are big.	*Les éléphants sont grands.*
Dogs and cats cry.	*Les chiens et les chats pleurent.*

Translate Orally from and into French

Kings talk a lot.	Les rois parlent beaucoup.
Princes eat lots of ice cream.	Les princes mangent beaucoup de glace.
What do kings do?	Les rois, que font-ils?
Dogs and cats can dance.	Les chiens et les chats peuvent danser.
The rich are the same everywhere.	Les riches sont partout les mêmes.
What do cats eat?	Les chats, que mangent-ils?

82

🔊 Talking to a Small Child at the Zoo
French Only
Parler à un petit enfant au zoo

🔊 Instructions: Listen to and read the following story. Make a list of ten new vocabulary words and make an effort to learn them.

Look at this strange animal.	🔊 *Regarde cet animal étrange.*
It is a camel.	*C'est un chameau.*
Do you know where camels live?	*Sais-tu où habitent les chameaux?*
Camels live in the desert where it's very hot.	*Les chameaux habitent dans le désert où il fait très chaud.*
What do you think they eat?	*Que penses-tu qu'ils mangent?*
They don't eat wheat or rice.	*Ils ne mangent pas de blé ou de riz.*
They don't eat fish or meat.	*Ils ne mangent pas de poisson ou de viande.*
They just eat grass, leaves, and thistles.	*Ils ne mangent que de l'herbe, des feuilles et des chardons.*
They especially like to eat thistles.	*Ils aiment en particulier manger des chardons.*
Do you know any story about camels?	*Connais-tu une histoire avec des chameaux?*
Do you know the story	*Connais-tu l'histoire de*
"The Camel Who Took a Walk"?	*«La chamelle qui partit se promener?»*
Someday I'll tell you that story.	*Un jour je te raconterai cette histoire.*
Would you like to be a camel?	*Voudrais-tu être un chameau?*
Why not?	*Pourquoi pas?*
What other kinds of animals live in the desert?	*Quelles autres espèces d'animaux vivent dans le désert?*
Tortoises also live in the desert.	*Les tortues habitent aussi dans le désert.*
What do tortoises look like?	*À quoi ressemblent les tortues?*
They have a hard shell.	*Elles ont une carapace.*
When they are frightened, they hide in their shell.	*Quand elles ont peur, elles se cachent dans leur carapace.*
They carry their own house with them.	*Elles portent leur propre maison avec elles.*
They move very slowly.	*Elles avancent très lentement.*
Have you heard the story	*As-tu entendu l'histoire*
"The Tortoise and the Hare"?	*«La tortue et le lièvre?»*
I'll tell it to you sometime.	*Je te la raconterai un jour.*
Look, there is a tortoise near the camel. Do you see it?	*Regarde, il y a une tortue près du chameau. La vois-tu?*
Camels and tortoises are friends.	*Les chameaux et les tortues sont des amis.*
Do you think they talk together?	*Penses-tu qu'ils se parlent?*
Which animals can speak?	*Quels animaux peuvent parler?*

Can dogs speak?	*Est-ce que les chiens peuvent parler?*
Can birds speak?	*Est-ce que les oiseaux peuvent parler?*
How do they communicate?	*Comment communiquent-ils?*
What language do they speak?	*Quelle langue parlent-ils?*

Can you speak animal language?	*Peux-tu parler la langue des animaux?*
Can you understand animal language?	*Peux-tu comprendre la langue des animaux?*
Is there anybody in the world who can speak animal language?	*Existe-t-il quelqu'un au monde qui puisse parler la langue des animaux?*

If you could talk with a camel,	*Si tu pouvais parler à un chameau,*
what would you like to tell him?	*que voudrais-tu lui dire?*
What would be the first question you'd ask him?	*Quelle serait la première question que tu lui poserais?*

What do you think the camel would ask you?   *Que penses-tu que le chameau te demanderait?*

Would you like to ride on a camel?	*Voudrais-tu monter un chameau?*
If you had to travel in a desert, would you prefer to ride a camel or a tortoise?	*Si tu devais voyager dans un désert, préfèrerais-tu monter sur un chameau ou sur une tortue?*

Or would you prefer to walk by yourself?	*Ou préférerais-tu marcher par toi-même?*
Why?	*Pourquoi?*

A camel is much faster than a tortoise and much stronger.   *Un chameau est beaucoup plus rapide qu'une tortue et beaucoup plus fort.*

Look, that camel has two humps on its back. Do you see them?	*Regarde, le chameau a deux bosses sur son dos. Les vois-tu?*
Do you know what the humps are for?	*Sais-tu à quoi servent les bosses?*

If you ate as much food as a camel does, would two humps grow on your back?   *Si tu mangeais autant de nourriture qu'un chameau, est-ce que deux bosses pousseraient sur ton dos?*

Of course not. You're not a camel.   *Bien sûr que non. Tu n'es pas un chameau.*

83
Des questions posées par un enfant
A Child's Questions

Instructions: Listen to the following conversation. Try to retell it!

Mama, why do you speak French?	*Maman, pourquoi parles-tu français?*
Because I was born in France.	*Parce que je suis née en France.*
Was I born in France?	*Est-ce que je suis né en France?*
No, you weren't born in France.	*Non, tu n'es pas né en France.*
And Daddy, was he born in France?	*Et Papa, est-il né en France?*
No, he wasn't born in France.	*Non, il n'est pas né en France.*
Grandma and Grandpa, were they born in France?	*Papi et Mamie, sont-ils nés en France?*
No, they weren't born in France.	*Non, ils ne sont pas nés en France.*
Why not?	*Pourquoi pas?*
Because they were born in America!	*Parce qu'ils sont nés en Amérique!*

THE ADVENTURE CONTINUES

About halfway through Isabelle's challenge, the rest of your meal arrives. With your appreciation for fine French cuisine increasing by the moment, you return to Isabelle's challenge. You are thrilled with the progress you are making in the language, and you look forward to proving your skills to Isabelle.

84
🎧 A Note of Humor: A Critical Mother
Une mère critique

🎧 Instructions: Listen to and read the following joke. Rewrite the ending in French!

🎧 One day, Charles's mother sent him a present for Christmas:
   two ties, a red one and a green one.
She also wrote him
   that she would come to visit him
   the following Sunday and asked him
   if he'd like to get her at the airport.
Charles knows that his mother is very critical.
He decided to put on the red tie.
When his mother arrived, he welcomed her with a hug.
She said: "Don't you like the green tie?"

Un jour, la mère de Charles lui a envoyé un cadeau pour Noël:
   deux cravates, une rouge et une verte.
Elle lui a aussi écrit
   qu'elle viendrait lui rendre visite
   le dimanche suivant et lui a demandé
   s'il voulait bien venir la chercher à l'aéroport.
Charles sait que sa mère a l'esprit critique.
Il a décidé de mettre la cravate rouge.
Quand sa mère est arrivée, il l'a accueillie par une embrassade.
Elle a dit: «N'aimes-tu pas la cravate verte?»

85

🎦 A Note of Humor: A Polite Rebuke
Une réprimande polie

Instructions: Listen to and read the following joke. Repeat it in French!

One day, an old man was riding his donkey along the road.	*Un jour, un vieil homme menait son âne, le long de la route.*
He met an impolite boy.	*Il rencontra un garçon impoli.*
The boy said:	*Le garçon dit:*
"Hi, donkey's father!"	*«Bonjour, père de l'âne!»*
"Hello, my son," replied the old man.	*«Bonjour, mon fils», répliqua le vieil homme.*

(Listen to the French again.)

86

🎦 *Ma première visite au Québec: quatrième partie*
My First Visit to Québec: Part Four

🎦 Instructions: Continue listening to this diglot-weave story.

🎦 *Le temps passa et* since *je* couldn't get her off my mind, *je décidais de téléphoner à l'hôtel de Bois-des-filion* where *je* had stayed during *la compétition de patin sur glace. Je* knew *que Camille* had *travaillé là* several winters in a row *et je pensais que* maybe, *peut-être je* could get *son numéro de téléphone ou son adresse à Québec.*

Un jour, je gathered *tout mon courage et je téléphonais:*

—*Allô.*

—*Allô, bonjour. Je m'appelle Tom Burr.*

—*Oui. En quoi puis-je vous être utile?*

—*Pardon?*

—*Comment puis-je vous aider?*

—*Oh, je suis un ami de Camille Ferrand et je* wondered if *vous avez son numéro de téléphone...*

—*Une minute s'il vous plaît.*

About *cinq minutes plus tard...*

—*Monsieur Burr?*

—*Oui.*

—*Voici le numéro de Camille. Avez-vous un stylo et du papier?*

—*Oui, je suis* ready...I mean...*je suis prêt.*

—*C'est le 827-57-9845.*

—*827-57-9855.*

—*Non, c'est le 827-57-9845.*

—*OK, j'ai compris, merci beaucoup madame.*

Je felt so proud *de mon accomplissement. Un mois* ago, *je* couldn't have *compris ce numéro de téléphone. Mais, maintenant* after having *étudié les numéros diligemment, je peux comprendre les numéros de téléphone et les heures de rendez-vous! Je* felt *très fier* indeed!

Deux jours plus tard, je décidais de téléphoner à Camille. Je wondered...*me demandais si elle* remembered *moi après un mois. Le* heart *battant, je* dialed *le numéro. Huit, deux, sept, cinq, sept, neuf, huit, quatre, cinq.*

Je let it *sonner quatre fois. Mon coeur battait* so fast, *je pensais que je* might have *une crise cardiaque avant qu'elle* would pick up *le téléphone...*

—*Allô.*

—*Allô...*

—*Qui est à l'appareil?*

—*C'est Tom Burr.*

—*Qui?*

—*Tom Burr...Bois-des-filion...compétition...*

—*Oh oui, je me souviens.*

—*Comment te souviens-tu de moi?*

—*Oh, c'est simple, je me souviens du rendez-vous...*

—*Camille,* don't be angry...*ne sois pas fâchée...*let me *expliquer ce qui s'est passé. Je suis venu* (came) *au rendez-vous à 9h et j'ai* waited *pendant deux heures. Puis un Monsieur est* *venu et m'a dit que tu étais venue à 7h. Je suis désolé, mais je n'avais pas compris l'heure de notre rendez-vous.*

—*Oh, et* all *ce temps, j'ai pensé que c'était une coutume américaine de* stand dates up. *Excusez-moi de* laugh *mais j'avais pensé à* every excuse possible *pour ton absence mais je n'avais jamais pensé à un* misunderstanding, *un malentendu.*

—*C'est moi qui m'excuse de ne pas avoir compris l'heure du rendez-vous mais je te promets que cela* will *jamais* happen again. *J'ai beaucoup étudié les chiffres.*

—By the way, *comment as-tu trouvé mon numéro de téléphone?*

—*J'ai téléphoné à l'hôtel de Bois-des-filion où tu travaillais…il y a une compétition de patin à glace* next month *et je me demandais si* it would *intéresser* you *de venir voir une compétition américaine. Ce n'est pas une compétition importante, c'est juste une compétition locale, mais je* have to be *un des juges et je* would very much like *ton aide et opinion…*

—When *est-ce* exactly?

—*Le 11 et 12 mars.*

—Well, *je suis très* busy *avec l'école et l'entraînement de patin à glace, mais…téléphone-moi samedi prochain et j'aurais une réponse.*

—*Entendu. À quelle heure samedi?*

—*À 7h, compris?*

—*Oui, 7—après 6 et avant 8—j'ai compris. Je te téléphonerai à 7h précises, samedi prochain.*

—*Au revoir Monsieur Tom.*

—*Au revoir Camille.*

Le following *samedi, à 7h précises…*

—*Allô.*

—*Allô, Camille, c'est Tom.*

—*Comment vas-tu Tom?*

—*Bien, merci, et toi?*

—*Très bien. Je suppose que tu* want to know *ma réponse pour la compétition à Rochester le mois prochain…en mars.*

—*Oui, bien sûr que je veux savoir ta réponse.*

—*Et bien, j'ai demandé à mes parents et ils sont d'accord.*

—*Super! Je suis très content.*

—*J'arriverai le soir du 10 mars, à 9 heures à l'aéroport de Rochester. C'est bon?*

—*Oui, le 10 mars, à 9 heures du soir à l'aéroport de Rochester. Est-ce exact?*

—*Oui, c'est exact. J'arrive* then *dans trois* weeks.

—*Très bien.*

—*Merci pour l'invitation.*

—*Merci de l'avoir acceptée. À bientôt.*

—*À bientôt, Tom.*

L'histoire goes on… *Aujourd'hui, c'est le 10 mars. Notre ami Tom est à l'aéroport depuis déjà une heure et* a half. It was so afraid to be late *qu'il est venu avec 2 heures d'avance. Il est arrivé à l'aéroport à 7h. Il ne voulait certainement pas* miss *cet important rendez-vous avec la belle Camille, la princesse enchanteresse. Il avait beaucoup pensé à elle pendant les deux mois de séparation et se réjouissait à la pensée de* see her again.

Le temps was ticking away *si lentement que Tom pensait que 9 heures* would *jamais* come. *Finalement, 9 heures est arrivé et l'avion de Québec aussi. Les passagers* got off *un par un. Tom* waited *et* waited, *se demandant si* there had been another *malentendu. Il* was about to *partir quand il* heard *la voix de l'ange: Tom!*

La voilà, la belle princesse. Oh, elle est even more *belle qu'avant! Elle* wore *un pantalon blanc et une blouse rose. Elle avait un beau pullover* tied around her shoulders. *Elle* looked *absolument ravissante.*

—*Bonsoir Tom.*

—*Bonsoir Camille. Comment s'est passé ce voyage?*

—*Oh très bien. C'est ma première visite aux États-Unis et je suis très contente.*

—*Allons* to get *tes bagages…*

Une heure plus tard, Tom et Camille were driving off *vers les lumières de la ville. Le* starry *ciel était clair. La* full *lune éclairait la route pour ces deux jeunes amoureux.*

Ce qui s'est passé après cela is left *à l'imagination* of the reader.

87

From Word to Discourse
Du mot au discours

Instructions: Read through this scatter chart. This should be a review of previously-learned French vocabulary.

SCATTER CHART

	il y a	*sur*
prenez	*mettez*	*donnez*
moi		*lui*
voici	*ici*	*là*
est / sont	*est-ce qu(e)...?*	
c'est	*n'est-ce pas?*	*cette / ces*
des	*une / deux*	
blanche(s)		*noire(s)*
couchée(s)	*debout*	
	tige(s)	
elle(s)	*l' / la / les*	*toute(s)*
aussi	*non plus*	*autre(s)*
mais	*petite(s)*	*longue(s)*
et		*oui non*
	ne, n', pas	

Sample Sentences

Instructions: Read through these sentences and see the words you've learned being used in phrases. Note that the starred sentences are grammatically incorrect.

1. Give me the small black rod. — *Donnez-moi la petite tige noire.*
2. Give him the long white rod. — *Donnez-lui la longue tige blanche.*
3. Take this rod and give it to me. — *Prenez cette tige et donnez-la moi.*

4.	Take the white rod and put it here.	*Prenez la tige blanche et mettez-la ici.*
5.	Take the black rod and put it there.	*Prenez la tige noire et mettez-la là.*
6.	Take all the rods and put them here.	*Prenez toutes les tiges et mettez-les ici.*
7.	This white rod is not long.	*Cette tige blanche n'est pas longue.*
		**Cette tige blanche est non longue.*
8.	Aren't these black rods small?	*Est-ce que ces tiges noires ne sont pas petites?*
		**Sont ces tiges noires pas petites?*
9.	No, these black rods are not small.	*Non, ces tiges noires ne sont pas petites.*
10.	These black rods are not long either.	*Ces tiges noires ne sont pas longues non plus.*
11.	This rod is long, but it is not black.	*Cette tige est longue mais elle n'est pas noire.*
		**Cette tige est longue mais c'est non noir.*
12.	That long rod is not (standing) upright, it's lying (down).	*Cette longue tige n'est pas debout. Elle est couchée.*
13.	These white rods are not lying, they are (standing) upright.	*Ces tiges blanches ne sont pas couchées, elles sont debout.*
14.	Don't give me the black rod, give me the white one.	*Ne me donnez pas la tige noire, donnez-moi la blanche.*
15.	Don't put the black one on the white one.	*Ne mettez pas la noire sur la blanche.*
		**Ne pas mettez la noire une sur la blanche une.*
16.	Don't take this white rod.	*Ne prenez pas cette tige blanche.*
17.	Don't take the black rod either.	*Ne prenez pas la tige noire non plus.*
		**Ne pas prenez la noire tige aussi.*
18.	Here is the small white rod. Take it but don't put it on the black rods.	*Voici la petite tige blanche. Prenez-la mais ne la mettez pas sur les tiges noires.*
19.	Take the other two white rods.	*Prenez les deux autres tiges blanches.*
		**Prenez les autres deux tiges blanches.*
20.	Don't give him these rods.	*Ne lui donnez pas ces tiges.*
		**Ne donnez pas lui ces tiges.*

TRANSLATION EXERCISE

Instructions: Can you give the French equivalent for the following? Check your translations against the sample sentences above.

Give him the long white rod. (2)
Take all the rods and put them here. (6)
Aren't these black rods small? (8)
These black rods are not long either. (10)
These white rods are not lying, they are standing. (13)
Don't give me the black rod, give me the white one. (14)
Don't take the black rod either. (17)
Here is the small white rod. Take it, but don't put it on the black rods. (18)
Take the other two white rods. (19)
Don't give him these rods. (20)

End Tape 3, Side B

Tape 4, Side A

88

📼 Focus on Scene
French Only
Concentration sur scène

Description: *Dans ce dessin il y a plusieurs choses. Au centre du dessin il y a une valise. Et debout, à côté de la valise, nous voyons deux adultes (un homme et une femme) d'un côté et deux enfants de l'autre. À l'extrême gauche du dessin, il y a deux maisons. À l'extrême droite du dessin, il y a quatre grands bâtiments, peut-être un centre ville. En haut, il y a un réveil. Le réveil indique 9:05. Au bas il y a une route, et sur la route il y a une voiture et un chauffeur. Devant la voiture il y a un sémaphore ou un feu qui est vert pour passer, orange pour ralentir, et rouge pour s'arrêter.*

Tape off. Follow instructions.

📼 Instructions. Make ten questions about this scene. For example: What is in this picture? Where is the car? Is the clock at the bottom? What is on the left? Is there a suitcase at the top? Write your questions in French using question patterns like: *Qu'est-ce qu'il y a dans…? Où est…? Est-ce que le…est à…? Est-ce qu'il y a…?*

1.

2.

3.

4.

5.

6.

7.

8.

9.

10.

CULTURE QUESTIONS—SECTION FOUR

Instructions: Answer these questions based on your reading. Feel free to check the appendix to find the answers.

1. Name three things that Belgians value.

2. About how many people in Québec claim English as their first language?

3. Of what three things do French people tend to be extremely proud?

4. True or False: French is the official language of the United Nations.

5. Name three of the most popular participation sports in France.

THE ADVENTURE CONTINUES

When you finish the exercises, Isabelle returns to your table. She checks your work carefully and asks how you enjoyed the meal. You assure her that it was delicious, especially a creamy leek soup that you tried.

"Oh, that?" she comments. "A Swiss friend of mine gave me that recipe years ago. It's still a customer favorite."

You ask her if she would consider sharing her recipe with you. She considers for a moment. "Well, you have made it this far," she concedes. "I suppose I could offer a bit of encouragement. Here." She writes out the recipe on a piece of paper Stump plucks from his pocket.

RECIPE: *VICHYSSOISE*

4 leeks (white part), thinly sliced

1 onion, thinly sliced

2 T butter

    5 potatoes, thinly sliced

    4 c chicken broth

    2 t salt

    2 c milk

    2 c light cream

    1 c whipping cream

    snipped chives

Cook leeks and onion in butter until tender but not brown. Add potatoes, broth, and salt. Cook covered for 35-40 minutes.

Rub mixture through a sieve; return to heat; add milk and light cream. Season to taste. Bring to boiling. Cool; rub through fine sieve. Chill before serving. When cold add whipping cream. Garnish with snipped chives. Makes about 10 servings.

THE ADVENTURE CONTINUES

"Merci beaucoup," you thank her when she finishes.

"Pas de quoi," she replies.

"You mentioned a Swiss friend," you comment. "Are you Swiss, then?"

She laughs softly. "Do I look Swiss?" she asks. "No, my friends, I come from Morocco. Have you ever been there?"

You reply that you have not, and you ask Isabelle to tell you about her homeland.

MOROCCO CULTURE OVERVIEW

Greetings in Morocco have a certain ceremonial aspect. In more sophisticated urban areas, men and women who are friends often greet by brushing cheeks or kissing. Most Moroccans greet friends by shaking hands and then placing the right hand over the heart. Traditional Moroccan food is served in one communal dish. People wash their hands both before and after the meal, and during the meal, they eat with their fingers, using the right hand only. Moroccan culture is deeply rooted in Islam, though popular folk beliefs are often incorporated into traditional Islamic practice. Islam is the official religion, and nearly 99 percent of the population belong to it. A hooded caftan, called a *djelleba,* is the traditional clothing. It is worn by men and women.

FACTS AND FIGURES ON MOROCCO

- Arabic is Morocco's official language. Berber and French are also widely spoken and understood. English is gaining popularity as an international language in Morocco.

- Soccer is Morocco's most popular sport.

- The population of Morocco is about 29.6 million.

- Morocco is a constitutional monarchy. The king names a prime minister and other ministers to run the government, but he retains executive authority. All citizens over age 20 can vote.

- Agriculture is the mainstay of Morocco's economy, but tourism is growing in importance.

THE ADVENTURE CONTINUES

"Well, I must prepare the dinner menus," Isabelle comments as she finishes her summary. "You two have more than earned your next clue—eggs. Another African has your next clue. Look for my friend Pierre. He comes from Senegal." Without another word, Isabelle rushes off. You and Stump pay your bill and leave the restaurant.

"I wonder how we're supposed to find Pierre," Stump wonders.

"We'll check the map when we get back to the Pétard's house," you tell him. "I'm sure Zsa-Zsa can help us."

That evening, you, Stump, and Zsa-Zsa check the map.

"That looks like the beach," Zsa-Zsa comments, pointing to the next spot on the map. "Perhaps Pierre is a lifeguard."

You nod. "We'll check on that first thing tomorrow morning."

You and Stump go to the computer room, where you email the submarine captain an update of your progress. He encourages you and asks if you will still be able to make the ten day deadline.

"That's a good question," Stump says solemnly. "Tomorrow's our seventh day, and I don't know how far from the treasure we are."

You email back to the submarine captain that you are unsure. He responds that, if necessary, he can give you one more day. However, he cannot extend his stay beyond eleven days.

Worried but too tired to do more, you and Stump retire for the night.

89
Chatter at a Royal Ball
Bavardages au bal royal

GETTING READY FOR CONVERSATION 10

Tape off. Study the first eight lines on your own. Then turn on the tape.

Instructions: Learn these words. Use them to master the conversation.

to suppose	*supposer*	great	*formidable*
to understand	*comprendre*	he and they	*lui et eux*
to want	*vouloir*	can, be able	*pouvoir*
he wants	*il veut*	he can	*il peut*
to have fear	*avoir peur*	perhaps	*peut-être*
he has fear	*il a peur*		
to know (someone)	*connaître*	the duke alone	*seul le duc*
to know (something)	*savoir*	a little	*un peu*

Sample Sentences

She knows a lot of Chinese (people).	*Elle connaît beaucoup de chinois.*
She knows a lot of Chinese (language).	*Elle sait beaucoup de chinois.*
He speaks French; she speaks <u>it</u> too.	*Il parle français; elle <u>le</u> parle aussi.*
He understands it but doesn't speak it.	*Il le comprend, mais ne le parle pas.*
He can speak it but doesn't want to.	*Il peut le parler mais il ne veut pas le parler.*
She speaks it <u>only</u> at church.	*Elle <u>ne</u> le parle <u>qu'</u>à l'église.*

CONVERSATION 10

Instructions: Try to recite the French on your own!

••: Only the duke speaks Chinese, right?	*Seul le duc parle chinois, n'est-ce pas?*
•: No. He doesn't speak it. Perhaps he understands it a little.	*Non. Il ne le parle pas. Peut-être il le comprend un peu.*
••: I suppose he <u>can</u> speak it, but he doesn't <u>want</u> to speak it.	*Je suppose qu'il <u>peut</u> le parler, mais il ne <u>veut</u> pas le parler.*
•: Oh, that's possible.	*Oh, c'est possible.*
••: It's the princess that speaks it well.	*C'est la princesse qui le parle bien.*
•: But she doesn't speak it often; she speaks it only at church.	*Mais elle ne le parle pas souvent; elle ne le parle qu'à l'église.*
••: I believe she likes to speak it there, but she doesn't like to speak it in the palace.	*Je crois qu'elle aime le parler à l'église, mais elle n'aime pas le parler dans le palais.*
•: With good reason. The king detests it.	*Elle a de bonnes raisons. Le roi le déteste.*
••: And with whom does she speak Chinese at the church?	*Et avec qui parle-t-elle chinois à l'église?*
•: Oh, she knows many Chinese who go to church with her.	*Oh, elle connaît beaucoup de chinois qui vont à l'église avec elle.*
••: And she talks it with them?	*Et elle le parle avec eux?*
•: I believe so.	*Je crois que oui.*
••: Great!	*Formidable!*

(Now listen to the conversation in French.)

Focus on the Language 45–49

Concentration sur la langue 45-49

FOCUS 45

la, le, l', les (feminine vs. masculine object pronouns)

1.	The king doesn't like the duchess.	*Le roi n'aime pas <u>la</u> duchesse.*
	He detests her.	*Il <u>la</u> déteste.*
	BUT NOT:	**Il <u>le</u> déteste.*
2.	The queen does not like the duke.	*La reine n'aime pas <u>le</u> duc.*
	She detests him.	*Elle <u>le</u> déteste.*
	BUT NOT:	**Elle <u>la</u> déteste.*
3.	He loves her.	*Il <u>l</u>'aime.*
	BUT NOT:	**Il <u>la</u> aime.*
4.	She loves him.	*Elle <u>l</u>'aime.*
	BUT NOT:	**Elle <u>le</u> aime.*

1. Language provides ways to refer back to a noun without using it again and again: The king came. I saw him. He is here. The queen came. I saw her. She's here. Words such as he, him, she, her that substitute for a noun are called pronouns. Him and her are object pronouns; he and she are subject pronouns.

2. French object pronouns have the same form as the definite article.

3. The pronoun that substitutes for *le duc* in 2 above is *le*. It can't be *la*, since *duc* is masculine.

4. The pronoun that stands for *la duchesse* in 1 above is *la*. It can't be *le*, since *duchesse* is feminine.

5. Both *la* and *le* lose their vowel before a word that begins in a vowel (examples 3, 4). You'll always see *Je l'aime*—you'll never see *Je la aime* or *je le aime!*

6. The plural form of both *la* and *le* is *les*. *Il <u>les</u> déteste.* He hates them. *Il <u>les</u> aime.* He loves them.

Translate Orally from and into French

Instructions: Orally translate the following sentences into French and back into English.

The duke is here, but the king detests <u>him</u>.	*Le duc est ici, mais le roi <u>le</u> déteste.*
The duchesse is here, but the king detests <u>her</u>.	*La duchesse est ici, mais le roi <u>la</u> déteste.*
The duke and the duchess are here, but the king detests <u>them</u>.	*Le duc et la duchesse sont ici, mais le roi <u>les</u> déteste.*
The dog is here, and the duke threatens to eat <u>it</u>.	*Le chien est ici, et le duc menace de <u>le</u> manger.*

FOCUS 46

Natural vs. Arbitrary Gender.

1.	The king sees the tower.		*Le roi voit la tour.*
	He sees it.		*Il la voit.*
		BUT NOT:	*Il le voit.*
2.	The king sees the drum.		*Le roi voit le tambour.*
	He sees it.		*Il le voit.*
		BUT NOT:	*Il la voit.*
3.	He sees the tower and the drum.		*Il voit la tour et le tambour.*
	He sees them.		*Il les voit.*
4.	The king knows the duke sings.		*Le roi sait que le duc chante.*
	The queen knows it too.		*La reine le sait aussi.*

1. Whereas nouns such as "king" and "queen" have "natural gender" that matches their sex, nouns such as "tower" and "drum" do not. English uses the pronoun "it" to substitute for "neuter" nouns. The book fell. I saw it. It is here. I gave it a kick. French has no neuter nouns, and no neuter pronoun. Every noun, as explained before, is either masculine or feminine: *le chocolat* and *le secret*, but *la tour* and *la cassette*.

2. As you can surmise from 1 and 2 above, the pronoun that substitutes for any noun must match the gender of that noun. If the noun-in-reference is feminine (as *la tour* in 1) the pronoun substitute must be *la*, not *le*; if the noun-in-reference is masculine (as *le tambour* in 2) the pronoun substitute must be *le*, not *la*. If the noun-in-reference is plural (as in 3) the pronoun substitute must be *les*, not *la* or *le*.

3. In example 4, the pronoun *le* stands not for just a word but for the whole clause "the duke sings."

Translate Orally from and into French

Instructions: Orally translate the following sentences into French and back into English.

The king knows the truth.	*Le roi sait la vérité.*
Yes, he knows it.	*Oui, il la sait.*
The king is making the drum.	*Le roi fait le tambour.*
Yes, he is making it.	*Oui, il le fait.*
He is making the drums.	*Il fait les tambours.*
Yes, he is making them.	*Oui, il les fait.*

FOCUS 47

Entirety vs. part: *le, l', les*, vs. *en*.

1a.	She drinks the milk.	*Elle boit le lait.*
1b.	She drinks it.	*Elle le boit.*
1c.	She drinks it all.	*Elle le boit tout.*
1d.	She drinks milk (or some milk).	*Elle boit du lait.*

| 1e. | She drinks it (or some of it). | *Elle en boit.* |
| 1f. | She drinks it a lot (or a lot of it). | *Elle en boit beaucoup.* |

Focus 23 noted that object pronouns *le, la, l'* which translate "it" (as well as "him" or "her"). In the data above, "it" is ambiguous. The "it" in 1b refers to all the milk mentioned in 1a, whatever the amount. But the "it" in 1e refers to only some of the milk, not a particular amount. Observe that *le* translates "it" in reference to an entire set amount, but *en* translates "it" in reference to a part of the whole. Often this "it" can be expressed as "some of it."

Also in Focus 46, note was taken of the pronoun *les* which translates "them." Now observe that "them" (like "it") is ambiguous in English. Not so in French, where it is translated by *les* or *en*.

2a.	He eats the chocolates.	*Il mange les chocolats.*
2b.	He eats them.	*Il les mange.*
2c.	He eats chocolates.	*Il mange des chocolats.*
2d.	He eats them.	*Il en mange.*

The "them" in 2b refers to the chocolates mentioned in 2a, a set quantity in the speaker's mind. The French has *les* for "them" in 2b. The "them" in 2d refers to chocolates in general, not a specific set of them. The French for "them" in this case is *en*, meaning not all of the chocolates in the world, not all of any specific quantity in mind, but only a part of the whole. Note that *les* translates "them" in reference to a whole amount, but *en* translates "them" in reference to a part of the whole. Note the relationship in the four sentences between *les* and *les* (2a, 2b) and *des* and *en* (2c, 2d).

Practice 1

Instructions: Determine which word is appropriate to translate the word "it" (*le* or *en*) or "them" (*les* or *en*). The answers are in the appendix.

1. He likes butter. He eats it.   ( )
2. Where is the butter I bought? He ate it.   ( )
3. He buys chocolates. He eats a lot of them.   ( )
4. He knows three hymns. He loves to sing them.   ( )
5. He has many favorite hymns. He loves to sing them.   ( )
6. He loves many of the hymns. He sings them.   ( )
7. He drinks a lot of milk. He drinks it every day.   ( )
8. He bought a quart of milk and drank it.   ( )
9. He bought eight litres of wine and drank it in two days.   ( )
10. He bought a barrel of wine and drank it every day.   ( )
11. He bought five hamburgers and ate them in one sitting.   ( )
12. He often buys five hamburgers and eats them.   ( )
13. He likes peanuts. He eats them by the handful.   ( )
14. He only knows three poems, but he recites them every day.   ( )
15. Who stole my milk. Marie stole it.   ( )
16. He buys chocolates every day. He eats them.   ( )
17. He buys chocolate every day. He eats it.   ( )

Translate Orally from and into French

Instructions: Orally translate the following sentences into French and back into English.

He is singing funeral chants.	*Il chante des chants funèbres.*
He sings them often.	*Il en chante souvent.*
He loves to sing them.	*Il aime en chanter.*
She sings only two funeral chants.	*Elle ne chante que deux chants funèbres.*
She sings them often.	*Elle les chante souvent.*
She loves to sing them.	*Elle aime les chanter.*
He drinks milk; he drinks it a lot.	*Il boit du lait; il en boit beaucoup.*
He is drinking it now.	*Il en boit maintenant.*
He has chocolates. He eats them.	*Il a des chocolats. Il en mange.*
He has some chocolate. He eats it.	*Il a du chocolat. Il en mange.*

Did you happen to notice?

1. Statements with *de la, du,* or *des* (indicating "some") use only *de* when negated: *Il boit du lait.* 'He drinks {of the} milk. BUT: *Il ne boit pas de lait.* "He doesn't drink {of} milk."

2. If a word suggests a partial amount of an indefinite quantity, *de* alone is used: *Il boit beaucoup de lait.* "He drinks a lot of milk." *Il mange assez de chocolat.* "He eats enough chocolate."

Translate Orally from and into French

Instructions: Orally translate the following sentences into French and back into English.

She drinks milk.	*Elle boit du lait.*
She drinks a lot of milk.	*Elle boit beaucoup de lait.*
He doesn't drink milk.	*Il ne boit pas de lait.*

Focus 48

Object Pronouns and Reflexive Pronouns.

1a.	She sees me.	*Elle me voit.*
1b.	I see myself.	*Je me vois.*
2a.	He sees him.	*Il le voit.*
2b.	He sees himself.	*Il se voit.*
2c.	She sees herself.	*Elle se voit.*
3a.	They see them.	*Ils les voient.*
3b.	They see themselves.	*Ils se voient.*

The form *me* serves in English and French as an object pronoun (1a). In French, *me* also serves as a reflexive pronoun (1b) that translated "myself."

The form *le* is an object pronoun (2a). *Se* is a reflexive pronoun (2b, 2c, 3b) that translates as "himself," "herself," or "themselves."

Translate Orally from and into French

Instructions: Orally translate the following sentences into French and back into English.

She wonders (asks herself).	*Elle se demande.*
I ask myself.	*Je me demande.*
I am mistaken (deceive myself).	*Je me trompe.*
He is mistaken.	*Il se trompe.*
I am preparing myself.	*Je me prépare.*
He is going to prepare himself.	*Il va se préparer.*
He begins to prepare himself.	*Il commence à se préparer.*
She says she's going to prepare herself.	*Elle dit qu'elle va se préparer.*
She decides to prepare herself.	*Elle décide de se préparer.*

Focus 49

To know a fact, *savoir,* vs. to know or be familiar with, *connaître.*

He knows that 2 + 2 = 4.	*Il sait que 2 + 2 = 4.*
BUT NOT:	*Il connaît que 2 + 2 = 4.*
He knows San Francisco (City).	*Il connaît San Francisco.*
He knew Saint Francis.	*Il connaissait Saint Francis.*
BUT NOT:	*Il savait San Francisco.*
	Il savait Saint Francis.

Though both *savoir* and *connaître* may be translated "know," *savoir* means "know" in a different sense than *connaître*. *Connaître* means "to be acquainted or familiar with." *Savoir* means "to know facts and such." One can *connaître* people, places (*il connaît Paris*), works of art (*il connaît la musique de Bach, les oeuvres de Victor Hugo.*), or a secret (*il connaît le secret.*)

Practice 2

Instructions: Determine which verb is appropriate, *savoir* or *connaître*. Write S for *savoir* and C for *connaître*. The answers are in the appendix.

1. The prince knows the answer. ( )
2. The prince knew everyone. ( )
3. The king knew what happened. ( )
4. The king knew the secret. ( )
5. The queen knows the palace. ( )
6. Who knows the best city? ( )
7. Who knows how many won? ( )
8. Who knows what happened? ( )
9. Who knows if John came? ( )
10. He knows the story well. ( )
11. He knows the music is great. ( )
12. I know John. ( )
13. I know John is rich. ( )

Translate Orally from and into French

Instructions: Orally translate the following sentences into French and back into English.

David knows Jean well.	*David connaît bien Jean.*
He knows that he knows Chicago.	*Il sait qu'il connaît Chicago.*
Yes, he knows it.	*Oui, il le sait.*

He knows Marie but she doesn't know it. She doesn't know him.	*Il connaît Marie, mais elle ne le sait pas. Elle ne le connaît pas.*
Anna knows many things.	*Anna sait beaucoup de choses.*
Marie knows many queens.	*Marie connaît beaucoup de reines.*
Anna knows the princess sings.	*Anna sait que la princesse chante.*

91

📼 Focus on Action
Concentration sur l'action

Tape off. Go through scatter chart (A), then (B) the self-quiz and review of pictographs on your own, very carefully. Then tape on and continue.

A. SCATTER CHART

go to the window, stop 🚶↗, 🛑 *allez à la fenêtre, arrêtez-vous*

smile, laugh, cry ☺, 😃, 😢 *souriez, riez, pleurez*

close the door, open the door ↓🚪, ↑🚪 *fermez la porte, ouvrez la porte*

dance, play, work ♪, 🎲, 🤖 *dansez, jouez, travaillez*

turn on the light, turn off the light ↑💡, ↓💡 *allumez la lumière, éteignez la lumière*

turn off the TV, turn on the TV ↓📺, ↑📺 *éteignez la télé, allumez la télé*

B. SELF-QUIZ

Instructions: Can you interpret these pictographs in French?

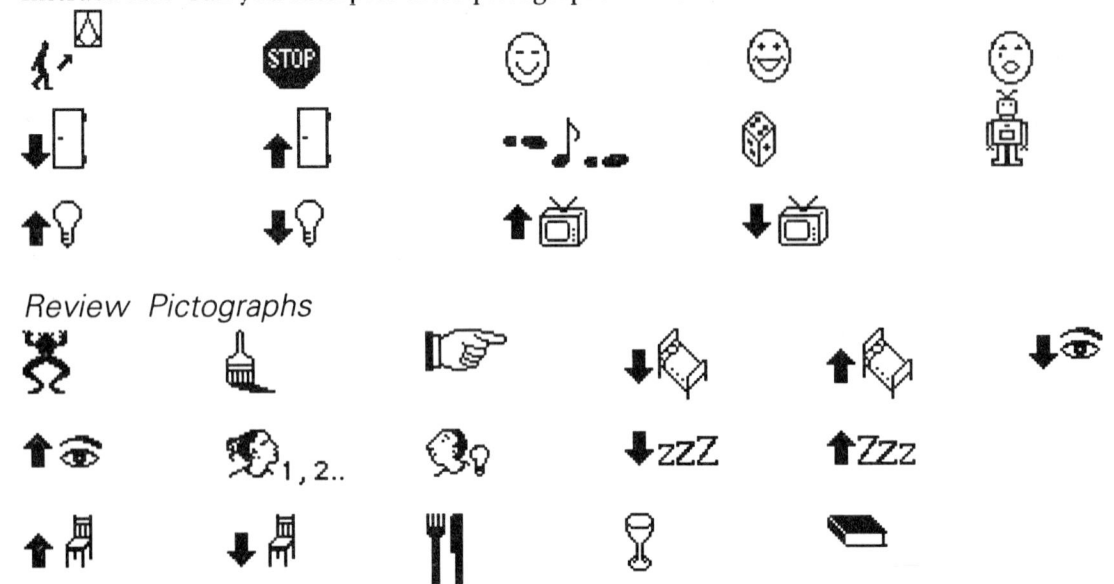

Review Pictographs

C. Multiple-Choice Frames

Instructions: Listen and identify which sector of the frame contains the depicted action(s). The script is in the appendix.

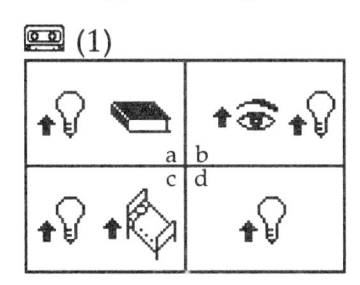

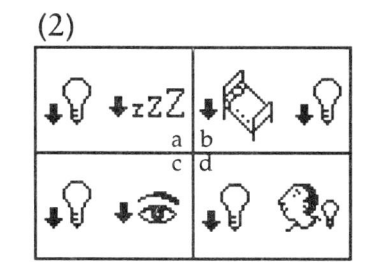

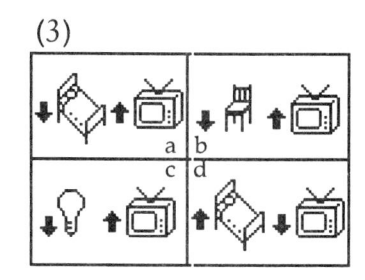

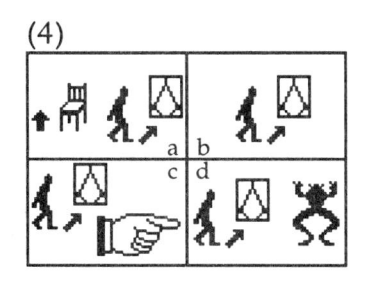

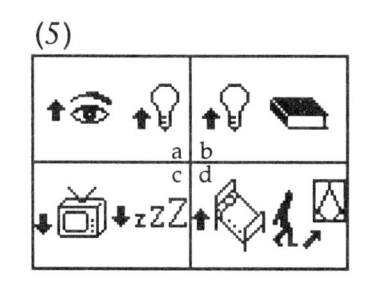

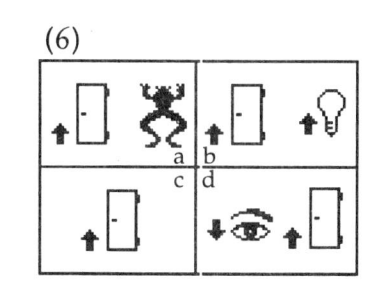

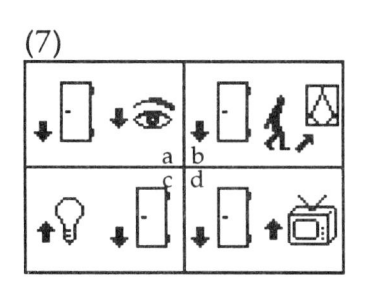

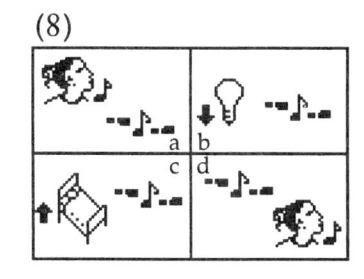

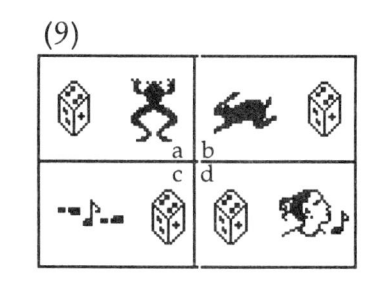

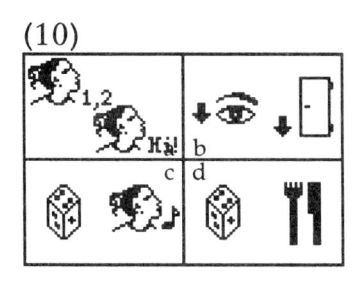

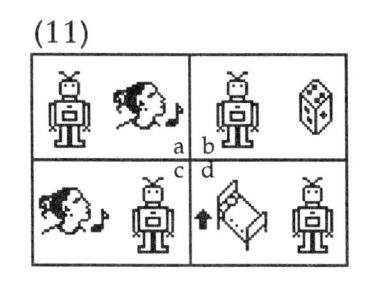

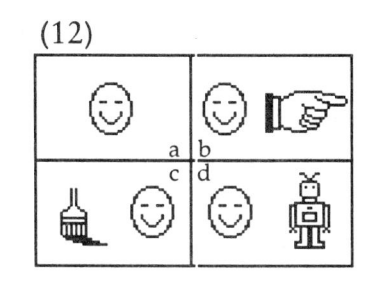

(13) (14) (15)

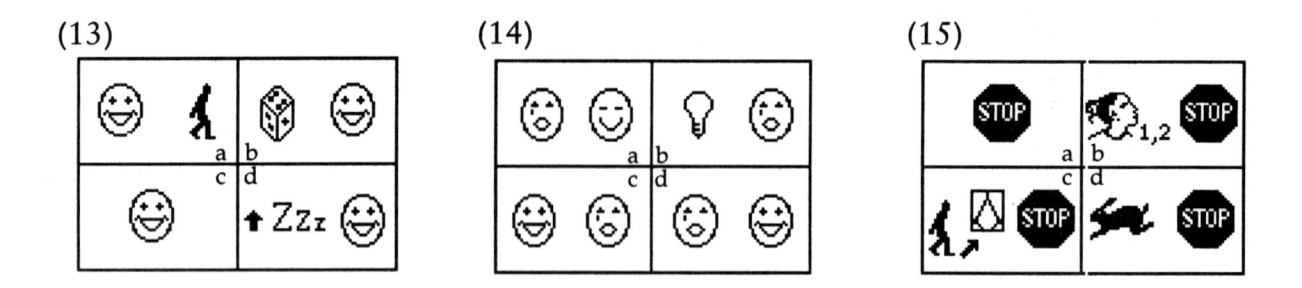

Tape off. Match the pictographs with the written French.

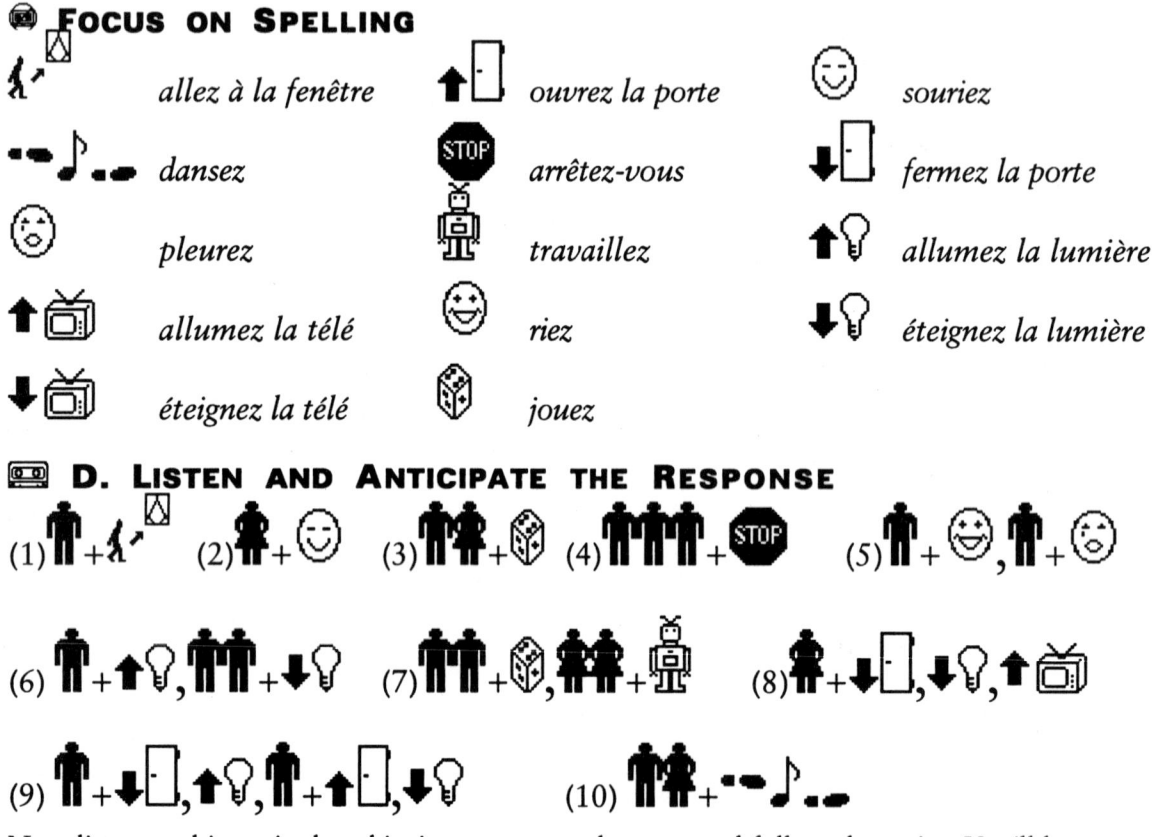

FOCUS ON SPELLING

allez à la fenêtre   *ouvrez la porte*   *souriez*

dansez   *arrêtez-vous*   *fermez la porte*

pleurez   *travaillez*   *allumez la lumière*

allumez la télé   *riez*   *éteignez la lumière*

éteignez la télé   *jouez*

D. LISTEN AND ANTICIPATE THE RESPONSE

(1) (2) (3) (4) (5)

(6) (7) (8)

(9) (10)

Now listen to this again, but this time turn over the page and follow the script. You'll hear three versions: one in present tense, one in future and one in past. Note that French spelling does not always correlate with the expected pronunciation.

Questions and Responses Tied to Pictographs

Instructions: Cover the question and response column. See if you can formulate a question asking what the people are doing in the present, future, and past progressive ("was [VERB]ing") tense. Then answer the question. Check the question and response columns to see if you are correct.

	Pictograph	Question	Response
1.		Que fait cet homme?	Il va à la fenêtre.
		Que va faire cet homme?	Il va aller à la fenêtre.
		Que faisait cet homme?	Il allait à la fenêtre.
2.		Que fait cette femme?	Elle sourit.
		Que va faire cette femme?	Elle va sourire.
		Que faisait cette femme?	Elle souriait.
3.		Que font ces gens?	Les deux jouent.
		Que vont faire ces gens?	Les deux vont jouer.
		Que faisaient ces gens?	Les deux jouaient.
4.		Que font ces gens?	Ils s'arrêtent.
		Que vont faire ces gens?	Ils vont s'arrêter.
		Que faisaient ces gens?	Ils s'arrêtaient.
5.		Que font ces gens?	L'un rit et l'autre pleure.
		Que vont faire ces gens?	L'un va rire et l'autre va pleurer.
		Que faisaient ces gens?	L'un riait et l'autre pleurait.
6.		Que font ces gens?	L'un allume la lumière et les deux autres éteignent la lumière.
		Que vont faire ces gens?	L'un va allumer la lumière et les deux autres vont éteindre la lumière.
		Que faisaient ces gens?	L'un allumait la lumière et les deux autres éteignaient la lumière.
7.		Que font ces gens?	Deux jouent et deux travaillent.
		Que vont faire ces gens?	Deux vont jouer et deux vont travailler.
		Que faisaient ces gens?	Deux jouaient et deux travaillaient.
8.		Que fait cette femme?	Elle ferme la porte, éteint la lumière et allume la télé.
		Que va faire cette femme?	Elle va fermer la porte, éteindre la lumière et allumer la télé.
		Que faisait cette femme?	Elle fermait la porte, éteignait la lumière et allumait la télé.
9.		Que font ces gens?	L'un ferme la porte et allume la lumière et l'autre ouvre la porte et éteint la lumière.
		Que vont faire ces gens?	L'un va fermer la porte et allumer la lumière et l'autre va ouvrir la porte et éteindre la lumière.
		Que faisaient ces gens?	L'un fermait la porte et allumait la lumière et l'autre ouvrait la porte et éteignait la lumière.
10.		Que font ces gens?	Ils dansent ensemble.
		Que vont faire ces gens?	Ils vont danser ensemble.
		Que faisaient ces gens?	Ils dansaient tous.

E. Act out or pantomime what you hear

Instructions: Pantomime what is called out on the tape. The script is in the appendix.

Come on now, really get into this!

F. Read and Perform the Action

Mangez!	Parlez!	Souriez!	Fermez la porte!	Fermez les yeux!	Mettez-vous debout!
Buvez!	Chantez!	Riez!	Ouvrez la porte!	Ouvrez les yeux!	Asseyez-vous!
Lisez!	Dormez!	Pleurez!	Levez-vous!	Allez à la fenêtre!	Arrêtez-vous!
Écrivez!	Comptez!	Dansez!	Travaillez!	Montrez du doigt!	Réveillez-vous!
Marchez!	Pensez!	Jouez!	Allumez la télé!	Allumez la lumière!	Allongez-vous!
Courez!	Peignez!	Sautez!	Éteignez la télé!	Éteignez la lumière!	

G. Review

Instructions: How many of these can you say in French?

THE ADVENTURE CONTINUES

Day Seven—0900 hours

Three Days to Rendezvous

The next morning, you and Stump head for the beach, armed with plenty of sunscreen. When you arrive at the beach, you ask the lifeguard on duty if she knows a man named Pierre who comes from Senegal.

"Mais oui," she replies. "He should be here in about two hours, if you care to wait for him."

You reply that you will. You and Stump spend about an hour reviewing the French that you have learned so far, and then you go for a swim in the island's clear, warm waters. By the time you are finished, a new lifeguard is seated in the lifeguard tower. You approach him and ask if he is Pierre.

"Oui," he replies. *"Je m'appelle Pierre Babin.* May I help you?"

You and Stump explain your search and mention Isabelle's clue. Pierre confirms that he has your next clue. He will give you this clue if you complete his challenge. To no one's surprise, he assigns you another set of French exercises and culture questions. Pierre returns to his post. You and Stump find a shady spot under a cluster of palm trees and get to work.

92

Chatter at a Royal Ball
Bavardages au bal royal

GETTING READY FOR MORE DESCRIPTION

Tape off. Do this first section on your own.

Instructions: Learn these words. Use them. Master the conversation.

listen	*écouter*
among them	*entre eux*
family	*famille*
smart	*intelligent(e)(s)*
those who	*ceux qui, celles qui*
Not everyone speaks.	*Tous ne parlent pas.*
Not everyone speaks it.	*Tous ne le parlent pas.*

MORE DESCRIPTION

••: In the royal family not everyone speaks Chinese. The duchess speaks it, but she speaks it only at church.

•: The duke doesn't speak it, and he understands it only a bit.

••: Of course the Chinese speak Chinese. At least those that go to church speak it.

•: But in the castle where they live they always speak French.

••: Why do they speak only French in the castle?

•: They don't speak Chinese in the castle because the king doesn't like it.

••: It's because he doesn't understand it. The queen doesn't either.

•: In the tower it's the same thing: the Chinese speak only French or Russian among themselves.

••: That's very interesting. The Chinese are very intelligent, aren't they?

Dans la famille royale, tous ne parlent pas chinois. La princesse le parle, mais elle ne le parle qu'à l'église.

Le duc ne le parle pas et il ne le comprend qu'un peu.

Bien sûr que les chinois parlent chinois. Au moins ceux qui vont à l'église le parlent.

Mais dans le château où ils vivent, ils parlent toujours français.

Pourquoi ne parlent-ils que le français dans le château?

Ils ne parlent pas chinois dans le château parce que le roi n'aime pas ça.

C'est parce qu'il ne le comprend pas. La reine non plus.

Dans la tour, c'est la même chose: les chinois ne parlent que français ou russe entre eux.

C'est très intéressant. Les chinois sont très intelligents, n'est-ce pas?

93

Une leçon de géographie
French Only
A Geography Lesson

Instructions: Listen to and read the following story. You will thereby learn geography-related vocabulary.

There are three main oceans on our planet: the Atlantic, the Pacific, and the Indian Ocean.	*Il y a trois océans principaux sur notre planète: l'Atlantique, le Pacifique, et l'Océan Indien.*
The United States of America is located in the northern hemisphere, on the North American continent.	*Les États-Unis d'Amérique sont situés dans l'hémisphère nord, sur le continent Nord-Américain.*
The U.S. shares a border with Canada to the north and Mexico to the south.	*Les USA ont une frontière avec le Canada au nord et le Méxique au sud.*
The United States of America is composed of fifty states; forty-eight are on the continent, one (Alaska) is way up here in the north, and the other (Hawaii) is way out here in the middle of the Pacific Ocean.	*Les États-Unis d'Amérique sont composés de cinquante états; quarante-huit sont sur le continent, un (Alaska) est tout là-haut au nord, et l'autre (Hawaï) est là-bas au milieu de l'Océan Pacifique.*
Alaska is the largest state, Texas is the second largest, and California is the third largest.	*L'Alaska est l'état le plus étendu, le Texas est le second, et la Californie est le troisième.*
California is a famous state located on the west coast, the Pacific coast.	*La Californie est un célèbre état situé sur la côte ouest, la côte Pacifique.*
Los Angeles and San Francisco are two famous cities in California.	*Los Angeles et San Francisco sont deux villes célèbres de Californie.*
The capital of the United States is not New York but Washington, D.C. (District of Columbia).	*La capitale des États-Unis n'est pas New-York mais Washington D.C. (District de Colombie).*
Washington is a city on the east coast, on the Atlantic coast.	*Washington est une ville sur la côte est, la côte atlantique.*
Now here are a few questions:	*Voici maintenant quelques questions:*
How many planets orbit around the sun?	*Combien de planètes orbitent autour du soleil?*
What is the name of our planet's satellite?	*Quel est le nom du satellite de notre planète?*
What is the name of the line between the two hemispheres?	*Quel est le nom de la ligne entre les deux hémisphères?*
How many continents are located in the southern hemisphere?	*Combien de continents sont situés dans l'hémisphère sud?*
What are the names of the continents located in the northern hemisphere?	*Quels sont les noms des continents situés dans l'hémisphère nord?*
Name the three main oceans.	*Nommez les trois océans principaux.*
What two countries share a border with the United States?	*Quels sont les deux pays qui font frontière avec les États-Unis?*
How many states make up the U.S., and what is the capital of the U.S.?	*Combien d'états composent les USA, et quelle est la capitale des USA?*

🎧 Storytime: Little Red Riding Hood
Le Petit Chaperon Rouge

🎧 Instructions: Listen to and read the familiar story. Circle all the French words you have heard before.

🎧 At one side of a woods
in a little white house
lives a little girl
with her mommy and daddy.
The little girl is called
Little Red Riding Hood.
On the other side of the woods
lives her grandma.

One day,
mother calls her little girl:
"Little Red Riding Hood!"
"Yes, mother."
"Grandma is sick.
Take her this basket of cookies."

The little girl takes the basket.
She leaves.
She walks through the woods.
A wolf comes.

*D'un côté de la forêt,
dans une petite maison blanche,
habite une petite fille
avec sa maman et son papa.
La petite fille s'appelle
le Petit Chaperon Rouge.
De l'autre côté de la forêt
habite sa grand-mère.*

*Un jour,
maman appelle sa petite fille:
«Petit Chaperon Rouge!»
«Oui, maman.»
«Grand-mère est malade.
Apporte-lui ce panier de biscuits.»*

*La petite fille prend le panier.
Elle part.
Elle marche à travers la forêt.
Un loup arrive.*

"Where are you going, little girl
  with your pretty little hood?"
  asks the wolf.
"To my grandmother's house."
"Where is your grandma's house?"
"On the other side of the woods."
"Oh, fine. Goodbye, little girl."

The wolf goes to the grandma's house.
He knocks on the door.
And the grandma says:
"Who is it?"
The wolf answers with the voice of a child:
"It's me, Little Red Riding Hood."
"Come in," says the grandma.

The wolf enters.
The grandma sees the wolf.
She gets frightened, and runs out.

The wolf gets in bed and puts on the
  grandma's cap.
Little Red Riding Hood comes.
She knocks on the door.
The wolf asks sweetly
  with the grandma's voice:
"Who is it?"
"Little Red Riding Hood."
"Come in, dear."

Little Red Riding Hood enters.
She sees the wolf in bed and thinks it is her
  grandma.
She says: "Oh, Grandma, you're sick.
Hmmm, and why do you have such big eyes?"
"The better to see you, my dear."
"Why do you have such big ears?"
"The better to hear you, my dear."
"Why do you have such a long nose?"
"The better to smell you, my dear."
"And why do you have such sharp teeth?"
"The better to EAT YOU, my dear."

Little Red Riding Hood cries:
"Oh, it's the wolf.
Help! Help!"
At that moment, the grandma enters with a dog.
The wolf is afraid of dogs.
He jumps out of bed and runs out of the house.
He manages to escape.
Little Red Riding Hood and her grandma and the
  dog eat all the cookies.

«Où vas-tu, petite fille,
  avec ton joli petit chaperon?»,
  demande le loup.
«À la maison de ma grand-mère.»
«Où est la maison de ta grand-mère?»
«De l'autre côté des bois.»
«Oh, très bien. Au revoir, petite fille.»

Le loup va à la maison de la grand-mère.
Il frappe à la porte.
Et la grand-mère dit:
«Qui est-ce?»
Le loup répond avec la voix d'un enfant:
«C'est moi, le Petit Chaperon Rouge.»
«Entre», dit la grand-mère.

Le loup entre.
La grand-mère voit le loup.
Elle prend peur et part en courant.

Le loup se met au lit et met le bonnet de la
  grand-mère.
Le Petit Chaperon Rouge arrive.
Elle frappe à la porte.
Le loup demande gentiment
  avec la voix de la grand-mère:
«Qui est là?»
«Le Petit Chaperon Rouge.»
«Entre ma chérie.»

Le Petit Chaperon Rouge entre.
Elle voit le loup au lit et pense que c'est sa grand-
  mère.
Elle dit: «Oh, grand-mère, tu es malade.
Hmmm, et pourquoi as-tu de si grands yeux?»
«Pour mieux te voir, ma chérie.»
«Pourquoi as-tu de si grandes oreilles?»
«Pour mieux t'entendre, ma chérie.»
«Pourquoi as-tu un si long nez?»
«Pour mieux te sentir, ma chérie.»
«Et pourquoi as-tu des dents si pointues?»
«Pour mieux TE MANGER, ma chérie.»

Le Petit Chaperon Rouge crie:
«Oh, c'est le loup.
À l'aide! À l'aide!»
À ce moment, la grand-mère entre avec un chien.
Le loup a peur des chiens.
Il saute du lit et sort en courant de la maison.
Il réussit à s'échapper.
Le Petit Chaperon Rouge et sa grand-mère et le chien
  mangent tous les biscuits.

95
A Child's Questions
Des questions posées par un enfant

Instructions: Listen to and read the following conversation. Recite the French on your own!

Mama, why do we have two cars?	*Maman, pourquoi avons-nous deux voitures?*
Because Daddy and I each need one.	*Parce que Papa et moi en avons besoin chacun d'une.*
Why does Daddy need a car?	*Pourquoi est-ce que Papa a besoin d'une voiture.*
Because he has to drive to work.	*Parce qu'il doit conduire pour aller au travail.*
Why do you need a car?	*Pourquoi est-ce que toi, tu as besoin d'une voiture?*
Because I have to do the shopping.	*Parce que je dois aller faire les commissions.*
Why don't I have a car too?	*Et moi, pourquoi je n'ai pas aussi une voiture?*
What would you need a car for?	*Pourquoi aurais-tu besoin d'une voiture?*
To drive to the moon.	*Pour conduire jusqu'à la lune.*
Oh, don't be silly!	*Oh, ne sois pas bête!*

96

What a Beautiful Sight!
French Only
Quel beau spectacle!

Instructions: Listen to and read the following story in French only. Do not look at the English column until you have listened to the French at least twice. Then check your comprehension with the English translation.

One day when I was small,
I looked out the window,
and here's what I saw:
   I saw a bird,
   I saw a tree,
   I saw a kite,
   I saw a plane,
   I saw a cloud,
   and I saw the sun.
And the sun shone in the sky.
	*Un jour quand j'étais petit,
	j'ai regardé par la fenêtre,
	et voici ce que j'ai vu:
	   j'ai vu un oiseau,
	   j'ai vu un arbre,
	   j'ai vu un cerf-volant,
	   j'ai vu un avion,
	   j'ai vu un nuage,
	   et j'ai vu le soleil.
	Et le soleil éclairait le ciel.*

The sun was behind the cloud, the cloud was behind the plane, the plane was behind the kite, the kite was behind the tree, the tree was behind the bird. And I thought: "What a beautiful sight!"	*Le soleil était derrière le nuage, le nuage était derrière l'avion, l'avion était derrière le cerf-volant, le cerf-volant était derrière l'arbre, l'arbre était derrière l'oiseau. Et j'ai pensé: «Quel beau spectacle!»*

I blinked and looked again,
and here is what I saw:
   I saw the same bird,
   I saw the same tree,
   I saw the same kite,
   I saw the same plane,
   I saw the same cloud,
   and I saw the same sun.
But now…
	*J'ai cligné des yeux et regardé à nouveau,
	et voici ce que j'ai vu:
	   j'ai vu le même oiseau,
	   j'ai vu le même arbre,
	   j'ai vu le même cerf-volant,
	   j'ai vu le même avion,
	   j'ai vu le même nuage,
	   et j'ai vu le même soleil.
	Mais maintenant…*

The bird was in front of the tree, the tree was in front of the kite, the kite was in front of the plane, the plane was in front of the cloud, the cloud was in front of the sun. And the sun shone in the sky. And I thought again: "What a beautiful sight!"	*L'oiseau était devant l'arbre, l'arbre était devant le cerf-volant, le cerf-volant était devant l'avion, l'avion était devant le nuage, le nuage était devant le soleil. Et le soleil éclairait le ciel. Et j'ai pensé une nouvelle fois: «Quel beau spectacle!»*

97

📼 Storytime: The Three Bears
Les trois ours

📼 Instructions: Listen to and read this familiar story. Circle all the words you've heard before.

📼 A family of bears.	*Une famille d'ours.*
A big bear: the daddy.	*Un gros ours: le papa.*
A middle-sized bear: the mama.	*Un ours moyen: la maman.*
A tiny bear: the son.	*Un petit ours: le fils.*
The morning.	*Le matin.*
The mama prepares breakfast.	*La maman prépare le petit-déjeuner.*
Puts it on the table.	*Le met sur la table.*
Calls: "Daddy Bear, Little Bear.	*Appèle: «Papa Ours, Petit Ours.*
Come and eat."	*Venez manger.»*
The food is very hot.	*La nourriture est très chaude.*
Too hot.	*Trop chaude.*
The Bear family goes out.	*La famille Ours sort.*
They walk in the woods.	*Ils marchent dans les bois.*
A little girl walks through the woods.	*Une petite fille marche à travers les bois.*
She sees a house.	*Elle voit une maison.*
It's the house of the bears.	*C'est la maison des ours.*
She knocks at the door.	*Elle frappe à la porte.*
There is no one home.	*Il n'y a personne à la maison.*
So she enters.	*Alors, elle entre.*
She sees three plates of food.	*Elle voit trois assiettes de nourriture.*
She is hungry.	*Elle a faim.*
She tries Papa Bear's plate.	*Elle goûte l'assiette de Papa Ours.*
It's a big plate, right?	*C'est une grande assiette, n'est-ce pas?*
Ahh! The food is too hot.	*Aïe! La nourriture est trop chaude.*
She tries Mama Bear's plate.	*Elle goûte l'assiette de Maman Ours.*
It's a middle-sized plate, right?	*C'est une assiette moyenne, n'est-ce pas?*
Ahh! It's too cold.	*Aïe! Elle est trop froide.*
She tries Baby Bear's plate.	*Elle goûte l'assiette de Bébé Ours.*
It's a little plate, right?	*C'est une petite assiette, n'est-ce pas?*
Hmm. Perfect.	*Mmmm. Parfait.*
She eats all the food.	*Elle mange toute la nourriture.*
She sees three chairs.	*Elle voit trois chaises.*
She sits in papa's chair.	*Elle s'assied sur la chaise de papa.*
It's big, right?	*Elle est grande, n'est-ce pas?*
Ahh! It's too hard.	*Oh! Elle est trop dure.*
She sits in mama's chair.	*Elle s'assied sur la chaise de maman.*
It's too soft.	*Elle est trop molle.*
She sits in baby's chair.	*Elle s'assied sur la chaise de bébé.*
It's a tiny chair, right?	*C'est une petite chaise, n'est-ce pas?*
Hmm. Perfect.	*Mmmm. Parfait.*
But the chair breaks.	*Mais la chaise se casse.*

She goes to the bedroom.	*Elle va à la chambre à coucher.*
She sees three beds.	*Elle voit trois lits.*
She lies down on papa's bed.	*Elle se couche sur le lit de papa.*
It's too hard.	*Il est trop dur.*
She lies down on mama's bed.	*Elle se couche sur le lit de maman.*
It's too soft.	*Il est trop mou.*
She lies on baby's bed.	*Elle se couche sur le lit de bébé.*
Hmm. Perfect.	*Mmmm. Parfait.*
And she falls asleep.	*Et elle s'endort.*
Now the bears return home.	*Maintenant, les ours rentrent à la maison.*
The daddy looks at his plate.	*Le papa regarde son assiette.*
He says: "Someone has tasted my food."	*Il dit: «Quelqu'un a goûté à ma nourriture.»*
The mama looks at her plate and says:	*La maman regarde son assiette et dit:*
"Someone has tasted my food, too."	*«Quelqu'un a aussi goûté à ma nourriture.»*
The baby looks at his plate.	*Le bébé regarde son assiette.*
"Someone has tasted my food, too.	*«Quelqu'un a aussi goûté à ma nourriture.*
And ate it all."	*Et l'a toute mangée.»*
The little bear cries.	*Le petit ours pleure.*
The bears see the chairs.	*Les ours voient les chaises.*
Papa looks at his chair and says:	*Papa regarde sa chaise et il dit:*
"Someone has sat in my chair."	*«Quelqu'un s'est assis sur ma chaise.»*
Mama looks at her chair and says:	*La maman regarde sa chaise et dit:*
"Someone has sat in my chair, too."	*«Quelqu'un s'est aussi assis sur ma chaise.»*
The baby looks at his chair and says:	*Le bébé regarde sa chaise et il dit:*
"And someone has sat in my chair, too and has broken it."	*«Et quelqu'un s'est aussi assis sur ma chaise et l'a cassée.»*
The little bear cries.	*Le petit ours pleure.*
The bears go to the bedroom.	*Les ours vont à la chambre à coucher.*
The daddy looks at his bed and says:	*Le papa regarde son lit et dit:*
"Someone has lain on my bed."	*«Quelqu'un s'est couché sur mon lit.»*
The mama looks at her bed and says:	*La maman regarde son lit et dit:*
"Someone has lain on my bed, too."	*«Quelqu'un s'est aussi couché sur mon lit.»*
The baby looks at his bed and says:	*Le bébé regarde son lit et dit:*
"And someone lay on my bed, too.	*«Et quelqu'un s'est aussi couché sur mon lit.*
And she is still there."	*Et elle y est encore.»*
The little girl wakes up.	*La petite fille se réveille.*
She sees the bears.	*Elle voit les ours.*
She is extremely frightened and screams.	*Elle est extrêmement effrayée et crie.*
She jumps from the bed and runs out.	*Elle saute du lit et s'enfuit.*
And she never returns to the woods.	*Et elle ne retourne plus jamais dans les bois.*

CULTURE QUESTIONS—SECTION FIVE

Instructions: Answer these questions based on your reading. Feel free to check the appendix to find the answers.

1. Name at least three countries where French is an official language.

2. Name two of Algeria's main exports.

3. Belgians do not serve french fries with ketchup. What do they use instead?

4. How do most Moroccans greet their friends?

5. What is a *djelleba*?

6. What is Luxembourg's official name?

THE ADVENTURE CONTINUES

You do a very thorough job on the exercises that Pierre assigned you. By the time you finish, he is off duty. He joins you in the shade and checks your work.

He nods his approval. "Very good—you pass."

"*Merci,*" you smile. "Isabelle told us you were from Senegal. What's life like there?"

Pierre grins. "Isabelle told me you were curious. Let me tell you about my homeland." With that, Pierre launches into a summary of Senegal.

SENEGAL CULTURE OVERVIEW

Senegal has many ethnic groups within its borders, each with its own history, traditions, and language. As a result, the Senegalese have become a multicultural people proud of their origins. Courtesy is very important in Senegal and is demonstrated through greetings and appropriate table manners. Most Senegalese take great care of their appearance. Many bathe more than once a day, and colognes and perfumes are very popular. Senegalese take great pride in their families and the families' history, and the elderly receive great respect. A little over 90 percent of Senegal's population is Muslim. About 6 percent follow tribal beliefs, and the remaining 3 percent are Christian.

FACTS AND FIGURES ON SENEGAL

- Senegal's population is about 9.55 million and is growing by 3.1% annually.

- French is Senegal's official language, but at least 24 other languages are spoken by Senegal's different ethnic groups. Wolof is the most commonly used of the native languages.

- In Senegal, women who have made a pilgrimage to Mecca wear a white scarf. Men who have made the pilgrimage wear a white turban as well as a white scarf.

- Dakar, Senegal's capital city, is an important port for West Africa.

- Senegal's economy is agriculture-based. The main cash crop is peanuts.

THE ADVENTURE CONTINUES

"There, does that satisfy your curiosity?" Pierre asks with a smile.

"*Oui,*" you respond.

"Your next clue is butter," Pierre continues. "My dear friend Cecile Champion has your next clue. You can find her in the forest. She'll be watching the birds."

"*Merci beaucoup* for your time," you thank him.

"*Bonne chance,*" he replies.

You and Stump return to the Pétard's residence. Stump goes over your clues.

"What on earth are we looking for?" he mumbles. "It sounds almost like a recipe, but I'm sure they wouldn't send us all this way for a recipe."

"Let's email the submarine captain," you suggest. "Maybe he will tell us now."

Stump does as you suggest.

"That information is still classified," the submarine captain writes back. "You will know it when you finally encounter it."

Stump closes the email program and sits thoughtfully in front of the computer. "Well, that was helpful," he comments. You detect a note of sarcasm in his voice.

"Don't worry, Stump," you console him. "I'm sure we'll find it in time."

Stump nods, and the two of you check the map for help on your next clue.

"Uh-oh," Stump comments. "I see a problem. Over here—" Stump indicates an area on the opposite side of the island. "—we have a small subtropical forest. However, the next point on the map is here in the middle of town."

"Hmmm," you say, pondering what Stump has said. "I think we should have a chat with Zsa-Zsa. Maybe she knows what is at that point."

You approach Zsa-Zsa, who examines your map carefully. "Let me see. . ." She squints at the map. "It's just off *Rue de St. Germain*. I believe that's a tour agency. Yes, that's right. They specialize in bird-watching excursions into the forest. Perhaps they know this Cecile Champion."

You nod. "Good thinking, Zsa-Zsa," you comment. "We'll visit the tour agency first thing in the morning."

You and Stump eat a light dinner and spend the rest of the evening studying.

End Tape 4, Side A

Tape 4, Side B

98

🔲 A Geometry Lesson
French Only
Une leçon de géometrie

🔲 Instructions: Listen to and read the following lesson on geometry. Try translating some of the sentences from French to English.

A rectangle, like a square has four straight lines and four right angles, is that not so? Yes, that is correct.	🔲 *Un rectangle, comme un carré, a quatre lignes droites et quatre angles droits, n'est-ce pas? Oui, c'est exact.*
Then what is the difference between a rectangle and a square? Listen. I will explain. A square is one kind of rectangle.	*Alors quelle est la différence entre un rectangle et un carré? Ecoutez. Je vais vous expliquer. Un carré est un genre de rectangle.*
Like any rectangle a square has four sides. But different from other rectangles, the four sides of a square are equal in length. Each side is parallel with the opposite side.	*Comme tous les rectangles, un carré a quatre côtés. Mais à la différence des autres rectangles, les quatre côtés d'un carré sont de la même longueur. Chaque côté est parallèle à l'autre côté.*
Here is a rectangle. This is one side. This is the opposite side. This side and the opposite side are parallel. The top side and the bottom side are also parallel.	*Voici un rectangle. Ceci est un côté. Ceci est le côté opposé. Ce côté et le côté opposé sont parallèles. Le haut et le bas sont aussi parallèles.*
What is the difference between a circle and an oval? In what way are a circle and an oval alike?	*Quelle est la différence entre un cercle et un ovale? En quoi est-ce qu'un cercle et un ovale se ressemblent?*
Can you explain? What color is this arrow? Black or white? It is white. Now look at this arrow. Is it the same color as the first? No it is not the same, it is a different color. It is black. Are the two arrows of the same form? No, not exactly.	*Pouvez-vous expliquer? De quelle couleur est cette flèche? Noire ou blanche? Elle est blanche. Maintenant regardez cette flèche. Est-elle de la même couleur que la première? Non, pas de la même couleur, elle est de couleur différente. Elle est noire. Est-ce que les deux flèches ont la même forme? Non, pas exactement.*

BOXES

Your task is to identify which of the three boxes contains what is described. [Check the appendix for the answers.]

1. Dans quelle boîte est-ce que toutes les flèches pointent vers la gauche?

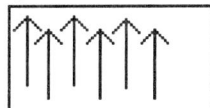

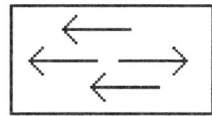

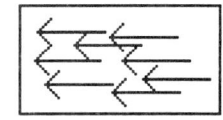

2. Voici trois boîtes. Chacune contient des flèches. Dans quelle boîte est-ce que toutes les flèches sont de la même couleur et de la même forme?

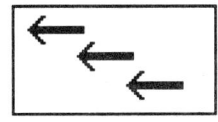

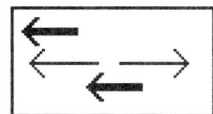

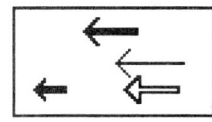

3. Voici trois boîtes. Chacune contient deux figures. Touchez la boîte qui contient deux figures différentes.

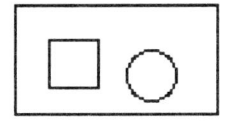

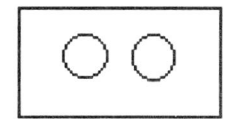

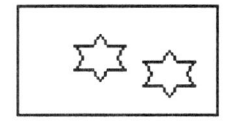

4. Dans laquelle de ces trois boîtes se trouvent deux lettres hors d'une figure et deux mêmes lettres dedans?

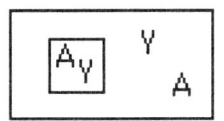

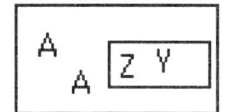

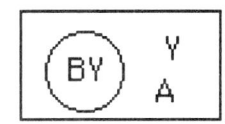

5. Chacune de ces trois boîtes contient deux figures. Quelle boîte contient deux figures de la même forme...deux figures identiques?

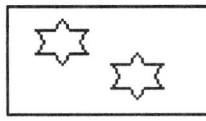

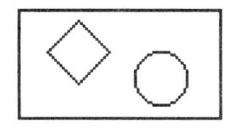

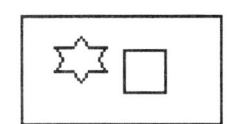

6. Chacune de ces trois boîtes contient des lettres et des chiffres. Trouvez la boîte dans laquelle tous les chiffres sont identiques et toutes les lettres différentes.

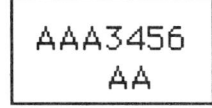

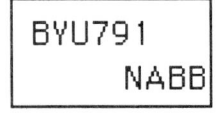

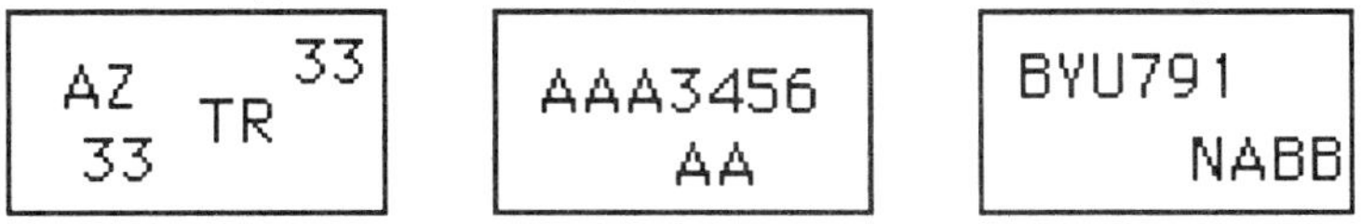

7. Voici trois boîtes. Dans chacune d'elle, il y a un cercle avec une ligne diagonale et plusieurs lettres et chiffres. Trouvez la boîte dans laquelle toutes les lettres sont à droite de la diagonale.

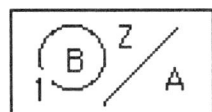

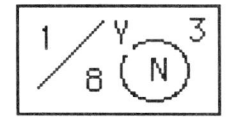

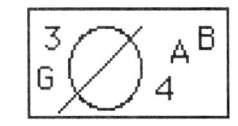

8. Dans laquelle de ces boîtes se trouvent des points et des lignes, mais pas de gros points ni de lignes épaisses?

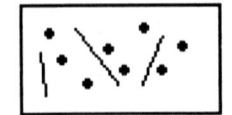

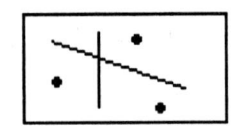

99

📼 *Un petit garçon et une fleur*
A Little Boy and a Flower

Instructions: Listen to and read the following story. Write a list of all the French words you have not used before. Memorize them and create a small story using those words.

A little boy found a pretty flower.	*Un petit garçon trouva une jolie fleur.*
"Because this is such a pretty flower, and because I love my sister, I'll pick it and give it to her."	*«Puisque c'est une si jolie fleur, et puisque j'aime ma sœur, je vais la cueillir et la lui donner.»*
So he picked the flower and took it to his sister.	*Alors il cueillit la fleur et l'apporta à sa sœur.*
"Here," he said, "take this! This flower is for you from me. It says: I love you."	*«Voici», dit-il, «Prends-la! Cette fleur est pour toi, de moi. Elle dit: je t'aime.»*
The sister took the flower and said: "Then we love each other. Thank you, dear brother."	*La sœur prit la fleur et dit: «Alors on s'aime. Merci, cher frère.»*
The sister took the flower to her father, gave it to him, and said, "Here, take this! This flower is for you from me. It says: I love you."	*La sœur apporta la fleur à son père, la lui donna, et dit, «Voici, prends-la! Cette fleur est pour toi, de moi. Elle dit: je t'aime.»*
The father took the flower and said: "Then we love each other. Thank you, dear daughter."	*Le père prit la fleur et dit: «Alors on s'aime. Merci, chère fille.»*
The father took the flower to his wife, gave it to her, and said, "Here, take this! This flower is for you from me. It says: I love you."	*Le père apporta la fleur à sa femme, la lui donna et dit, «Voici, prends-la! Cette fleur est pour toi, de moi. Elle dit: je t'aime.»*
The wife took the flower and said: "Then we love each other. Thank you, dear husband."	*La femme prit la fleur et dit: «Alors on s'aime. Merci, cher mari.»*

Listen again, French only.

100

Une leçon de géographie
French Only
A Geography Lesson

Instructions: Listen to and read the following lesson in French. Pick out ten new vocabulary words and do your best to learn them.

Last time we discussed the general situation of our planet, the earth, in the solar system.	*La dernière fois nous avons parlé de la situation générale de notre planète, la terre, dans le système solaire.*
We identified its geography and briefly discussed the United States.	*Nous avons identifié sa géographie et parlé brièvement des États-Unis.*
Today, I would like to take you on a little trip around a beautiful part of our world. I would like us to visit Europe.	*Aujourd'hui, j'aimerais vous emmener faire un petit voyage autour d'un joli coin de notre monde. J'aimerais que nous visitions l'Europe.*
Here is a map of Europe.	*Voici une carte de l'Europe.*
If you remember, Europe is one of the three continents in the northern hemisphere.	*Si vous vous souvenez, l'Europe est un des trois continents de l'hémisphère nord.*
Let's start with these islands here.	*Commençons par ces îles-ici.*
These are what we call the British Isles.	*Ce sont ce qu'on appelle les Îles Britanniques.*
Here is an easy question for you:	*Voici une question facile:*
What language is spoken in England?	*Quelle langue est parlée en Angleterre?*
English, just like in the United States and many other countries.	*L'anglais, tout comme aux États-Unis et dans beaucoup d'autres pays.*
Just across the English Channel is France.	*Juste de l'autre côté de la Manche se trouve la France.*
What is the capital of France?	*Quelle est la capitale de la France?*
Paris, of course!	*Paris, bien sûr!*
What do you know about Paris?	*Que savez-vous de Paris?*
Right, that's where the Eiffel Tower is!	*C'est juste, c'est là où se trouve la Tour Eiffel!*
Look here, this is a peninsula.	*Regardez ici, c'est une péninsule.*
On this peninsula, we find Spain and Portugal, homelands of the beautiful Spanish and Portuguese languages.	*Sur cette péninsule, nous trouvons l'Espagne et le Portugal, terres natales des belles langues espagnole et portugaise.*
Do you know anyone who speaks Spanish or Portuguese?	*Vous connaissez quelqu'un qui parle espagnol ou portugais?*
This country right here in the shape of a boot is Italy.	*Ce pays-là qui a la forme d'une botte est l'Italie.*
And this one that resembles a hand is Greece.	*Et celui-là qui ressemble à une main est la Grèce.*
Wouldn't you like to live there and swim in the Mediterranean Sea?	*N'aimeriez-vous pas vivre là et nager dans la mer méditerranée?*
I would!	*Moi, oui!*

Right here in the middle is located the tiny country of Switzerland.	Ici, au milieu, se trouve la minuscule Suisse.
An interesting characteristic of Switzerland is that <u>in spite of</u> its small size, it has three national languages: Italian, French, and German.	Une caractéristique intéressante de la Suisse est que <u>malgré</u> sa petite taille, il y a trois langues nationales: l'italien, le français, et l'allemand.
Where else is German spoken?	Où encore est parlé l'allemand?
In Germany of course, but also here in Austria.	En Allemagne bien sûr, mais aussi ici en Autriche.
There is another language that is closely related to German.	Il y a une autre langue qui est étroitement reliée à l'allemand.
It is Dutch.	C'est le hollandais.
Do you know where Dutch is spoken?	Savez-vous où on parle le hollandais?
Yes, here in Holland.	Oui, ici en Hollande.
Next to Holland, we have here Belgium and Luxemburg.	À côté de la Hollande, nous avons la Belgique et le Luxembourg.
These two countries are also French-speaking.	Ces deux pays sont aussi de langue française.
Here to the north, we have what we call Scandinavia.	Au Nord ici, nous avons ce qu'on appelle la Scandinavie.
Five countries are included in Scandinavia: Denmark, Finland, Sweden, Norway, and <u>way out here</u> we have Iceland.	Cinq pays sont inclus dans la Scandinavie: le Danemark, la Finlande, la Suède, la Norvège, et <u>tout là-bas</u>, nous avons l'Islande.
It must be cold there!	Il doit faire froid là!
All the countries <u>about which</u> we have talked so far form Western Europe.	Tous les pays <u>dont</u> nous avons parlé jusqu'à présent forment l'Europe de l'ouest.
In Eastern Europe are found Poland, the Czech Republic, Hungary, Bulgaria, Romania, etc.	En Europe de l'est se trouve la Pologne, la Tchécoslovaquie, la Hongrie, la Bulgarie, la Roumanie, etc.
There is another important country in Eastern Europe.	Il y a un autre pays important en Europe de l'est.
Can you guess?	Pouvez-vous deviner?
It's Russia of course.	C'est la Russie bien sûr.
Part of Russia is included in Eastern Europe and the rest in Asia.	Une partie de la Russie est inclue dans l'Europe de l'est et le reste est en Asie.
It is such a large country!	C'est un si grand pays!
It stretches from Germany here to Japan way over there.	Il s'étend de l'Allemagne ici au Japon tout là-bas.
It is <u>by far</u> the largest country in the world.	C'est <u>de loin</u> le plus grand pays du monde.
Well, our session is over.	Et bien, notre séance est terminée.
Did you like our little tour?	Est-ce que notre petit tour vous a plu?
Isn't Europe fascinating?	L'Europe, n'est-elle pas fascinante?
So many countries, so many languages, so many cultures...	Tant de pays, tant de langues, tant de cultures...

🎦 THE ADVENTURE CONTINUES

Day Eight—0930 hours

Two Days to Rendezvous

As soon as the island's businesses open the next morning, you and Stump walk to the point marked on the map. There, you find the tour agency that Zsa-Zsa mentioned. You and Stump walk into its cool, tastefully furnished office. You approach the receptionist at the main desk.

"*Pardonnez-moi, mademoiselle,*" you begin, "but we are looking for a woman *qui s'appelle* Cecile Champion. Do you know her?"

"*Oui!* I know her," the receptionist replies in halting English. "She is one of our best tour guides. You hope to meet her?"

"Yes," you reply. "Is she here?"

The receptionist shakes her head. "She is on tour now. She returns late tomorrow. Should I take a message?"

"Yes, please," you say. "We would like to meet with her as soon as she returns." You leave your code names and the Pétard's phone number. The receptionist raises her eyebrows upon hearing your code names, but she agrees to relay the message to Cecile.

You thank her for her time and leave the tour agency's office.

"What do we do now?" Stump asks glumly.

You shrug. "We wait," you suggest, "and we study more French so we can pass Cecile's challenge quickly when we get it."

You and Stump return to the Pétard's home. You email the submarine captain and inform him of the delay. He writes back that he will arrange to have the rendezvous the eleventh day instead of the tenth. Then you and Stump focus on learning more French. You complete several more French activities before you stop for the day.

101

In the Aquarium
French Only
Dans l'aquarium

Instructions: Listen to and read through this story. How many French words do you already know? Recite the French along with the voice on the tape.

Look at that big fish.	*Regarde ce grand poisson.*
It's a shark.	*C'est un requin.*
Sharks live in oceans.	*Les requins vivent dans les océans.*
They have a lot of sharp teeth.	*Ils ont beaucoup de dents bien aiguisées.*
Their skin is not smooth like yours.	*Leur peau n'est pas lisse comme la tienne.*
It's very rough,	*Elle est très rugueuse,*
like sandpaper.	*comme du papier de verre.*
Sharks are dangerous.	*Les requins sont dangereux.*
They're mean.	*Ils sont méchants.*
They're fearless.	*Ils n'ont aucune peur.*
Some sharks attack people.	*Certains requins attaquent les gens.*
A shark can take off your leg in one bite.	*Un requin peut t'arracher une jambe en une bouchée.*
That's why many people are afraid of sharks.	*C'est pourquoi beaucoup de gens ont peur des requins.*
Are you afraid of sharks?	*As-tu peur des requins?*
If you were fishing and caught a shark, what would you do?	*Si tu pêchais et que tu attrapais un requin, que ferais-tu?*
Would you give it a kiss and throw it back?	*Lui donnerais-tu un baiser et le rejeterais-tu ensuite?*

Or would you like to take it home to cook it and eat it? | Ou voudrais-tu le prendre à la maison pour le cuire et pour le manger?

When fish are caught on a hook, do they cry? | *Quand les poissons sont pris à un hameçon, est-ce qu'ils pleurent?*

If you hit a shark with a stick, would the shark cry? | *Si tu frappais un requin avec un bâton, est-ce que le requin se mettrait à pleurer?*

Can you tell a male shark from a female shark? | *Peux-tu distinguer entre un requin mâle et un requin femelle?*

Do sharks lay eggs, or do they give birth to their young alive? | *Est-ce que les requins pondent des œufs, ou donnent-ils naissance à leurs petits vivants?*

Are all sharks big? | *Est-ce que tous les requins sont grands?*
No, some of them are <u>as small as</u> a cat, and others are as big as a bus. | *Non, certains d'entre eux sont <u>aussi petits qu'</u>un chat et d'autres, aussi grands qu'un bus.*

Would you like to play with a shark? | *Voudrais-tu jouer avec un requin?*
If you ever see one, don't try to play with it, ok? | *Si jamais tu en voyais un, n'essaie pas de jouer avec lui, d'accord?*

102

🎧 Focus on Scene
French Only
Concentration sur scène

Description: *Dans ce dessin, il y a plusieurs objets. En haut du dessin, il y a un train qui va de gauche à droite. Au-dessous du train et au centre de l'image, au dessus de la ligne horizontale, il y a trois instruments de communication à distance. Celui de gauche est le plus ancien des trois: la lettre. Celui de droite est le plus récent: le poste de télévision. Celui du milieu est le téléphone. Au-dessous de la ligne horizontale, nous voyons deux moyens de transport, l'un plus rapide que l'autre. Ce sont un avion et un camion. L'avion est à gauche du camion et se dirige vers la gauche. Le camion se dirige vers la droite. En bas à gauche nous voyons deux genres d'armes: un pistolet et un couteau, un couteau de chasse. Le pistolet est placé à gauche du couteau. À l'opposé de ces deux objets, à droite, nous voyons deux genres d'animaux: une tortue et un dinosaure. Ce dernier est à droite.*

🎧 Instructions: Form ten questions in French about this scene. For example: What is in this picture? Where is the truck? Is the train at the bottom left? What is at the bottom right? Is the airplane headed to the left?

1.
2.
3.

4.
5.
6.
7.
8.
9.
10.

103

📼 Storytime: The Story of the Three Thieves
L'histoire des trois voleurs

📼 Instructions: Listen to and read the following story. Rewrite the ending in French!

📼 There were once three thieves.	*Il était une fois trois voleurs.*
One dark night they set about to rob the house of a rich man.	*Une nuit sombre, ils entreprirent de cambrioler la maison d'un riche.*
The leader of the thieves said: "I'll go first. You wait here for me, ok?"	*Le chef des voleurs dit: «J'irai en premier. Attendez-moi ici, d'accord?»*
He crawled in through a window and began to grope his way across the dark room.	*Il se glissa à l'intérieur en passant par une fenêtre, et il commença à tâtonner à travers la pièce obscure.*
Suddenly he bumped into a chair and knocked it over.	*Tout à coup, il heurta une chaise et il la renversa.*
The noise woke up the man. He called out: "Who's that?"	*Le bruit réveilla l'homme. Il cria: «Qui est là?»*
The thief answered: "Meow!"	*Le voleur répondit: «Miaou!»*
Thinking it was only a cat, the rich man went back to sleep.	*Pensant que ce n'était qu'un chat, le riche se rendormit.*
The thief took some things and crawled outside through the window.	*Le voleur prit quelques objets et se glissa dehors par la fenêtre.*
His friends asked: "How did it go?"	*Ses amis lui demandèrent: «Comment ça a été?»*
He told them: "I accidentally knocked over a chair and woke up the man.	*Il leur dit: «J'ai renversé une chaise par accident et j'ai réveillé l'homme.*
He called out: 'Who's that?' I answered: 'Meow!' and he thought it was only a cat."	*Il a crié: «Qui est là?» J'ai répondu: «Miaou!» et il a pensé que ce n'était qu'un chat.»*
The other thieves said: "Whew! That was close!"	*Les autres voleurs dirent: «Et bien! Il s'en est fallu de peu!»*
The second thief said: "I'll be next, ok?"	*Le deuxième voleur dit: «Je serai le suivant, d'accord?»*
He crawled in through the window and began to grope his way across the dark room.	*Il se glissa à l'intérieur par la fenêtre et il commenca à tâtonner à travers la pièce sombre.*
Suddenly he bumped into the chair and knocked it over.	*Tout à coup, il heurta une chaise et il la renversa.*
Again the noise woke up the man. He called out: "Who's that?"	*Le bruit réveilla à nouveau l'homme. Il cria: «Qui est là?»*
The thief answered: "Meow!"	*Le voleur répondit: «Miaou!»*
Thinking it was only a cat, the rich man went back to sleep.	*Pensant que ce n'était qu'un chat, le riche se rendormit.*

The thief took some things and crawled back out the window.	*Le voleur prit quelques objets et se glissa dehors par la fenêtre.*
The leader of the thieves asked: "How did it go?"	*Le chef lui demanda: «Comment ça a été?»*
He said: "The same thing that happened to you happened to me.	*Il dit: «La même chose qui t'est arrivée à toi m'est arrivée aussi.*
I accidentally knocked over a chair and woke up the man.	*J'ai renversé par accident une chaise et j'ai réveillé l'homme.*
He called out: 'Who's that?'	*Il a crié: «Qui est là?»*
I said 'Meow!' just like you did, and he went back to sleep."	*J'ai dit: «Miaou!» tout comme tu l'as fait, et il s'est rendormi.»*
The third thief said: "I'll be next, ok?"	*Le troisième voleur dit: «Je serai le suivant, d'accord?»*
This thief wasn't very smart.	*Ce voleur n'était pas très intelligent.*
He crawled in through the window and began to grope his way across the dark room.	*Il se glissa à l'intérieur par la fenêtre et il commença à tâtonner à travers la pièce sombre.*
Suddenly he bumped into the chair and knocked it over.	*Tout à coup, il heurta une chaise et il la renversa.*
Of course the noise woke up the man.	*Bien sûr, le bruit réveilla l'homme.*
He called out: "Who's that?"	*Il cria: «Qui est là?»*
The thief replied: "Another cat."	*Le voleur répondit: «Un autre chat.»*

104

🔲 *Dans la salle de classe de chimie*
French Only
In the Chemistry Classroom

🔲 Instructions: Listen to and read the following lesson on chemistry. Circle all the French words you have heard before.

Here are two glasses of water. In the one glass there is cold water; in the other glass there is hot water. It is boiling hot—too hot to drink. Here is some ice. Watch. If I put the ice in the cold water, what will happen? It will begin to melt very slowly. You see, it may take three or four minutes to melt. Why will it melt? Because the water is a bit warmer than the ice.	🔲 *Voici deux verres d'eau.* *Dans l'un des verres il y a de l'eau froide;* *dans l'autre il y a de l'eau chaude.* *C'est de l'eau bouillante—trop chaude à boire.* *Voici de la glace. Regardez.* *Si je mets de la glace dans l'eau froide,* *que se passera-t-il?* *Elle commencera à fondre très lentement.* *Tu vois, ça prendra peut-être trois ou quatre* *minutes pour fondre.* *Pourquoi cela fondra-t-il? Parce que* *l'eau est un peu plus chaude que la glace.*
If I put the ice in the hot water, what will happen? It will melt very rapidly. Why? Because the water is much warmer than the ice. What effect will the ice have on the hot water? It will cool it down a bit. Now perhaps it is no longer too hot to drink.	*Si je mets la glace dans l'eau chaude,* *que se passera-t-il?* *Elle fondra très rapidement.* *Pourquoi? Parce que l'eau est* *beaucoup plus chaude que la glace.* *Quel effet aura la glace sur* *l'eau chaude?* *Elle la refroidira un peu.* *Maintenant elle n'est peut-être plus trop chaude* *à boire.*
Taste it. Fresh water. Salty. Sweet. Here are three glasses of water. You can taste each one and see that the water is fresh. It is not salty. It is not sweet. Here are three spoons, each containing a different substance. They look alike, but they're different. One is salt. One is sugar. One is sand.	*Goûte-la. Eau fraîche.* *Salée. Sucrée.* *Voici trois verres d'eau.* *Vous pouvez goûter chacun et voir* *que l'eau est fraîche.* *Elle n'est pas salée. Elle n'est pas sucrée.* *Voici trois cuillères, chacune contenant* *une substance différente.* *Elles se ressemblent mais elles sont différentes.* *L'une est du sel. Une autre est du sucre. Puis, une est* *du sable.*
Try to guess which is which. Watch, I'll pour the stuff from this spoon into one of the glasses of water. Then I'll stir it a little bit. What do you think will happen? If it's sand, then it won't dissolve.	*Essayez de deviner laquelle est laquelle.* *Regardez, je vais vider le truc de cette cuillère* *dans un des verres d'eau.* *Ensuite je vais mélanger un peu.* *À ton avis que se passera-t-il?* *Si c'est du sable, alors ça ne se dissoudra pas.*

But if it's salt or sugar it will quickly dissolve.	Mais si c'est du sel ou du sucre ça se dissoudra vite.
Watch. What did you see?	Regardez. Qu'avez-vous vu?
Did it dissolve?	Ça s'est dissout?
Yes. So we know the substance wasn't sand.	Oui. Alors on sait que la substance n'était pas du sable.
It must have been either salt or sugar.	Ça devait être soit du sel ou du sucre.
Now I'll pour a little of the stuff from this spoon into this other glass of water.	Maintenant je verserai un peu du truc de cette cuillère dans cet autre verre d'eau.
Then I'll stir it a little bit.	Ensuite je vais le mélanger un peu.
What do you think will happen?	À ton avis, que se passera-t-il?
It will either dissolve or not.	Ça se dissoudra ou pas.
If it's salt or sugar it will dissolve, but if it's sand it won't.	Si c'est du sel ou du sucre ça se dissoudra, mais pas si c'est du sable.
All right. It didn't dissolve.	Bien. Il ne s'est pas dissout.
Can you tell which it was?	Peux-tu dire lequel était-ce?
How can you tell whether it was salt or sugar?	Comment peux-tu dire si c'était du sel ou du sucre?
Can you tell by looking at it?	Peux-tu deviner rien qu'en le regardant?
Not at all.	Non, pas du tout.
It still looks like the fresh water.	Ça ressemble encore à de l'eau fraîche.
Can you tell by smelling it?	Peux-tu deviner rien qu'en le sentant?
Not very well.	Pas très bien.
It still smells like the fresh water.	Ça sent encore l'eau fraîche.
Can you tell by tasting it? Yes.	Peux-tu deviner rien qu'en la goûtant? Oui.
It has a different taste.	Ça a un goût différent.
It tastes sweet.	Ça a un goût sucré.
By tasting it you can know whether the substance was salt or sugar.	En la goûtant tu peux savoir si la substance était du sel ou du sucre.
Taste of this glass of water.	Goûte ce verre d'eau.
How was it, salty or sweet?	Comment était-ce, salé ou sucré?
Sweet is right.	Sucré, correct.
So the stuff in the second spoon was sugar, not salt.	Alors le truc dans la deuxième cuillère était du sucre, pas du sel.
Marie, you guessed right.	Marie, tu as bien deviné.
Pierre, you guessed wrong.	Pierre, tu as mal deviné.
Do you know now what stuff was in the first spoon?	Sais-tu maintenant ce qui était dans la première cuillère?
How can you know it was salt?	Comment peux-tu savoir que c'était du sel?
You didn't taste it.	Tu ne l'as pas goûté.
Now we know that the stuff in the first spoon was salt,	Maintenant on sait que le truc dans la première cuillère était du sel,
and the stuff in the second spoon was sugar.	et le truc dans la deuxième cuillère était du sucre.
So now it's easy to predict what'll happen when we pour the stuff from the third spoon into the third glass of water, right?	Alors maintenant il est facile de prédire ce qui se passera quand nous mettrons le truc de la troisième cuillère dans le troisième verre d'eau, n'est-ce pas?
What is the stuff in the third spoon? Sand.	Quel est le truc de la troisième cuillère? Du sable.
We know sand doesn't dissolve in water.	Nous savons que le sable ne se dissout pas dans l'eau.
Watch. You see, the substance didn't dissolve.	Regarde. Tu vois, la substance ne s'est pas dissoute.
It was really sand.	C'était vraiment du sable.
We were able to correctly predict the outcome.	Nous avons pu prédire correctement ce qui allait suivre.

Here is some special paper. If you put it
in sweet water it will change color.
It will not change color if you put it in
fresh water or salty water.
I'll shift these two glasses now
so you can't tell
which one has sweet water
and which one has salty water.
Now I'll dip this special paper in one
of the two glasses of water.
Watch. Did it change color? No.
So this water has no sugar.
The other one must be the sweet water.
We can tell by dipping the special paper
in it.
You see, it changed color. That proves
that this water contains sugar.

We have seen that certain substances
dissolve in water and others do not.
Here are two glasses of water, here's a
bottle containing a colorless liquid,
and here's a bottle containing another
kind of colorless liquid.
One is vegetable oil. The other is vinegar.
I won't tell you which is which.
Try to guess.

What will happen if we pour some oil
into the water?
Will it dissolve?

*Voici du papier spécial. Si tu le mets
dans de l'eau sucrée il change de couleur.
Il ne changera pas de couleur si tu le
mets dans de l'eau fraîche ou salée.
Je vais changer ces deux verres maintenant
pour que vous ne puissiez pas dire
lequel a de l'eau sucrée
et lequel a de l'eau salée.
Maintenant je vais plonger ce papier
spécial dans l'un des deux verres d'eau.
Regardez. A-t-il changé de couleur? Non.
Alors cette eau n'a pas de sucre.
L'autre doit être l'eau sucrée.
Nous pouvons le savoir en plongeant
le papier spécial dedans.
Regardez, il a changé de couleur. Ça prouve
que cette eau contient du sucre.*

*Nous avons vu que certaines substances
se dissolvent dans l'eau et pas d'autres.
Voici deux verres d'eau, voici une
bouteille contenant un liquide incolore,
et voici une bouteille contenant un autre
genre de liquide incolore.
L'une est de l'huile végétale. L'autre est du vinaigre.
Je ne dirai pas lequel est lequel.
Essayez de deviner.*

*Que se passera-t-il si nous versons de l'huile
dans l'eau?
Va-t-elle se dissoudre?*

105

🔲 Voice in the Darkness
French Only
La voix dans les ténèbres

🔲 Instructions: Listen to and read this poem in French.

In darkness I cried out to you.	🔲 *Dans les ténèbres je t'ai appelé.*
In darkness you cried out to me	*Dans les ténèbres tu m'as appelé.*
I recognized your voice.	*J'ai reconnu ta voix.*
You recognized my voice.	*Tu as reconnu ma voix.*
"Come," I said.	*«Viens», j'ai dit.*
You answered, "Where are you, Daddy?	*Tu as répondu, «Où es-tu, papa?*
I don't see you."	*Je ne te vois pas.»*
"Here. I'm here. Come here," I said.	*«Là. Je suis là. Viens là», ai-je dit.*
"I'm afraid, Daddy" you said.	*«J'ai peur, papa», as-tu dit.*
Don't be afraid, my son. Wait,	*«N'aies pas peur, mon fils. Attends,*
I'll come to you."	*Je viendrai à toi.»*
"It is dark, Daddy. I can't see anything.	*«Il fait noir, papa. Je n'y vois rien.*
I'm afraid. I'm afraid."	*J'ai peur. J'ai peur.»*
"Don't lose courage, little son.	*«Ne perds pas courage, mon petit.*
I'm coming right now."	*J'arrive tout de suite.»*
"Hurry, Daddy. I'm waiting for you."	*«Dépêche-toi, papa. Je t'attends.»*

106

🔲 A Note of Humor: *Un fils paresseux*
French Only
A Lazy Son

🔲 Instructions: Listen to and read the following joke. Try to tell it in French to a friend!

A son complained to his father:	🔲 *Un fils se plaignait à son père:*
"I don't want to go to school."	*«Je ne veux pas aller à l'école.»*
The father said: "Johnny, give	*Le père dit: «Jeannot, donne-*
me three reasons why you shouldn't go."	*moi trois raisons de ne pas y aller.»*
The son answered:	*Le fils répondit:*
"I am bored at school.	*«Je m'ennuie à l'école.*
There's too much work to do,	*Il faut travailler trop dur,*
and my teachers don't like me."	*et mes professeurs ne m'aiment pas.»*
"I understand your feelings, Johnny.	*«Je comprends tes sentiments, Jeannot.*
Sometimes I felt the same way.	*Parfois, j'ai ressenti la même chose.*
Let me give you three reasons why you should go:	*Laisse-moi te donner trois raisons d'y aller:*

There are things that we should do even if we don't like them.	*Certaines choses nous devons les faire, même si nous n'en avons pas envie.*
You are forty-seven years old now.	*Tu as quarante-sept ans.*
You are the principal!"	*Tu es le principal!»*

107

Chatter at a Royal Ball
Bavardages au bal royal

GETTING READY FOR CONVERSATION 15

By yourself—tape off.

Instructions: Go over these new words until you feel comfortable with them. Then observe them in use in the conversation below!

to learn	*apprendre*	to respond	*répondre*
to hear	*entendre*	crazy things	*des bêtises*
to meet, encounter	*rencontrer*	so many languages	*tant de langues*
to fall from/off a tower	*tomber d'une tour*	to fall in love	*tomber amoureux/amoureuse*

What will become of her?	*Que va-t-elle devenir?*
What became of her?	*Qu'est-elle devenue?*
She met a Russian prince.	*Elle a rencontré un prince russe.*
She fell in love <u>with</u> a Russian prince.	*Elle est tombée amoureuse <u>d'</u>un prince russe.*
He wrote crazy things to her.	*Il lui a écrit des bêtises.*
She began to write letters to him.	*Elle a commencé à lui écrire des lettres.*
She still writes poems.	*Elle écrit toujours des poèmes.*
He responded to her.	*Il lui a répondu.*
He has made a big mistake.	*Il a fait une grand erreur.*
I remember him.	*Je me souviens de lui.*
She learned Russian.	*Elle a appris le russe.*

CONVERSATION 15

Instructions: Recite the English before the French voice speaks on the tape!

- • •: And the beautiful princess who knew so many languages? You remember her, don't you? She wrote a famous poem in Arabic <u>about</u> love.

  Et la belle princesse qui savait tant de langues? Tu te souviens d'elle, n'est-ce pas? Elle a écrit un poème célèbre en arabe <u>au sujet de</u> l'amour.

- •: Yes, I remember her. She knew King Hussein and wrote him crazy things in Arabic.

  Oui, je me souviens d'elle. Elle connaissait le roi Hussein et lui écrivait des bêtises en arabe.

- • •: What became of her, do you know?

  Qu'est-elle devenue, le sais-tu?

- •: Well, she still writes poems in Arabic, but she met a Russian prince.

  Et bien, elle écrit toujours des poèmes en arabe, mais elle a rencontré un prince russe.

- • •: I can't believe it.

  Je ne peux pas le croire.

- •: Yes, she fell in love with a handsome young Russian prince.

  Oui, elle est tombée amoureuse d'un beau jeune prince russe.

- • •: So she learned Russian and began to write him crazy things in Russian?

  Alors elle a appris le russe et a commencé à lui écrire des bêtises en russe?

•:	Exactly.	*C'est exact.*
••:	Has the Russian prince responded to her letters?	*Le prince russe, a-t-il répondu à ses lettres?*
•:	I don't know, but if he has, he has certainly made a big mistake.	*Je ne sais pas, mais s'il a répondu, il a certainement fait une grande erreur.*
••:	And now what is she going to do, do you know?	*Et maintenant que va-t-elle faire, le sais-tu?*
•:	Well, they say she's going to live in Siberia.	*Et bien, on dit qu'elle va vivre en Sibérie.*
••:	In Siberia?	*En Sibérie?*
•:	Oh, poor thing! What will become of her?	*Oh, la pauvre! Que va-t-elle devenir?*

Listen again, French only.

THE ADVENTURE CONTINUES

You stop late that afternoon. You and Stump prepare the leek soup recipe that you learned from Isabelle, and you and the Pétards stay up late into the night discussing French cuisine and culture.

Day Nine—1000 hours

Two Days to New Rendezvous

You and Stump work through six more French exercises this morning and early this afternoon.

End Tape 4, Side B

108

🎧 A Note of Humor: The Crocodile
Le crocodile

🎧 Instructions: Listen to and read the following story. Rewrite the ending in French!

🎧 A pale, nervous man came into the office of a psychiatrist who was a personal friend.	*Un homme pâle et nerveux entra dans le bureau d'un psychiatre qui était un ami personnel.*
The doctor said: "Pierre, my friend, I see that you are under great stress. Tell me what your problem is."	*Le docteur dit: «Pierre, mon ami, je vois que tu souffres d'une grande dépression. Raconte-moi ton problème.»*
"Oh Doctor, please help me. I am extremely frightened."	*«Oh docteur, s'il te plaît, aide-moi. J'ai très peur.»*
"What is it that frightens you?"	*«Qu'est-ce qui te fait peur?»*
"There's a crocodile under my bed."	*«Il y a un crocodile sous mon lit.»*
"A crocodile under your bed?"	*«Un crocodile sous ton lit?»*
"Yes, there's a crocodile under my bed one meter long. I'm afraid it's going to eat me."	*«Oui, il y a un crocodile sous mon lit qui est long d'un mètre. J'ai peur qu'il me mange.»*
"Don't worry, Pierre," said the doctor. "It's only an illusion.	*«Ne t'inquiète pas, Pierre», a dit le docteur. «Ce n'est qu'une illusion.*
I have many patients who have a similar problem. It's really nothing serious.	*J'ai beaucoup de patients qui ont un problème similaire. Ce n'est vraiment rien de grave.*
I have some pills that will cure your ailment in a short time.	*J'ai des pilules qui vont guérir ton mal en peu de temps.*
Here, take three of these little pills three times a day: three in the morning, three at noon, and three at night before going to bed.	*Tiens, prends trois de ces petites pilules trois fois par jour: trois le matin, trois à midi, et trois le soir avant d'aller au lit.*
I can assure you, you'll soon be well again.	*Je peux te l'assurer, tu te porteras bientôt mieux.*
Come back and see me in three weeks, will you?"	*Reviens me voir dans trois semaines, d'accord?»*
"Thank you doctor, thank you very much."	*«Merci docteur, merci beaucoup.»*
In three weeks the man came again to the office.	*Trois semaines plus tard, l'homme retourna au cabinet du docteur.*
He was even paler and thinner than before.	*Il était encore plus pâle et plus maigre qu'avant.*
He said: "Oh doctor, I still have the same problem. And it's getting worse and worse.	*Il dit: «Oh, docteur, j'ai toujours le même problème. Ça va de pire en pire.*
The crocodile is still under my bed, only now it is one-and-a-half meters long.	*Le crocodile est toujours sous mon lit, mais maintenant il est long d'un mètre et demi.*
I'm sure it's going to eat me.	*Je suis sûr qu'il va me manger.*
Oh, what'll I do? You've gotta help me."	*Oh, qu'est-ce-que je vais faire? Tu dois m'aider.»*
"Have you taken the three pills three times a day as I prescribed?"	*«As-tu pris les trois pilules trois fois par jour comme je te l'avais dit?»*

"Yes, yes, of course. Three in the morning, three at noon, and three at night before going to bed."	«Oui, oui, bien sûr. Trois le matin, trois à midi, et trois le soir avant d'aller au lit.»
"Well then, I'll give you these new pills. They are more powerful than the others.	«Et bien, je vais te donner ces nouvelles pilules. Elles sont plus fortes que les autres.
Take six of them, three times a day: six in the morning, six at noon, and six at night before going to bed.	Prends-en six, trois fois par jour: six le matin, six à midi, et six le soir avant d'aller au lit.
I can assure you, you'll soon be well again. Come back and see me in six weeks, will you?"	Je peux te l'assurer, tu te portiras bientôt mieux. Reviens me voir dans six semaines, d'accord?»
"Thank you doctor, thank you very much."	«Merci docteur, merci beaucoup.»
In six weeks the man came again to the office.	Après six semaines, l'homme revint au cabinet du docteur.
He was even thinner, paler, and more nervous than before.	Il était encore plus maigre, plus pâle et plus nerveux qu'avant.
He said: "Oh doctor, I still have the same problem, and it's getting worse.	Il dit: «Oh docteur, j'ai toujours le même problème. Ça va de pire en pire.
The crocodile is still under my bed, only now it is two meters long. I know it's going to eat me."	Le crocodile est toujours sous mon lit, mais maintenant, il est long de deux mètres. Je sais qu'il va me manger.»
"Have you taken the six pills three times a day as I prescribed?"	«As-tu pris les six pilules trois fois par jour comme je l'avais prescrit?»
"Yes, yes, of course. Six in the morning, six at noon, and six at night before going to bed."	«Oui, oui, bien sûr. Six le matin, six à midi, et six le soir avant d'aller au lit.»
"Well then, I'll give you these new pills.	«Et bien, je vais te donner ces nouvelles pilules.
They are extremely powerful. I want you to take nine of them, three times a day: nine in the morning, nine at noon, and nine at night before going to bed.	Elles sont extrêmement fortes. Je veux que tu en prennes neuf, trois fois par jour: neuf le matin, neuf à midi, et neuf le soir avant d'aller au lit.
I can assure you you'll soon be well again. Come back and see me in nine weeks, will you?"	Je peux te l'assurer, tu te porteras bientôt mieux. Reviens me voir dans neuf semaines, d'accord?»
Nine weeks went by but the man didn't come.	Neuf semaines passèrent mais l'homme ne revint pas.
Ten weeks, eleven weeks, twelve weeks.	Dix semaines, onze semaines, douze semaines.
At the end of twelve weeks, the doctor by chance was walking along a street and he passed the house of his sick friend.	Au bout de douze semaines, le docteur se promenait au hasard le long d'une rue et il passa devant la maison de son ami malade.
He decided to stop and call on him.	Il décida de s'arrêter et de lui rendre visite.
He knocked on the door. His friend's wife answered the door. She was crying.	Il frappa à la porte. La femme de son ami ouvrit la porte. Elle pleurait.
"Good evening, Mrs. Durant, I came to see how Pierre is doing."	«Bonsoir, Madame Durant, je suis venu voir comment se portait Pierre.»
"Oh doctor, haven't you heard?"	«Oh docteur, n'êtes-vous pas au courant?»
"What?"	«Quoi?»
"Pierre is dead."	«Pierre est mort.»
"Dead?"	«Mort?»
"Yes, he was eaten by the crocodile."	«Oui, il a été dévoré par le crocodile.»

Listen again, French only.

109

📼 Storytime: The Farmer and the Turnip
French Only
Le fermier et le navet

📼 Instructions: Listen to and read the following story. Learn basic vocabulary about gardening.

Once upon a time there was a farmer.
The farmer planted some seeds.
and he watered them,
and the sun shone,
and after a time,
  a tiny plant grew out.
And he watered it,
and the sun shone,
and the little plant grew,
and he watered it,
and the sun shone,
and the little plant grew even more.
And he watered it,
and the sun shone,
and the little plant grew and grew.
And one day the farmer said:
"The plant is ripe."

So the farmer took hold of the plant,
and tugged and tugged and tugged,
but the plant didn't come out.
So the farmer called his wife:
"Wife, come here, wife."
So the wife came and took hold of the farmer,
and the farmer grabbed the plant,
and they tugged and they tugged and they tugged,
but the plant didn't come out.

So the farmer called his daughter:
"Daughter, come here, daughter."
And so the daughter came,
and she grabbed on to the wife,
and the wife grabbed on to the farmer,
and the farmer grabbed the plant,
and they tugged and tugged and tugged,
but the plant didn't come out.

So they called the dog:
"Dog, come here, dog."
The dog came, and the dog grabbed on to the daughter,
and the daughter grabbed on to the wife,

📼 *Il était une fois un fermier.*
Le fermier planta quelques graines,
et il les arrosa,
et le soleil brilla,
et au bout de quelques temps,
  une plante minuscule poussa.
Et il l'arrosa,
et le soleil brilla,
et la petite plante poussa,
et il l'arrosa,
et le soleil brilla,
et la petite plante grandit encore plus.
Et il l'arrosa,
et le soleil brilla,
et la petite plante poussa et poussa.
Et un jour le fermier dit:
«La plante est mûre.»

Alors, le fermier saisit la plante,
et il tira et tira et tira,
mais la plante ne sortit pas.
Alors le fermier appela sa femme:
«Femme, viens ici, femme.»
Alors la femme vint et tint le fermier,
et le fermier tint la plante,
et ils tirèrent et tirèrent et tirèrent,
mais la plante ne sortit pas.

Alors le fermier appela sa fille:
«Fille, viens ici, fille.»
Alors la fille vint
et elle tint la femme,
et la femme tint le fermier,
et le fermier tint la plante,
et ils tirèrent et tirèrent et tirèrent,
mais la plante ne sortit pas.

Alors ils appelèrent le chien:
«Chien, viens ici, chien.»
Le chien vint et le chien tint la fille,

et la fille tint la femme,

and the wife grabbed on to the farmer,	*et la femme tint le fermier,*
and the farmer grabbed the plant,	*et le fermier tint la plante,*
and they tugged and they tugged and they tugged,	*et ils tirèrent et tirèrent et tirèrent,*
but the plant didn't come out.	*mais la plante ne sortit pas.*

So the farmer called the cat: "Cat, come here, cat."
So the cat came,
and the cat grabbed on to the dog,
and the dog grabbed on to the daughter,
and the daughter grabbed on to wife,
and the wife grabbed on to the farmer,
and the farmer grabbed the plant,
and they tugged and they tugged and they tugged,
and the plant didn't come out.
Then, at that moment, a little mouse came by,

and the mouse said:
"What goes on here?"
And the farmer explained that they were not able
to get the plant out.
Then the mouse said:
"I can help."
And they all laughed at him: "Ha-ha-ha-ha.
You, so small, how are you going to help us?"
But the mouse convinced them.
And so the mouse grabbed on to the cat,
and the cat grabbed on to the dog,
and the dog grabbed on to the the daughter,
and the daughter grabbed on to the wife,
and the wife grabbed on to the farmer,
and the farmer grabbed the plant
and they tugged and tugged and tugged,
and the plant came out.

Alors le fermier appela le chat: «Chat, viens ici, chat.»
Alors le chat vint,
et le chat tint le chien,
et le chien tint la fille,
et la fille tint la femme,
et la femme tint le fermier,
et le fermier tint la plante,
et ils tirèrent et tirèrent et tirèrent,
et la plante ne sortit pas.
Alors, à ce moment précis, une petite souris passa
   par là,
et la souris dit:
«Que se passe-t-il ici?»
Et le fermier expliqua qu'ils n'arrivaient pas
à déraciner la plante.
Alors la souris dit:
«Je peux aider.»
Et ils se sont tous moqués d'elle: «Ha, ha, ha, ha.
Toi, si petite, comment vas-tu nous aider?»
Mais la souris les a convaincus.
Et la souris tint le chat,
et le chat tint le chien,
et le chien tint la fille,
et la fille tint la femme,
et la femme tint le fermier,
et le fermier tint la plante,
et ils tirèrent et tirèrent et tirèrent,
et la plante sortit.

110

🎧 The Story of Chicken Little
L'histoire d'un Petit Poussin

🎬 Instructions: Read and listen to this familiar story. Read along in French with the voice on the tape.

🎧 This is the story of Chicken Little, a chickie that became alarmed and set itself to believe that the sky was falling.
One day this chickie was in the garden eating, when a leaf, a very large leaf, fell on her head.

The poor chickie was startled and imagined that the sky was falling.
It started to run, screaming: "Peep, peep, Mommy, where are you Mommy?"
"Cluck, cluck, here I am, chickie.
What is it?"
"The sky is falling!
The sky is falling!"
"How do you know, Chickie?"
"I saw it with my very eyes, and a piece fell BOOM! on my head. I tell you the truth."
"Let's flee!" screamed the hen. "Let's flee, run!
Duck, Duck, where are you, Duck?"
"Quack, quack, here I am. What happened? What happened?"
"The sky is falling!
The sky is falling!"
"How do you know, Hen?"
"The chickie told me."
"How do you know, Chickie?"
"I saw it with my very eyes, and a piece fell BOOM! on my head. I tell you the truth."
"Let's flee!" screamed the duck. "Let's flee, run!"
"Goose, Goose, where are you, Goose?"
"Honk, honk, here I am. What happened?"
"The sky is falling!
The sky is falling!"
"How do you know, Duck?"
"The hen told me."
"How do you know, Hen?"
"The chickie told me."
"How do you know, Chickie?"
"I saw it with my very eyes, and a piece fell BOOM! on my head. I tell you the truth."
"Let's flee!" screamed the goose. "Let's flee, run!"
"Turkey, Turkey, where are you, Turkey?"
"Gobble, gobble. Here I am, Goose.

Ceci est l'histoire de Petit Poussin, un petit poussin qui a pris peur et s'est mis en tête que le ciel tombait.
Un jour, ce petit poussin était dans un jardin en train de manger, quand une feuille, une très grande feuille lui est tombée sur la tête.
Le pauvre petit poussin en a été surpris et il s'est imaginé que le ciel tombait.
Il s'est mis à courir en criant: «Cui, cui, maman, où es-tu maman?»
«Cot, Cot, je suis ici Petit Poussin.
Que se passe-t-il?»
«Le ciel est en train de tomber.
Le ciel est en train de tomber!»
«Comment le sais-tu, Petit Poussin?»
«Je l'ai vu de mes propres yeux, et BOUM! un morceau m'est tombé sur la tête. Je te dis la vérité.»
«Fuyons!» a dit la poule. «Fuyons, courons!
Canard, Canard, où es-tu Canard?»
«Coin, coin, me voici. Que s'est-il passé? Que s'est-il passé?»
«Le ciel est en train de tomber!
Le ciel est en train de tomber!»
«Comment le sais-tu, Poule?»
«Le poussin me l'a dit.»
«Comment le sais-tu, Petit Poussin?»
«Je l'ai vu de mes propres yeux, et BOUM! un morceau m'est tombé sur la tête. Je te dis la vérité.»
«Fuyons!», a crié le canard. «Fuyons, courons!»
«Oie, Oie, où es-tu, Oie?»
«Honk, Honk, me voici. Que s'est-il passé?»
«Le ciel est en train de tomber!
Le ciel est en train de tomber!»
«Comment le sais-tu, Canard?»
«La poule me l'a dit.»
«Comment le sais-tu, Poule?»
«Le petit poussin me l'a dit.»
«Comment le sais-tu, Petit Poussin?»
«Je l'ai vu de mes propres yeux, et BOUM! un morceau m'est tombé sur la tête. Je te dis la vérité.»
«Fuyons!», a crié l'oie. «Fuyons, courons!»
«Dinde, Dinde, où es-tu, Dinde?»
«Glou, glou. Me voici, Oie.

What happened? What happened?"
"The sky is falling! The sky is falling!"

"How do you know, Goose?"
"The duck told me."
"How do you know, Duck?"
"The hen told me."
"How do you know, Hen?"
"The chickie told me."
"How do you know, Chickie?"
"I saw it with my very eyes, and a piece fell BOOM! on my head. I tell you the truth."
"Let's flee!" screamed the turkey. "Let's flee, run!"
"Fox, Fox, where are you, Fox?"
"Yif, yif. Here I am.
What happened?
"The sky is falling! The sky is falling!"

"How do you know, Turkey?"
"The goose told me."
"How do you know, Goose?"
"The duck told me."
"How do you know, Duck?"
"The hen told me."
"How do you know, Hen?"
"The chickie told me."
"How do you know, Chickie?"
"I saw it with my very eyes, and a piece fell BOOM! on my head. I tell you the truth."
The fox thought a little and said:
"Don't be afraid. I will save you.
Come with me to my den."
And all the animals went in with the fox into her den.

Que s'est-il passé? Que s'est-il passé?»
«Le ciel est en train de tomber! Le ciel est en train de tomber!»

«Comment le sais-tu, Oie?»
«Le canard me l'a dit.»
«Comment le sais-tu, Canard?»
«La poule me l'a dit.»
«Comment le sais-tu, Poule?»
«Le petit poussin me l'a dit.»
«Comment le sais-tu, Petit Poussin?
«Je l'ai vu de mes propres yeux, et BOUM! un morceau m'est tombé sur la tête. Je te dis la vérité.»
«Fuyons!», a crié la dinde. «Fuyons, courons! Renard, Renard, où es-tu Renard?»
«Yif, yif. Me voici.
Que s'est-il passé?»
«Le ciel est en train de tomber! Le ciel est en train de tomber!»

«Comment le sais-tu, Dinde?»
«L'oie me l'a dit.»
«Comment le sais-tu, Oie?»
«Le canard me l'a dit.»
«Comment le sais-tu, Canard?»
«La poule me l'a dit.»
«Comment le sais-tu, Poule?»
«Le petit poussin me l'a dit.»
«Comment le sais-tu, Petit Poussin?»
«Je l'ai vu de mes propres yeux, et BOUM! un morceau m'est tombé sur la tête. Je te dis la vérité.»
Le renard y a réfléchi un peu et il a dit:
«N'ayez pas peur. Je vous sauverai.
Venez avec moi dans ma tanière.»
Et tous les animaux sont entrés avec le renard dans sa tanière.

111

No One Pays Any Attention to Me!
French Only
Personne ne s'intéresse à moi!

Instructions: Read and listen to this conversation between a doctor and a patient. Rewrite the ending of this story in French!

Doctor:	Please come in. Sit down.	*Docteur:*	*Veuillez entrer. Asseyez-vous!*
Patient:	Thank you, Doctor.	*Patient:*	*Merci, docteur.*
Doctor:	Tell me, what is your problem?	*Docteur:*	*Dites-moi, quel est votre problème?*
Patient:	Oh, Doctor, please help me.	*Patient:*	*Oh, docteur, s'il vous plaît, aidez-moi.*
	Tell me what to do.		*Dites-moi ce que je dois faire.*
	I feel I am worthless.		*J'ai l'impression de n'avoir aucune valeur.*
	I feel no one cares about me.		*J'ai l'impression que personne ne s'intéresse à moi.*
	No one pays attention to me.		*Personne ne fait attention à moi.*
	Everyone treats me as if I didn't matter.		*Tout le monde me traite comme si je ne comptais pas.*
	Everyone treats me as if I didn't even exist.		*Tout le monde me traite comme si je n'existais même pas.*
Doctor:	Next!	*Docteur:*	*Au suivant!*

112

Conversations and Snatches of Conversations
French Only
Conversations et extraits de conversations

Instructions: Listen to and read the following conversation pieces.

I am American. I'm an American florist.	*Je suis américain. Je suis un fleuriste américain.*
I am also an American florist.	*Je suis aussi une fleuriste américaine.*
Very interesting!	*Très intéressant!*
My name is Sophie.	*Je m'appelle Sophie.*
And I am Richard.	*Et moi Richard.*
It's a pleasure.	*C'est un plaisir.*
Same here.	*Pour moi aussi.*
Who's there?	*Qui est-ce?*
It's me.	*C'est moi.*
Who are you?	*Qui êtes-vous?*
It's me, Sophie.	*C'est moi, Sophie.*
Sophie?	*Sophie?*
Sophie Dupont.	*Sophie Dupont.*
Oh, Sophie, come in, please.	*Oh, Sophie, entrez, s'il vous plaît.*
Your name, monsieur?	*Votre nom, monsieur?*
My name is Bill Clinton.	*Mon nom est Bill Clinton.*
Truly?	*Vraiment?*
It's true. I am Bill Clinton.	*C'est vrai. Je suis Bill Clinton.*
And me, I'm Marilyn Monroe.	*Et moi, je suis Marilyn Monroe.*
Who are you? Are you with us?	*Qui êtes-vous? Êtes-vous avec nous?*
Yes, we are with you.	*Oui, nous sommes avec vous.*
And that man there, who is he?	*Et cette homme là, qui est-ce?*
He is with us. Don't worry.	*Il est avec nous. Ne vous inquiétez pas.*
We are all with you.	*Nous sommes tous avec vous.*
Ok, come with me.	*O.K., venez avec moi.*
Let's go!	*Allons-y!*
Go over there...with him.	*Allez là-bas...avec lui.*
No, stop. Wait.	*Non, arrêtez-vous. Attendez.*
Come with us.	*Venez avec nous.*
Hurry!	*Vite!* (be <u>vite</u> with your <u>feet</u>)
Shh, quiet!	*Shh, silence!*
Let's go!	*Allons-y!*
Hello...Hello.	*Allô...allô.*
Do you speak English?	*Parlez-vous anglais?*
Just a minute, please.	*Un instant, s'il vous plaît.*
Do you speak Spanish or German?	*Parlez-vous espagnol ou allemand?*
No, but I speak Italian a little bit.	*Non, mais je parle un petit peu italien.*

Do you speak English?	Parlez-vous anglais?
Of course. All the world speaks English, right?	Bien sûr. Tout le monde parle anglais, n'est-ce pas?

How much do you want from me?	Combien voulez-vous de moi?
Five francs.	Cinq francs.
And from me?	Et de moi?
Three francs.	Trois francs.
How much does this cost?	Combien ça coûte?
Four francs.	Quatre francs.
Not expensive. And that?	Pas cher. Et ça?
Three francs.	Trois francs.

Breathe deeply. Feel yourself relax.

Count up to four.	Comptez jusqu'à quatre.
One, two, three, four.	Un, deux, trois, quatre.
Again. Louder!	Encore. Plus fort!
One, two, three, four.	Un, deux, trois, quatre.
One time more! A bit louder!	Une fois de plus! Un peu plus fort!
One, two, three, four.	Un, deux, trois, quatre.
That's fine. That's enough.	C'est bien. Cela suffit.

How much does this cost?	Combien ça coûte?
One hundred dollars.	Cent dollars.
A hundred dollars!? It's a rip-off!	Cent dollars? C'est du vol!
I agree. They're thieves.	Je suis d'accord. Ce sont des voleurs.

What's that?	Qu'est-ce que c'est?
Ice cream.	De la glace.
And that?	Et cela?
Cake.	Du gâteau.
Waiter!	Garçon!
I hear you.	Je vous écoute.
The bill, please.	La note, s'il vous plaît.
Right away.	Tout de suite.

Meet my friend Natasha.	Je te présente mon amie Natasha.
It's a pleasure to meet you.	Enchanté de faire votre connaissance.
And Natasha, here is my friend Bob.	Et Natasha, voici mon ami Bob.
Nice to meet you.	Enchantée.

Allow me to introduce myself.	Permettez-moi de me présenter.
Please do.	Je vous en prie.
My name is Sophie.	Je m'appelle Sophie.
And I am Catherine.	Et moi Catherine.

I've been studying English for years.	J'étudie l'anglais depuis des années.
You speak it well.	Vous le parlez bien.
I manage.	Je me débrouille.

Do you understand French?	Vous comprenez le français?
Yes.	Oui.
And your husband?	Et votre mari?
Not much. Hardly at all.	Pas beaucoup. À peine.

113

Beautiful Girl at the University
Jolie fille à l'université

Instructions: Listen to and read the following dialogue. Circle the French words you've already heard before.

	Autumn, September, a new semester	*Automne, septembre, un nouveau semestre*
V:	Hello!	*Bonjour!*
N:	Hi!	*Salut!*
V:	I have a question.	*J'ai une question.*
N:	Please.	*Je t'en prie.*
V:	Where are you going?	*Où vas-tu?*
N:	Over there.	*Là-bas.*
V:	To the post office?	*À la poste?*
N:	Yes, to the post office to mail a letter.	*Oui, à la poste, poster une lettre.*
V:	How about that, how interesting!	*Ça alors, que c'est intéressant!*
N:	How do you mean, interesting?	*Que veux-tu dire, intéressant?*
V:	I am also going to the post office.	*Je vais aussi à la poste.*
N:	Really? What for?	*Vraiment? Pourquoi faire?*
V:	I work there.	*J'y travaille.*
	Listen, I have an idea.	*Écoute, j'ai une idée.*
N:	What is it?	*Qu'est-ce que c'est?*
V:	Let's go together, ok?	*Allons-y ensemble, d'accord?*
N:	Ok.	*D'accord.*
	Why not?	*Pourquoi pas?*
	With pleasure.	*Avec plaisir.*

Listen to the French again.

V:	By the way, my name is Vincent.	*Au fait, je m'appelle Vincent.*
	And, your name is…Rose, right?	*Et tu t'appelles…Rose, n'est-ce pas?*
N:	No, my name is Nicole.	*Non, je m'appelle Nicole.*
V:	Nicole, it's a pleasure to meet you.	*Nicole, c'est un plaisir de faire ta connaissance.*
N:	For me too.	*Pour moi aussi.*
V:	Say, how do you spend your time?	*Dis, comment passes-tu ton temps?*
N:	Here, at the university?	*Ici, à l'université?*
	I am a pianist.	*Je suis pianiste.*
V:	Truly, and I am a singer.	*Vraiment, et je suis chanteur.*
N:	How about that!	*Ça alors!*
	You know, my husband is also a musician.	*Tu sais, mon mari est aussi un musicien.*
	He is a pianist.	*C'est un pianiste.*
V:	Excellent. Oh, yes, I forgot.	*Excellent. Ah, oui, j'oubliais.*
N:	What?	*Quoi?*
V:	Excuse me.	*Excuse-moi.*
	It's time for me to go home.	*Je dois rentrer à la maison.*
N:	So soon.	*Si vite.*
V:	Yes, unfortunately.	*Oui, malheureusement.*
	I am late for a class.	*Je suis en retard pour une classe.*
	Forgive me.	*Pardonne-moi.*
N:	It's nothing.	*Ce n'est rien.*

V:	Look, here is my bus.	*Regarde, voilà mon bus.*
N:	Well, that means goodbye.	*Et bien, ça veut dire au revoir.*
V:	Goodbye!	*Au revoir!*
	Regards to your husband.	*Le bonjour à ton mari.*
N:	Thanks!	*Merci!*
V:	Till we meet again!	*À la prochaine!*
N:	Bye!	*Au revoir!*

🔊 Listen to the French again.

THE ADVENTURE CONTINUES

When you and Stump have completed those six French exercises, you decide to spend the rest of the day reviewing what you have learned so far. You are delighted with the progress you have made, and you want to make sure you retain your knowledge of the French language and of French-speaking cultures.

After dinner that evening, you receive a call from Cecile Champion.

"I just got back," she tells you. "Katrine, our receptionist, gave me your message. When would you like to speak with me?"

"As soon as possible," Stump inserts before you can formulate a more polite response.

"Pierre told us we needed to speak with you," you add.

Cecile thinks for a moment. "Can you come to the tour office now? I will be here catching up on paperwork and messages for a couple of hours."

"We'll be there as soon as we can," you tell her.

"Then I will see you when you arrive," she responds. She hangs up the phone. You and Stump rush out the door and walk swiftly to the tour offices you visited the day before. Cecile greets you at the door of the tour office.

"Let us dispense with formalities," she begins. "Pierre sent you. How may I help you?"

You and Stump explain your search and your tight deadline. Cecile nods. "It is a good thing I called immediately upon my return," she comments. "Yes, I have your next clue. Like those before me, I have a challenge you must complete before you receive your clue."

Cecile assigns you another set of French exercises and another series of culture questions. "Bring your work to me tomorrow," she tells you.

You and Stump agree and return to the Pétard's residence, where you get right to work. You complete several French activities before you retire for the night.

114

🎧 Openers and Rejoinders
French Only
Présentations et répliques

🎧 Instructions: Read and listen to these conversation pieces. Make new conversations of your own based on these phrases. Then recite them out loud!

Is everyone ready?	🎧 *Est-ce que tout le monde est prêt?*
Not yet.	*Pas encore.*
Yvon, are you ready?	*Yvon, es-tu prêt?*
Yes, I'm ready.	*Oui, je suis prêt.*
Valerie, are you ready?	*Valérie, es-tu prête?*
Yes, I'm ready now.	*Oui, je suis prête maintenant.*
Then we're off!	*Alors, allons-y!*
Are you with us?	*Es-tu avec nous?*
Yes, I'm with you.	*Oui, je suis avec vous.*
Then let's go!	*Alors, allons-y!*
I'm leaving you.	*Je te quitte.*
Oh!	*Oh!*
I'm never coming back.	*Je ne reviendrai jamais.*
Oh!	*Oh!*
Good luck.	*Bonne chance.*
Farewell!	*Bon voyage!*
How many cars do you have?	*Combien de voitures avez-vous?*
Cars? In America? Three.	*Des voitures? En Amérique? Trois.*
One big one and two small ones.	*Une grosse et deux petites.*
They are new?	*Elles sont toutes neuves?*
No. One new one, and two old ones.	*Non. Une neuve et deux vieilles.*
How much does a new car cost in America?	*Combien coûte une voiture neuve en Amérique?*
About $20,000 or $30,000.	*Environ 20.000 ou 30.000 dollars.*
For this one I paid $20,000.	*Pour celle-ci j'ai payé 20.000 dollars.*
You must be very rich.	*Vous devez être très riche.*
Not really.	*Pas vraiment.*
It's your number.	*C'est votre numéro!*
Are you sure <u>of it</u>?	<u>*En*</u> *êtes-vous sûr?*
Absolutely.	*Absolument.*
It means I won the prize?	*Ça veut dire que j'ai gagné le prix?*
That's right.	*C'est exact.*
Heavens! I can't believe it.	*Ciel! Je ne peux pas le croire.*
I don't know anything.	*Je ne sais rien.*
What does that mean?	*Qu'est-ce que cela veut dire?*
It means I know nothing.	*Ça veut dire que je ne sais rien.*

Give me, please, the number of the Royal Hotel.	Donnez-moi, s'il vous plaît, le numéro de l'Hôtel Royal.
One minute...59-81-72-27.	Un instant...59-81-72-27.
Repeat, please, a bit louder.	Répétez, s'il vous plaît, un peu plus fort.
59-81-72-27. Do you understand?	59-81-72-27. Vous comprenez?
Yes, thank you.	Oui, merci.
You're welcome.	De rien.
I have a headache.	J'ai mal à la tête.
And I have a toothache.	Et j'ai mal aux dents.
Where is the aspirin?	Où avons-nous de l'aspirine?
Where is the dentist?	Où est le dentiste?
We're proud of you.	Nous sommes fiers de toi.
No reason to be. I didn't do anything special.	Aucune raison. Je n'ai rien fait de particulier.
There is reason. You're our heroine.	Il y a une raison. Tu es notre héroïne.
Are you going with us?	Tu viens avec nous?
Yes, wait for me.	Oui, attendez-moi.
Then hurry up!	Alors, dépêche-toi!
Nonsense!	Idiotie!
No, it's absolutely true.	Non, c'est absolument vrai.
I don't believe it.	Je ne le crois pas.
I'm telling the truth.	Je dis la vérité.
You're lying.	Tu mens.
Believe me! I'm not lying.	Crois-moi! Je ne mens pas.
Nonsense!	Idiotie!
I can prove it.	Je peux le prouver.
Get out of bed! You're so lazy!	Sors du lit! Tu es tellement paresseux!
I'm sick. I can't budge!	Je suis malade. Je ne peux pas bouger!
Lazy! Lazy! Lazy!	Paresseux! Paresseux! Paresseux!
Where's your daddy?	Où est ton papa?
He is on duty today.	Il est de garde aujourd'hui.
And your mother?	Et ta maman?
She's in town today.	Elle est en ville aujourd'hui.
Ha ha ha ha!	Ha ha ha ha!
Don't make fun of me!	Ne te moque pas de moi!
But you're so funny!	Mais tu es si marrante!
Why are you laughing?	Pourquoi ris-tu?
You make me laugh.	Tu me fais rire.
Why?	Pourquoi?
You put your shirt on backwards.	Tu as mis ta chemise à l'envers.
Are you married?	Êtes-vous mariée?
No, I'm single. Are you married?	Non, je suis célibataire. Êtes-vous marié?
No, I'm single too.	Non, je suis célibataire aussi.
There's a letter on the table for you.	Il y a une lettre sur la table pour toi.
Oh, I hadn't noticed. Who from?	Oh, je n'avais pas remarqué. De qui?
From your girlfriend.	De ta petite amie.

What do you want from me?	*Que voulez-vous de moi?*
Respect. Nothing more.	*Du respect. Rien de plus.*
That shouldn't be too hard.	*Ça ne devrait pas être trop difficile.*
What's that?	*Qu'est-ce que c'est?*
Ice cream.	*De la glace.*
I want some.	*J'en veux.*
Chocolate?	*Au chocolat?*
No, strawberry.	*Non, à la fraise.*
What'll you have?	*Et toi, que prendras-tu?*
The same.	*La même chose.*

End Tape 5, Side A

Tape 5, Side B

115

Second Meeting at the University
Deuxième rencontre à l'université

Instructions: Listen to and read the following dialogue. Make a list of ten words you are not familiar with and memorize them.

	It is spring, April	*C'est le printemps, avril*
N:	Vincent?	*Vincent?*
V:	Rose, hello!	*Rose, bonjour!*
N:	Hi, Vincent.	*Salut, Vincent.*
	You forgot my name, it's Nicole.	*Tu as oublié mon nom, c'est Nicole.*
V:	Nicole, forgive me.	*Nicole, pardonne-moi.*
	I guess I have Rose in my head.	*Il semble que j'ai Rose dans la tête.*
N:	Who is this Rose?	*Qui est cette Rose?*
V:	She is just a friend.	*C'est juste une amie.*
	Many years ago.	*D'il y a bien des années.*
	So be it. How are things?	*Peu importe. Comment vas-tu?*
N:	Quite well, thanks.	*Assez bien, merci.*
V:	And how is your husband?	*Et comment va ton mari?*
N:	Fine, everything is fine with us.	*Bien, tout va bien chez nous.*
	How are you doing? Everything ok?	*Comment vas-tu? Tout va bien?*
	I have not seen you for a long time.	*Je ne t'ai pas vu depuis longtemps.*
V:	I have not seen you since fall.	*Je ne t'ai pas vue depuis l'automne.*
	And it's already 1993.	*Et c'est déjà 1993.*
	By the way, happy new year.	*En fait, bonne année.*
N:	Same to you.	*Pour toi aussi.*
	Are you coming from work?	*Tu reviens du travail?*
V:	No, from a singing lesson.	*Non, d'une leçon de chant.*
	I am going to the library.	*Je vais à la bibliothèque.*
N:	Still working at the post office?	*Tu travailles toujours à la poste?*
V:	No, I quit in February.	*Non, j'ai arrêté en février.*
	To tell the truth, they fired me.	*À vrai dire, j'ai été licencié.*
N:	That's too bad.	*C'est dommage.*
	What happened?	*Que s'est-il passé?*
	Why did they fire you?	*Pourquoi t'ont-ils licencié?*
V:	Because I could not come on time.	*Parce que je ne pouvais pas arriver à l'heure.*
N:	How so?	*Comment ça?*
V:	I am used to studying till midnight in the library.	*J'ai l'habitude d'étudier jusqu'à minuit à la bibliothèque.*
	I can't get up at five in the morning.	*Je ne peux pas me lever à cinq heures du matin.*

(Listen to the French again.)

N:	I understand that.	*Je comprends ça.*
V:	But now my father is angry with me.	*Mais maintenant mon père est en colère contre moi.*
N:	Why that?	*Pourquoi donc?*
V:	He says I am a fool.	*Il dit que je suis un idiot.*
	I should have bought an alarm clock.	*J'aurais dû m'acheter un réveil.*

N:	In my opinion, it would have been better to go to bed earlier.	À mon avis, ça aurait été mieux d'aller au lit plus tôt.
V:	And flunk out of school?	Et échouer à l'école?
N:	Such is life.	C'est la vie.
	Are you looking for a job?	Cherches-tu du travail?
V:	Of course. Otherwise I'd have no money.	Bien sûr. Autrement je n'aurais pas d'argent.
N:	Where do you work now?	Où travailles-tu maintenant?
V:	At the bookstore.	À la librairie.
N:	That's where my sister works.	C'est là que travaille ma sœur.
V:	Really, I didn't know.	Vraiment, je ne savais pas.
	What is her name?	Comment s'appelle-t-elle?
N:	Rose, her name is Rose. Believe it or not.	Rose, elle s'appelle Rose. Incroyable mais vrai.
V:	You're kidding.	Tu blagues.
N:	No, I am not kidding.	Non, je ne blague pas.
	I am telling the truth.	Je dis la vérité.
	She works in the computer section.	Elle travaille au rayon des ordinateurs.
V:	Is she as beautiful as you?	Est-elle aussi jolie que toi?
N:	Oh, she is much, much more beautiful than me.	Oh, elle est beaucoup, beaucoup plus belle que moi.
V:	Introduce me to her, will you?	Présente-la moi, veux-tu?
N:	I will do that, some day.	Je le ferai, un jour.
V:	I've got to go now.	Je dois y aller maintenant.
	I am going to a piano lesson.	Je vais à une leçon de piano.
	Nice to see you again.	Ravi de t'avoir revue.
N:	So long!	À la prochaine!

Listen to the French again.

Instructions: Now listen to these dialogue fragments in French only. Try your best to understand them!

Excusez-moi, s'il vous plaît. Dites-moi, où sont les toilettes?
Pour les dames, c'est par là, à droite. Pour les messieurs, c'est à gauche.
Merci.

Qui est-ce là, à gauche? Tu la connais?
Oui, c'est mon amie. Elle parle bien espagnol.
J'aimerais parler espagnol avec elle si tu me la présentais.
Volontiers.

Tu as quelque chose dans la main, qu'est-que c'est?
C'est un cadeau.
Pour qui?
Pour mon ami, Sébastian.

J'en parlerais à mon amis Yves.
Tu te trompes beaucoup si tu crois qu'il est un de tes amis.

Pardonnez-moi Monsieur, pourriez-vous me dire où se trouve la banque de France?
C'est du côté de la poste.
Et où est la poste?
La poste est en face de la bibliothèque.
Je ne sais pas où est la bibliothèque.
C'est près du musée.

Pardonnez-moi, je suis une étrangère ici, je ne sais pas où se trouve le musée.
Là-bas. Pas loin d'ici.
Merci.
De rien.

Comment dit-on chien en chinois?
Gou.
Répétez lentement s'il vous plaît.

Quel âge as-tu?
25 ans.
On a la même âge!
Tu as aussi 25 ans?

Quand êtes-vous arrivés?
Hier soir.
Et quand partez-vous?
Demain matin.
Demain matin? À quelle heure?
De bonne heure, vers 5 heures.
Laissez-moi vous accompagner.
Avec plaisir.

À quelle heure avez-vous l'intention d'arriver?
À 8 heures.
À 8 heures précises?
Disons vers 8 heures.
Vers 8 heures?
Il vaut mieux dire entre 8 et 9 heures.

Qu'est-ce qui ne va pas?
Je suis en colère.
Et pourquoi?
Parce que tu ne veux pas jouer aux cartes avec moi.
En mon avis tu devrais oublier toute cette affaire.
Je ne peux pas.
Pourquoi?
Parce que je suis en colère, voilà pourquoi.

J'ai entendu dire que votre fils était à l'armée.
Oui, mon fils aîné est à l'armée.
Est'ce qu'il s'y plaît?
Pas vraiment.

Je suis très fier de mon fils.
Pourquoi?
Il sait épeler son nom dans les deux sens.
Comment s'appelle-t-il?
Bob.

Voulez-vous manger?
Non, je n'ai pas faim. J'ai soif.
Et bien, allons boire un coup.

As-tu déjà payer l'amende?
Pas encore. Je la paierai demain.
Combien ça va coûter? Tu le sais?
Pas exactement. Demain, je le saurai.

Quel est ton jour de congés?
Cette semaine, lundi. La semaine prochaine, mardi.

J'aimerais quelques conseils.
Au sujet de...
Au sujet de l'amour.
Oh, ce sera un plaisir pour moi.

C'est une absurdité.
Non, c'est absolument vrai.
C'est impossible.
Je t'assure que c'est ainsi.
Vraiment?
Je peux même le prouver.

116

Isabelle and Vincent
Isabelle et Vincent

Instructions: Listen to and read the following conversation. Read along in French with the voices on the tape.

Summer, July — *Été, juillet*

V:	Hi!	*Salut!*
I:	Hello!	*Bonjour!*
V:	How are things?	*Comment va la vie?*
I:	Very well, thanks.	*Très bien, merci.*
V:	We met at the concert last week, remember?	*Nous nous sommes rencontrés au concert la semaine dernière, t'en souviens-tu?*
I:	Yes, I remember, of course I remember. Nice to see you again.	*Oui, je m'en souviens, bien sûr, je m'en souviens. Ravie de te revoir.*
V:	Forgive me, I forgot your name.	*Pardonne-moi, j'ai oublié ton nom.*
I:	My name is Isabelle, and yours is Vincent, right?	*Je m'appelle Isabelle, et toi Vincent, n'est-ce pas?*
V:	Yes, and what's that?	*Oui, et qu'est-ce que c'est que ça?*
I:	That's my dog.	*C'est mon chien.*
V:	Your dog! He looks like a wolf!	*Ton chien! Il ressemble à un loup!*
I:	Yes, actually his father was a wolf.	*Oui, en fait son père était un loup.*
V:	Tell me, where is your home?	*Dis-moi, où est ta maison?*
I:	On the other side of the park, and yours?	*De l'autre côté du parc, et la tienne?*
V:	On this side of the park.	*De ce côté du parc.*
I:	By the university?	*À côté de l'université?*
V:	Exactly. I was told that you were a pianist?	*Exactement. On m'a dit que tu étais pianiste?*
I:	No, I am not a pianist, I am a Russian spy.	*Non, je ne suis pas une pianiste, je suis une espionne russe.*
V:	Hmm, how interesting, and I am an American secret agent.	*Mmm, que c'est intéressant, et je suis un agent secret américain.*
I:	I know that.	*Je sais.*
V:	How did you find out?	*Comment as-tu su?*
I:	My husband is also a secret agent. He told me. Well, got to go.	*Mon mari est aussi un agent secret. Il me l'a dit. Bon, je dois y aller.*
V:	Wait a second, I've got one last question.	*Attends une seconde, j'ai une dernière question.*
I:	What is it?	*Qu'est-ce que c'est?*
V:	Tell me, what's your dog's name?	*Dis-moi, comment s'appelle ton chien?*
I:	Napo, his name is Napo.	*Napo, il s'appelle Napo.*
V:	Why do you call him Napo?	*Pourquoi l'appelles-tu Napo?*
I:	Hard to say, Napoleon.	*Difficile à dire, Napoléon.*
V:	Well, got to go. Goodbye Napo. Goodbye Isabelle.	*Bon, je dois y aller. Au revoir Napo. Au revoir Isabelle.*
I:	Good luck!	*Bonne chance!*

(Listen to the French again.)

117
Chatter at a Royal Ball
French Only
Bavardages au bal royal

Instructions: Listen to and read the following conversations. You've already learned these before; this should be a review.

🔊 Back now to the scene of the royal ball.

CONVERSATION 1

••: Who is singing?
•: The king. The king is singing.
••: Which king?
•: The one who likes to play funeral chants on the drum.
••: The king who likes to play funeral chants on the drum is singing?
•: Yes, and he sings well, doesn't he?
••: Well enough. He sings better than he plays.

Qui chante?
Le roi. Le roi chante.
Quel roi?
Celui qui aime jouer des chants funèbres au tambour.
Le roi qui aime jouer des chants funèbres au tambour chante?
Oui, et il chante bien, n'est-ce pas?
Assez bien. Il chante mieux qu'il ne joue.

CONVERSATION 2

••: The queen is singing also.
•: Which queen?
••: The one who was crying in the bathroom with the princess.
•: The queen who was crying in the bathroom with the princess is singing?
••: Yes, she is singing in the tower with the king.
•: The king and the queen are singing funeral chants in the tower?
••: Yes. And don't they sing well?
•: Well yes, they sing more or less well. But why do they sing funeral chants?
••: Who knows?

La reine chante aussi.
Quelle reine?
Celle qui pleurait dans la salle de bain avec la princesse.
La reine qui pleurait dans la salle de bain avec la princesse chante?
Oui. Elle chante dans la tour avec le roi.
Le roi et la reine chantent des chants funèbres dans la tour?
Oui. Et ne chantent-ils pas bien?
Bien oui, ils chantent plus ou moins bien. Mais pourquoi chantent-ils des chants funèbres?
Qui sait?

CONVERSATION 3

••: Bobi and Misti are singing too. They are singing with the king and queen in the tower.
•: Bobi and Misti?
••: The cat and the dog.
•: A king and a queen with a dog and a cat? They're singing in the tower?
••: It appears so.
•: Do they sing well?
••: Yes, they sing well enough.
•: And the princess, is she singing too?
••: No, the princess isn't singing. She cries more than she sings.

Bobi et Misti chantent aussi. Ils chantent avec le roi et la reine dans la tour.
Bobi et Misti?
Le chat et le chien.
Un roi et une reine avec un chien et un chat? Ils chantent dans la tour?
Il semble que oui.
Est-ce qu'ils chantent bien?
Oui, ils chantent assez bien.
Et la princesse, chante-t-elle aussi?
Non, la princesse ne chante pas. Elle pleure plus qu'elle ne chante.

      She doesn't sing well.
      In fact, she sings worse than the dog!   *Elle ne chante pas bien.*
                                                                            En fait, elle chante plus mal que le chien!
- •: But better than the cat, right? — *Mais mieux que le chat, n'est-ce pas?*
- ••: Of course. Imagine! — *Bien sûr. Tu t'imagines!*
- •: Oh gee! — *Oh là là!*

CONVERSATION 4

- ••: The king that loves to play the drum is singing now, right? — *Le roi qui aime jouer du tambour chante maintenant, n'est-ce pas?*
- •: Yes. He's not playing. — *Oui. Il ne joue pas.*
- ••: Doesn't he play anymore? — *Est-ce qu'il ne joue plus?*
- •: Oh he still plays. He often plays. He's going to play tonight. But he prefers to sing. — *Oh, il joue encore. Il joue souvent. Il va jouer ce soir. Mais il préfère chanter.*
- ••: Who is it he is singing with? — *Avec qui est-ce qu'il chante?*
- •: With the queen. Both are singing, and she is playing drum now. — *Avec la reine. Tous les deux chantent et elle joue du tambour maintenant.*
- ••: And the dog and the cat, what are they doing now? — *Et le chien et le chat, que font-ils maintenant?*
- •: Both are singing with the king and the queen. — *Les deux chantent avec le roi et la reine.*
- ••: Really? Where? Where are they singing? — *Vraiment? Où? Où est-ce qu'ils chantent?*
- •: Over there. Listen. — *Là bas. Écoute.*
- ••: It's sensational. Imagine! — *C'est sensationnel. Imagine-toi!*
- •: They like to sing together. — *Ils aiment chanter ensemble.*
- ••: That's great! — *C'est formidable!*
- •: They say that the cat has decided to sing with the princess. — *On dit que le chat a décidé de chanter avec la princesse.*
- ••: When? — *Quand?*
- •: Now. — *Maintenant.*
- ••: That's horrible! — *C'est horrible!*
- •: Listen! They're starting to sing already. — *Écoute! Ils commencent déjà à chanter.*
- ••: Yukh! How much does this concert cost? — *Beurk. Combien coûte ce concert?*

THE ADVENTURE CONTINUES

Day Ten—0800 hours

One Day to New Rendezvous

You wake up early the next morning and get back to work on Cecile's challenge. You set a goal to finish by noon. You work your way through more exercises.

118

Afanti and the Pauper
French Only
Afanti et le pauvre

Instructions: Listen to and read the following story. Do not read along in English until after you've listened to the story in French at least once. Work toward full comprehension.

Once there was a poor man who had no food to eat.	Il était une fois un pauvre qui n'avait rien à manger.
In his hunger, he walked the streets of the city.	Affamé, il marchait par les rues de la ville.
Passing a restaurant, he smelled the delicious food.	En passant devant un restaurant il a senti de la nourriture délicieuse.
He stopped and stood inhaling the smells.	Il s'est arrêté et s'est tenu debout pour humer les odeurs.
After a while, the restaurant owner came out.	Après un certain temps, le propiétaire du restaurant est sorti.
"What are you doing here?" he asked the pauper.	«Que fais-tu ici?» a-t-il demandé au pauvre.
"Good sir, I haven't eaten in two days.	«Mon bon monsieur, je n'ai pas mangé depuis deux jours.
I am dying of hunger.	Je meurs de faim.
I thought perhaps by smelling your good food I could derive some sustenance."	J'ai pensé que, peut-être, en respirant votre bonne nourriture, je pourrais en gagner quelque force.»
"How long have you been here?"	«Depuis combien de temps es-tu ici?»
"Only for a few minutes."	«Depuis à peine quelques minutes.»
"Then you must pay me."	«Alors, tu dois me payer.»
"Why should I pay you? I haven't consumed any food."	«Pourquoi devrais-je vous payer? Je n'ai pas consommé de nourriture.»
"By smelling the food you've consumed the flavor.	«En respirant la nourriture, tu as consommé la saveur.
And if you do not pay me, I'll have you arrested and thrown in jail."	Et si tu ne me paies pas, je te ferai arrêter et jeter en prison.»
"But I am poor. I have no money.	«Mais je suis pauvre. Je n'ai pas d'argent.
I can't pay you.	Je ne peux pas vous payer.
Please let me go."	S'il vous plaît, laissez-moi partir.»
Just then a policeman came by, and asked: "What's going on here?"	À ce moment précis un policier est passé par là, et il a demandé: «Que ce passe-t-il ici?»
The restaurant owner answered:	Le propriétaire du restaurant a répondu:
"This man has consumed my food but refuses to pay for it."	«Cet homme a consommé ma nourriture, mais il refuse de la payer.»
The policeman took the poor man to the police station and locked him in a cell.	Le policier a amené le pauvre homme à la station de police et l'a enfermé dans une cellule.
The poor man asked that his friend Afanti come at once.	Le pauvre homme a demandé que son ami Afanti vienne tout de suite.
Afanti came and heard what had happened.	Afanti est venu et a entendu ce qui s'était passé.
He told the judge that he himself would pay the restaurant owner.	Il a dit au juge qu'il payerait lui-même le propriétaire du restaurant.
Afanti and the pauper went to the restaurant	Afanti et le pauvre sont allés ensemble au

together.
Afanti asked how much the man
owed for the food.
"One kuai five mao," said the owner.
Afanti reached in his pocket
and pulled from it a bag of coins.
He held the bag up and shook it
by the ear of the restaurant owner.
The owner heard the coins jingle
and reached up to take the money,
but Afanti quickly withdrew it, smiling.
"My friend was able to smell your restaurant
food," he said,
"and now you were able to hear this money.
That satisfies completely his debt to you."

restaurant.
Afanti a demandé combien l'homme
devait pour la nourriture.
«Un kuai, cinq mao», a dit le propriétaire.
Afanti a mit sa main dans sa poche
et en a sorti un sac de monnaie.
Il a tenu le sac en l'air et l'a
secoué près de l'oreille du propriétaire du restaurant.
Le propriétaire a entendu la monnaie cliqueter
et a étendu la main pour prendre l'argent,
mais Afanti l'a rapidement retiré, en souriant.
«Mon ami a pu sentir la nourriture de votre
restaurant», a-t-il dit,
«et maintenant, vous avez pu entendre cet argent.
Ceci satisfait pleinement sa dette envers vous.»

119

The Story of the Hare and the Tortoise
French Only
L'histoire du lièvre et de la tortue

Instructions: Listen to and read the following story. Follow along with the French voice on the tape. Then review the English portion and see how much you understood!

Everyone knows a hare runs very fast,	*Tout le monde sait qu'un lièvre court très vite,*
even faster than a dog or a horse,	*plus vite même qu'un chien ou qu'un cheval,*
and perhaps almost as fast as a deer.	*et peut-être presque aussi vite qu'une biche.*
On the other hand, a tortoise cannot run.	*Par contre, une tortue ne peut pas courir.*
He can only crawl along slowly.	*Elle ne peut que ramper lentement.*
One day a small hare was admiring his long	*Un jour, un petit lièvre admirait ses longues*
hindlegs and said arrogantly:	*pattes de derrière et il a dit avec fierté:*
"Of all the animals, I am the fastest.	*«De tous les animaux, je suis le plus rapide.*
No animal can beat me.	*Aucun animal ne peut me battre.*
No animal can run as fast as I can."	*Aucun animal ne peut courir aussi vite que moi.»*
The other animals saw the hare was proud,	*Les autres animaux ont vu que le lièvre était fier,*
but at first no one dared take up his challenge.	*mais, au début, personne n'osait relever son défi.*
Suddenly a tortoise said:	*Tout à coup, une tortue a dit:*
"I know you can run fast,	*«Je sais que tu peux courir vite,*
but that doesn't matter.	*mais cela n'a aucune importance.*
If we race I will win."	*Si nous faisons une course, je gagnerai.»*
All the animals turned	*Tous les animaux se sont retournés*
and looked at the tortoise.	*et ils ont regardé la tortue.*
They thought: "How dare you?	*Ils ont pensé: «Comment oses-tu?*
It is foolish to have a foot race	*C'est une folie de faire une course à pied*
with a hare."	*contre un lièvre.»*
The hare burst out laughing:	*Le lièvre a éclaté de rire:*
"You can't even run,	*«Tu ne peux même pas courir,*
you can only crawl."	*tu peux seulement ramper.»*
The tortoise said: "Don't you dare race me?"	*La tortue a dit: «N'oses-tu pas courir contre moi?»*
"Okay," the hare said.	*«D'accord», a dit le lièvre.*
"We'll meet tomorrow near the pine tree	*«Nous nous rencontrerons demain, près du sapin*
on the hill.	*sur la colline.*
Tonight you'd better get a good rest."	*Cette nuit, tu ferais bien de te reposer.»*
The next day the race began.	*La course a commencé le jour suivant.*
All the animals looked on.	*Tous les animaux ont regardé.*
The hare took off very fast,	*Le lièvre est parti très vite,*
and of course the tortoise crawled very slowly.	*et, bien sûr, la tortue a rampé très lentement.*
After a minute the hare looked back,	*Après une minute, le lièvre a regardé en arrière*
but couldn't see the tortoise.	*mais il ne pouvait pas voir la tortue.*
He thought to himself:	*Il a pensé à voix basse:*
"Why should I kill myself running?	*«Pourquoi devrais-je me tuer à courir?*

I'll stop under this tree and have a rest."	*Je vais m'arrêter sous cet arbre et me reposer.»*
So he stopped and lay down	*Il s'est donc arrêté et il s'est couché*
to wait for the tortoise.	*pour attendre la tortue.*
Before long he fell asleep.	*Peu après, il s'est endormi.*
Meanwhile the tortoise continued crawling.	*Pendant ce temps-là, la tortue continuait à ramper.*
She moved very slowly,	*Elle avançait très lentement,*
but she didn't stop;	*mais elle ne s'est pas arrêtée;*
she didn't give up.	*elle n'a pas abandonné.*
After a while, she passed under the tree	*Après un certain temps, elle est passée sous l'arbre*
and saw the hare sleeping.	*et elle a vu le lièvre qui dormait.*
She thought: "Although I am tired,	*Elle a pensé: «Bien que je sois fatiguée,*
I can't stop. I must press on."	*je ne peux pas m'arrêter. Je dois aller de l'avant.»*
After a long time, the hare woke up	*Après un long moment, le lièvre s'est soudainement*
with a start.	*réveillé.*
He didn't know how long he'd been sleeping.	*Il ne savait pas combien de temps il avait dormi.*
Suddenly he remembered the race.	*Tout à coup, il s'est souvenu de la course.*
He looked back but didn't see the tortoise.	*Il a regardé en arrière, mais il n'a pas vu la tortue.*
He looked ahead and saw that the tortoise	*Il a regardé en avant, et il a vu que la tortue*
was almost at the finish line.	*était déjà presque à la ligne d'arrivée.*
He ran as fast as he could	*Il a couru aussi vite qu'il a pu,*
but could not catch up with the tortoise.	*mais il n'a pas pu rattraper la tortue.*
The hare lost the race	*Le lièvre a perdu la course*
and hung his head in shame.	*et il a baissé la tête de honte.*
The tortoise won.	*La tortue a gagné.*
And all the animals cheered.	*Et tous les animaux ont applaudi.*

120

📼 Five Blind Men Describe an Elephant
Cinq aveugles décrivent un éléphant

📼 Instructions: Listen to and read the following story. How many words do you already know?

📼 One day five blind men were chatting, and the subject turned to elephants. One of them said: "I've grown this old and I still don't know what an elephant looks like."	*Un jour, cinq aveugles bavardaient et ils se sont mis à parler d'éléphants.* *L'un d'eux a dit:* *«J'ai atteint un âge déjà avancé et je ne sais toujours pas à quoi ressemble un éléphant.»*
"Neither do I." "Me, I haven't seen one either." "Same here." "What in fact does an elephant look like?"	*«Moi non plus.»* *«Moi, je n'en ai pas encore vu non plus.»* *«Moi non plus.»* *«En fait, à quoi ressemble un éléphant?»*

All five had the same opinion,
   so they at once decided to ask
   someone to take them to an elephant
   so they could feel it.
	Tous les cinq avaient la même opinion
	   et ils ont donc tout de suite décidé de demander
	   à quelqu'un de les amener vers un éléphant pour
	   qu'ils puissent le toucher.

One day the group of blind men finally got
   the chance to "see" what an elephant was.
	Un jour, le groupe d'aveugles a finalement eu
	   la chance de «voir» ce qu'était un éléphant.

With great delight they went up to the elephant
   and attentively began to feel it.
	C'est avec grand plaisir qu'ils sont allés vers l'éléphant et
	   qu'ils ont commencé à le toucher attentivement.

"Aha! Now I know, an elephant has the shape of a wall." "No! An elephant has the shape of a thick rope." "No! No! An elephant looks like a big fan!"	*«Ah ha! Maintenant je sais, un éléphant a la forme d'un mur.»* *«Et non, un éléphant a la forme d'une corde épaisse.»* *«Non! Non! Un éléphant ressemble à un grand ventilateur.»*
"You are all wrong! An elephant looks like a pillar." "All of you are wrong. An elephant looks like a snake."	*«Vous avez tous tort! Un éléphant ressemble à une colonne.»* *«Vous avez tous tort. Un éléphant ressemble à un serpent.»*

Each thought only his own opinion was right.
Since each thought that the part that he touched
   constituted the whole elephant,
     they would not listen to one another or accept
     another's opinion.
And so it finally ended in a quarrel.
	Chacun pensait que seule son opinion était correcte.
	Puisque chacun pensait que la partie qu'il touchait
	   constituait l'éléphant en entier,
	     ils ne voulaient pas s'écouter les uns les autres, ou
	     accepter l'opinion d'un autre.
	Et cela s'est ainsi finalement terminé par une dispute.

End Tape 5, Side B

Tape 6, Side A

121

Three Little Pigs (Version One)
French Only
Les trois petits cochons

Instructions: Listen to the following story in French. Do you understand it? Which words do you already know?

Trois petits cochons. Frères. Trois maisons. Une maison en paille.

Une maison en planches. Une maison en briques. Un loup. Il vient affamé.

Il vient à la maison en paille. Il souffle. La maison en paille tombe.

Mais le petit cochon s'échappe. Le loup vient une fois de plus.

Il vient à la maison en planches. Il vient très affamé.

Il souffle. La maison en planches tombe. Mais le petit cochon s'échappe.

Le loup vient une fois de plus. Il vient à la maison en briques. Il est TRÈS affamé.

Il souffle. Il souffle une fois de plus. Mais la maison en briques ne tombe pas.

Et le loup part TRÈS TRÈS affamé.

122

Three Little Pigs (Version 2)
Les trois petits cochons

Instructions: Listen to and read the following story. Work toward full comprehension.

There were once three pigs.	*Il était une fois trois cochons.*
Three little pigs.	*Trois petits cochons.*
They were brothers.	*Ils étaient frères.*
But they had different characters.	*Mais ils avaient des caractères différents.*
One day they were talking.	*Un jour, ils parlaient.*
They wanted to build themselves a house.	*Ils voulaient construire une maison.*
As they were talking	*Pendant qu'ils parlaient*
they saw a man in a truck	*ils ont vu un homme dans un camion*
with a load of straw.	*avec un chargement de paille.*
"Let's build a house of straw!"	*«Construisons une maison en paille!»,*
said the first little pig.	*a dit le premier petit cochon.*
"No, we don't want a house	*«Non», a dit son frère, «nous ne*
of straw," said his brother.	*voulons pas de maison en paille.»*
"Well, then, I am going to build	*«Bon», a dit le premier petit cochon,*
it myself," said the first little pig.	*«Alors, je la construirai moi-même.»*
Then he went to talk with the man	*Alors il est allé parler avec l'homme*
and said to him:	*et lui a dit:*
"Please, sir, sell me your straw	*«S'il vous plaît, Monsieur, vendez-moi votre paille*
so that I can build my house."	*pour que je puisse construire ma maison.»*
"Very well," said the man.	*«D'accord», a dit l'homme.*
And he sold the straw to the first little pig,	*Et il a vendu la paille au premier petit cochon*
who rapidly built himself a house of straw.	*qui a rapidement construit une maison en paille.*
The second little pig saw a man in a truck	*Le deuxième petit cochon a vu un homme dans un*
with a load of sticks.	*camion avec un chargement de planches.*
"Me and you, let's build us a house of sticks,"	*«Toi et moi, construisons une maison en planches»,*
he said to the other little pig.	*a-t-il dit à l'autre petit cochon.*
"No, I don't want a house of sticks,"	*«Non, je ne veux pas de maison en planches»,*
said the other little pig.	*a dit l'autre petit cochon.*
"Well, then, I am going to build it myself,"	*«Bon», a dit le deuxième petit cochon, «et bien*
said the second little pig.	*je vais la construire moi-même.»*
Then he went to talk with the man,	*Alors, il est allé parler avec l'homme*
and he said to him:	*et lui a dit:*
"Please, sir, sell me your sticks	*«S'il vous plaît, Monsieur, vendez-moi vos planches*
so that I can build my house."	*pour que je puisse construire ma maison.»*
"Very well," said the man.	*«D'accord», a dit l'homme.*
And he sold the sticks to the the second little pig,	*Et il a vendu les planches au deuxième petit cochon,*
who quickly built himself a house of sticks.	*qui a rapidement construit une maison en planches.*
The third little pig didn't want	*Le troisième petit cochon ne*
a house of straw.	*voulait pas de maison en paille.*
Nor did he want a house of sticks.	*Et il ne voulait pas non plus de maison en planches.*
But he saw a man in a truck	*Mais il a vu un homme dans un camion*
with a load of bricks.	*avec un chargement de briques.*

Then he decided to build a house of bricks.

He went to talk with the man.
"Please, sir, sell me your bricks
so that I can build my house."
"Very well," said the man.
And he sold the bricks to the third little pig,
who carefully built himself a house of bricks.

Soon came a big, bad wolf.
He was hungry.

He came to the first little pig's house,
and knocked on the door and said to him:
"Little pig, little pig, let me come in."
"No way, Mr. Wolf,
I won't let you come in."
"Then I'll huff and I'll puff
till your house tumbles down."
And he huffed and he puffed
till the house tumbled down.
But the little pig went running
to the house of the second pig.
The big, bad wolf couldn't catch him.
And the little pig escaped.
The big, bad wolf was angry,
but he tried to not let it be seen
how angry he was.

He came to the house of the second little pig,
the house of sticks, and said:
"Little pig, little pig, let me come in."
"No way, Mr. Wolf,
I won't let you come in."
"Then I'll huff and I'll puff
till it tumbles your house down."
And he huffed and he puffed
till the house tumbled down.
But the two little pigs
went running to the house of their brother,
the house of bricks.
The big, bad wolf was unable
to catch them.
And the little pigs escaped.
Now indeed the big, bad wolf
was really angry.
And he was hungry.
But he tried to not let it be seen
how angry he was.

He came to the house of the third little pig,
the house of bricks, and said:
"Little pig, little pig, let me come in."
"No way, Mr. Wolf,

Alors, il a décidé de construire une maison en briques.

Il est allé parler avec l'homme.
«S'il vous plaît, Monsieur, vendez-moi vos briques,
pour que je puisse construire ma maison.»
«D'accord», a dit l'homme.
Et il a vendu les briques au troisième petit cochon,
qui a soigneusement construit une maison en briques.

Peu après, un grand méchant loup est venu.
Il avait faim.

Il est venu à la maison du premier petit cochon,
et frappé à la porte et lui a dit:
«Petit cochon, petit cochon, laisse-moi entrer.»
«Pas question, Monsieur Loup,
je ne vous laisserai pas entrer.»
«Alors je soufflerai et je soufflerai,
jusqu'à ce que ta maison s'écroule.»
Et il a soufflé et il a soufflé
jusqu'à ce que la maison s'écroule.
Mais le petit cochon est parti en courant
vers la maison du deuxième cochon.
Et le grand méchant loup n'a pas pu l'attraper.
Et le petit cochon s'est enfui.
Le grand méchant loup était en colère,
mais il a essayé de ne pas montrer
combien il était en colère.

Il est arrivé à la maison du deuxième petit cochon,
la maison en planches, et il a dit:
«Petit cochon, petit cochon, laisse-moi entrer.»
«Pas question, Monsieur Loup,
je ne vous laisserai pas entrer.»
«Alors je soufflerai et je soufflerai
jusqu'à ce que ta maison s'écroule.»
Et il a soufflé et il a soufflé
jusqu'à ce que la maison s'écroule.
Mais les deux petits cochons
sont partis en courant vers la maison en briques de leur frère.
Le grand méchant loup n'a pas été capable de
les attraper.
Et les petits cochons se sont enfuis.
Maintenant, le grand méchant loup
était vraiment en colère.
Et il avait faim.
Mais il a essayé de ne pas montrer
combien il était en colère.

Il est arrivé à la maison du troisième petit cochon,
la maison en briques, et a dit:
«Petit cochon, petit cochon, laisse-moi entrer.»
«Pas question, Monsieur Loup,

I won't let you come in."
"Then I'll huff and I'll puff
till it tumbles your house down."
Then he huffed and he puffed,
and he puffed and he huffed,
but he could not tumble the house
of bricks down.
Finally the wolf went away,
but very angry and very hungry.
Then the first and the second little pig
said to the third little pig:
"Thanks, brother, for building a strong house."
And the three little pigs lived happily
in the house of bricks for many years.

But the wolf died of hunger.
Poor thing!

je ne vous laisserai pas entrer.»
«Alors, je soufflerai et je soufflerai
jusqu'à ce que ta maison s'écroule.»
Alors, il a soufflé et il a soufflé,
et il a soufflé et il a soufflé,
mais il ne pouvait pas faire écrouler
la maison en briques.
Finalement le loup est parti,
mais très en colère et très affamé.
Alors, le premier et le deuxième petit cochon
ont dit au troixième petit cochon:
«Merci, frère, d'avoir construit une maison solide.»
Et les trois petits cochons ont vécu heureux
dans la maison en briques pendant de nombreuses
années.
Mais le loup est mort de faim.
Le pauvre!

123

The Hunter and the Thief
Le chasseur et le voleur

Instructions: Listen to and read the following story. Then answer the questions at the end of the story.

In a minute, I'll tell you a story.	*Dans une minute, je vais vous raconter une histoire.*
Here's what my story will be about:	*Voici de quoi parlera mon histoire:*
In it a woman will prepare food.	*Une femme préparera de la nourriture.*
Here's the woman who will prepare the food.	*Voici la femme qui préparera la nourriture.*
After this a mouse will come and eat the food.	*Après cela une souris viendra et mangera la nourriture.*
Here's the mouse that will eat the food.	*Voici la souris qui mangera la nourriture.*
After this a cat will come and catch the mouse.	*Après cela un chat viendra et attrapera la souris.*
Here's the cat that will catch the mouse.	*Voici le chat qui attrapera la souris.*
After this a snake will come and swallow the cat.	*Après cela un serpent viendra et avalera le chat.*
Here's the snake that will swallow the cat.	*Voici le serpent qui avalera le chat.*
After this an eagle will come and pounce on the snake.	*Après cela un aigle viendra et s'abattra sur le serpent.*
Here's the eagle that will pounce on the snake.	*Voici l'aigle qui s'abattra sur le serpent.*
After this a hunter will come and kill the eagle.	*Après cela un chasseur viendra et tuera l'aigle.*
Here's the hunter that will kill the eagle.	*Voici le chasseur qui tuera l'aigle.*
After this a thief will come and steal the eagle.	*Après cela un voleur viendra et volera l'aigle.*
Here's the thief that will steal the eagle.	*Voici le voleur qui volera l'aigle.*
After this a policeman will come and arrest the thief.	*Après cela un policier viendra et arrêtera le voleur.*
Here's the police that will arrest the thief.	*Voici le policier qui arrêtera le voleur.*
And the thief will go to jail.	*Et le voleur ira en prison.*
Here's the thief that will go to jail.	*Voici le voleur qui ira en prison.*
Poor woman! Poor mouse!	*Pauvre femme! Pauvre souris!*
Poor cat! Poor snake!	*Pauvre chat! Pauvre serpent!*
Poor eagle! Poor hunter!	*Pauvre aigle! Pauvre chasseur!*
And poor thief!	*Et pauvre voleur!*

* * * * *

Here now is my story.	*Voici maintenant mon histoire.*
At first the woman prepares the food.	*D'abord la femme prépare la nourriture.*
Here's the woman preparing the food.	*Voici la femme préparant la nourriture.*
After this the mouse comes and eats the food.	*Après cela la souris vient et mange la nourriture.*
Here's the mouse eating the food.	*Voici la souris mangeant la nourriture.*
After this the cat comes and catches the mouse.	*Après cela le chat vient et attrape la souris.*
Here's the cat catching the mouse.	*Voici le chat attrapant la souris.*
After this the snake comes and swallows the cat.	*Après cela le serpent vient et avale le chat.*
Here's the snake swallowing the cat.	*Voici le serpent avalant le chat.*
After this the eagle comes and pounces on the snake.	*Après cela l'aigle vient et s'abat sur le serpent.*
Here's the eagle pouncing on the snake.	*Voici l'aigle s'abattant sur le serpent.*

After this the hunter comes and kills the eagle.	Après cela le chasseur vient et tue l'aigle.
Here's the hunter killing the eagle.	Voici le chasseur tuant l'aigle.
After this the thief comes and steals the eagle.	Après cela le voleur vient et vole l'aigle.
Here's the thief stealing the eagle.	Voici le voleur volant l'aigle.
After this the policeman comes and arrests the thief.	Après cela le policier vient et arrête le voleur.
Here's the policeman arresting the thief.	Voici le policier arrêtant le voleur.
And the thief goes to jail.	Et le voleur va en prison.
And here's the thief in jail.	Et voici le voleur en prison.
Poor woman! Poor mouse!	Pauvre femme! Pauvre souris!
Poor cat! Poor snake!	Pauvre chat! Pauvre serpent!
Poor eagle! Poor hunter!	Pauvre aigle! Pauvre chasseur!
And poor thief!	Et pauvre voleur!

* * *

Now let's see how well you learned the story.	Maintenant voyons si vous avez bien appris cette histoire.
What happened first?	Que s'est-il passé d'abord?
The woman prepared some food.	La femme a préparé de la nourriture.
Here's the woman preparing the food.	Voici la femme préparant la nourriture.
What happened after that?	Que s'est-il passé après cela?
After that a mouse came and ate the food.	Après cela la souris est venue et a mangé la nourriture.
Here's the mouse eating the food.	Voici la souris mangeant la nourriture.
What happened after that?	Que s'est-il passé après cela?
After that the cat came and caught the mouse.	Après cela le chat est venu et a attrapé la souris.
Here's the cat catching the mouse.	Voici le chat attrapant la souris.
What happened after that?	Que s'est-il passé après cela?
After that the snake came and swallowed the cat.	Après cela le serpent est venu et a avalé le chat.
Here's the snake swallowing the cat.	Voici le serpent avalant le chat.
What happened after that?	Que s'est-il passé après cela?
After that the eagle came and pounced on the snake.	Après cela l'aigle est venu et s'est abattu sur le serpent.
Here's the eagle pouncing on the snake.	Voici l'aigle s'abattant sur le serpent.
What happened after that?	Que s'est-il passé après cela?
After that the hunter came and killed the eagle.	Après cela le chasseur est venu et a tué l'aigle.
Here's the hunter killing the eagle.	Voici le chasseur tuant l'aigle.
What happened after that?	Que s'est-il passé après cela?
After that the thief came and stole the eagle.	Après cela le voleur est venu et a volé l'aigle.
Here's the thief stealing the eagle.	Voici le voleur volant l'aigle.
What happened after that?	Que s'est-il passé après cela?
After that the policeman came and arrested the thief.	Après cela le policier est venu et a arrêté le voleur.
Here's the policeman arresting the thief.	Voici le policier arrêtant le voleur.
What happened after that?	Que s'est-il passé après cela?
The thief went to jail.	Le voleur est allé en prison.
And here's the thief in jail.	Et voici le voleur en prison.

QUESTIONS

What did the mouse do?	Qu'a fait la souris?
The mouse ate up the food.	La souris a mangé la nourriture.
What did the cat do?	Qu'a fait le chat?
The cat caught the mouse.	Le chat a attrapé la souris.

What did the snake do?	*Qu'a fait le serpent?*
The snake swallowed the cat.	*Le serpent a avalé le chat.*
What did the eagle do?	*Qu'a fait l'aigle?*
The eagle pounced on the snake.	*L'aigle s'est abattu sur le serpent.*
What did the hunter do?	*Qu'a fait le chasseur?*
The hunter killed the eagle.	*Le chasseur a tué l'aigle.*
What did the thief do?	*Qu'a fait le voleur?*
The thief stole the eagle.	*Le voleur a volé l'aigle.*
What did the policeman do?	*Qu'a fait le policier?*
The policeman arrested the thief.	*Le policier a arrêté le voleur.*
Where is the thief now?	*Où est le voleur maintenant?*
The thief is in jail.	*Le voleur est en prison.*

124
Les pêcheurs silencieux
The Silent Fishermen

Instructions: Listen to and read the following story. Rewrite the ending in French!

Early one Saturday morning	De bonne heure un samedi matin,
a fisherman and his son went out fishing.	un pêcheur et son fils partirent à la pêche.
Because fishermen don't like to talk a lot,	Puisque les pêcheurs n'aiment pas beaucoup parler,
the men in our story were as	les hommes de notre histoire étaient
quiet as fish.	aussi silencieux que des poissons.
Not until noon, when the clouds appeared	Ce ne fut qu'à midi, quand des nuages apparurent
on the horizon,	à l'horizon,
did the son say to the father:	que le fils dit au père:
"Looks like it's gonna rain."	«On dirait qu'il va pleuvoir.»
The father looked up for a while	Le père leva les yeux un instant
and nodded.	et hocha la tête.
But he didn't say a word.	Mais il ne dit pas un mot.
The day went by like that.	La journée se déroula ainsi.
On Sunday they took a rest.	Le dimanche ils se reposèrent.
But as usual, they said nothing	Mais comme d'habitude,
to each other.	ils ne se dirent rien.
On Monday they went fishing again.	Le lundi, il retournèrent à la pêche.
But they were still silent.	Mais ils étaient toujours silencieux.
Tuesday, Wednesday, Thursday, Friday,	Mardi, mercredi, jeudi, vendredi,
all passed in the same way.	tous les jours se déroulèrent de la même manière.
It was only on Friday evening	Ce n'est que vendredi soir,
when it was raining hard,	alors qu'il pleuvait très fort,
that the father wiped his forehead	que le père s'essuya le front
with his hand and said:	avec la main et dit:
"Yes, you're right."	«Oui, tu as raison.»

CULTURE QUESTIONS—SECTION SIX

Instructions: Answer these questions based on your reading. Feel free to check the appendix to find the answers.

1. Name three major industries in Québec.

2. How is traditional Moroccan food served?

3. What is Morocco most popular sport?

4. What is Senegal's most widely understood native language?

5. What city in Senegal is an important port for West Africa?

6. What river forms Luxembourg's southern border?

THE ADVENTURE CONTINUES

You finish Cecile's challenge in plenty of time to return it to her. You and Stump rush to her office and show her your work.

She nods her approval. "Excellent work. I can see you have devoted many hours to learning the French language and culture. Now, I have heard you have a healthy interest in learning of other cultures in which French is spoken."

You confirm what she has heard, though you wonder from whom she heard it.

"Then," she continues, "if you wish, I will tell you of my own beautiful homeland, Switzerland."

You tell her that you would love to learn more about Switzerland, and she begins her summary.

SWITZERLAND CULTURE OVERVIEW

The Swiss tend to consider their country to be ideal. They have a tremendous appreciation for nature and beauty, and they are very sensitive to environmental issues. Switzerland is a beautiful country, with high mountains and clear lakes. When people from other countries describe scenic beauty, they often use Switzerland as a standard. The Swiss value hard work, thrift, independence, tolerance, and punctuality. In fact, there is a saying that if a person is late, he is either not wearing a Swiss watch or not riding a Swiss train. Almost half the population of Switzerland is Roman Catholic, and most of the rest of the population belong to different Christian faiths.

FACTS AND FIGURES ON SWITZERLAND

- Switzerland's population is about 6.96 million and is growing by 0.6% annually.

- Switzerland is nicknamed the "roof of Europe" because of the Alps.

- Switzerland has four official languages: German, French, Italian, and Romansch.

- Soccer and cycling are Switzerland's most popular sports.

- The Swiss Confederation was founded on 1 August 1291—more than seven centuries ago!

- Switzerland's federal government consists of the bicameral Federal Assembly and the Assembly's president.

- Switzerland exports fine watches, cheeses, machinery, textiles, chemicals, and precision instruments.

THE ADVENTURE CONTINUES

Cecile finishes her summary. You can tell from the expressions that play across her face that she is very proud of her homeland and that she misses it. In a soft voice, you ask her why she left it.

She shrugs expressively. "I am a field biologist," she explains. "I knew I could do our world more good out here than back in Switzerland where so many are already interested in caring for our world. Anyway, you have earned your final clue—salt and vanilla. Marie-Loire works at the resort hotel as an entertainment co-ordinator. If you can pass her challenge, she will guide you to the treasure you seek."

You thank her for taking the time to see you. Then you and Stump rush to the resort hotel, hoping that you can find Marie-Loire quickly. You find her office in the hotel without difficulty, and to your relief, she is in her office and has time to talk to you. You explain your search to her and relay what Cecile told you.

Marie-Loire nods her comprehension. "I can guide you to the treasure you seek," she tells you in delightfully accented English, "though it will be up to you to obtain the treasure. Before I can guide you to the treasure, though, you must complete my challenge—more French exercises. Because this is your last challenge before seeing the treasure, this challenge will be longer and more difficult than those you have had before. You have twenty-four hours to complete it. *Bonne chance!*"

You and Stump thank her and hurry back to the Pétard residence. You get to work immediately on Marie-Loire's challenge. You know that you have to work with the submarine captain's deadline as well as Marie-Loire's. You complete eight of the fifteen exercises in the challenge before you fall asleep.

125

📼 *Les pêcheurs silencieux*
The Silent Fishermen

📼 Instructions: Listen to this story written only in French. Work toward full comprehension.

📼 *De bonne heure un samedi matin, un pêcheur et son fils partirent à la pêche. Puisque les pêcheurs n'aiment pas beaucoup parler, les hommes de notre histoire étaient aussi silencieux que des poissons. Ce ne fut qu'à midi, quand des nuages apparurent à l'horizon, que le fils dit au père: «On dirait qu'il va pleuvoir.»*

Le père leva les yeux un instant et hocha la tête. Mais il ne dit pas un mot. La journée se déroula ainsi. Le dimanche ils se reposèrent. Mais comme d'habitude, ils ne se dirent rien. Le lundi, il retournèrent à la pêche.

Mais ils étaient toujours silencieux. Mardi, mercredi, jeudi, vendredi, tous les jours se déroulèrent de la même manière. Ce n'est que vendredi soir, alors qu'il pleuvait très fort, que le père s'essuya le front avec la main et dit: «Oui, tu as raison.»

126

📼 The Three Billygoats Gruff
French Only
Les trois boucs

📼 Instructions: Listen to and read the following story. Circle all the vocabulary words that are new to you and try to learn them.

There were three goats	📼 *Il était une fois trois boucs*
that lived in the mountains.	*qui vivaient dans les montagnes.*
They were brothers.	*Ils étaient frères.*
There was a big goat,	*Il y avait un grand bouc,*
a middle-sized goat,	*un bouc moyen,*
and a little goat.	*et un petit bouc.*
The goats liked very much	*Les boucs aimaient beaucoup*
to eat green grass	*manger de l'herbe verte*
in the mountains.	*dans les montagnes.*
And they never went down to the valley.	*Et ils ne descendaient jamais dans la vallée.*
They never had crossed the bridge.	*Ils n'avaient jamais traversé le pont.*
One day the small goat noticed	*Un jour, le petit bouc a remarqué*
that on the other side of	*que de l'autre côté du pont,*
the bridge there was a lot of green grass.	*il y avait beaucoup d'herbe verte.*
Then the small goat thought	*Alors, le petit bouc a envisagé*
about crossing the bridge	*de traverser le pont*
and descending to the valley	*et de descendre dans la vallée*

to eat that green grass.
He didn't know that beneath the bridge
there was a troll,
very ugly and very fierce.

Well, the little goat neared the bridge,
and soon began to cross it.
But when he was crossing the bridge
his footsteps sounded:
TIP, TAP, TIP, TAP…
Upon hearing the footsteps of the small goat,
the troll jumped from the water
and yelled with a fierce voice:
"Who is crossing my bridge?"
"It's me, the little goat."
"And why do you come here?"
"I am going to go down to the valley
to eat the green grass over there."
"Get off of my bridge!
If not, I will eat you."
"Oh, please, don't eat me.
I am very small.
Better wait until
my brother passes by here.
He is bigger
and fatter than me."
"Ok, go ahead then this time."

A little later,
the middle-sized goat saw that his
little brother was in the valley
below and was happy there,
eating green grass.
Now he thought of crossing the
bridge to go down into the valley
where there was a lot of green grass.
He neared the bridge
and began to cross
without knowing of the troll
that lives below.
But when he went crossing the
bridge, his footsteps sounded:
TIP, TAP, TIP, TAP…
Upon hearing the foosteps of the
middle-sized goat on the bridge,
the ugly troll jumped from the
water and yelled with a fierce voice:
"Who is crossing my bridge?"
"I am, the middle-sized billygoat."
"And why do you come here?"
"I am going to go down to the
valley to eat the green grass there
with my brother."
"Get off of my bridge!

pour manger cette herbe verte.
Il ne savait pas que sous le pont
il y avait un génie
très laid et très féroce.

Alors, le petit bouc s'est approché du pont
et s'est tout de suite mis à le traverser.
Mais, quand il était en train de traverser le pont,
ses pas résonnaient:
TIP, TAP, TIP, TAP…
Quand il a entendu les pas du petit bouc,
le génie est sorti de la rivière
et a crié d'une voix féroce:
«Qui traverse mon pont?»
«C'est moi, le petit bouc.»
«Et pourquoi viens-tu ici?»
«Je vais descendre dans la vallée
pour y manger l'herbe verte.»
«Va-t'en de mon pont.
Sinon, je te mangerai.»
«Oh, s'il vous plaît, ne me mangez pas.
Je suis très petit.
Il vaut mieux attendre
que mon frère passe par ici.
Il est plus grand
et plus gras que moi.»
«D'accord, vas-y pour cette fois.»

Un peu plus tard,
le bouc moyen a vu que son
petit frère était dans la vallée,
en bas, et qu'il y était heureux,
à manger de l'herbe verte.
Il a alors envisagé de traverser le
pont pour descendre dans la vallée
où il y avait de l'herbe verte.
Il s'est approché du pont
et a commencé à le traverser
ne sachant rien du génie
qui vivait au-dessous.
Mais quand il a traversé le pont,
ses pas résonnaient:
TIP, TAP, TIP, TAP…
Quand il a entendu les pas du bouc
moyen sur le pont,
le vilain génie est sorti de l'eau
et a crié avec une voix féroce:
«Qui traverse mon pont?»
«C'est moi, le bouc moyen.»
«Et pourquoi viens-tu ici?»
«Je descends dans la vallée
pour y manger de l'herbe verte
avec mon frère.»
«Va-t'en de mon pont!

If not, I will eat you."	*Sinon, je vais te manger.»*
"Oh, please, don't eat me.	*«Oh, s'il vous plaît, ne me mangez pas.*
I am still very small.	*Je suis encore très petit.*
Better wait until	*Il vaut mieux attendre*
my big brother passes by here.	*que mon grand frère passe par ici.*
He is bigger	*Il est plus grand*
and fatter than I."	*et plus gras que moi.»*
"Ok, then, pass this time."	*«Alors d'accord, passe cette fois-ci.»*
A little time later	*Quelques temps plus tard,*
the big billygoat (the big brother)	*le grand bouc (le frère aîné)*
sees that his little brothers are	*voit que ses petits frères sont*
in the valley happily	*heureux dans la vallée*
eating green grass.	*à manger de l'herbe verte.*
Now he thinks of crossing the	*Il envisage maintenant de traverser*
bridge and going down to the	*le pont et de descendre dans la*
valley to eat that grass.	*vallée pour y manger cette herbe.*
He nears the bridge	*Il s'approche du pont*
and begins to cross it	*et commence à le traverser*
without knowing of the ugly troll.	*ne sachant rien au sujet du vilain génie.*
But as he was crossing the bridge,	*Mais, quand il a traversé le pont,*
his footsteps were heard:	*on entendait ses pas:*
TOPE, TOPE, TOPE, TOPE,	TOC, TOC, TOC, TOC
and the bridge rocked from such weight.	*et le pont se balançait sous un tel poids.*
Upon hearing the footsteps	*Quand il a entendu les pas*
and feeling the bridge sway,	*et qu'il a senti le pont se balancer,*
the ugly troll jumped from the water,	*le vilain génie est sorti de l'eau,*
and he yelled with a fierce voice:	*et il a crié d'une voix féroce:*
"Who is crossing my bridge?"	*«Qui traverse mon pont?»*
"I am, the big billygoat."	*«C'est moi, le bouc.»*
"And why did you come here?"	*«Et pourquoi viens-tu ici?»*
"I'm going to go down to the valley	*«Je vais descendre dans la vallée*
to eat some grass there	*pour y manger de l'herbe*
with my little brothers."	*avec mes petits frères.»*
"Get off my bridge.	*«Va-t'en de mon pont.*
Otherwise, I'm going to eat you."	*Sinon, je vais te manger.»*
"Well, come ahead."	*«D'accord, viens donc.»*
The ugly troll moved up close,	*Le vilain génie s'est approché,*
but the big billygoat lowered his	*mais le bouc a baissé sa*
head, and with his horns	*tête, et avec ses cornes,*
he gave a tremendous blow to the troll.	*il a donné un grand coup au génie.*
He fell into the water and drowned.	*Il est tombé dans l'eau et il s'est noyé.*
And from that day onward,	*Et à partir de ce jour,*
the ugly troll hasn't bothered the billygoats.	*le vilain génie n'a plus dérangé les boucs.*
The billygoats can cross the bridge	*Les boucs peuvent traverser le pont*
whenever they want, and they can	*quand ils le veulent et ils peuvent*
eat the grass in the valley	*manger l'herbe de la vallée*
as well as in the mountains.	*aussi bien que celle de la montagne.*

127

🎧 Mercury and the Woodcutters
Mercure et les bûcherons

🎧 Instructions: Listen to and read the following story. Read the French along with the voice on the tape.

🎧 A woodcutter was cutting wood	Un bûcheron coupait du bois
along the riverside.	le long de la rivière.
By accident he let his axe fall	Il laissa tomber sa hache dans
into the river.	la rivière par accident.
Because he had lost his worktool,	Parce qu'il avait perdu son outil,
he sat down on a riverbank	il s'assit sur la rive
and contemplated his misfortune.	pour considérer sa mésaventure.
To his astonishment, Mercury	À son grand étonnement, Mercure
suddenly appeared before him	soudain apparut devant lui
and asked:	et lui demanda:
"What happened?	«Que s'est-il passé?
Why are you sad?"	Pourquoi es-tu triste?»
After the woodcutter told him of his	Après que le bûcheron lui ai raconté
misfortune,	sa mésaventure,
Mercury jumped into the river	Mercure sauta dans la rivière
and came up	et il lui remonta
holding a golden axe.	une hache en d'or à la main.
He said: "Is this yours?"	Il dit: «Est-ce la tienne?»
"No, it's not mine.	«Non, ce n'est pas la mienne.
Mine is made of iron."	La mienne est en fer.»
Then Mercury jumped again	Alors Mercure sauta de nouveau
into the river,	dans la rivière
and this time came up with a silver axe.	et, cette fois-ci, il revint avec une hache en argent.
"Is this one yours?"	«Est-ce la tienne?»
"No, it's not mine.	«Non, ce n'est pas la mienne.
Mine is made of iron."	La mienne est en fer.»
A third time	Mercure plongea une troisième
Mercury dove into the river.	fois dans la rivière.
This time he brought	Cette fois ci, il rapporta la
the woodcutter's lost axe.	hache perdue du bûcheron.
"Is this one yours?"	«Est-ce que celle-ci est la tienne?»
"Yes, that's mine. Thank you!"	«Oui, c'est la mienne. Merci!»
Mercury said:	Mercure dit:
"You are an honest man.	«Tu es un homme honnête.
Therefore I will give you	Je te donnerai donc
the golden axe	la hache en or
and the silver axe	et la hache en argent
as well as your iron axe."	ainsi que ta hache en fer.»
Back home, the woodcutter told	De retour à la maison, le bûcheron
his strange experience to his	raconta son étrange expérience
relatives and neighbors.	à sa famille et à ses voisins.
One of them thought he would	L'un d'eux pensa qu'il tenterait
try his luck,	sa chance

so he took his axe and went to the river. He threw his axe in the water and then sat down on the riverbank and pretended to bemoan his misfortune. Just as he had hoped, Mercury appeared before him and asked: "What happened? Why are you grieving?" The woodcutter said: "My axe accidentally fell in the river. Would you dredge it up for me?" Mercury said: "I will try and see." He dove to the bottom of the river and came up with a golden axe. "Is this yours?" he asked. "Yes, it's mine. And last week I lost another axe. Would you see if you can find it?" Mercury dove into the water and soon came back with a silver axe. "Is this your lost axe?" "Yes, yes," the woodcutter said greedily. Then Mercury said to him: "You have lied to me. You are both greedy and dishonest. Therefore I will give you neither the golden axe nor the silver axe. And I will not fetch up the iron axe you threw into the river either."	*et il prit donc sa hache et alla à la rivière. Il jeta sa hache dans l'eau et il s'assit sur la rive de la rivière et il prétendit gémir de sa malchance. Tout comme il l'avait espéré, Mercure apparut devant lui et lui demanda:* «Que s'est-il passé? Pourquoi es-tu triste?» *Le bûcheron dit:* «Ma hache est accidentellement tombée dans la rivière. Voudrais-tu aller me la chercher?» *Mercure dit:* «Je vais essayer.» *Il plongea au fond de la rivière et il revint avec une hache en or.* «Est-ce la tienne?» *demanda-t-il.* «Oui, c'est la mienne. *et la semaine dernière, j'ai perdu une autre hache.* Voudrais-tu voir si tu peux la trouver?» *Mercure plongea dans l'eau et revint bientôt avec une hache d'argent.* «Est-ce que c'est la hache que tu as perdue?» «Oui, oui», *dit le bûcheron avec avarice. Mercure lui dit alors:* «Tu m'as menti. Tu es à la fois cupide et malhonnête. En conséquence, je ne te donnerai ni la hache en or ni la hache en argent. Et je n'irai pas non plus chercher la hache en fer que tu as jetée dans la rivière.»

128 *Proverbes*
Proverbs

Instructions: Read through these proverbs. The translations are not literal—we've included the proverbs as they are known in English and in French.

All that glitters is not gold.	*Tout ce qui brille n'est pas or.*
All's well that ends well.	*Tout est bien qui finit bien.*
Better late than never.	*Mieux vaut tard que jamais.*
Birds of a feather flock together.	*Qui se ressemble s'assemble.*
He who laughs last laughs best.	*Rira bien qui rira le dernier.*
Heaven helps those who help themselves.	*Aide-toi, et le ciel t'aidera.*
Man proposes but God disposes.	*L'homme propose mais Dieu dispose.*
No news is good news.	*Pas de nouvelles, bonnes nouvelles.*
Nothing ventured, nothing gained.	*Qui ne risque rien n'a rien.*
One shouldn't speak ill of one's neighbors.	*On ne doit pas dire du mal de ses voisins.*
Practice makes perfect.	*Usage rend maître.*
Speech is silver, silence is gold.	*La parole est d'argent, mais le silence est d'or.*
Tell me what he eats and I'll tell you what he is.	*Dis-moi ce qu'il mange et je te dirai ce qu'il est.*
The walls have ears.	*Les murs ont des oreilles.*
Where there's a will, there's a way.	*Vouloir, c'est pouvoir.*
Where there's smoke, there's fire.	*Il n'y a pas de fumée sans feu.*

129

The Little Red Hen
La petite poule rousse

Instructions: Listen to and read the following story. Rewrite the ending in French!

Once upon a time there was a red hen who worked very hard. In fact, she was called: "The-Hen-Who-Works-Hard." One day she found a grain of wheat. "Cluck-cluck," she said. "Come see. I found a grain of wheat. Will you help me plant it?" "Quack-quack, not me," said the duck. "Honk-Honk, not me," said the goose. "Gobble-gobble, neither I," said the turkey. "Then, I'll do it myself," said the hen. And she did.	*Il était une fois une poule rousse qui travaillait très dur. En fait, on l'appelait: «La-Poule-Qui-Travaille-Dur.» Un jour, elle a trouvé un grain de blé. «Cotte-Cotte», dit-elle. «Venez voir. J'ai trouvé un grain de blé. M'aiderez-vous à le planter?» «Coin-Coin, pas moi», a dit le canard. «Honk-Honk, pas moi», a dit l'oie. «Glou-glou, ni moi», a dit la dinde. «Alors, je le ferai moi-même», a dit la poule. Et elle l'a fait.*
"Who will help me harvest the wheat?" said the hen. "Not me," said the duck. "Not me," said the goose. "Neither I," said the turkey. "Then I'll do it myself," said the hen. And she did.	*«Qui m'aidera à récolter le blé?» a dit la poule. «Pas moi», a dit le canard. «Pas moi», a dit l'oie. «Ni moi», a dit la dinde. «Alors, je le ferai moi-même», a dit la poule. Et elle l'a fait.*
"Very well, and now, who will help me carry that wheat to the mill?" "Not me," said the duck. "Not me," said the goose. "Neither I," said the turkey. "Then I'll carry it myself," said the hen. And she did. She came back with the flour.	*«Très bien, et maintenant, qui m'aidera à porter ce blé au moulin?» «Pas moi», a dit le canard. «Pas moi», a dit l'oie. «Ni moi», a dit la dinde. «Alors, je le porterai moi-même», a dit la poule. Et elle l'a fait. Et elle est revenue avec la farine.*
"Very well," she said. "And now, who will help me make bread?" "Not me," said the duck. "Not me," said the goose. "Neither I," said the turkey. "Then I'll make it myself," said the hen. And she did. Mmmm, warm bread. Delicious.	*«Très bien», dit-elle. «Et maintenant, qui m'aidera à faire du pain?» «Pas moi», a dit le canard. «Pas moi», a dit l'oie. «Ni moi», a dit la dinde. «Alors, je le ferai moi-même», a dit la poule. Et elle l'a fait. Mmmm, du pain chaud. Délicieux.*
"And now," said the hen, "who wants a piece of that bread?" "Me," said the duck. "Me," said the goose. "Me too," said the turkey.	*«Et maintenant», a dit la poule, «qui veut un morceau de ce pain?» «Moi», a dit le canard. «Moi», a dit l'oie. «Moi aussi», a dit la dinde.*

"Oh, but you didn't help me plant the seed. You didn't help me to harvest it. You didn't help me to carry the wheat to the windmill and bring back the flour. You didn't help me to make the bread. You didn't help me at all. I did everything myself." Then the hen called her chickies: "Cluck-cluck, come my chickies. Here is some bread for you." And they ate all the bread. But the duck, the goose, and the turkey didn't get the least piece.	«Oh, mais vous ne m'avez pas aidée à planter la semence. Vous ne m'avez pas aidée à la moissonner. Vous ne m'avez pas aidée à porter le blé au moulin et à rapporter la farine. Vous ne m'avez pas aidée à faire le pain. Vous ne m'avez pas aidée du tout. J'ai dû tout faire moi-même.» Alors la poule a appelé ses poussins: «Cotte-Cotte, venez mes poussins. Voici du pain pour vous.» Et ils ont mangé tout le pain. Mais le canard, l'oie, et la dinde n'ont pas reçu le moindre morceau.

130

Treatment for Melancholy
Traitement contre la mélancolie

Instructions: Listen to and read the following story. Learn words about emotions in French.

A man went to see a doctor. The doctor asked him: "What is your complaint?" "I am depressed," said the man. "I am not happy. I am always sad. I often cry. I never laugh. It is years since I have laughed. Is there anything that can cure me of my depression? Can you prescribe medication? Can you treat me or counsel me? Is there something that can make me laugh again?" "I believe your depression can be cured. Go to the circus. The circus has a clown who is extremely funny. For sure he'll make you laugh." "I don't believe it." "Why don't you believe it? I guarantee the clown will make you laugh until you're sick to your stomach." "No, you are wrong," said the poor man. "Why?" said the doctor. The man said: "I am the clown."	Un homme est allé voir un docteur. Le docteur lui a demandé: «De quoi vous plaignez-vous?» «Je suis déprimé», a dit l'homme. «Je ne suis pas heureux. Je suis toujours triste. Je pleure souvent. Je ne ris jamais. Cela fait des années que je n'ai pas ri. Y a-t-il quelque chose qui puisse me guérir de ma dépression? Pouvez-vous me prescrire des médicaments? Pouvez-vous me donner un traitement ou me conseiller? Y-a-t-il quelque chose qui puisse à nouveau me faire rire?» «Je crois que votre dépression peut être guérie. Allez au cirque. Le cirque a un clown qui est extrêmement drôle. Il vous fera certainement rire.» «Je ne le crois pas.» «Pourquoi ne le croyez-vous pas? Je vous garantis que ce clown vous fera rire jusqu'à ce que vous ayez mal à l'estomac.» «Non. Vous avez tort», a dit le pauvre homme. «Pourquoi?», a dit le docteur. L'homme a dit: «Je suis le clown.»

131
Learning Words in Clusters
Apprentissage de mots en série

Instructions: Go through the following word lists. Circle all the words you already know; underline the words you still need to learn. Then go ahead and familiarize yourself with each word as best as possible!

WORD SET 1
Location and Direction

to the west	*vers l'ouest*
to the east	*vers l'est*
to the north	*vers le nord*
to the south	*vers le sud*
on the left	*à gauche*
on the right	*à droite*
far from here	*loin d'ici*
near here	*près d'ici*
below	*au dessous*
downward	*vers le bas* (base)
above	*au dessus*
upward	*vers le haut*
forward	*en avant*
backward	*en arrière*
behind, in back	*derrière*
everywhere	*partout*

WORD SET 2
General Time Expressions

four seasons	*quatre saisons*
in winter	*en hiver*
in autumn	*en automne*
in summer	*en été*
in spring	*au printemps*
today	*aujourd'hui*
tomorrow	*demain*
day after tomorrow	*après-demain*
yesterday	*hier*
day before yesterday	*avant-hier*
seldom	*rarement*
usually	*habituellement*
sometimes	*parfois*
never	*jamais*
often	*souvent*
always	*toujours*
	(lit. all days)

WORD SET 3
Panorama

mountain	*(la) montagne*
hill	*(la) colline*
lake	*(le) lac*
pond	*(l') étang* (m)
river	*(la) rivière*
village	*(le) village*
city	*(la) ville*
road	*(la) route*
bridge	*(le) pont*
forest	*(la) forêt*
tree	*(l') arbre* (m)
garden	*(le) jardin*
field	*(le) champs*
fence	*(la) barrière*

WORD SET 4
Household

room	*(la) pièce* ("P.S.")
bathroom	*(la) salle de bain*
bathtub	*(la) baignoire*
living room	*(la) salle de séjour*
	(*séjour* "stay, sojourn")
sofa	*(le) sofa/canapé*
armchair	*(le) fauteuil*
bedroom	*(la) chambre*
bed	*(le) lit* (litter)
kitchen	*(la) cuisine*
table	*(la) table*
chair	*(la) chaise*
cupboard	*(le) placard*
shelf	*(l') étagère* (f)
	(*étage* "stage, story")
stool	*(le) tabouret*
rug	*(le) tapis* (tapestry)

WORD SET 5
Clothing and Things Worn

dress	(la) robe
suit	(le) costume
suit-coat	(le) veston
pants	(le) pantalon
shirt	(la) chemise
blouse	(le) chemisier
sweater	(le) pullover, tricot
tie	(la) cravate
socks	(les) chaussettes (f)
shoes	(les) chaussures (f)
belt	(la) ceinture (cinch)
hat	(le) chapeau
ring	(la) bague
necklace	(le) collier (collar)
watch	(la) montre
gloves	(les) gants (m) (elegant with gants)

WORD SET 6
Foods

food	(la) nourriture
seasoning	(l') assaisonnement (f)
salt	(le) sel (f)
soup	(la) soupe
salad	(la) salade
lettuce	(la) laitue
fish	(le) poisson
lobster	(la) langouste/ (le) homard
meat	(la) viande
pork	(le) porc
mutton	(le) mouton
roast beef	(le) rosbif
sausage	(la) saucisse
bread	(le) pain
butter	(le) beurre
ice cream	(la) glace

WORD SET 8
Fruits and Vegetables

fruit	(le) fruit
lemon	(le) citron (citrus)
orange	(l') orange (f)
plum	(la) prune
peach	(la) pêche
pear	(la) poire
cherries	(les) cerises (f)
apple	(la) pomme
potato	(la) pomme de terre
tomato	(la) tomate
cucumber	(le) concombre

WORD SET 7
Sea and Sky

sky	(le) ciel
cloud	(le) nuage
sun	(le) soleil
moon	(la) lune (lunar)
stars	(les) étoiles (f)
sea	(la) mer
storm	(l') orage (m)
fog	(le) brouillard
rain	(la) pluie
weather	(le) temps
wind	(le) vent
wave	(la) vague
land	(la) terre
beach	(la) plage
bay	(la) baie
harbor	(le) port

WORD SET 9
Wild Animals

lion	(le) lion
tiger	(le) tigre
leopard	(le) léopard
elephant	(l') éléphant (m)
hippopotomus	(l') hippopotame (m)
rhinocerus	(le) rhinocéros
ostrich	(l') autruche (m)
vulture	(le) vautour
bear	(l') ours (m)
wolf	(le) loup
fox	(le) renard
bird	(l') oiseau (m)
eagle	(l') aigle (m)
owl	(le) hibou
bat	(la) chauve-souris

WORD SET 10
Domestic Animals

horse	(le) cheval
cow	(la) vache
donkey	(l') âne (f)
camel	(le) chameau
sheep	(le) mouton (mutton)
lamb	(l') agneau (m)
goat	(la) chèvre (Chevrolet)
pig	(le) cochon (kosher)
rabbit	(le) lapin (lapel)
rooster	(le) coq
duck	(le) canard

WORD SET 11
City

building	(le) bâtiment
store	(le) magasin
hospital	(l') hôpital (m)
theater	(le) théatre
factory	(l') usine (f)
bakery	(la) pâtisserie
school	(l') école (f)
church	(l') église (f)
cemetary	(le) cimetière
park	(le) parc
airport	(l') aéroport (m)
airplane	(l') avion (m)
helicopter	(l') hélicoptère (m)
train station	(la) gare
train	(le) train
bus	(l') autobus (m)
crowd	(la) foule
stadium	(le) stade

WORD SET 12
Seashore and Boating

cliff	(le) rocher
lighthouse	(le) phare
boat	(le) bateau
sailing ship	(le) voilier
sail	(la) voile
steamship	(le) bateau à vapeur
wheel	(la) roue
anchor	(l') ancre (f)
whale	(la) baleine
skipper, captain	(le) capitaine
seaman, sailor	(le) marin
bottom	(le) fond
	(deep=profond)

WORD SET 13
Clothing

clothing	(les) vêtements (m)
underwear	(les) sous-vêtements (m)
scarf	(l') écharpe (f)
shawl	(le) châle
button	(le) bouton
zipper	(la) fermeture éclair
snap	(le) bouton-pression
shorts	(le) short
bra	(le) soutien-gorge
jersey, vest	(le) maillot
swimsuit	(le) maillot de bain
apron	(le) tablier

WORD SET 14
Bedroom

bed	(le) lit (litter)
mattress	(le) matelas
blanket	(la) couverture
sheet	(le) drap
pillow	(l') oreiller (m)
	(ear=oreille)
cushion	(le) coussin
hanger	(le) cintre
wall	(le) mur (mural)
floor	(le) sol (soil)
ceiling	(le) plafond
	("platform")
light	(la) lumière
lamp	(la) lampe
door	(la) porte
window	(la) fenêtre

End Tape 6, Side A

132

🔲 Little Red Riding Hood
Le Petit Chaperon Rouge

🔲 Instructions: Listen to and read the following story. Read the French along with the voice on the tape.

🔲 In a house on one side of the woods	*Dans une maison, d'un côté du bois*
there lives a little girl with her mother	*vit une petite fille avec sa mère*
and father.	*et son père.*
She's called Little Red Riding Hood.	*Elle s'appelle le Petit Chaperon Rouge.*
Her grandmother lives	*Sa grand-mère habite*
on the other side of the woods.	*de l'autre côté du bois.*
One day the mother calls the girl:	*Un jour, la mère appelle sa fille:*
"Little Red Riding Hood."	*«Petit Chaperon Rouge.»*
"Yes, Mother."	*«Oui maman.»*
"Red Riding Hood, your grandma is sick.	*«Petit Chaperon Rouge, ta grand-mère est malade.*
Take her this basket of cookies.	*Apporte-lui ce panier de biscuits.*
Take it to her, please."	*Apporte-le lui, s'il te plaît.»*
"Yes, Mother, with pleasure."	*«Oui maman, avec plaisir.»*
"But be careful, dear.	*«Mais fais attention, ma chérie.*
Don't talk with anyone.	*Ne parle avec personne.*
They say that there's a ferocious wolf	*On dit qu'il y a un loup féroce*
in the woods."	*dans le bois.»*
"Okay, Mother. Don't worry."	*«D'accord, maman. Ne t'inquiète pas.»*

The girl enters the woods	*La fille entre dans les bois*
carrying the basket of cookies.	*en portant un panier de biscuits.*
The fierce wolf is sitting	*Le loup féroce est assis*
at the side of the road.	*sur le côté de la route.*
He sniffs.	*Il renifle.*
"Hmm, cookies.	*«Mmm, des biscuits.*
They smell very good.	*Ils sentent très bon.*
I am hungry."	*J'ai faim.»*
Then he sees Red Riding Hood.	*Il voit alors le Petit Chaperon Rouge.*
"Good morning, little girl.	*«Bonjour, petite fille.*
Where are you going?"	*Où vas-tu?»*
"I'm going to my grandma's house	*«Je me rends chez ma grand-mère*
with this basket of cookies."	*avec ce panier de biscuits.»*
"Oh, your grandma is sick?"	*«Oh, ta grand-mère est malade?»*
"Yes, she's a little sick."	*«Oui, elle est légèrement malade.»*
"And where does your grandma live?"	*«Et où habite ta grand-mère?»*
"She lives on the other side	*«Elle habite de l'autre côté*
of the woods."	*du bois.»*
"Oh yes, I know her."	*«Oh oui, je la connais.»*
"Are you the wolf?"	*«Es-tu le loup?»*
"Yes, but you needn't fear.	*«Oui, mais n'aie pas peur.*
I love little girls.	*J'aime les petites filles.*
What is your name?"	*Quel est ton nom?»*
"I'm called Little Red Riding Hood."	*«Je m'appelle le Petit Chaperon Rouge.»*
"Enchanted to meet you.	*«Enchanté de faire ta connaissance.*
Don't worry. I won't hurt you.	*Ne t'inquiète pas. Je ne te ferai pas de mal.*
Well then, I have to go now.	*Et bien, je dois m'en aller.*
Goodbye, Little Red Riding Hood."	*Au revoir, Petit Chaperon Rouge.»*
"Goodbye, Mr. Wolf."	*«Au revoir, Monsieur le Loup.»*
Red Riding Hood	*Le Petit Chaperon Rouge*
continues on her way, whistling.	*continue son chemin en sifflant.*
The wolf runs through the woods	*Le loup court à travers les bois*
till he comes	*jusqu'à ce qu'il arrive*
to the grandma's house.	*à la maison de la grand-mère.*
He knocks on the door.	*Il frappe à la porte.*
"Who is it?"	*«Qui est là?»*
The wolf imitates the voice of the little girl:	*Le loup imite la voix de la petite fille:*
"It's me, Little Red Riding Hood.	*«C'est moi, Petit Chaperon Rouge.*
I have a basket of cookies for you."	*J'ai un panier de biscuits pour toi.»*
"Come in."	*«Entre.»*
The wolf goes in.	*Le loup entre.*
Grandma is in bed.	*La grand-mère est au lit.*
She sees the wolf.	*Elle voit le loup.*
"You, you're not my granddaughter,	*«Tu n'es pas ma petite-fille.*
but rather the wolf."	*mais tu es en fait le loup.»*
"Exactly.	*«Exactement.*
I am not your granddaughter,	*Je ne suis pas ta petite-fille,*
but rather the wolf.	*mais je suis en fait le loup.*
But don't be frightened."	*Mais n'aie pas peur.»*
The wolf goes into the kitchen	*Le loup entre dans la cuisine*
looking for cookies.	*à la recherche de biscuits.*
Meanwhile grandma	*En attendant, grand-mère*

quickly gets out of bed	*sort rapidement du lit*
and runs out of the house.	*et sort en courant de la maison.*
The wolf knows that Little Red	*Le loup sait que le Petit Chaperon*
Riding Hood will come soon.	*Rouge arrivera bientôt.*
He puts on the grandma's bonnet	*Il met le bonnet de la grand-mère*
and gets into bed.	*et se met au lit.*
Little Red Riding Hood knocks on the door.	*Le Petit Chaperon Rouge frappe à la porte.*
"Who is it?" says the wolf.	*«Qui est là?», dit le loup.*
"Little Red Riding Hood.	*«Le Petit Chaperon Rouge.*
I have a basket of cookies for you."	*J'ai un panier de biscuits pour toi.»*
"Come in, my dear."	*«Entre, ma chérie.»*
She goes in.	*Elle entre.*
The wolf imitates the grandma's voice:	*Le loup imite la voix de la grand-mère:*
"Red Riding Hood, good morning."	*«Bonjour, Petit Chaperon Rouge.»*
"Good morning, Grandma.	*«Bonjour, grand-mère.*
How are you?"	*Comment vas-tu?»*
"A little better, thank you.	*«Un peu mieux, merci.*
Come here and let me see what	*Viens ici et fait moi voir ce que*
you have brought me."	*tu m'as apportée.»*
Little Red Riding Hood takes the basket	*Le Petit Chaperon Rouge prend le panier*
and puts it on the bed.	*et le pose sur le lit.*
Then she looks at the wolf.	*Elle regarde alors le loup.*
She looks at him up close.	*Elle le regarde de près.*
"Grandma, you are very sick."	*«Grand-mère, tu es très malade.»*
"Not really, my dear."	*«Pas vraiment, ma chérie.»*
"You have such big eyes."	*«Tu as de si grands yeux.»*
"I know, my dear."	*«Je sais, ma chérie.»*
"Grandma, why do you have	*«Grand-mère, pourquoi as-tu*
such big eyes?"	*de si grands yeux?»*
"The better to see you, my dear."	*«Pour mieux te voir, ma chérie.»*
"You have huge ears."	*«Tu as de grandes oreilles.»*
"I know, my dear."	*«Je sais, ma chérie.»*
"Grandma, why do you have such huge ears?"	*«Grand-mère, pourquoi as-tu de si grandes oreilles?»*
"The better to hear you, my dear."	*«Pour mieux t'entendre, ma chérie.»*
"You have such a long nose."	*«Tu as un si long nez.»*
"I know, my dear."	*«Je sais, ma chérie.»*
"Grandma, why do you have such a long nose?"	*«Grand-mère, pourquoi as-tu un si long nez?»*
"The better to smell you, my dear."	*«Pour mieux te sentir, ma chérie.»*
"Grandma, you have really changed."	*«Grand-mère, tu as vraiment changé.»*
"So what? Don't you still love me?	*«Et alors, ne m'aimes-tu plus?*
Come here and give me a kiss."	*Viens et donne-moi un baiser.»*
"But Grandma, you have such sharp teeth."	*«Mais grand-mère, tu as des dents si pointues.»*
"I know, my dear."	*«Je sais, ma chérie.»*
"Why do you have such sharp teeth?"	*«Pourquoi as-tu des dents si pointues?»*
"The better to EAT YOU, my dear."	*«Pour mieux TE MANGER, ma chérie.»*
"Oh, I'm scared. You are the ferocious wolf."	*«Oh, j'ai peur. Tu es le loup féroce.»*
Just at that moment the grandma returns with a dog.	*À ce moment-là, la grand-mère revient avec un chien.*
They enter.	*Ils entrent.*
"Help! Help!" cries Little Red Riding Hood.	*«À l'aide! À l'aide!» crie Le Petit Chaperon Rouge.*

"Help!" cries the wolf, "A dog!"	*«À l'aide», crie le loup, «un chien!»*
At once the wolf jumps out of the bed,	*En un seul coup le loup saute hors du lit,*
runs out of the house,	*sort de la maison en courant*
and escapes into the forest.	*et s'enfuit dans la forêt.*
So the grandma, the dog,	*Alors, la grand-mère, le chien,*
and Little Red Riding eat the cookies.	*et le Petit Chaperon Rouge mangent les biscuits.*
And when Little Red Riding Hood returns home	*Et quand le Petit Chaperon Rouge rentre à la maison*
she doesn't tell her mother anything	*elle ne dit rien à sa mère de ce*
about what happened.	*qui s'est passé.*
And for his part, the wolf decides	*Et de son côté, le loup décide*
to never talk to little girls again,	*de ne plus jamais parler aux petites filles*
and also to try to never frighten people again.	*et aussi de ne plus jamais faire peur aux gens.*

Now listen to this story again, French only.

THE ADVENTURE CONTINUES

Day Eleven—0630 hours

Day of Rendezvous

You get up bright and early the next morning and get back to work on Marie-Loire's challenge. You and Stump set a goal of finishing early that afternoon. You work through the remaining exercises quickly but accurately.

133

🎧 A Milkmaid's Fantasy
French Only
La fantaisie d'une laitière

🎧 Instructions: Listen to and read the following story. Work toward full comprehension.

A dairymaid was walking down a road carrying on her head a pot of milk that she had stolen.	🎧 *Une laitière marchait le long d'une route portant sur la tête un pot de lait qu'elle avait volé.*
She was going to the market to sell it.	*Elle allait au marché le vendre.*
Walking along, she said to herself:	*En marchant, elle se dit:*
I'll sell this milk and buy some eggs.	*Je vais vendre ce lait et acheter des oeufs.*
The eggs will give me chicks.	*Les oeufs me donneront des poussins.*
When the chicks have grown, I'll sell them and buy a little pig.	*Quand les poussins auront grandi, je les vendrai et achèterai un petit cochon.*
When the little pig is grown, it will give me lots of other little pigs.	*Quand le petit cochon aura grandi, il me donnera plein d'autres petits cochons.*
I'll sell them and buy a piece of land.	*Je les vendrai et j'achèterai un morceau de terrain.*
On the land I'll plant grapevines.	*Sur ce terrain je planterai de la vigne.*
From the grapes I'll make wine, and in a few years I'll be able to buy a good-sized farm.	*Des raisins je ferai du vin, et dans quelques années je pourrai acheter une ferme de belle taille.*
On the farm I'll have pigs, cows, chickens, and I'll grow more grapevines.	*Dans la ferme j'aurai des cochons, des vaches, des poules, et je cultiverai davantage de vignes.*
From the pigs I'll have ham, from the cows I'll have milk and meat, from the chickens I'll have eggs and meat, and from the grapes I'll have wine.	*Des cochons, j'obtiendrai du jambon, des vaches, j'aurai du lait et de la viande, des poules, j'aurai des oeufs et de la viande, de la vigne, j'aurai du vin.*
In time for sure I'll be rich.	*Avec le temps, pour sûr je serai riche.*
Just at that moment she tripped on a rock in the road and the milk was all spilt on the ground.	*Juste à ce moment-là, elle trébucha sur une pierre sur la route et le lait fut entièrement renversé sur le sol.*
And with the milk her dreams of riches vanished.	*Et avec le lait s'évanouirent ses rêves de richesse.*

134

🔊 Two Stubborn Goats
Deux chèvres têtues

🔊 Instructions: Listen to and read the following story. How many words do you already know?

🔊 In ancient Greece there was a man called Aesop who could tell stories.	*Dans la Grèce antique, il y avait un homme qui s'appelait d'Ésope qui pouvait raconter des histoires.*
The stories he told more than 2000 years ago still circulate in our day.	*Les histoires qu'il a racontées, il y a plus de 2000 ans, circulent toujours de nos jours.*
One of the stories he told is about two stubborn goats.	*Une des histoires qu'il a racontées concerne deux chèvres têtues.*
One day a large tree fell across a river, creating a narrow bridge.	*Un jour, un grand arbre est tombé à travers la rivière, créant un pont étroit.*
It happened that two goats intended to cross the bridge at the same time from opposite sides,	*Il est arrivé que deux chèvres avaient l'intention de traverser le pont en partant en même temps des deux côtés opposés,*
but the bridge was so narrow that only one could cross it at a time.	*mais le pont était si étroit qu'une seule pouvait le traverser à la fois.*
What do you think happened?	*Que pensez-vous qu'il soit arrivé?*
Of course, they knocked heads at the middle of the bridge,	*Bien sûr, elles se sont cogné la tête au milieu du pont,*
but both obstinately refused to cede to the other.	*mais toutes les deux ont obstinément refusé de céder à l'autre.*
Both struggled to push the other back.	*Toutes deux se sont débattues pour pousser l'autre en arrière.*
They pushed until both fell in the river and drowned.	*Elles se sont poussées jusqu'à ce que toutes les deux tombent dans la rivière et se noyent.*

135

🎞 The Little Red Hen
French Only
La petite poule rousse
«Les paresseux ne mangeront pas le pain du travailleur»

🎞 Instructions: Listen to and read the following story. Learn vocabulary about specific ingredients in French.

It is a story about a hen
who knew how to work.
She was not lazy, she liked to work.
This story is about her neighbors,
who didn't know how to work
and who didn't like to work.
They only liked to eat and play.
One day, this productive hen found a
grain of wheat. "Ah," she thought,
"it's a good seed. If we plant it,
it will produce a lot of wheat."

"Cot-Cot, come and see, I found a good
grain of wheat," she announced to her
friends.
"Who will help me to plant it?"
"Not me," said the duck, who was watching
a TV show. "I have other things to do."

(In reality, the duck didn't have anything
else to do than to watch TV all day).
"Not me," said the goose, who was playing
solitaire. "I am very busy."
(In reality, the goose didn't have anything
to do at all. She only wanted to play,
she didn't want to work.)
"Not me," said the turkey, who was reading
a magazine. "I am not in the mood to work
today."
(In reality, the turkey never was
in the mood to work. She was very lazy.)
"Then, very well," said the diligent little hen,
"I'll plant it myself." So she worked
diligently and prepared the ground with
much precaution, placed the grain of wheat,
covered it up with soil, and watered it.
"There," she said. "Now we will have to wait
and see what happens." After a few days
it germinated, and in a few weeks
it became ripe and yellow. It was ready

🎞 *C'est une histoire au sujet d'une poule*
qui savait travailler.
Elle n'était pas paresseuse, elle aimait travailler.
Cette histoire est au sujet de ses voisins
qui ne savaient pas comment travailler
et qui n'aimaient pas travailler.
Ils n'aimaient que manger et jouer.
Un jour, cette poule productive a trouvé un
grain de blé. «Ah», a-t-elle pensé,
«c'est une bonne semence. Si nous la plantons,
elle produira beaucoup de blé.»

«Cotte-Cotte, venez voir, j'ai trouvé un bon
grain de blé», a-t-elle annoncé à ses
amis.
«Qui m'aidera à le planter?»
«Pas moi», a dit le canard, qui était en train de
regarder une émission à la télévision. «J'ai
d'autres choses à faire.»
(En réalité, le canard n'avait rien d'autre à faire
que de regarder la télévision toute la journée.)
«Pas moi», a dit l'oie qui jouait au
solitaire. «Je suis très occupée.»
(En réalité, l'oie n'avait rien
à faire du tout. Elle ne voulait que jouer,
elle ne voulait pas travailler.)
«Pas moi», a dit la dinde qui était en train de lire
un magazine. «Je ne suis pas d'humeur à travailler
aujourd'hui.»
(En réalité, la dinde n'était jamais
d'humeur à travailler. Elle était très paresseuse.)
«Alors, très bien», a dit la poule diligente,
«je le planterai moi-même.» Alors, elle a travaillé
avec diligence et elle a préparé le sol avec
beaucoup de précaution, y a placé le grain de blé,
l'a recouvert avec de la terre et l'a arrosé.
«Voilà», a-t-elle dit. «Maintenant nous devrons
attendre et voir ce qui va se passer.» Après
quelques jours, il a germé et en quelques semaines
il est devenu mûr et jaune. Il était prêt

for harvest.

So the diligent hen called her friends: "Now the wheat is ripe and ready to be harvested. Who will help me collect it?"
"Not me," said the duck, who was still watching TV. "I've other things to do."
"Not me," said the goose, who was still playing solitaire. "I'm very busy."
"Not me," said the turkey, who was still reading a magazine. "I'm not in the mood to work today."
"Very well then," said the diligent hen, "I'll do it myself. But I still think that you could help me." So she cut the wheat with her beak and winnowed it with her wings.

"Now," she said to her friends, "who will help me carry this wheat to the windmill?"
"Not me," said the duck. "I have other more important to do."
"Not me," said the goose. "I'm not finished with this game."
"Not me," said the turkey. "I just don't feel up to work right now."
"Very well," said the hen, "so I'll do it myself." So she carried the wheat to the windmill, where it was ground. It was made into flour. Then she brought the flour back home.

"And now," said she, "who will help me make bread out of this flour?"
"Not me," said the duck.
"Not me," said the goose.
"Not me," said the turkey.
Each was minding his own business.
"Very well then," said the diligent hen, "I'll do it myself." So she prepared the dough, heated the oven, and then she baked the bread. And when she took it out of the oven…Mmmm, it smelled good.

"So," said the diligent hen, "who wants a piece of that bread?"
"I want a piece," said the duck.
"I also want a piece," said the goose.
"Me too, I want to have a piece," said the turkey.
And they all ran into the kitchen thinking they could get a piece of warm bread.
"Oh, but you didn't help me to plant the seed. You didn't help me to harvest it.

pour la moisson.

Alors, la poule diligente a appelé ses amis: «Maintenant le blé est mûr et prêt à être moissonné. Qui m'aidera à le récolter?»
«Pas moi», a dit le canard qui regardait encore la télévision. «J'ai d'autres choses à faire.»
«Pas moi», a dit l'oie qui jouait encore au solitaire. «Je suis très occupée.»
«Pas moi», a dit la dinde qui lisait encore un magazine. «Je ne suis pas d'humeur à travailler aujourd'hui.»
«Très bien alors», a dit la poule diligente, «je le ferai moi-même. Mais je pense malgré tout que vous pourriez m'aider.» Alors, elle a coupé le blé avec son bec et l'a vanné avec ses ailes.

«Maintenant», a-t-elle dit à ses amis, «qui m'aidera à porter ce blé au moulin?»
«Pas moi», a dit le canard. «J'ai d'autres choses plus importantes à faire.»
«Pas moi», a dit l'oie. «Je n'ai pas fini cette partie.»
«Pas moi», a dit la dinde. «Je n'ai simplement pas envie de travailler en ce moment.»
«Très bien», a dit la poule, «alors je le ferai moi même.» Alors, elle a porté le blé au moulin où il a été moulu. Il a été transformé en farine. Puis elle a rapporté la farine à la maison.

«Et maintenant», a-t-elle dit, «qui m'aidera à faire du pain de cette farine?»
«Pas moi», a dit le canard.
«Pas moi», a dit l'oie.
«Pas moi», a dit la dinde.
Chacun était occupé à ses propres affaires.
«Très bien alors», a dit la poule diligente, «je le ferai moi-même.» Alors, elle a préparé la pâte, chauffé le four, et ensuite, elle a cuit le pain. Et quand elle l'a sorti du four…Mmmm, cela sentait bon.

«Alors», a dit la poule diligente, «qui veut un morceau de ce pain?»
«J'en veux un morceau», a dit le canard.
«J'en veux aussi un morceau», a dit l'oie.
«Moi aussi, je veux en avoir un morceau», a dit la dinde.
Et ils ont tous couru dans la cuisine pensant pouvoir recevoir un morceau de pain chaud.
«Oh, mais vous ne m'avez pas aidée à planter la semence. Vous ne m'avez pas aidée à la moissonner.

You didn't help me to carry the wheat
to the windmill and bring back the flour.
You didn't help me to make the bread.
You didn't help me at all."

Then the diligent hen called her chicks:
"Cot-Cot, come my chickies, here is bread
for you." And the hen and the chickies
ate all the bread.
And nothing was left for the duck, the
goose, and the turkey.
For the idler shall not eat the bread of
the laborer.

*Vous ne m'avez pas aidée à porter le blé
au moulin et à rapporter la farine.
Vous ne m'avez pas aidée à faire le pain.
Vous ne m'avez pas aidée du tout.»*

*Alors, la poule diligente a appelé ses poussins:
«Cotte-Cotte, venez mes poussins, voici du pain
pour vous.» Et la poule et ses poussins
ont mangé tout le pain.
Et il n'en est rien resté pour le canard,
l'oie, et la dinde.
Car les paresseux ne mangeront pas le pain
du travailleur.*

136

🔊 A Hungry Giant
French Only
Un géant affamé

🔊 Instructions: Listen to and read the following story. Read along with the voice on the tape.

Have you ever seen a giant? Do you know how big a giant is? Do you know how much a hungry giant can eat? Well, I haven't ever seen a giant, but one time my father saw one. Anyway he told me he saw one.	🔊 *As-tu déjà vu un géant?* *Sais-tu combien mesure un géant?* *Sais-tu combien* *un géant affamé peut manger?* *Et bien, je n'ai jamais vu de géant,* *mais une fois mon père en a vu un.* *En tout cas, il m'a dit* *qu'il en avait vu un.*
This happened when he was a boy just your age. One morning before breakfast, he took a walk and saw a fly that was caught in a spider's web. He watched the spider come and eat the fly. "Good," thought my father. "The spider ate the fly. I don't like flies."	*Cela s'est passé quand il était* *un garçon de ton âge.* *Un matin avant le petit déjeuner,* *il s'est promené et a vu une mouche* *qui s'était laissée prendre* *dans une toile d'araignée.* *Il a regardé l'araignée s'approcher* *et manger la mouche.* *«Très bien», a pensé mon père.* *«L'araignée a mangé la mouche.* *Je n'aime pas les mouches.»*
A moment later a bird came and ate the spider. "Good," thought my father. "The bird ate the spider. I don't like spiders."	*Un moment plus tard un oiseau est venu* *et a mangé l'araignée.* *«Très bien», a pensé mon père.* *«L'oiseau a mangé l'araignée.* *Je n'aime pas les araignées.»*
But the next moment a cat came along and ate the bird. And my father thought: "Too bad, the cat ate the bird. I like birds."	*Mais, de suite après,* *un chat est venu et a mangé l'oiseau.* *Et mon père a pensé:* *«Dommage, le chat a mangé l'oiseau.* *J'aime bien les oiseaux.»*
But the next moment a snake came along and ate the cat. And my father thought: "Too bad, I like cats."	*Mais, de suite après,* *un serpent est venu* *et a mangé le chat.* *Et mon père a pensé:* *«Dommage, j'aime bien les chats.»*
But the next moment a pig came along and ate the snake. And my father thought:	*Mais, de suite après, un cochon est venu* *et a mangé le serpent.* *Et mon père a pensé:*

"Good, the pig ate the snake.
"I don't like snakes."

Before long a leopard came along
and ate the pig.
And my father thought:
"Wow, a leopard ate the pig.
This is exciting!"

A while later a crocodile came along
and ate the leopard.
And my father thought:
"Wow, a crocodile ate the leopard.
This is really exciting.
What will happen now?"

Before long a hippopotamus came along
and ate the crocodile.
And my father thought:
"Wow, a hippopotamus ate
the crocodile.
What will happen now?"

A moment later,
a whale came along
and ate the hippopotamus.
And my father thought:
"Wow, this is too much.
Just imagine:
A whale has eaten a hippopotamus,
the hippopotamus has eaten a crocodile,
the crocodile has eaten a leopard,
the leopard has eaten a pig,
the pig has eaten a snake,
the snake has eaten a cat,
the cat has eaten a bird,
the bird has eaten a spider,
and the spider has eaten a fly.
That's amazing.
I've never seen such a thing."

Just then a hand
reached down from the sky
and picked up the whale.
My father looked up
just as the giant
swallowed it whole.
And he thought:
"Wow, this is the first time
I've seen a giant.
Maybe he's still hungry.
I'd better get out of here."
And he ran home
as fast as he could.

*«Très bien, le cochon a mangé le serpent.
Je n'aime pas les serpents.»*

*Sous peu, un léopard est venu
et a mangé le cochon.
Et mon père a pensé:
«Ça alors, un léopard a mangé le cochon.
C'est sensationnel!»*

*Un peu plus tard, un crocodile est venu
et a mangé le léopard.
Et mon père a pensé:
«Ça alors, un crocodile a mangé le léopard.
C'est vraiment sensationnel!
Que va-t-il se passer maintenant?»*

*Peu après, un hippopotame est venu
et a mangé le crocodile.
Et mon père a pensé:
«Ça alors, un hippopotame a mangé
le crocodile.
Que va-t-il se passer maintenant?»*

*Un moment plus tard,
une baleine est venue
et a mangé l'hippopotame.
Et mon père a pensé:
«Ça alors, c'est trop.
Rends-toi compte:
Une baleine a mangé un hippopotame,
l'hippopotame a mangé un crocodile,
le crocodile a mangé un léopard,
le léopard a mangé un cochon,
le cochon a mangé un serpent,
le serpent a mangé un chat,
le chat a mangé un oiseau,
l'oiseau a mangé une araignée,
et l'araignée a mangé une mouche.
C'est incroyable.
Je n'ai jamais rien vu de pareil.»*

*Juste à ce moment-là, une main
est venue du ciel
et a saisi la baleine.
Mon père a levé la tête
juste au moment où le géant
l'avalait toute entière.
Et il a pensé:
«Ça alors, c'est la première fois
que je vois un géant.
Peut-être a-t-il encore faim.
Je ferai mieux de partir d'ici.»
Et il est rentré chez lui en courant
aussi vite qu'il pouvait.*

And there, as he ate a big bowl of mush, he thought of the fly and the spider and the bird and the cat and the snake and the pig and the leopard and the crocodile and the hippopotamus and the whale. But most of all he thought of the giant and how hungry he must have been.	*Et là, pendant qu'il mangeait un grand bol de bouillie de blé, il a pensé à la mouche et à l'araignée et à l'oiseau et au chat et au serpent et au cochon et au léopard et au crocodile et à l'hippopotame et à la baleine. Mais il a surtout pensé au géant et à quel point il devait avoir faim.*

137

Poor King Midas
French Only
Le pauvre roi Midas

Instructions: Listen to and read the following story. Learn as many new vocabulary words as you can!

Once upon a time there was a young king whose wife died, leaving him an only daughter.	*Il était une fois un jeune roi dont la femme était morte, le laissant avec une seule fille.*
The king's name was Midas.	*Le nom du roi était Midas.*
His little girl was very beautiful and he loved her very much.	*Sa petite fille était très belle et il l'aimait beaucoup.*
In the treasure chamber of King Midas there was a ton of gold: gold dust, gold bars, gold coins, gold crowns, gold platters, gold goblets, gold statues, gold jewelry, even gold cooking pots.	*Dans la trésorerie du roi Midas, il y avait une tonne d'or: de la poudre d'or, des lingots d'or, de la monnaie en or, des couronnes en or, des assiettes en or, des gobelets en or, des statues en or, des bijoux en or, et même des ustensiles de cuisine en or.*
Every day he would go down into his treasure chamber, locking the door carefully behind him, and there he would play with his riches, gloating in the power and influence he thought these would bring someday.	*Il descendait tous les jours à la trésorerie, refermant la porte derrière lui avec soin, et il y jouait avec ses richesses, se vantant de sa force et de son l'influence, pensait-t-il ces choses lui procureraient un jour.*
He would lick the gold as if it were candy.	*Il léchait l'or comme si c'était une friandise.*
He would sit on the floor and count his money for hours. He would toss it into the air and laugh as it rained gold on his head.	*Il s'asseyait par terre et comptait son argent pendant des heures. Il le jetait en l'air et riait alors qu'il pleuvait de l'or sur sa tête.*
Like a pig he would wallow in the gold dust, bury himself in it, dance on it.	*Il se vautrait comme un cochon dans la poudre d'or, s'y enterrait, et y dansait au-dessus.*
"Oh, except for my daughter, my precious little Marigold, gold is my treasure.	*«Oh, à l'exception de ma fille, ma précieuse petite Marior, l'or est mon seul trésor.*
My beautiful daughter is very precious to me, but her beauty, like that of a flower, will fade.	*Ma jolie fille m'est très chère, mais sa beauté, comme celle d'une fleur, se fânera.*
Only gold is forever beautiful.	*Seul l'or est beau pour toujours.*
Oh, how I love to touch it.	*Oh, comme j'aime le toucher.*
If I can only get enough gold I will be happy forever."	*Si seulement je pouvais obtenir assez d'or, je serai heureux pour toujours.»*
One day as he was thus gloating over his treasure, he suddenly became aware that there was someone standing beside him.	*Un jour, alors qu'il se vantait de cette manière au sujet de son trésor, il s'est soudainement aperçu qu'il y avait quelqu'un qui se tenait à côté de lui.*
It was an immortal visitor come down from heaven.	*C'était un visiteur immortel descendu du ciel.*
This is the conversation they had:	*Ceci est la conversation qu'ils ont eu:*
—Well, King Midas, I see that you have quite a lot of gold.	*—Et bien, roi Midas, je vois que tu as beaucoup d'or.*
—Oh, it's not so much. Really, it's only a little.	*—Oh, ce n'est pas tellement. Vraiment, ce n'est que peu.*
—So, you are not satisfied then?	*—Alors, tu n'es pas satisfait?*

—No. I am not satisfied. I want more, much more.
—How much would it take to satisfy you?
—Oh, I wish I could create gold by the touch of my hand.
—Create gold by your touch? Are you sure that with such power you would be satisfied?
—Of course. I'd never tire of it. Nothing else in the world would bring me such happiness.
—And are you sure you would never regret it if everything you touched turned to gold?
—Surely I would never regret having this marvelous power. I'd give anything if whatever I touched turned into gold.
—Then it shall be as you wish. From tomorrow at sunrise, whatever your hand touches, it will turn immediately into gold.

As soon as he woke up the next morning, King Midas began to experiment with his marvelous power.

It was true just as the immortal visitor had promised; everything he touched turned to gold.

He picked up his red velvet slippers to put them on, and they immediately turned into gold.

They were very heavy and not very comfortable but, King Midas thought, they were certainly shinier now.

He went out and took a walk in his flower garden, touching the flowers one by one to test his magic gift.

Sure enough, no sooner did he touch a flower than it turned into gold.

"Isn't that marvelous?" King Midas laughed. And the sound of his laughter startled the birds.

As he danced about, touching all the flowers and laughing, he would have turned all the flowers to gold, but realizing it was time for breakfast, the king returned to his room to dress.

At that moment, his servant brought in his breakfast on a tray.

King Midas reached out to take his bread and fruit, and putting them into his mouth without looking, he found that they too had had turned to gold.

He almost broke his teeth trying to bite into them.

He took a cup of tea, but before he could bring it to his lips, the cup and the tea turned to gold.

—*Non, je ne suis pas satisfait. J'en veux plus, bien plus.*
—*Combien te faudrait-il pour te satisfaire?*
—*Oh, je voudrais tellement pouvoir créer de l'or par mon toucher.*
—*Créer de l'or par ton toucher? Es-tu sûr qu'avec un tel pouvoir tu serais satisfait?*
—*Bien sûr. Je ne m'en fatiguerai jamais. Il n'y a rien au monde qui me procurerait un tel bonheur.*
—*Et, es-tu sûr que tu ne regretteras jamais que tout ce que tu touches se transforme en or?*
—*Je ne regretterai assurément jamais d'avoir ce merveilleux pouvoir. Je donnerais n'importe quoi si tout ce que je touchais se transformait en or.*
—*Il sera alors fait selon ta volonté. Dès demain, au lever du soleil, quoi que tu touches avec ta main, se transformera immédiatement en or.*

Dès qu'il s'est réveillé le lendemain matin, le roi Midas s'est mis à expérimenter son merveilleux pouvoir.

C'était vrai, comme le visiteur immortel l'avait promis, tout ce qu'il touchait se transformait en or.

Il a ramassé ses pantoufles en velour rouge pour les mettre et elles se sont immédiatement transformées en or.

Elles étaient très lourdes et pas très confortables mais le roi Midas a pensé qu'elles brillaient vraiment plus maintenant.

Il est sorti et il est parti se promener dans son jardin de fleurs, touchant les fleurs une à une pour tester son pouvoir magique.

Assurément, aussitôt qu'il touchait une fleur, elle se transformait en or.

«N'est-ce pas merveilleux?» Le roi Midas se mit à rire. Et le son de son rire a fait sursauter les oiseaux.

Et il se mit à danser joyeusement touchant toutes les fleurs en riant. Il aurait transformé toutes les fleurs en or, mais, en se rendant compte qu'il était temps de prendre le petit déjeuner, le roi est rentré dans sa chambre pour s'habiller.

À ce moment, son serviteur lui a apporté son petit déjeuner sur un plateau.

Le roi Midas étendit la main pour prendre son pain et des fruits, et en les mettant dans la bouche sans regarder, il a découvert qu'eux aussi s'étaient transformés en or.

Il s'est presque cassé les dents en essayant d'y mordre dedans.

Il a pris une tasse de thé, mais avant qu'il ne puisse la porter aux lèvres, la tasse de thé s'était transformée en or.

The thought passed through his mind: "If I can't eat or drink, I'll soon starve to death."	*Cette pensée lui a traversé l'esprit: «Si je ne peux pas manger ou boire, je mourrai bientôt de faim.»*
But looking at the bread and fruit, he marveled at their beauty.	*Mais en regardant le pain et les fruits, il s'est émerveillé devant leur beauté.*
Just then his little girl came running in, carrying her dolly and laughing joyously.	*À ce moment précis, sa petite fille est entrée en courant, en portant sa poupée et en riant joyeusement.*
Looking at her, the king thought: "She is as radiant as the sun."	*En la regardant, le roi a pensé: «Elle est aussi radiante que le soleil.»*
He reached out his arms to take her, but as he touched his daughter's hand, instantly she and her dolly turned into a statue of gold.	*Il a étendu les bras pour la prendre dans ses bras mais, dès qu'il lui eut touché la main, en un instant, elle et sa poupée se sont transformées en une statue d'or.*
Seized with panic, King Midas fell to his knees and cried out:	*Pris de panique, le roi Midas est tombé à genoux et s'est mis à pleurer:*
"No! No! Marigold, my daughter, my precious daughter, what have I done? What have I done?	*«Non! Non! Marior, ma fille, ma précieuse petite fille, qu'ai-je fait? Qu'ai-je fait?*
Oh God, forgive me! In my selfishness, in my lust for gold I have destroyed my daughter.	*Oh mon Dieu, pardonne-moi! Dans mon avarice, dans ma convoitise pour l'or, j'ai détruit ma fille.*
Oh God, what can I do? What can I do?"	*Oh mon Dieu, que puis-je faire? Que puis-je faire?»*
Just then the immortal visitor appeared again before him.	*À ce moment précis, le visiteur immortel est à nouveau apparu devant lui.*
Reaching down and patting the sobbing king on the shoulder, he said:	*Se penchant vers lui et en consolant le roi en lui tapotane sur l'épaule, il a dit:*
"King Midas, you're weeping. What happened?"	*«Roi Midas, tu pleures. Que s'est-il passé?»*
"I am of all men most miserable."	*«Je suis le plus misérable des hommes.»*
"Good King Midas," said the immortal visitor. "Is it that I did not keep the promise I made to you?"	*«Bon roi Midas», a dit le visiteur immortel. «Cela vient-il du fait que je n'ai pas tenu la promesse que je t'avais faite?»*
"No, no. You granted me my wish. Whatever I touched turned to gold."	*«Non, non. Tu m'as accordé mon vœu. Tout ce que j'ai touché s'est transformé en or.»*
The immortal visitor said: "You told me that that power would bring you great happiness, but now you are weeping, and you tell me you are the most miserable man in the world. How can this be?"	*Le visiteur immortel a dit: «Tu m'as dit que ce pouvoir t'apporterait de grandes joies, mais maintenant tu pleures, et tu me dis que tu es l'homme le plus misérable du monde. Comment est-ce possible?»*
"Oh, immortal visitor, I was foolish. I didn't realize how evil my selfish wish was.	*«Oh, visiteur immortel, j'étais fou. Je ne me rendais pas compte à quel point mon vœu était mauvais.*
Now the lust for gold has destroyed my soul and robbed me forever of all happiness, for I have destroyed my daughter."	*Maintenant, la convoitise pour l'or a détruit mon âme et m'a ôté toute joie pour toujours, car j'ai détruit ma fille.»*
"But King Midas, isn't gold the most desirable, the most beautiful thing in all the world?"	*«Mais, roi Midas, l'or n'est-il pas la chose la plus désirable, la plus belle chose au monde?»*
"Oh no, I detest the sight of gold."	*«Oh non, j'en déteste la vue.»*
"Tell me, King Midas, is gold not the most valuable thing in all the world?"	*«Dis-moi, roi Midas, l'or n'est-il pas la chose qui a le plus de valeur au monde?»*
"Immortal visitor, tell me wherein gold has its value."	*«Visiteur immortel, dis-moi en quoi l'or a de la valeur.»*
"Well, King Midas, surely it is more valuable than a cup of tea, right?"	*«Et bien, roi Midas, il a sûrement plus de valeur qu'une tasse de thé, n'est-ce pas?»*
"No. A simple cup of tea is of more worth than all the gold I possess."	*«Non. Une simple tasse de thé vaut plus que tout l'or que je possède.»*
"Surely gold is more valuable than a crust of bread, do you not agree?"	*«L'or vaut sûrement plus qu'une croûte de pain, n'es-tu pas d'accord?»*

"No. A crust of bread is of more worth than all the gold I possess."

"King Midas, is gold not more valuable than a daughter's love?"

"Oh, immortal stranger, you don't understand.
I have come to realize that the common things of life—our children, our friends, and even the ordinary things we see and touch every day—are our real treasures.
Now I know that the poor who appreciate these common things are happier than kings with treasures of gold."

Seeing that the king's sorrow was sincere, the immortal visitor took pity on him and said:
"Would you have me remove the power I gave you and let you restore your daughter's life?"
"Oh noble stranger, if you will do this, I will give you all the gold in my treasury."
"Then, King Midas, go and wash your hands in the river. And bring back a pail of water.
With the water from the river sprinkle whatever you have touched and it will return at once to its normal state.
Then, King Midas, use your gold to help the people."

Hearing this, King Midas took a pail and ran to the river, washed his hands, and ran back to his palace with the pail of water.

He splashed water on the gold statue of his daughter, who immediately was restored to life.

Then King Midas fell to his knees, took his little girl in his arms, and with tears running down his cheeks, exclaimed:

"God has forgiven me. He has restored my precious daughter to me."

King Midas kept his promise to use his gold to help the people.

And after that he lived a long and happy life, for he appreciated his family, his friends, and even the ordinary things of life that all of us see and touch every day.

«Non. Une croûte de pain vaut plus que tout l'or que je possède.»

«Roi Midas, l'or n'a-t-il pas plus de valeur que l'amour d'une fille?»

*«Oh visiteur immortel, tu ne comprends pas.
Je suis arrivé à la conclusion que les choses les plus communes de la vie—nos enfants, nos amis et même les choses ordinaires que nous voyons et que nous touchons chaque jour—sont de réels trésors.
Je sais maintenant que les pauvres qui apprécient les choses les plus communes sont plus heureux que les rois aux trésors d'or.»*

*Voyant que la peine du roi était sincère, le visiteur immortel prit pitié de lui et dit:
«Voudrais-tu que je reprenne les pouvoirs que je t'ai donnés et que je te laisse redonner vie à ta fille?»
«Oh noble étranger, si tu fais cela, je te donnerai tout l'or de ma trésorerie.»
«Alors, roi Midas, va te laver dans la rivière. Et ramène un seau d'eau.
Arrose tout ce que tu as touché avec l'eau de la rivière et tout reviendra à son état naturel.*

Ensuite, roi Midas, utilise ton or pour aider le peuple.»

En entendant cela, le roi Midas a pris un seau et a couru jusqu'à la rivière, s'y est lavé les mains et a couru de retour au palais avec le seau d'eau.

Il a aspergé d'eau la statue en or de sa fille qui a immédiatement retrouvé la vie.

Alors, le roi Midas est tombé à genoux, a pris la petite fille dans ses bras et s'est exclamé les larmes lui coulant le long des joues:

«Dieu m'a pardonné. Il m'a rendu ma précieuse fille.»

Le roi Midas a tenu sa promesse d'utiliser son or pour aider le peuple.

Après cela, il a vécu une longue vie heureuse, car il a apprécié sa famille, ses amis et même les choses ordinaires de la vie que nous voyons et que nous touchons tous les jours.

138

🎧 A Greedy Dog
Un chien vorace

🎞️ Instructions: Listen to and read the following story. Rewrite the ending in French!

🎧 There was once a dog who hung all the time around a butcher shop in hope of getting a bone to chew on or a piece of meat to eat. The butcher didn't want the dog to hang around so he shooed him off: "Get out of here, dog. Go away! Go home! Beat it!" But one day while the butcher wasn't looking, the dog came and stole a piece of meat and ran away. Crossing a bridge some distance from the butcher shop, he stopped and looked at the still water below. What do you think he saw? Mirrored on the water, he saw a dog just like himself, holding in his mouth a large piece of meat. Greedily he thought: I'll dive in and get that other piece of meat too. When he jumped into the water to try to get the other piece, he let go of the piece that he already had. Because of his greed, the silly dog lost even the meat that he had stolen at the butcher shop. He ended up having no meat at all.	*Il était une fois un chien qui traînait tous les jours autour d'une boucherie dans l'espoir d'obtenir un os à ronger ou un morceau de viande à manger. Le boucher ne voulait pas voir le chien traîner, alors il lui criait après: «Sors de là, chien. Va-t'en. Rentre chez toi. Fiche le camp.» Mais un jour pendant que le boucher ne regardait pas, le chien s'approcha, vola un morceau de viande et s'enfuit en courant. En traversant un pont à une certaine distance de la boucherie, il s'arrêta et regarda l'eau tranquille au-dessous. Que pensez-vous qu'il vit? Se miroitant sur l'eau il vit un chien juste comme lui, tenant dans sa gueule un gros morceau de viande. Goulument il pensa: je vais plonger et attraper cet autre morceau de viande aussi. Quand il sauta dans l'eau pour essayer de récupérer l'autre morceau, il laissa partir le morceau qu'il avait déjà. À cause de sa voracité, ce chien bête perdit même la viande qu'il avait volée à la boucherie. Il finit par n'avoir plus de viande du tout.*

139

The Most Beautiful Thing in the World
La plus belle chose au monde

Instructions: Cover the column in English and read the French. See how much you understand, and then look at the English.

Once there was a young artist who wanted to paint the most beautiful thing in the world.	*Il était une fois un jeune artiste qui voulait peindre la plus belle chose au monde.*
Not knowing where it was or where to find it, he left his family and went out into the world to search for it.	*Ne sachant pas où elle était ni où la trouver, il quitta sa famille et partit parcourir le monde à sa recherche.*
As he traveled about, he saw an old priest. He said to him: "Father, you have lived very long and you look wise. Can you tell me what is the most beautiful thing in the world is?"	*En voyageant, il vit un vieux prêtre. Il lui dit: «Père, vous avez vécu très longtemps et vous avez l'air très sage. Pouvez-vous me dire ce qu'est la plus belle chose au monde?»*
The old priest replied: "That is very simple: surely faith is the most beautiful thing in the world."	*Le vieux prêtre répondit: «C'est très simple: la foi est certainement la plus belle chose au monde.»*
Pondering the priest's answer, but unsure how to paint faith, the young artist traveled on until he came to an old farmer.	*Réfléchissant à la réponse du prêtre, mais ne sachant pas comment peindre la foi, le jeune artiste continua à voyager jusqu'à ce qu'il rencontre un vieux fermier.*
"Kind sir," he said to the farmer, "you have lived close to nature. Can you tell me what the most beautiful thing in the world is?"	*«Bon monsieur», dit-il au fermier, «vous avez vécu près de la nature. Pouvez-vous me dire ce qu'est la plus belle chose au monde?»*
The farmer replied: "That is easy: surely hope is the most beautiful thing in the world."	*Le fermier répondit: «C'est facile: l'espoir est certainement la plus belle chose au monde.»*
Pondering the answers of the farmer and the priest, yet not knowing how he could depict faith and hope, the artist traveled on until he came to a young bride.	*Réfléchissant aux réponses du fermier et du prêtre, et ne sachant toujours pas comment peindre la foi et l'espoir, l'artiste continua à voyager jusqu'à rencontrer une jeune mariée.*
He said to her: "How happy you look! Can you tell me what is the most beautiful thing in the world?"	*Il lui dit: «Comme vous avez l'air heureuse! Pouvez-vous me dire quelle est la plus belle chose au monde?»*
The bride replied: "That is easy: surely love is the most beautiful thing in the world."	*La mariée répondit: «C'est facile: l'amour est certainement la plus belle chose au monde.»*
Not knowing how he could depict love, the artist traveled on until he came to a wounded soldier limping home from war.	*Ne sachant pas comment peindre l'amour, l'artiste continua à voyager jusqu'à rencontrer un soldat blessé rentrant de la guerre chez lui en boitant.*
He asked him: "Can you tell me what is the most beautiful thing in the world?"	*Il lui demanda: «Peux-tu me dire quelle est la plus belle chose au monde?»*
The soldier replied: "That is easy: surely peace is the most beautiful thing in the world."	*Le soldat répondit: «C'est facile: la paix est certainement la plus belle chose au monde.»*
The young artist pondered what the priest, the farmer, the bride, and the soldier had said, but thought:	*Le jeune artiste réfléchit à ce que le prêtre, le fermier, la mariée, et le soldat avaient dit, mais pensa:*
How can I depict faith, hope, love, and peace in one picture?	*Comment puis-je peindre la foi, l'espoir, l'amour, et la paix en une seule image?*

Thinking there was nothing further he could learn, he turned back and returned home.	*Pensant qu'il ne pouvait pas en apprendre davantage, il fit demi-tour et rentra chez lui.*
The moment he entered his home, he saw the following:	*Au moment où il entra chez lui, il vit la chose suivante :*
In the forehead of his mother he saw faith.	*Sur le front de sa mère, il vit la foi.*
In the eyes of his children he saw hope.	*Dans les yeux de ses enfants, il vit l'espoir.*
In the smile of his wife he saw love.	*Dans le sourire de sa femme, il vit l'amour.*
And around his house he saw peace.	*Et autour de sa maison, il vit la paix.*
At once the young artist set about to paint the picture of the most beautiful thing in the world.	*Aussitôt le jeune artiste se mit à peindre la plus belle chose au monde.*
And that picture was nothing more than his own home and family.	*Et ce tableau n'était rien de plus que son propre foyer et sa famille.*
Let us not forget that in our own home we find faith, hope, love, and peace,	*N'oublions pas que dans nos propres foyers nous trouvons la foi, l'espoir, l'amour, et la paix,*
and these are surely the most beautiful things in the world.	*et ce sont certainement les choses les plus belles au monde.*

THE ADVENTURE CONTINUES

You finish Marie-Loire's challenge early that afternoon. You and Stump rush to her office. She is a little surprised to see you so soon, but she makes time to check your work.

She nods. "Excellent work. I am surprised you could complete my challenge so quickly—you really must have worked hard. You pass my challenge with flying colors. Follow me."

Marie-Loire leads you out of the hotel and hails a taxi. As you and she ride to the other side of town, you ask her where she comes from.

"I grew up in Tahiti," she tells you with a smile. "My parents still live there. Would you like to hear about my country?"

You express your eagerness to learn about another French-speaking culture, and Marie Loire tells you a bit about Tahiti.

TAHITI CULTURE OVERVIEW

Tahitians place great emphasis on *joie de vivre*—joy of life. Their lifestyle is relaxed and comfortable, and they treat their guests as old friends. Tahitians enjoy a variety of French and Chinese foods as well as their own traditional foods. Tahitians value personal relationships and try to live as simply and happily as possible. Family ties are very important to Tahitians. The people of Tahiti embraced Christianity around the turn of the 18th century. Today, nearly 55 percent of the population follow Protestant beliefs. Another 30 percent are Roman Catholic. Approximately 6 percent belong to The Church of Jesus Christ of Latter-day Saints, and a little over 2 percent of the population are Seventh-Day Adventists. Other Christian faiths are also represented on the island, as are Judaism and Buddhism.

FACTS AND FIGURES ON TAHITI

- Tahiti is just one of the Society Islands. The Society Islands are one of the island groups in French Polynesia.

- Tahiti's largest city, Papeete, is both Tahiti's and French Polynesia's capital city.

- Tahiti's population is about 230,000.

- French is the official language for French Polynesia, and almost everyone in Tahiti speaks it. However, Tahitian is the official language for the Society Islands.

- The Tahitian alphabet has 13 letters.

- Soccer is Tahiti's national sport.

- One of the Society Islands, Tetiaroa, is owned by Marlon Brando.

- Because of Tahiti's tradition of hospitality, tipping taxi drivers or other service personnel is not commonly accepted.

- Tourism and agriculture are the mainstays of Tahiti's economy.

THE ADVENTURE CONTINUES

Just as Marie-Loire finishes her summary, the taxi driver stops the taxi in front of a small cottage with a tile roof and bright turquoise walls. You insist on paying the taxi fare, and after paying, you follow Marie-Loire to the cottage. An old woman with white hair, dark eyes, and laugh lines answers the door and welcomes you to her abode. She greets Marie-Loire as an old friend. You and Stump introduce yourselves.

"Yes, I know who you are," she tells you. "My friends have told me all about you. *Je m'appelle Anne-Charlotte. Bienvenue.*"

You follow Marie-Loire into Anne-Charlotte's cottage. A party is going on, and the odors wafting from the kitchen are truly sensational. Anne-Charlotte excuses herself and walks into the kitchen. You walk around the room, greeting the other guests at the party. To your surprise, you know all of them. You greet Gilles, Jean-Luc, Isabelle, and all the others who helped you in your search.

Gilles takes you aside and explains that Anne-Charlotte is the sole possessor of the ultimate crepes recipe. This recipe is the object of your quest. Before he can explain more, Anne-Charlotte returns to the main room, carrying a platter heaped high with delicate-looking crepes. You sample one and discover that they have a tasty apricot filling. These crepes are the most delicious you have ever tasted—tender, rich, and delicately flavored. You approach Anne-Charlotte and ask if you can buy her recipe.

"No," she replies. "You cannot buy my recipe. But I will give it to you if you can complete my challenge."

You and Stump look at each other. You do not have time to complete another series of French exercises, but what choice do you have? You accept Anne-Charlotte's challenge. To your relief, she does not assign any French exercises. Instead, she hands you a list of culture questions. You and Stump smile and start work immediately.

Culture Test

Instructions: Answer these questions based on your reading. Feel free to check the appendix to find the answers.

1. About how many people speak French as their native language?

2. Why is French called a Romance language?

3. When did Algeria win its independence?

4. What famous desert dominates the southern part of Algeria?

5. What are the two main groups into which Belgian culture is divided?

6. What kind of government does Belgium have?

7. What are Canada's official languages?

8. What city in Québec is known for its excellent subway system?

9. What is the dominant religion in France?

10. True or False: The first French cookbooks were written about a hundred years ago.

11. Where is Mt. Blanc, Europe's highest mountain?

12. What is Morocco's official language?

13. What is the mainstay of Morocco's economy?

14. Name Luxembourg's three official languages.

15. What are two favorite pastimes in Luxembourg?

16. What famous bicycle race passes through Luxembourg?

17. What is Senegal's dominant religion?

18. What is Senegal's official language?

19. What is Senegal's main cash crop?

20. What is Switzerland's nickname?

21. Which French-speaking country is famous for its scenic beauty?

22. Name Switzerland's four official languages.

23. What are Switzerland's most popular sports?

24. When was the Swiss Confederation founded?

25. Tahiti is part of what island group?

26. What is Tahiti's largest city?

27. How many letters does the Tahitian alphabet have?

28. What is Tahiti's national sport?

You and Stump finish the test quickly. You check your answers and submit the test for Anne-Charlotte's approval.

She nods when she finishes checking your answers. "Perfect!" she exclaims. She leaves the room for a moment and returns with a copy of her wonderful recipe. "This recipe has been in my family for hundreds of years," she explains. "I am a widow with no children of my own. I wanted to pass the recipe on to someone who would appreciate the language and the cultures behind the recipe. My friends arranged the challenges you passed. So, your quest is complete. Congratulations!" She hands you the recipe.

RECIPE: *CREPES*

1 c flour

1 c skim milk

1 t sugar

3 eggs

1/3 stick of butter

pinch of salt

1 t vanilla

1/2 t rum extract (optional)

Mix everything in a blender until it makes smooth batter (about 30 seconds). In a very hot pan, spread a thin layer of batter. Cook 20 seconds on each side.

THE ADVENTURE CONTINUES

You thank Anne-Charlotte for her recipe. Just then, the Pétards rush in.

"We are so sorry to be late!" Zsa-Zsa exclaims. "So good to see you again, Anne-Charlotte! Rumpelstiltskin and Stumpelriltskin, excellent work! You have accomplished exactly what you were supposed to do."

Zsa-Zsa continues and lists what you have accomplished during your stay on *l'île de Providence*.

- You have learned a lot of vocabulary on a wide variety of topics.

- You have mastered question words that will let you request and understand information.

- You have mastered basic grammar and verb conjugations, without spending hours memorizing dull lists.

- You have learned a number of conversations, and your knowledge of the language will allow you to modify these conversations to fit different situations.

- You know how to use the language and could communicate in a French-speaking country.

"And best of all," she finishes, "You had fun! Now, hurry so you can make your rendezvous."

You thank the Pétards for their hospitality and then go around the room bidding everyone farewell. They respond with *"Salut!"* and *"Au revoir."* Then, with the recipe in hand, you rush to the wharf, where you are just in time to meet your ride to the submarine.

On board the submarine, the captain and his team of experts debrief you. When they finish, you and the captain chat while the submarine's cook prepares a batch of Anne-Charlotte's delicious crepes.

You munch them contentedly when they are done. You wonder what your next assignment will be—now that you have learned French, perhaps your superiors will send you to France or one of the other countries you studied! The submarine captain takes you by surprise, though. You nearly choke on what he says next.

"You have proven your ability to learn a language," he begins, "so choose your next adventure—Spanish for *Isla de Providencia* or German for *Flucht nach Deutschland.*"

End Tape 6, Side B

Appendix—Answer Keys

Chapter 1 Self-Quiz
(1) c. (2) a. (3) j. (4) d. (5) e. (6) i. (7) f. (8) g. (9) h. (10) b.
(11) a. (12) e. (13) g. (14) f. (15) b. (16) c. (17) d. (18) i. (19) j. (20) h.
(21) d. (22) g. (23) c. (24) a. (25) f. (26) e. (27) j. (28) b. (29) h. (30) i

Chapter 2 Part 2 Self-Test
Sentences 1, 2, 4, 6, and 8 are incorrect.

Chapter 2 Part 4 Self-Test
1(a), 2(b), 3(b), 4(b), 5(a), 6(a), 7(a), 8(b)

Chapter 4 Part A: Translation from French
1. She cooks. 2. Paul likes his sister. 3. He likes to help her (or him).

Chapter 4 Part B: Translation from English
1. *Il est un jeune homme.* 2. *Elle a un frère.* 3. *Paul est le frère de Marie.* 4. *Elle aime l'aider.* 5. *Ils cuisinent ensemble.*

Chapter 5 Multiple-Choice Frames

A	*quatre* (a)	*deux* (b)	*trois* (d)
B	*six* (b)	*cinq* (c)	*quatre* (d)
C	*cinq* (b)	*deux* (d)	*six* (c)
D	*quatre* (b)	*trois* (c)	*deux* (d)
E	*trois points et une ligne* (b)	*deux points* (a)	*un point et une ligne* (d)
F	*deux points et un chiffre* (c)	*deux lignes et un chiffre* (b)	*deux points et une ligne* (a)
G	*deux points et une ligne* (d)	*trois points et une ligne* (c)	*quatre points* (a)
H	*deux chiffres* (a)	*deux points* (b)	*deux lignes* (c)
I	*les chiffres un, deux, et quatre* (b)	*les chiffres un, trois, et quatre* (d)	*les chiffres un, trois, et deux* (c)
J	*six chiffres* (a)	*quatre chiffres et quatre points* (c)	*trois lignes et cinq points* (d)

Chapter 5 Listen and Draw
A) ••   (B) _____   (C) 2 5 6   (D) • __ 4   (E) ••• __ __

Chapter 13 Look and Listen
1. *Un gros point et un petit point.* 2. *Une longue ligne et une ligne courte.* 3. *Une ligne épaisse et un petit chiffre, le chiffre cinq.* 4. *Un gros point et une ligne courte.* 5. *Deux petits points et trois lignes courtes.* 6. *Trois gros points, trois petits points, et deux petits chiffres, les chiffres six et un.*

Chapter 13 Multiple-Choice Frames

A	*un petit point* (a)	*un petit chiffre* (b)	*un gros point* (c)	*un gros chiffre* (d)
B	*le chiffre six et un petit point* (a)	*une ligne épaisse* (b)	*un gros point* (c)	*une ligne fine* (d)
C	*une ligne épaisse et deux lignes fines* (a)	*une ligne fine et deux lignes épaisses* (b)	*un petit point et une ligne épaisse* (c)	*deux gros points et un petit point* (d)
D	*le chiffre deux* (a)	*le chiffre sept* (c)	*deux lignes* (d)	
E	*le chiffre huit* (b)	*le chiffre sept* (a)	*le chiffre cinq* (d)	
F	*six points* (c)	*le chiffre huit* (b)	*le chiffre neuf* (a)	

G	*dix* (d)	*huit* (c)	*neuf* (a)
H	*huit* (a)	*onze* (b)	*neuf* (c)
I	*dix, huit* (b)	*neuf, dix* (d)	*dix, neuf* (c)
J	*douze, onze* (a)	*douze, sept* (d)	*douze, neuf* (c)

Chapter 13 Listen and Draw

	Drawing	Transcript
1.	• 11 ___	*Un petit point, un gros chiffre onze, et une ligne fine.*
2.	___ ___ ___ 9	*Trois lignes courtes et fines et le chiffre neuf.*
3.	• • • • • • • _____	*Sept petits points et une ligne longue et fine.*
4.	12, 11, 10, 9, 8	*Cinq chiffres, les chiffres douze, onze, dix, neuf, et huit.*

Chapter 14 Nine Sentences to Read Out Loud 1

1. Cet homme est roi. 2. Cet homme est ce roi. 3. Ce roi est un homme. 4. Ce serviteur est roi. 5. Ce serviteur est ce roi. 6. Ce roi est un serviteur. 7. Qui est ce roi? 8. Un homme est un roi. 9. Un roi est un homme.

Chapter 14 Nine Sentences to Read Out Loud 2

1. Qui est reine? 2. Cette femme-là est reine. 3. Elle est servante. 4. Cette reine-là est une servante. 5. Elle est cette femme-ci. 6. Qui est cette femme-là? 7. Elle est reine. 8. Qui est une servante? 9. Une reine est une servante.

Chapter 15 Translation Exercise 1

1. Joseph est un ami de Josette, qui est princesse. 2. L'amie de Nanette n'est pas princesse. 3. L'ami de Pierre était prince, oui. 4. Il était ici avec Robert, qui est un ami de la princesse. 5. Qui est Josette? C'est la princesse qui était ici avec Robert. 6. Roland était prince et est prince. 7. Richard n'était pas prince et n'est pas prince. 8. Qui était ici avec Nanette? 9. C'était un monsieur qui est peut-être un ami de la princesse.

Chapter 15 Translation Exercise 2

1. Josette est une amie. 2. Marie aussi, n'est-ce pas? 3. Est-ce que Marie est une amie? 4. Oui, c'est aussi une amie. 5. Mais la princesse qui était ici n'est pas une amie. 6. Mademoiselle Renard est une princesse sans ami. 7. Marie et Robert n'étaient pas ici avec le prince. 8. Ils étaient avec l'amie de la princesse. 9. Qui était ici et qui était là? 10. Je ne sais pas, mais bien sûr qu'ils n'étaient pas là. 11. C'était moi.

Chapter 15 Translation Exercise 3

1. D'où est Robert? 2. Est-ce qu'il est de Paris? 3. Qui est d'ici et qui est de Paris? 4. Où est le prince qui était ici avec la princesse de Monaco? 5. La princesse n'est pas de Monaco, elle est de Paris. 6. D'où? De Paris...pas de Monaco. 7. Le prince et la princesse sont ici. 8. Les princes sont de Paris, mais les princesses sont de Monaco. 9. Est-ce qu'ils sont ici? Pas maintenant, mais ils étaient ici.

Chapter 20 Multiple-Choice Frames

A	*un point et une ligne verticale* (a)	*un point et une ligne horizontale* (c)	*un point et une ligne diagonale* (d)
B	*deux lignes diagonales* (b)	*deux lignes horizontales* (d)	*une ligne verticale et une diagonale* (a)
C	*deux longues lignes horizontales et une ligne horizontale courte* (a)	*quatre courtes lignes diagonales et une ligne verticale* (d)	*quatre courtes lignes diagonales et une ligne horizontale* (b)
D	*un gros chiffre, une ligne verticale, et un petit chiffre* (d)	*un gros chiffre, une ligne horizontale, et un petit chiffre* (a)	
E	*un point suivi d'une ligne* (c)	*un chiffre suivi d'un point* (a)	*un point suivi d'un chiffre* (d)

F *une ligne horizontale suivie d'une ligne diagonale* (b)   *une ligne verticale suivie d'une ligne diagonale* (c)   *une ligne diagonale suivie d'une ligne verticale* (a)

G *le chiffre douze suivi d'un point* (a)   *le chiffre deux suivi d'une ligne horizontale* (d)   *le chiffre deux suivi d'une ligne diagonale* (c)

H *un petit chiffre suivi d'un gros point* (d)   *un petit chiffre suivi d'un gros chiffre* (b)   *un gros chiffre suivi d'un petit chiffre* (a)

I *un petit point suivi d'un gros point* (a)   *un gros point suivi d'un petit point* (b)   *un petit chiffre suivi d'un petit point* (d)

J *une ligne horizontale et une ligne diagonale suivies d'un gros chiffre* (c)   *une ligne horizontale et une ligne diagonale suivies d'un petit chiffre* (d)   *une ligne verticale suivie d'une ligne diagonale suivie d'un gros point* (b)

Chapter 20 Read and Draw

1. _____ | 2. /\ | | |__ __   3. 9 7   4. • ● \/\ \

Chapter 21 Practice

1. Il y a une autre chose, une chose noire. 2. Est-ce que cette chose noire est petite? 3. Non, cette chose noire est longue. 4. La chose noire est sur la chose blanche. 5. Cette petite chose est ici, debout sur la chose noire. 6. La chose noire est couchée là. 7. Ces choses noires sont longues, mais ces choses blanches sont petites. 8. Oui, l'une est petite et les autres sont longues. 9. Est-ce que toutes les choses noires sont longues? Non, il y a des choses longues et des petites. 10. Est-ce que les choses blanches sont noires? Non, les choses blanches sont blanches, et les choses noires sont noires.

Chapter 27 Translation

1. There are a ballerina, an actress, and a drum player. 2. The actress loves the drum player. 3. The drum player doesn't love the actress. 4. He detests the actress. 5. He loves the ballerina. 6. He doesn't dance with the actress. 7. He dances with the ballerina. 8. He doesn't sing with the actress. 9. No, the drum player sings with the ballerina. 10. The ballerina doesn't like the actress. 11. The actress doesn't like the ballerina.

Chapter 28 Listen and Look

1. *La flèche blanche pointe vers la droite, la flèche noire pointe vers la gauche.*
2. *Les deux flèches blanches pointent vers la droite, et les deux flèches noires pointent vers le bas.*
3. *Deux flèches noires pointant l'une vers l'autre.*
4. *Une ligne verticale entre deux points.*
5. *Une flèche noire au-dessus d'un gros point et une flèche blanche au-dessus d'un petit point.*
6. *Une flèche noire pointant vers la gauche au-dessus d'une ligne, et une flèche noire pointant vers la droite au-dessous d'une ligne.*
7. *Deux flèches blanches au-dessus d'une longue ligne.*
8. *Une ligne verticale entre deux flèches, l'une blanche pointant vers la droite et l'autre noire pointant vers la gauche.*

Chapter 28 Multiple-Choice Frames

A *une ligne diagonale entre deux points* (a)   *un chiffre entre deux lignes diagonales* (d)   *un point entre deux lignes verticales* (b)

B *une flèche noire pointant vers la gauche* (b)   *une flèche noire et une flèche blanche pointant vers la droite* (c)   *une flèche blanche pointant vers la droite* (a)

C *deux flèches noires pointant vers la gauche* (b)   *deux flèches noires pointant vers la droite* (c)   *deux flèches noires pointant vers le haut* (d)

D *un point au-dessous d'une ligne horizontale* (c)   *une ligne horizontale au-dessus d'un point* (c)   *une ligne verticale au-dessus d'un point* (d)

E *trois points entre deux lignes diagonales* (d)   *trois points entre deux lignes verticales* (c)   *trois points au-dessus d'une ligne horizontale* (b)

Chapter 28 Read and Draw
1. | • | 2. ⬇   3. /⟹/   4. 4̲ 5̄   5. ➡➡ ⬅⬅

Chapter 29 Culture Questions—Section 1
1. English

2. the language of love

3. 1830

4. "The Tell"

Chapter 34 Reading Activity 1
1. Cet homme-ci est un bon roi.   2. Est-ce qu'il est bon?   3. Un bon roi est un bon homme. 4. Ce serviteur-ci est un roi.   5. Est-ce qu'il est un bon roi?   6. Il est un méchant serviteur et il est un méchant roi.   7. Qui est cette femme-ci?   8. Est-ce qu'elle est reine?   9. Cette femme-là qui est reine est une méchante reine.   10. Elle est une femme bonne.

Chapter 34 Reading Activity 2
1. Cet homme-ci est roi.   2. Est-ce qu'il est un bon roi?   3. Non, il n'est pas un bon roi.   4. Il est un méchant homme, et il est un très méchant roi.   5. Un méchant homme n'est pas un bon roi. 6. Qui est cette femme-ci?   7. Est-ce qu'elle est reine?   8. Elle est une femme bonne, mais elle n'est pas une bonne reine.   9. Elle est une très méchante reine.

Chapter 41 Forms of Questions

1.	Qu'est-ce que le roi chante?	Le roi, que chante-t-il?	Que chante le roi?
2.	Quand est-ce que le roi chante?	Le roi, quand chante-t-il?	Quand chante le roi?
3.	Est-ce que la princesse pleure beaucoup?	La princesse pleure-t-elle beaucoup?	
4.	Où est-ce qu'elle pleure?	Où pleure-t-elle?	
5.	Pourquoi est-ce qu'elle pleure?	Pourquoi pleure-t-elle?	
6.	Est-ce qu'elle ne chante pas?	Ne chante-t-elle pas?	
7.	Qu'est-ce que fait le prince?	Le prince, que fait-il?	Que fait le prince?

Chapter 41 Culture Questions—Section Two
1. Arabic

2. French and Dutch (Flemish)

3. French

4. any 3 of the following: hockey, baseball, curling, rugby, skiing, tennis, & lacrosse

Chapter 42 Sample Story Plot
1. Une dame va à la pharmacie.   2. Elle achète une bouteille d'orangeade.   3. Elle porte la bouteille à une amie, une jeune fille.   4. La jeune fille va à la pharmacie.   5. Elle achète une bouteille de limonade.   6. Elle apporte la bouteille à la dame.   7. La limonade est bonne. 8. L'orangeade n'est pas bonne.   9. La jeune fille porte la bouteille d'orangeade à la pharmacie et dit, «La bouteille n'est pas bonne.»   10. La femme à la pharmacie dit, «La bouteille est bonne.»   11. La jeune fille dit, «Non, l'orangeade n'est pas bonne. La bouteille est bonne, mais l'orangeade dans la bouteille n'est pas bonne.»   12. La pharmacienne dit, «O.K., l'orangeade dans la bouteille n'est pas bonne.»   13. La jeune fille dit, «O.K.», et achète une bouteille de limonade.   14. Elle dit, «La limonade est bonne.»   15. «Oui», dit la pharmacienne, «la limonade est bonne.»

Chapter 43 Multiple-Choice Frames
A.   Deux lignes verticales parallèles   Deux lignes horizontales   Deux lignes non-parallèles (a).
   (c)   parallèles (b)

330

B. *Un point suivi d'une ligne diagonale suivie de lignes perpendiculaires* (d)
C. *Deux points suivis d'une ligne crochue* (a)
D. *Une ligne crochue au-dessous d'une ligne droite* (b)
E. *Une ligne courbe au-dessus de lignes parallèles diagonales* (a)

Deux lignes perpendiculaires suivies de lignes parallèles suivies d'un point (b)
Une ligne courbe suivie de deux points (d)
Une ligne courbe suivie d'une ligne droite (a)
Une ligne courbe entre quatre lignes droites verticales et parallèles (d)

Deux lignes parallèles verticales suivies de deux lignes perpendiculaires (a).
Une ligne crochue suivie de deux points (c)
Une ligne droite suivie d'une ligne courbe (d)
Deux lignes verticales parallèles entre deux lignes courbes (c)

Chapter 43 Listen and Draw
Drawing   Transcription
1. / /   *Deux lignes diagonales parallèles.*
2. | —   *Une ligne droite verticale suivie d'une ligne droite horizontale.*
3. ▬▬▬ | | *Une ligne épaisse horizontale suivie de deux fines lignes verticales.*

Chapter 43 Reading Comprehension
1. A straight line and a curved line cannot be parallel, but two curved lines can be parallel, can't they?   2. These two lines aren't parallel, because one is straight and the other is curved.   3. Vertical lines are parallel. Horizontal lines are also parallel. Diagonal lines can be parallel.   4. Certain perpendicular lines can form the letters: L, T, E, F, H.   5. Certain curved lines can also form the letters: C, S, J, U.   6. Perpendicular lines can be thick or thin, but they can't be curved, can they?

Chapter 48 Multiple-Choice Frames
A. *Un triangle* (c)
B. *Un triangle au-dessous d'un carré* (c)
C. *Un cercle au-dessus d'un autre cercle* (b)
D. *Une grosse figure suivie d'une petite figure* (a)
E. *Un carré et une croix au-dessus d'une ligne* (a)

Un carré (d)
Un triangle au-dessus d'un carré (d)
Un cercle suivi d'un autre cercle (c)
Deux petites figures (b)
Une croix et un triangle au-dessous d'une ligne (d)

Une étoile (b)
Un triangle suivi d'un carré (a)
Un triangle suivi d'un autre triangle (d)
Une petite figure suivie d'une grosse figure (d)
Une croix et un triangle au-dessus d'une ligne (b)

Chapter 48 Listen and Draw
Drawing   Transcription
1. □ △ ☆ ○   *Un carré, un triangle, une étoile, et un cercle.*
2. W V   *Deux lignes crochues formant des lettres.*
3. △ ✚ ☆   *Une croix entre un triangle et une étoile.*
4. | ∫   *Une ligne droite et une ligne courbe, les deux sont épaisses.*
5. ☆ ☆ ☆ ☆ ☆ ✚ ✚   *Cinq étoiles suivies de deux croix.*

Chapter 48 Reading Comprehension
1. What letter is this? Is this a D or an O? This is a D.   2. What type of figure is this? Is it a circle or a square?   3. All these triangles point up, and all these arrows point down. There are as many triangles as arrows.   4. These two figures are between two short, thick, vertical lines.   5. Are circles, squares, points, and lines figures? The circles and the squares are (figures) it (le), but not the points and lines.   6. These figures are formed of lines.

Chapter 49 Nine Sentences to Read Out Loud 1
1. *Ce méchant roi a un grand chien et un petit chien.*   2. *Le grand chien est bon, mais le petit chien est méchant.*   3. *Le grand chien aime le roi.*   4. *Le roi aime le petit chien et le*

grand chien. 5. La reine a un loup. 6. Elle aime le loup. 7. Mais le loup déteste la reine. 8. Le chien sait que le loup déteste la reine. 9. Le roi qui aime le petit chien déteste le grand méchant loup.

Chapter 49 Nine Sentences to Read Out Loud 2
1. Ce méchant roi a un bon chien et un méchant chien. 2. Le bon chien est petit; le méchant chien est grand. 3. Le bon chien aime le roi, et le roi aime le bon chien. 4. Elle aime les chats. 5. La reine voit que le roi aime le bon chien et que le bon chien aime le roi. 6. La reine a des chats. 7. Mais les chats détestent la reine. 8. Le chien voit que les chats détestent la reine. 9. Et il croit que le roi voit que les chats détestent la reine.

Chapter 52 Translation Exercise
1. Donnez-lui la longue tige blanche. 2. Prenez toutes les tiges et mettez-les ici. 3. Ces tiges noires ne sont pas petites? 4. Ces tiges noires ne sont pas longues non plus. 5. Ces tiges blanches ne sont pas debout, elles sont couchées. 6. Ne me donnez pas la tige noire, donnez-moi la blanche. 7. Ne prenez pas cette tige noire non plus. 8. Voici la petite tige blanche. 9. Prenez-la, mais ne la mettez pas sur les tiges noires. 10. Prenez les deux autres petites tiges blanches et mettez-les là-bas.

Chapter 55 Sample Story Plot
1. Un vendeur vend des bonbons dans le marché. 2. Pierre vient au marché. 3. Pierre demande si les bonbons sont bons. 4. Le vendeur répond que les bonbons sont très bons. 5. Il donne un bonbon à Pierre. 6. Pierre prend le bonbon. 7. Il goûte le bonbon et il dit, «Mmm, oui, les bonbons sont très bons.» 8. Le vendeur vend un kilo de bonbons à Pierre. 9. Alors Pierre apporte les bonbons à son frère. 10. Il donne un bonbon à son frère. 11. Le frère prend le bonbon. 12. Il goûte le bonbon et il dit, «Mmm, les bonbons sont très bons.» 13. Il mange et mange. Il mange le kilo de bonbons. 14. Pierre demande si les bonbons sont bons. 15. Son frère répond, «Non, les bonbons ne sont pas très bons.» 16. Alors le frère va au marché. 17. Il achète un kilo de bonbons. 18. Il apporte les bonbons à sa sœur Michelle. 19. Michelle prend les bonbons. 20. Elle mange les bonbons. 21. Alors elle dit, «Les bonbons sont très bons.»

Chapter 56 Culture Questions—Section Three
1. Islam

2. chocolates, mussels, waffles, and french fries

3. *Québécois*

4. Catholicism

5. soccer and rugby

Chapter 57 Multiple-Choice Frames
1.	*Mangez!* (a)		
2.	*Buvez!* (b)	*Mangez!* (a)	*Mangez et buvez!* (c)
3.	*Buvez et mangez!* (a)	*Mangez et buvez!* (b)	*Asseyez-vous!* (d)
4.	*Asseyez-vous et mangez!* (d)	*Asseyez-vous et buvez!* (b)	*Mettez-vous debout!* (a)
5.	*Mettez-vous debout et buvez!* (b)	*Mettez-vous debout et asseyez-vous!* (a)	*Asseyez-vous et mettez-vous debout!* (c)
6.	*Lisez* (d)	*Asseyez-vous et lisez!* (a)	*Mettez-vous debout et lisez!* (c)
7.	*Buvez et lisez!* (c)	*Asseyez-vous et lisez!* (b)	*Mettez-vous debout et lisez!* (a)
8.	*Écrivez!* (c)	*Écrivez et lisez!* (a)	*Mangez et écrivez!* (d)
9.	*Lisez et écrivez!* (a)	*Mangez et buvez!* (b)	*Mettez-vous debout et écrivez!* (c)
10.	*Parlez!* (b)	*Asseyez-vous et parlez!* (c)	*Buvez et parlez!* (a)
11.	*Chantez!* (a)	*Chantez et parlez!* (c)	*Mettez-vous debout et chantez!* (d)
12.	*Mangez et parlez!* (b)	*Chantez et parlez!* (d)	*Lisez et écrivez!* (a)

13. *Marchez!* (c)   *Mettez-vous debout et marchez!* (a)   *Marchez et parlez!* (d)
14. *Courez!* (b)   *Marchez et courez!* (a)   *Mettez-vous debout et courez!* (d)
15. *Lisez et écrivez!* (a)   *Marchez et courez!* (b)   *Chantez et parlez!* (d)

Chapter 57 Listen and Anticipate Response
1. *Que fait cet homme? Il mange.*
2. *Que fait cette femme? Elle boit.*
3. *Que font ces gens? Ils chantent.*
4. *Que font ces gens? Ils parlent. Tous les trois parlent.*
5. *Que font ces gens? L'un se met debout, et l'autre s'assoit.*
6. *Que font ces gens? L'un court, et l'autre marche.*
7. *Que font ces gens? Deux écrivent et deux lisent.*
8. *Que fait cette femme? Elle mange, boit, et chante.*
9. *Que font ces gens? L'un se met debout et court, et l'autre s'assoit et lit.*
10. *Que font ces gens? Ils mangent. Les deux mangent.*

Chapter 57 Act Out or Pantomime What You Hear

Mettez-vous debout. Buvez. Asseyez-vous et mangez. Lisez et écrivez. Mettez-vous debout et marchez. Chantez et parlez. Asseyez-vous et écrivez. Lisez et parlez. Mettez-vous debout, marchez et courez. Asseyez-vous.

Chapter 58 Six Sentences to Read Out Loud 1
1. Ce sont des chiens et des chats. 2. Les chiens sont grands mais les chats sont petits. 3. Les chats disent que tous les grands chiens sont méchants. 4. Mais des grands chats sont méchants aussi. 5. Les petits chiens disent que les grands chats ne sont pas de bons chats. 6. Ils sont grands mais ils ne sont pas bons.

Chapter 58 Six Sentences to Read Out Loud 2
1. Ces chiens sont dans la forêt. 2. Un loup est aussi dans la forêt. 3. Le chien est ici avec le loup. 4. Un chien est aussi dans la maison. 5. Est-il dans la maison avec le chat? 6. Et le chat où était-il?

Chapter 69 Sample Plot One
1. In this story there is a cat and a dog. 2. Both are singing in the bathroom. 3. But the dog is not content. 4. Why isn't the dog content? 5. Because he detests the cat. 6. And why does the dog detest the cat? 7. It's because the cat sings better. 8. What is it the dog swears to do? 9. He swears to attack the cat. 10. Yes, he swears that one day he's gonna attack the cat. 11. And finally, one day he does attack the cat! 12. Very shocking, isn't it? 13. That's all.

Chapter 69 Sample Plot Two
1. In this story there's a palace. 2. The king is in the palace. 3. The king has a treasure. 4. The king has jewels. 5. He loves the jewels. 6. It's a secret where he keeps the jewels. 7. But the beautiful secretary knows the secret. 8. The duchess also knows where the king keeps the jewels. 9. In this story there's also a thief. 10. This thief also is in the palace. 11. He doesn't know where the jewels are. 12. But he thinks they are in the bathroom. 13. He enters the bathroom. 14. He searches and searches, but he doesn't find the jewels. 15. He thinks that the jewels are in the tower. 16. He climbs up (mounts) the tower. 17. He searches and searches, but doesn't find the jewels. 18. He thinks now that the jewels are in the chamber of the queen. 19. He enters the queen's chamber. 20. He searches and searches, and finally finds the jewels.

Chapter 76 Multiple-Choice Frames
1. *Allongez-vous!* (b)   *Allongez-vous et lisez!* (a)   *Asseyez vous et mangez!* (d)
2. *Levez-vous!* (c)   *Allongez-vous et levez-vous!* (a)   *Levez-vous et marchez!* (b)

3.	*Levez-vous et parlez! (d)*	*Allongez-vous et mangez! (a)*	*Levez-vous et asseyez-vous! (c)*
4.	*Fermez les yeux! (c)*	*Allongez-vous et fermez les yeux! (a)*	*Fermez les yeux et chantez! (d)*
5.	*Ouvrez les yeux! (a)*	*Fermez les yeux et ouvrez les yeux! (c)*	*Ouvrez les yeux et levez-vous! (d)*
6.	*Ouvrez les yeux et lisez! (c)*	*Allongez-vous et fermez les yeux! (a)*	*Fermez les yeux et parlez! (d)*
7.	*Dormez! (d)*	*Allongez-vous et dormez! (a)*	*Fermez les yeux et dormez! (c)*
8.	*Réveillez-vous (c)*	*Réveillez-vous et levez-vous! (d)*	*Réveillez-vous et lisez! (a)*
9.	*Sautez! (a)*	*Courez et sautez! (b)*	*Mettez-vous debout et sautez! (d)*
10.	*Comptez! (c)*	*Fermez les yeux et comptez! (b)*	*Comptez et chantez! (a)*
11.	*Peignez! (b)*	*Peignez et chantez! (a)*	*Peignez et comptez! (c)*
12.	*Montrez du doigt! (d)*	*Montrez du doigt et peignez! (a)*	*Réveillez-vous et peignez! (b)*
13.	*Dormez et peignez! (b)*	*Montrez du doigt et parlez! (c)*	*Réveillez-vous et montrez du doigt! (d)*
14.	*Pensez! (a)*	*Pensez et parlez! (b)*	*Pensez et écrivez! (d)*
15.	*Réveillez-vous et pensez! (c)*	*Allongez-vous et fermez les yeux! (d)*	*Comptez et pensez! (b)*

Chapter 76 Act Out or Pantomime What You Hear
Mettez-vous debout! Buvez et mangez! Asseyez-vous et comptez! Lisez, comptez et écrivez! Mettez-vous debout et marchez! Chantez et parlez! Sautez et comptez! Fermez les yeux et buvez! Levez-vous, ouvrez les yeux et montrez du doigt! Asseyez-vous, peignez et écrivez! Lisez et parlez! Allongez-vous et fermez les yeux! Ouvrez les yeux! Mettez-vous debout, marchez et courez! Asseyez-vous! Fermez les yeux et pensez! Dormez! Réveillez-vous et sautez! Asseyez-vous et lisez! Allongez-vous, fermez les yeux et dormez.

Chapter 88 Culture Questions—Section Four
1. hard work, cultural appreciation, and family ties

2. less than one million

3. their culture, heritage, and nation

4. true

5. any 3 of the following: fishing, cycling, tennis, hiking, skiing, & sailing

Chapter 90 Practice 1
(1) *en.* (2) *le.* (3) *en.* (4) *les.* (5) *les.* (6) *les.* (7) *en.* (8) *le.* (9) *les.* (10) *en.* (11) *les.* (12) *en.* (13) *en.* (14) *les.* (15) *le.* (16) *les.* (17) *en.*

Chapter 90 Practice 2
(1) S. (2) C. (3) S. (4) C. (5) C. (6) C. (7) S. (8) S. (9) S. (10) C. (11) S. (12) C. (13) S.

Chapter 91 Multiple-Choice Frames
1.	*Allumez la lumière! (d)*	*Allumez la lumière et lisez! (a)*	*Ouvrez les yeux et allumez la lumière! (b)*
2.	*Éteignez la lumière et dormez! (a)*	*Éteignez la lumière et pensez! (d)*	*Éteignez la lumière et fermez les yeux! (c)*
3.	*Allongez-vous et allumez la télé! (a)*	*Levez-vous et éteignez la télé! (d)*	*Éteignez la lumière et allumez la télé! (c)*
4.	*Allez à la fenêtre (b)*	*Allez à la fenêtre et sautez! (d)*	*Mettez-vous debout et allez à la fenêtre! (a)*
5.	*Allumez la lumière et lisez! (b)*	*Eteignez la télé et dormez! (c)*	*Levez-vous et allez à la fenêtre! (d)*
6.	*Ouvrez la porte! (c)*	*Fermez les yeux et ouvrez la porte! (d)*	*Ouvrez la porte et allumez la lumière! (b)*
7.	*Fermez la porte et allez à la fenêtre! (b)*	*Fermez la porte et allumez la télé! (d)*	*Allumez la lumière et fermez la porte! (c)*

8. *Chantez et dansez! (a)*	*Levez-vous et dansez! (c)*	*Éteignez la lumière et dansez! (b)*
9. *Jouez et chantez! (d)*	*Courez et jouez! (b)*	*Dansez et jouez! (c)*
10. *Comptez et parlez! (a)*	*Jouez et chantez! (c)*	*Fermez les yeux et fermez la porte! (b)*
11. *Chantez et travaillez! (c)*	*Levez-vous et travaillez! (d)*	*Travaillez et jouez! (b)*
12. *Souriez! (a)*	*Souriez et travaillez! (d)*	*Souriez et montrez du doigt! (b)*
13. *Riez! (c)*	*Réveillez-vous et riez! (d)*	*Jouez et riez! (b)*
14. *Riez et pleurez! (c)*	*Pleurez et riez! (d)*	*Pensez et pleurez! (b)*
15. *Arrêtez-vous! (a)*	*Allez à la fenêtre et arrêtez-vous! (c)*	*Courez et arrêtez-vous! (d)*

Chapter 91 Act Out or Pantomime What You Hear

Mettez-vous debout! Buvez et mangez! Allez à la fenêtre et arrêtez-vous! Asseyez-vous et souriez! Lisez, comptez et écrivez! Mettez-vous debout et marchez! Chantez et parlez! Dansez et comptez! Marchez et ouvrez la porte! Fermez la porte! Éteignez la lumière et allumez la télé! Fermez les yeux et buvez! Levez-vous, ouvrez les yeux et montrez du doigt! Asseyez-vous, peignez et écrivez! Lisez et parlez! Riez et pleurez! Allongez-vous et fermez les yeux! Ouvrez les yeux! Mettez-vous debout, marchez et courez! Sautez! Asseyez-vous! Fermez les yeux et pensez! Dormez! Réveillez-vous et travaillez! Asseyez-vous, jouez et lisez! Allongez-vous, fermez les yeux et dormez!

Chapter 97 Culture Questions—Section Five

1. any 3 of the following: Belgium, Canada, France, Haiti, Luxembourg, Senegal, Switzerland, and Tahiti

2. any 2 of the following: oil, petroleum products, natural gas, and wine

3. mayonnaise

4. shaking hands and placing their right hands over their hearts

5. a hooded kaftan that is Morocco's traditional clothing

6. the Grand Duchy of Luxembourg

Chapter 98 Boxes

1. *La boîte de droite.* 2. *La boîte de gauche.* 3. *La boîte de gauche.* 4. *La boîte de gauche.* 5. *La boîte de gauche.* 6. *La boîte de gauche.* 7. *La boîte du milieu.* 8. *La boîte de droite.* Also, *la boîte du milieu.*

Chapter 124 Culture Questions—Section Six

1. mining, forestry, & manufacturing

2. in one communal dish

3. soccer

4. Wolof

5. Dakar

6. the Moselle River

Chapter 139 Culture Test

1. 90 million

2. It developed from Latin.

3. 3 July 1962

4. the Sahara Desert

5. Walloons and Flemish

6. constitutional monarchy

7. English and French

8. Montréal

9. Catholicism

10. False. (They were written in the Middle Ages.)

11. France

12. Arabic

13. agriculture

14. Luxembourgish, French, and German

15. cycling and hiking

16. *Tour de France*

17. Islam

18. French

19. peanuts

20. the roof of Europe

21. Switzerland

22. German, French, Italian, and Romansch

23. soccer and cycling

24. 1 August 1291

25. the Society Islands

26. Papeete

27. 13

28. soccer

Appendix II—Verbs

Fifty Common Verbs

parler	to talk	*danser*	to dance
chanter	to sing	*compter*	to count
jouer	to play	*être*	to be
avoir	to have	*aller*	to go
sauter	to jump	*défendre*	to defend/prohibit
détester	to hate	*embrasser*	to kiss
aider	to help	*observer*	to observe
habiter	to live	*appeller*	to call
apporter	to take	*marcher*	to walk
demander	to ask	*frapper*	to knock/hit
répondre	to respond	*entrer*	to go in
mettre	to put	*arriver*	to arrive
voir	to see	*entendre*	to hear
sentir	to smell/feel	*manger*	to eat
crier	to cry out	*pleurer*	to cry
réussir	to succeed	*échapper*	to escape
étudier	to study	*apprendre*	to learn
écrire	to write	*dormir*	to sleep
sortir	to go out	*partir*	to leave
exercer	to exercise	*préferer*	to prefer
menacer	to threaten	*regretter*	to be sorry
décider	to decide	*craindre*	to be afraid
finir	to finish	*choisir*	to choose
accepter	to accept	*oublier*	to forget
essayer	to try	*arrêter*	to stop

Verb Conjugations

Present tense (I am verbing, I do verb, and I verb)

-er verbs	-ir verbs	-re verbs
Je chante	*Je choisis*	*Je rends*
Tu chantes	*Tu choisis*	*Tu rends*
Il chante	*Il choisit*	*Il rend*
Elle chante	*Elle choisit*	*Elle rend*
On chante	*On choisit*	*On rend*
Nous chantons	*Nous choisissons*	*Nous rendons*
Vous chantez	*Vous choisissez*	*Vous rendez*
Ils/Elles chantent	*Ils/Elles choisissent*	*Ils/Elles rendent*

For –er verbs you drop the –er ending and add:

Je -e
Tu -es
Il/Elle/On -e
Nous -ons
Vous -ez
Ils/Elles -ent

For most –ir verbs you drop the –ir ending and add:

Je -is
Tu -is
Il/Elle/On -it

Nous -issons
Vous -issez
Ils/Elles -issent

For –re verbs you drop the –re ending and add:

Je -s
Tu -s
Il/Elle/On (add nothing)
Nous -ons
Vous -ez
Ils/Elles -ent

Irregular Verb Conjugations

être	avoir	faire	aller
Je suis	J'ai	Je fais	Je vais
Tu es	Tu as	Tu fais	Tu vas
Il est	Il a	Il fait	Il va
Elle est	Elle a	Elle fait	Elle va
On est	On a	On fait	On va
Nous sommes	Nous avons	Nous faisons	Nous allons
Vous êtes	Vous avez	Vous faites	Vous allez
Ils/Elles sont	Ils/Elles ont	Ils/Elles font	Ils/Elles vont

Past Tense Verb Conjugations (I verbed, I did verb, I have verbed)

-er verbs	-ir verbs	-re verbs
J'ai chanté	J'ai choisi	J'ai rendu
Tu as chanté	Tu as choisi	Tu as rendu
Il a chanté	Il a choisi	Il a rendu
Elle a chanté	Elle a choisi	Elle a rendu
On a chanté	On a choisi	On a rendu
Nous avons chanté	Nous avons choisi	Nous avons rendu
Vous avez chanté	Vous avez choisi	Vous avez rendu
Ils/Elles ont chanté	Ils/Elles ont choisi	Ils/Elles ont rendu

The construction looks like this:

SUBJECT + CONJUGATION OF AVOIR (OR ÊTRE) + PAST PARTICIPLE

(In most instances) The past participle can be formed by taking the infinitive form of the verb (i.e. chanter, choisir, rendre), dropping the two-letter ending, and adding:

(for –er verbs) **é**
(for –ir verbs) **i**
(for –re verbs) **u**

Almost every verb will make the past tense (or the *passé composé*) with the verb *avoir*. Here is a list of the verbs that use *être* instead:

aller	arriver	entrer	monter	tomber	naître
venir	partir	sortir	descendre	passer	mourir
revenir		rentrer			devenir
		rester			

(most are verbs of motion or action)

Imperfect tense (I was verbing, I used to verb, I verbed)

-er verbs	-ir verbs	-re verbs
Je chantais	*Je finissais*	*Je rendais*
Tu chantais	*Tu finissais*	*Tu rendais*
Il chantait	*Il finissait*	*Il rendait*
Elle chantait	*Elle finissait*	*Elle rendait*
On chantait	*On finissait*	*On rendait*
Nous chantions	*Nous finissions*	*Nous rendions*
Vous chantiez	*Vous finissiez*	*Vous rendiez*
Ils/Elles chantaient	*Ils/Elles finissaient*	*Ils/Elles rendaient*

For all French verbs you drop the *-ons* from the verb already conjugated in the present-tense *nous* form and add:

Je -ais
Tu -ais
Il/Elle/On -ait
Nous -ions
Vous -iez
Ils/Elles -aient

For example: *chanter => nous chantons => chantons => je chantais, tu chantais*, etc.

Future Tense – I will verb

For regular –er and –ir verbs don't drop anything, for regular –re verbs drop the final -e, and add:

Je -ai
Tu -as
Il/Elle/On -a
Nous -ons
Vous -ez
Ils/Elles -ont

For example:

parler	**finir**	**vendre**
je parlerai	*je finirai*	*je vendrai*
tu parleras	*tu finiras*	*tu vendras*
il/elle/on parlera	*il/elle/on finira*	*il/elle/on vendra*
nous parlerons	*nous finirons*	*nous vendrons*
vous parlerez	*vous finirez*	*vous vendrez*
ils/elles parleront	*ils/elles finiront*	*ils/elles vendront*

Conditional Tense – I would verb

For regular –er and –ir verbs don't drop anything, for regular –re verbs drop the final -e, and add:

Je -ais
Tu -ais
Il/Elle/On -ait
Nous -ions
Vous -iez
Ils/Elles -aient

For example:

parler	***finir***	***vendre***
je parlerais	*je finirais*	*je vendrais*
tu parlerais	*tu finirais*	*tu vendrais*
il/elle/on parlerait	*il/elle/on finirait*	*il/elle/on vendrait*
nous parlerions	*nous finirions*	*nous vendrions*
vous parleriez	*vous finiriez*	*vous vendriez*
ils/elles parleraient	*ils/elles finiraient*	*ils/elles vendraient*

Sentence Construction

When forming a sentence these words (parts of speech) always come before the verb:

SUBJECT + (NE) + (ME + (LE + (LUI + (Y) + (EN) + **VERB** + (PAS)
                    TE   LA   LEUR)
                    SE   LES)
                    NOUS
                    VOUS)

Reflexive Verbs

When conjugating reflexive verbs there are two things to consider:
1) the verb must be conjugated with the subject of the sentence.
2) the *se* (the word in front of the verb) must also be conjugated with the subject of the sentence.

For example:

The verb *se demander* would be conjugated like this:
Je me demande
Tu te demandes
Il se demande
Elle se demande
On se demande
Nous nous demandons
Vous vous demandez
Ils/Elles se demandent

Note that each subject has a different word to describe the subject, but the verb is still conjugated, as it would be normally.

Many verbs say different things if you don't include the reflexive when needed. For example *Je demande* means I request but *Je me demande* means I wonder. The verb *tromper* means to deceive and the verb *se tromper* means to be mistaken.